T0320024

A Global History of Runaways

THE CALIFORNIA WORLD HISTORY LIBRARY

Edited by Edmund Burke III, Kenneth Pomeranz, and Patricia Seed

University of California Press, one of the most distinguished university presses in the United States, enriches lives around the world by advancing scholarship in the humanities, social sciences, and natural sciences. Its activities are supported by the UC Press Foundation and by philanthropic contributions from individuals and institutions. For more information, visit www.ucpress.edu.

University of California Press
Oakland, California

Library of Congress Cataloging-in-Publication Data

Names: Rediker, Marcus, editor. | Chakraborty, Titas, 1983- editor. | Rossum, Matthias van, 1984- editor.
Title: A global history of runaways : workers, mobility, and capitalism 1600–1850 / edited by Marcus Rediker, Titas Chakraborty, Matthias van Rossum.
Description: Oakland, California : University of California Press, 2019 | Series: The California world history library | Includes bibliographical references and index. |
Identifiers: LCCN 2018061420 (print) | LCCN 2019004045 (ebook) | ISBN 9780520973060 (Epub) | ISBN 9780520304352 (cloth : alk. paper) | ISBN 9780520304369 (pbk. : alk. paper)
Subjects: LCSH: Labor mobility--History. | Imperialism--Economic aspects. | Capitalism--History.
Classification: LCC HD5717 (ebook) | LCC HD5717 .G57 2019 (print) | DDC 331.12/90903--dc23
LC record available at https://lccn.loc.gov/2018061420

28   27   26   25   24   23   22   21   20   19
10   9   8   7   6   5   4   3   2   1

A Global History of Runaways

Workers, Mobility, and
Capitalism 1600–1850

———

Edited by

Marcus Rediker, Titas Chakraborty,
Matthias van Rossum

UNIVERSITY OF CALIFORNIA PRESS

CONTENTS

ILLUSTRATIONS AND TABLES

MAPS

FIGURES

TABLES

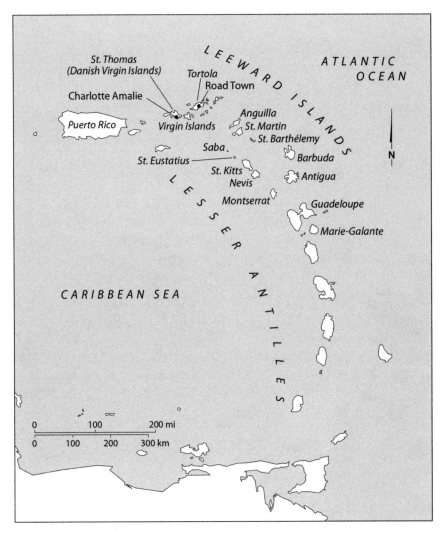

MAP 1. Leeward Islands, Caribbean Sea

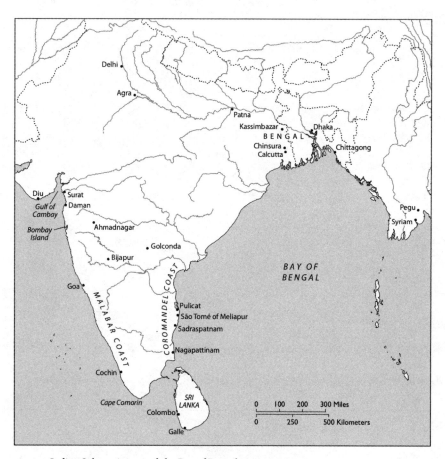

MAP 2. Indian Subcontinent and the Bay of Bengal, ca. 1700

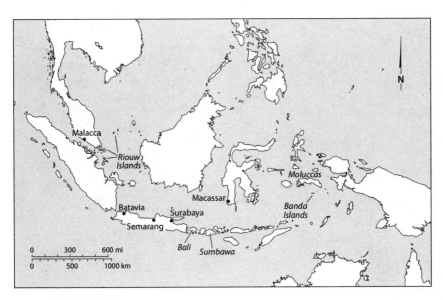

MAP 3. Dutch East India, ca. 1750

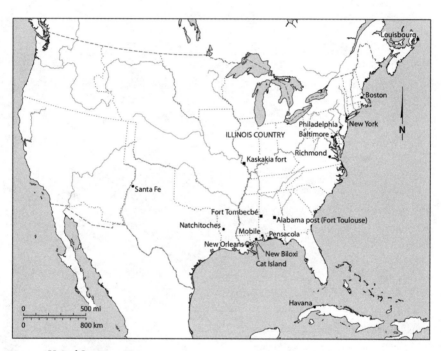

MAP 4. United States, ca. 1850

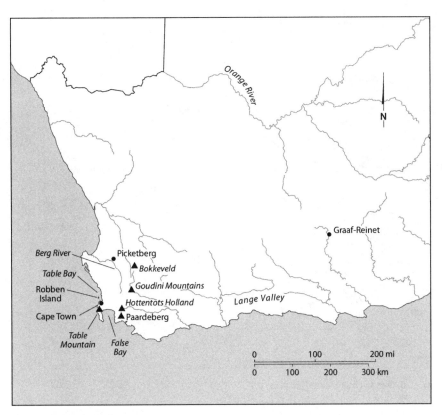

Orange River

N

Graaf-Reinet

Berg River
Picketberg
▲ Bokkeveld
Table Bay
▲ Goudini Mountains
Robben
Island
Hottentots Holland
Lange Valley
Cape Town
▲ Paardeberg
Table
Mountain
False
Bay

0		100		200 mi
0	100	200	300 km	

MAP 5. Cape of Good Hope, ca. 1780

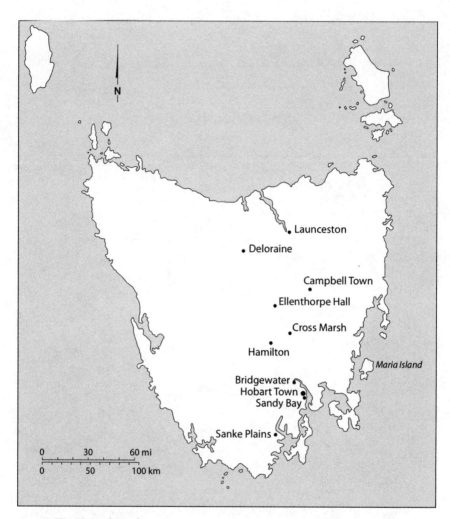

MAP 6. Van Diemen's Land, ca. 1840

Introduction

Flight as Fight

Leo Lucassen and Lex Heerma van Voss[1]

One evening in March 1760, three Bengal sailors, Dedaroe, Jadoe, and Pieroe, keeping guard in the port of Batavia (present-day Jakarta), noticed a man who suspiciously hid his face with a piece of cloth while navigating past them. They asked the passenger of the vessel to identify himself and recognized him as a fellow sailor from Bengal, Baboe. Baboe had been in the service of the Dutch East India Company, but had deserted his work on the Batavia wharf. He had survived for a year and a half by performing wage labor in Batavia. In the town he had met another Bengal, Alladie, who served as a boatswain on the English vessel *Pocock.* Alladie had engaged Baboe to work on the *Pocock,* and he was now trying to smuggle his new hire aboard ship. The Dutch authorities had Alladie whipped and banned from Batavia for his role in the attempted desertion. As a Company servant under Dutch law, Baboe thus escaped severe, possibly capital punishment. He was sentenced to two years of forced labor in the ropewalk on the Island Edam off the coast of Java.[2]

We hear Baboe's voice only through the documents produced in the Courts of the Dutch, and we do not know why he absconded from his work at the wharf. Something in his living and working conditions made him decide that he would be better off outside the orbit of the Dutch company. He actually ran away from a hospital for "Moorish" workers, and the reason he was hospitalized may have shaped his decision. He managed to hide and survive in Dutch Batavia, doing what was described as "coolie" work. The Dutch and the English alike were short on hands, and Alladie was able to offer Baboe a monthly wage close to the level usual for European sailors. By sentencing Baboe to convict labor, the colonial authorities killed two birds with one stone: his punishment relieved the labor shortage of the Company.

Because of labor shortages in their far-flung colonial empires, all European colonial powers resorted to harsh discipline in recruiting and retaining workers. This was true for nominally free wage workers, like many sailors and soldiers, who signed on for a considerable time period and were not allowed to leave their jobs. It was by definition true for unfree workers like convicts and enslaved workers. Often, as in Baboe's case, the available sources were written by the oppressors, offering no clues as to the motives of the runaway, nor about the network he used to survive for a year and a half in a foreign town. Other workers, like Alladie, with similar backgrounds and positions, might have helped him. But the deportment of Dedaroe, Jadoe, and Pieroe shows that this need not necessarily be the case. Even if we lack these details, it is clear that Baboe put much at stake by running away, risking harsh punishment and surviving in the urban jungle of Batavia. We can safely qualify his flight as part of a fight against oppression.

The establishment of European empires and the rise of capitalism around the globe beginning in the sixteenth century constitute the backdrop and essential contexts for this volume. Imperial expansion was a Herculean task; it required many kinds of work—the production of commodities for trade, such as sugar, tobacco, and spices; the movement of riverine boats and transoceanic vessels connecting ports with vast hinterlands; and the maintenance of factories and forts and military labor to safeguard imperial possessions. The nascent system of global capitalism required that workers from Europe, the Americas, Asia, and Africa be mobilized in ways that were novel, cooperative, and systemic. Over the early modern era, the slaves, servants, convicts, soldiers, and sailors who made the new global economy possible numbered in the millions.

Comparing and connecting the Portuguese, British, Danish, Dutch, French, Mughal, and American empires, the essays that follow demonstrate how trading settlements and networks, military expeditions, and plantation societies were built and maintained, requiring many varieties and vast quantities of labor.[3] The carriers, fighters, and builders crucial to these imperial projects were mobilized through a wide range of strategies, all of them entailing significant constraint and coercion. As capitalists and imperial planners organized the global cooperation of their workers they discovered that these workers sometimes translated that cooperation into projects of their own. In short, they resisted.

At the heart of a new imperial and capitalist order lay the vexed and contested issue of workers' mobility. No matter where global workers originated, no matter what labors they did, and no matter where they did them, large numbers of them ran away from their employers. In response empire builders created rules, regulations, laws, and treaties around the world, from the Atlantic to the Indian and Pacific Oceans, to criminalize running away and to make sure that mobility served business and state interests. They implemented a wide range of violent, terror-filled punishments designed to limit mobility to prescribed circuits.

Yet the lack of complete political power (in India, for example) and the issue of labor scarcity in many parts of the world (the Americas, especially) made it difficult to enforce the regulations of worker mobility. European sailors and soldiers entering Bengal's labor market quickly adopted the practice of floating around from one employer to another. Likewise in Europe, soldiers working in Denmark came from Norway and Iceland. Even in mature colonies, running away from work remained a more or less continuous threat. In the convict colony of Australia, special prisons were erected for "absconding" convicts, who repeatedly undermined colonial objectives. Employers and states in turn experimented with more totalizing forms of surveillance and confinement globally, in the process transforming not only their colonies but their metropoles as well.

Between 1600 and 1850 the entwined processes of imperial expansion and capitalist commercialization took many forms and created multiple labor regimes around the world. Timothy Coates describes deserters and runaways in three different parts of the Portuguese empire. Titas Chakraborty examines English and Dutch imperial expansion into Bengal, where East India trading companies mobilized native and European laborers on a mass scale to produce and transport silk textiles, saltpeter, opium, and tea. Matthias van Rossum explores how the Dutch East India Company mobilized a mixed, multi-ethnic labor regime of enslaved, corvée, and waged workers across the lands and seas of Asia. Timothy Coates, Johan Heinsen, James Dator, and Anita Rupprecht show how Portuguese, Danish, French, and English imperial planners built plantation colonies based on the combined work of European convicts and indentured servants as well as African slaves and, later, "liberated" apprentices. Yevan Terrien analyzes the geopolitically important military/agricultural outpost of early French colonial Louisiana, which depended on a mixture of enslaved and waged workers to support the rich sugar colonies in the Caribbean. Nicole Ulrich studies the mobile crew of European and indigenous servants, slaves, soldiers, and sailors in the Cape of Good Hope under Dutch rule in the late seventeenth and early eighteenth centuries. Jesse Olsavsky and Mary Mitchell treat slavery and runaways in the nineteenth-century U.S. "empire of cotton," which grew from massive land purchases, Indian removal, and imperial war to become a mature and hugely profitable plantation system. Hamish Maxwell-Stewart and Michael Quinlan present the history of labor and desertion in the Australian colony of Tasmania, which was practically "an open air panopticon" for captive, convict labor.

Who were these workers? Most of them were the vanquished, victims of expropriation of one kind or another in their native lands, who were thrown onto the roads and ways and eventually ships, often bound for far-flung colonies. Indentured servants arrived in the Leeward Islands from Nantes, Dublin, and London after expulsion from their home economies. Many of the indentured Europeans and all of the enslaved Africans were captive, stolen people, who had lost control not only over their means of living but also their bodies. Convicts and corvée workers came from Europe and Asia to labor for Danish and Dutch overseas companies in the East and West Indies. Convict labor often led to wage labor: criminals in French prisons were packed off as soldiers to colonial Louisiana. Danish convicts had their alienation inscribed on their foreheads; such branded "thief marks" formally excluded them and their children from Danish society. Even free wage laborers such as European sailors and soldiers were set in motion under conditions of coercion through conscription and violent discipline. Many of these workers had been peasants and artisans who lost their land, tools, and skills. Forced movement was a means of creating and imposing social control within a global accumulation of capital.

Although workers had come to the colonies by different routes, the use of fast feet created common experiences. Slaves, servants, and waged workers often found themselves cooperating on the same work sites. Some continued their cooperation subversively when they absconded. Running away could turn slaves into sailors, and soldiers into peasants. They frequently formed motley crews: Johannes Kodij, Maart from Bengal, Imandie from Naoer, Poese de Rozairo from Mozambique, Mira Kaffier from Madras, and Gregorius Jeremias from Oejang Sala all served under Captain Scott on a vessel en route to Malacca in March 1784. Desertion enabled such workers to scramble the neat categories of the global social division of labor and indeed to challenge them. The struggle over mobility was a potentially unifying experience.

Why, in the face of extreme punishments, did workers run, repeatedly and collectively? Running away was intimately linked to ideas of improving one's life by regaining some measure of control over the body, labor, and subsistence. Perhaps the most common reason for running away was dissatisfaction with working conditions. Grueling labor at sea or ashore drove sailors and soldiers in Louisiana, Indonesia, and Australia to fly from their masters. The super-exploitation of enslaved people in the Americas propelled runaways to inaccessible, defensible places where they built independent maroon communities. Others escaped aboard deep-sea vessels in what N. A. T. Hall called "maritime marronage."[4]

How to improve one's life depended on a worker's objectives and options. A major motivation of runaways was to form or renew family ties that had been torn asunder by forced labor. In the Cape Colony, Adam, a slave, had to run away to form his family with a Khoesan woman, Jannetje, and their son April. Tom, a liberated African from Tortola, assisted his wife, Jane, to run away as he could not bear her suffering at the hands of her employer. On reaching Mobile on the Gulf coast of North America, French soldiers complained that they came to the region to "settle down" as skilled workers, not to perform military drudgery. Other workers simply wanted more control over their time. Corvée workers in Dutch Ceylon ran away to protest the lengthening of the workday throughout the eighteenth century. Bondspeople in New Orleans temporarily escaped in and around the city to take time off from work, as did convicts in Van Diemen's Land. Soldiers and sailors ran away from work and "straggled" across town and country almost everywhere they were stationed. The struggle over time was nearly universal among coerced workers.

Some decisions to run depended on understanding the value of labor and its geopolitical setting. When "liberated" Africans were given menial jobs as apprentices, they ran away, knowing that skilled work would improve both their material lives and social status. Similarly, European sailors and soldiers frequently absconded to the armies of local and imperial elites in Mughal India, escaping the lowest positions in the company hierarchy and turning their martial skills in ordnance into higher wages. Both Irish indentured servants and enslaved Africans used their knowledge of the physical and political geography of the plantation regime in the early eighteenth-century Leeward Islands to play French and British colonial authorities against each other. French authorities were forced to promise runaway slaves "very pleasing and easy servitude" to avert desertion to their imperial enemies.

Running away has sometimes been presented by historians as an "individualist" form of resistance, to be contrasted with "collective" struggle epitomized in insurrection. The essays of this volume contradict this facile binary. First of all, most deserters ran away in groups, many of them repeatedly.[5] Some, like the Danish convicts Peder Vognmand and Jens Pedersen, left behind a trail of documentation that explained their every move. Even individual runaways depended on collective networks to make their way toward freedom. Frederick, an African apprentice in Tortola, made it to St. Thomas with the help of a free black woman, Sally Keys, "known for her sympathy towards the apprentices." Those who had experience in desertion encouraged others: runaways who returned to French Guadeloupe after three years' absence "encouraged" another desertion of six people a few years later.

Running produced innovation from above. Joint escapes sometimes encouraged imperial and class authorities to introduce new racial categories to divide them. Christopher Codrington, governor of the English Leeward Islands, proposed to "solve" the problem of desertion by decreasing the influx of white landless servants from Europe and building a racialized plantation regime based on the labor of enslaved Africans. They too of course ran away, but now poor, free whites were paid to catch and return them. This new "racial contract between the big planters, the small farmers, and the landless white laborers," writes James Dator, "offered a psychological wage large enough to reinforce the ideology of containment."

Deserters repeatedly shaped crises of sovereignty by creating and exploiting interimperial competition. Runaways in Louisiana and the Danish West Indies took advantage of the weaknesses of imperial control and fled the colonial settlement. Asian workers played one company against another, deserting here and there for better wages and privileges. Indentured servants in the Caribbean deserted from one empire to another, and runaway slaves formed maroon communities that initially challenged the colonial order and then gained a modicum of independence from it. In the United States slaves deserted to the north and helped abolitionists both to resist and critique American imperial expansion.

Desertion also contributed to the transformation of labor regimes in both colonies and modern states. Uncontrollable running essentially forced the Danish West India Company to abandon convict labor in St. Thomas and to initiate a transition toward full dependence on enslaved workers. Similarly, in the Leeward Islands, desertion pushed planters to decrease their employment of indentured servants and to shift their labor investment toward African slaves—who themselves created new headaches for their bosses by running away. In French Louisiana and precolonial Bengal, footloose workers shaped the relationship between European powers and indigenous polities. In Tortola the desertion of workers created frictions between the interests of local planters and metropolitan imperial planners, guiding how the latter conceptualized and implemented abolition. Runaway slaves from the American South educated abolitionist Vigilance Committees and the larger antislavery movement in the North, helping to create both the theory and the practice of abolition and finally creating a crisis that would lead to the Civil War. In this explosive situation the actions of runaways were genuinely revolutionary.

The essays in this volume seek to answer seven questions:

1. What were the causes of desertion? (in each specific time and place of study)
2. What is the "political economy of desertion"?
3. What kinds of knowledge made desertion possible?
4. How did workers understand and justify their mobility?
5. What has been the impact and historical significance of desertion / mobility?
6. How is desertion (and the diversity of deserters) related to class formation?
7. How is desertion related to other forms of resistance and class struggle?

Given the scarcity of sources, it is obviously not always possible to answer all of these questions in every case. The remainder of this introduction will formulate more general observations while placing the theme, period, and regions under study in a broader temporal, geographical, and theoretical frame.

CAPITALISM AND GLOBAL EMPIRES

This volume explores running away in the Atlantic and Indian Ocean regions during the first round of globalization, roughly the sixteenth, seventeenth, and eighteenth centuries, as a new kind of empire developed. Previous empires, even if they sometimes had overseas colonies, were primarily landed. The new empires consisted of a European metropolitan country and a string of dispersed colonies and trading posts, which often needed military and naval defense.[6] These empires were formed by the main seafaring states of Western Europe, and usually included

Caribbean or American colonies to produce silver, sugar, and tobacco and Asian strongpoints to supply the home market with spices, cotton, silk, porcelain, coffee and tea. Trade between Asia and Europe increased twenty-five-fold between the early sixteenth and late eighteenth centuries, and the trade between Europe and the Americas even more so.[7]

Vast armies of workers were needed to produce raw materials and goods for European markets. In India and China relatively strong states usually enabled local traders, producers, and workers to profit from European demand. Elsewhere in Asia and the Americas the European states and mercantile companies established a more direct rule and often forced local workers or free or unfree workers brought from elsewhere to produce the goods. Free workers were not easily convinced to take up these jobs as colonies were considered dangerous and unhealthy. If local labor was unavailable, the colonial empires resorted to unfree labor, bringing in convicts or enslaved workers. Many of the capitalist empires therefore included one or more African posts or colonies to procure enslaved Africans to work the plantations in the Americas.

Sailors, soldiers, indentured servants, convicts, and enslaved workers were crucial to make this global merchant capitalism work. The first two groups were male. The majority of indentured servants and convicts and the majority of the enslaved transported across the Atlantic were male, but over time a more even sexual balance resulted in slave communities.[8] As Hamish Maxwell-Stewart and Michael Quinlan note in their essay, more than four times as many men were transported as convicts to Australia than women. All in all, men made up the bulk of the deserters discussed in this volume. But Maxwell-Stewart and Quinlan also point out that, proportionally, female convicts were a bit more likely to be posted missing than male. Convict and slave runaways included both men and women.

LABOR HISTORY

As Van Rossum and Kamp state: "Mobility and desertion must be seen as integral parts of workers' strategies, part of repertoires of individual and collective acts, ranging from obedience and career making to strikes and mutinies. Desertion is crucial in this respect as it was not only a rejection of one's work and working conditions, but was also related to finding a better future, lying either in a new employment elsewhere, or in alternative ways of livelihood."[9] Within labor history, the decision of workers to withdraw their labor from their employers is an obvious tactic of resistance, employed in strikes. In the situations described in this volume, the power of the employers was so great that workers had to desert surreptitiously. They left not only the workplace, but also their communities, thereby becoming migrants.

Yet not all deserters aimed to burn their bridges. Hirschman's voice-exit typology can be used to categorize the types of desertion and running away.[10]

1. Bending and breaking the rules (acquiescence / voice);
2. Renegotiating labor conditions (voice);
3. Escaping from labor relations (exit).

Breaking the rules was running away with the aim to extend one's personal freedom without questioning the coerced labor relation as such. The runaway did not necessarily accept the labor system but considered the consequences of a more principled opposition (voice, exit) too grave. The many forms of "petit marronage" fit in this category. Absconding to visit one's relatives who lived on another plantation and returning after a few days, or escaping the brutal conditions of plantations for a brief time, were part of a wider repertoire of resistance and mobility. This phenomenon fits within a much longer tradition, for example the celebration of "blue Monday" by artisanal and industrial workers.[11] Somewhat similar was the temporary (and seasonal) exit of Russian peasants (*Otchotniki*), who combined work for their lord with wage labor in cities. In the first half of the nineteenth century some 136,000 in Moscow and 228,000 in St Petersburg—almost half the population—made such seasonal exits.[12] Many lords disliked the practice but were forced to give in, even though they required the workers to pay for internal passports and to leave their relatives as collateral. Such forms of agency could be a first step toward a more fundamental opposition to slavery or other forms of coerced labor.

Renegotiating labor conditions was running away to find a better deal elsewhere or to force employers to change the conditions of the existing working or contractual conditions.[13] Threatening to desert or actually doing so was sometimes a strategy to force employers to improve labor conditions and raise pay without fundamentally changing the labor relation as such. Rediker, for example, showed how in the early modern Atlantic maritime workers took advantage of labor shortages to "renegotiate" their service contract through desertion.[14] These types of desertion were part of the broader process of individual and collective bargaining.[15]

It seems no coincidence that desertion among sailors emerged as a strategy alongside the introduction of wage labor in the late medieval Mediterranean, where between 1250 and 1350 "owner-captains" negotiated sailors' wages as traditional, personal bonds between capital and labor broke down in medieval shipping. Only then did desertion from merchant ships become a significant problem in ports such as Venice, Genoa, and Pisa. Merchants offered sailors advance pay in order to procure labor and limit turnover. But sailors took the advance wages and tried to disappear into the increasingly anonymous ports of the later Middle Ages.[16] Shipowners fought back by employing professional agents to capture and return the sailors. Soldiers also deserted to get a better deal by enrolling again in another regiment of the same army. This was quite common in eighteenth-century Europe, for example during the Austrian War of Succession (1740–48), when illegal reenrollment was called "billardage," and those who did so illegally were known as "rouleurs."[17]

Escaping from labor relations altogether involved leaving one's cultural zone and explicitly linked running away to social change.[18] We can link this exit option to a classification of three modes of labor relations as developed by the International Institute of Social History.[19]

1. Escaping tributary labor relations (serfs, soldiers, convicts)
2. Escaping temporary coerced commodified labor relations (soldiers, sailors, servants, apprentices)
3. Escaping permanently coerced commodified labor relations (slaves)

Escaping tributary labor was not limited to convicts who populate the chapters by Heinsen and Maxwell-Stewart and Quinlan.[20] It includes people sentenced to (heavy) labor in faraway penal colonies for very long periods or for life, such as Van Diemen's Land and Andaman Islands (Britain), Guiana and New Caledonia (France), Siberia (Russia), Angola and Mozambique (Portugal), and other colonies.[21] It also includes peasants who since at least the early Middle Ages ran away in large numbers to cities to avoid corvée labor. Only when feudalism waned in Western Europe in the fifteenth century did this type of running away dwindle. Between 1727–42 some 325,000 Russian serfs headed to sparsely settled lands in the Kazan and Voronezh provinces to the East and the South, where they set themselves up as state peasants with families and sometimes entire villages.[22] The number of fugitives swelled in the nineteenth century, when Siberia became a popular destination. State officials in the South and the East welcomed runaway peasants in the southern steppes and in Siberia until well into the eighteenth century, showing how the interests of the nobility and the state could diverge.[23]

Others who tried to escape tributary labor were men whose military service was a form of corvée. This phenomenon had deep roots throughout Eurasia and Africa. In contrast to mercenaries, many states forced men into military service. Although conscription only became widespread after the French Revolution,[24] earlier forms of obligatory military service fit the tributary labor relation model: "The precise form that the tributary labor relationship takes can vary from legal enslavement (as in the Ottoman *devşirme*) to levies for specific campaigns, hereditary obligations (as in the case of the Ming where households were obliged to provide one member of the household for military service instead of corvée or tax obligations) and early and modern forms of conscription."[25]

Feudal military mobilization was especially widespread in the early modern period and before, ranging from the French *milice royal*,[26] to the Ottoman *timar* system and the German and Habsburg *Wehrbauer* to Russian Cossacks.[27] In many parts of the world, like India, China, and the Middle East, military service mixed tributary service, mercenary work, and slavery.[28] Perquisites and privileges deterred some military workers from running away—for example, the elite Turkish slaves in the Ghulam/Mamluk in the Abbasid Caliphate from the ninth century onward.[29] But among other segments of the army, especially the draftees and pressed soldiers, running away was endemic.[30]

Fleeing the army or the navy without consent almost always involved migrations beyond cultural boundaries. Desertion and draft dodging in France during the French Revolution was common and involved hundreds of thousands of men, many of whom moved to other cities or polities, thereby changing their legal status.[31] Many deserters found employment in local French industries, or organized themselves as bands of woodcutters and quarrymen. Others went to ports like Bordeaux, hoping to escape to the colonies or the United States.[32] Many fled to other polities that had ideological, (geo)political, or military reasons to welcome them, as when soldiers conscripted in eighteenth-century Habsburg army deserted to the Ottoman empire.[33]

As numerous contributors to this volume make clear,[34] commodified labor in many parts of the world, including Europe, was until the nineteenth century organized through various sorts of contracts that tied workers to employers. In Western Europe this goes back to the English *Ordinance of Labourers* (1351), which included penalties for workers who departed their workplace prematurely.[35] Although people in principle entered labor contracts freely, they could not leave without permission until the contract expired, which added the element of force to the labor relation.[36] How many broke their contracts and left prematurely, and where they ran to, has not been systematically studied. Yet it is clear that soldiers, sailors, and domestic workers, many of whom were pressed into service one way or another, ran away in great numbers.[37] Their labor conditions were often bad, pay was low, and (corporal) punishments were more the rule than the exception. This was true for many parts of the world including eighteenth-century North America, where in 1759 Benjamin Franklin remarked that the majority of labor was performed by "indentured servants brought from Great Britain."[38] Many of them absconded after receiving a recruiter's "farthing," often soon after landing in the colonies, or jumping ship after having left an English port.[39]

Rates of desertion among soldiers and sailors in the early modern period varied. The rate in German armies in the late seventeenth and eighteenth centuries was between five and fifty percent,[40] whereas the Dutch Republic had a staggering high level of 40 percent at the end of the eighteenth century.[41] Given the risk of punishment many soldiers absconded to other polities, like the French soldiers who ran to territories of the Holy Roman Empire or the Dutch Republic.[42] Runaways who crossed not only a political but also a religious border could increase their welcome when they converted. A good example was the siege of Eger (present-day Hungary) by the Ottomans in 1596, when 250 Christian soldiers fled to the Ottoman empire "and became Turk," just like 500 Walloon soldiers did four years later.[43] Sailors in service of the European East India companies were less inclined to abscond. Mutinies occurred regularly aboard European ships in Asia, but these were perhaps limited by fewer options to flee within Asia.[44]

Finally we arrive at those people who had the best reason to escape, because they had been enslaved against their will, most of them with slim chances of ever being freed again. The most extreme example were chattel slaves whose descendants inherited their oppressed condition. Their rate of escape depended on geography and other circumstances, but as conditions were appalling and discipline brutal, many did try to run away. Their owners therefore did everything they could to prevent their escape, not only because they had invested heavily in "human capital," but also because runaways undermined the legitimacy of the slave system and enticed others to follow their example. The chapters by Mitchell, Oslavsky, Dator, and Ulrich, on the U.S. South, the Caribbean, and the Cape Colony in South Africa, illuminate the runaway practices of enslaved Africans who were brought against their will to the Americas or who were forcefully moved within Africa.

Slaves left plantations, or farms, planning to settle permanently in areas where the slave regime had limited access, such as swamps, hills, and forests, or the borderlands of the Cape Colony. Sometimes colonial rulers accepted this *grand marronage* and recognized maroon communities through treaties.[45] Powerful maroon communities developed in Jamaica, Brazil, and Suriname, but much less so in the U.S. South.[46] Another form of escaping slavery was to flee to other polities, often overseas. The most obvious destinations were states where slavery was abolished, like Mexico in 1824,[47] English territories in the Caribbean after 1838, then France in 1848, and finally Canada.

States that had institutionalized slavery could also offer runaway slaves protection, as for example in New Spain in the eighteenth century. Spanish colonial rulers in what is now Venezuela and Mexico welcomed former slaves as new settlers in thinly populated parts of the empire, not unlike rulers of Russian peripheries had done in Tsarist Siberia. Ex-slaves who converted to Catholicism became especially effective "agents of empire."[48] These groups of runaways could also include European indentured servants, as in Barbados in the middle of the seventeenth century ("several Irish servants and negroes") and eighteenth-century Virginia.[49] Ethnically mixed groups of runaways also formed communities in Asia and South Africa.[50]

By far the best-known example of fleeing to another polity is the "underground railroad" by which southern U.S. slaves, helped by free blacks and whites who principally opposed slavery, were smuggled to Northern states and Canada in the nineteenth century.[51] The numbers are uncertain, but may amount to 100,000,[52] of whom some 30,000 reached Canada.[53] Although we have no good quantitative evidence, scholars estimate that the numbers of runaways who remained in the South were much larger than those who escaped to the North or to Mexico.[54] By far most of them took to cities in the South where they hoped to blend in with the existing communities of free blacks.[55] Even on small Caribbean slave islands, cities functioned as places of refuge, as on the Danish island of St. Croix, with small cities such as Christiansted, Frederiksted, and Charlotte Amalie, where free blacks but also poor whites hid runaway slaves.[56]

Much less is known about runaway slaves in other parts of the world, like Africa and Asia. We have some indications that slaves in Africa, or those being threatened by slave raiders, fled to territories where African rulers could not reach them, but the possibility of "fleeing the state"[57] seems to have been limited.[58] More is known about enslaved sailors, soldiers, and commoners in the early modern Mediterranean. Due to the scarcity of rowers for the galleys and the constant frictions between Christian and Muslim polities, slave raiding by both sides was common practice after the late Middle Ages.[59] This included, on the Christian side, vagrants and gypsies who were caught in German and French states and sold as rowers to city states like Venice, Rovereto, and Genua.[60] In total in the period 1500–1800 slave raiders may have taken a million Europeans, more than half a million North African Muslims, and 375,000 African slaves to Spain and Portugal to work on sugar plantations in the Mediterranean and the Canary Islands.[61] Many of these captives were released after ransoms were paid, or were freed by force. How many ran away is unclear.

Table 0.1 shows that the causes for running away boil down to dissatisfaction with coercion, prevailing labor relations, and pay and work conditions. Whether people ran away depended on a mix of concerns, ranging from (political or natural) geography (was there a viable place to run to?), to knowledge and networks, to the force of the punitive regime and its disciplining effects. The motivations to run determined the form of running away. In situations without obvious places to escape to, and where workers were in no position to bargain, *breaking the rules* within the dominant coercive labor relation was the only option. People often disobeyed the rules despite the prospect of harsh punishments. There are ample indications that breaking the rules was motivated by a sense of injustice and the wish to reestablish some sort of autonomy.

The transition from breaking the rules to running away as a *negotiating* strategy was gradual and depended on the bargaining power of the workers involved. When labor or skills were scarce and employers had no immediate alternative, workers often used desertion as a weapon to negotiate better terms. Their action did not change the labor system as such, but it did stimulate class (or at least occupational-group) consciousness and established the limits of the employer's disciplinary power. Some runaways would develop a more radical approach that could lead to *escape* with no intention to return, to move toward a new polity with more favorable labor conditions or to join a maroon society. Escaping could—and often did—result in new labor relations, such as self-employment or freer forms of wage labor.

TABLE 0.1 The relationship between forms of running away and the seven leading questions of this volume.

	Causes	Political Economy	Knowledge	Workers' Justification	Impact	Class Formation	Class Struggle
Bending and Breaking the Rules	Dissatisfaction with prevailing labor relations	Coerced labor relations	Collective knowledge about limits of opposition	Reaction to violations of the moral economy and feelings of injustice	*Low*	Mainly leaves the status quo intact	Virtually absent
Renegotiating	Dissatisfaction with pay and work conditions	Rising impact of commodified labor	Geographical and labor market knowledge	Conscious bargaining strategy	*Medium* Stimulated individual and collective bargaining	Increased class consciousness	Shows that class struggles long predated the industrial era
Escaping	Resistance against social control and (extreme) coercion	Varies from patriarchy to chattel slavery	Geographical and political-economic knowledge	From individual motives to better one's live to collective resistance against extreme coercion	*Large* Due to erosion of: (1) prevailing family systems; (2) labor relations	Can lead to new class formations (wage labor, self-employment)	May take the form of class struggle but not necessarily so

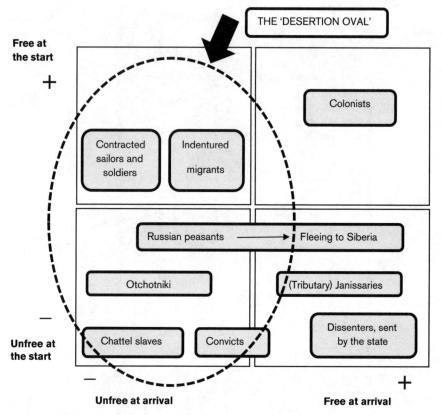

FIGURE 0.1. Desertion Oval.

The greater the coercion workers faced, the greater their likelihood of looking for alternatives and voting with their feet. Yet this was only possible if they had the necessary knowledge and alternatives. The "Desertion Oval" in Figure 0.1 shows that the phenomenon of running away was largely limited to labor relations in which migrants were bonded at the source of their work, with chattel slavery as the strongest example.

Yet not all deserters were unfree at their origin and at destination: indentured servants, soldiers, and sailors were also likely to run away. Being unfree at the origin, however, did not necessarily lead to escape. Bonded migrants who were offered a privileged position at destination, even if they formally remained slaves, lacked the incentive to leave. For most of them the trade-off was acceptable. The formerly Christian Janissaries in the Ottoman empire and Russian religious dissenters in the nineteenth century exemplify the point.

MIGRATION HISTORY

The history of desertion must be connected to the blossoming field of migration history. Although the transportation of slaves, and to some extent that of soldiers and sailors, has been the subject of increasing interest among historians of migration,[62] what happened after arrival, or during the time that these migrants navigated the colonial circuit, has not been a topic of systematic study. Migration and mobility as forms of resistance, linked to forced labor, however, has a long history, reaching back—at least—to the Babylonian empire.[63] This is not surprising since forced labor has been common throughout history. Today people continue to migrate to escape oppressive labor relations, such as the Eritreans who are pressed into military service at home or indigenous Guatemalans facing labor demands by the state.[64] Geographical mobility has long been central to escaping repressive labor relations.

This point is well illustrated by Linda Rupert in her work on marronage from the Dutch island of Curaçao to the "Tierra Firme" of the Spanish empire. She writes, "The stories of these intrepid individuals require us to rethink the traditional narrative of marronage. As dozens of cases in the Venezuelan archives attest, these immigrants were as much running towards something known and attractive—the promise of legal freedom, land, and economic opportunities—as they were fleeing away from an oppressive slave society. Like immigrants throughout history, their journeys were based on calculated, carefully informed decisions."[65]

Rupert reconstructed the patterns and mechanisms of running away of almost 600 slaves from Curaçao to what is now Venezuela, between 1729 and 1774, as part of a much larger emigration. By 1720 already some 20,000 maritime maroons from Dutch, Danish, and Caribbean plantation islands had fled to the mainland. Until the end of the eighteenth century the Spanish imperial rulers welcomed them, especially if they converted to Catholicism, settled in sparsely populated regions, and thus acted as agents of empire. This strategy of the Spanish colonial authorities was also implemented in Puerto Rico toward runaways from the Danish Caribbean island of St. Croix and for slaves who escaped from South Carolina to Spanish Florida in the eighteenth century.[66]

Mainstream migration historians—who limit themselves largely to international mobility and to free self-deciding individuals—have paid little attention to these movements. Unfree movers, like slaves and convicts, but also those who more or less freely entered labor contracts, like sailors and soldiers, as well as other "organizational migrants," are often left out of the picture.[67] Their subsequent position as (oppressive) agents of empire further bolsters their exclusion from the field.[68]

In order to analyze running away as a form of migration it is necessary to go beyond the modernist and Eurocentric definition of the phenomenon. Since the 1980s many scholars have criticized the "tyranny du national"[69] and pointed at the structural similarities of international and internal migrations, and at the same time stressed that temporal and seasonal moves should be included.[70] Moreover, mainstream migration history also reproduced the modernization paradigm, assuming that mass migration only really began with the ascent of industrial capitalism during the first round of globalization after 1820, enabled by the transportation and communication revolution of the long nineteenth century.

As Patrick Manning and others have shown, however, human societies have always been inherently mobile, long before the assumed mobility transition.[71] Temporary migrants, such as soldiers and sailors, were an important part of this mobility, not least because of their role as empire builders. These "organizational migrants" differed from other labor migrants in that the decision of where to migrate was taken by the institution or organization they joined. Although most of these migrants entered their contracts freely, the prevailing labor conditions—in terms of pay, food, working hours, and not least discipline—often caused conflicts, which led to mutiny and desertion. A second category of migrants that stands out in this volume are those who were forced into slavery, in Africa and elsewhere, and subsequently transported, whether within a polity or to another continent. Although slavery (and runaway slaves) has a much longer history, chattel slavery was boosted between 1600 and 1850 by the demand for labor at production sites, especially by the emerging plantation economies in the Caribbean, but also in the Indian Ocean.

Deserters ran to sparsely populated frontier areas of colonial empires, to another polity, or simply to another regiment or ship, but an especially attractive destination was a city, a port city in particular. In this respect chattel slaves in the Americas resembled serfs in Russia. As the chapter by Mitchell shows, hiding in urban co-ethnic communities within a relatively anonymous environment provided protection. Moreover, as Marcus Rediker has pointed out, deserters spread radical ideas through port cities,[72] showing how runaways contributed to broader cross-cultural interactions in the realm of knowledge and cultural practices.

Runaways bridged labor and migration by acting as intermediaries and facilitators.[73] Flight was made possible by networks of materially self-interested or ideologically principled people who helped deserters run to safe places. The offer of support through the "underground railroad," free blacks in cities, or employers looking for soldiers in revolutionary France or convicts in Van Diemen's Land[74] created networks and enabled transport. These networks often determined the direction and destination of the flight.

FLIGHT AS FIGHT

The history of runaways illuminates the globalizing world in the early modern period with tentacles deep into the nineteenth century. The essays in this volume highlight unexpected links between very different forms of resistance against oppressive labor relations and thus de-exocitizes the experiences of African origin maroons in the New World as well as those of Asian deserters in India. Both groups reacted similarly as bonded and indentured laborers inside and outside Europe,[75] whether they were employed as sailors, soldiers, servants, artisans, or agricultural workers. In many instances they acted together.

An emphasis on labor relations reveals commonalities in the actions of runaways around the world who fought bonded labor, opposed injustice, and pursued a better life. But that is not all. Running away was not restricted to the Atlantic and the Indian Ocean worlds between 1600 and 1850, but is a much broader phenomenon, both spatially and historically, depending on the prevailing labor relations and the availability of spaces of refuge. Whether the first round of globalization constituted a peak in the number of runaways, due to the expansion of the industrial plantation complex, trade, and the concomitant use of soldiers and sailors far away from home, is a topic for additional comparative research. It is already clear that the mechanisms and agency laid bare in this volume will illuminate similar situations in different temporal and geographical cases and as such can function as important heuristic and theoretical tools.

NOTES

1. Most of the papers collected in this volume were presented at a workshop at the International Institute of Social History in Amsterdam on 22–23 October 2015 and at the Department of History / Dietrich School of Arts and Sciences of the University of Pittsburgh on 4–5 May 2016. All were reworked again after the second workshop. This introduction reflects ideas that we gleaned from the debates among the participants at the workshops and from the editors of this volume. The introduction is thus in many ways a result of collective work, but the two authors alone are responsible for any errors.

2. Matthias van Rossum, *Werkers van de wereld: Globalisering, Arbeid en Interculturele Ontmoetingen Tussen Aziatische en Europese Zeelieden in dienst van de VOC, 1600–1800* (Hilversum: Verloren, 2014), 201–3; Van Rossum, "'Working for the Devil': Desertion in the Eurasian Empire of the VOC," in *Desertion in the Early Modern World,* ed. Matthias van Rossum and Jeanette Kamp (London: Bloomsbury, 2016), 127–58.

3. Unless otherwise noted, the examples and quotations in what follows are taken from the accompanying essays.

4. N. A. T. Hall, "Maritime Maroons: 'Grand Marronage' from the Danish West Indies," *William and Mary Quarterly* 42, no. 4 (October 1985): 476–98.

5. Terrien shows that in Louisiana between 1715 and 1760, only one-fourth of desertions were by single soldiers, and half ran in groups of four or more. In a paper presented at our first workshop, but not included in this volume, Karwan Fatah-Black gave as comparable figures for runaway sailors in Surinam (1767–1802), 34 percent deserting singly and 31 percent in groups of more than four.

6. Jane Burbank and Frederick Cooper, eds., *Empires in World History: Power and the Politics of Difference* (Princeton, NJ: Princeton University Press, 2010); Herbert Münkler, *Imperien: Die Logik der Weltherrschaft vom Alten Rom bis zu den Vereinigten Staaten* (Berlin: Rowohlt, 2005).

7. Pim de Zwart, *Globalization and the Colonial Origins of the Great Divergence: Intercontinental Trade and Living Standards in the Dutch East India Company's Commercial Empire, c. 1600–1800* (Leiden: Brill, 2016).

8. Herbert S. Klein, *The Atlantic Slave Trade* (Cambridge: Cambridge University Press, 1999), 161–68; David Eltis, *The Rise of African Slavery in the Americas* (Cambridge: Cambridge University Press, 2000), 85–113.

9. Matthias van Rossum and Jeanette Kamp, eds., *Desertion in the Early Modern World* (London: Bloomsbury, 2016), 4.

10. Albert O. Hirschman, *Exit, Voice, and Loyalty: Responses to Decline in Firms, Organizations, and States* (Cambridge, MA: Harvard University Press, 1970). Hirschman suggested three possible answers to policies formulated by authorities or products from companies: loyalty (follow the policies, buy the product), voice (make one's objections to them known) or exit (switch to an alternative). We follow Van Rossum in adopting acquiescence for Hirschman's loyalty, as loyalty assumes a much too positive attitude to expect from these workers toward their working and living conditions or the authorities that enforced them: E. A. Hoffmann, "Exit and Voice: Organizational Loyalty and Dispute Resolution Strategies," *Social Forces* 84, no. 4 (2006): 2313–30.

11. H. G. Gutman, "Work, Culture and Society in Industrializing America, 1815–1919," *American Historical Review* 78 (1973): 531–88; Kate Trenschel, *Under the Influence: Working-Class Drinking, Temperance, and Cultural Revolution in Russia, 1895–1932* (Pittsburgh: University of Pittsburgh Press, 2006), 26; George S. Kealy, *Toronto Workers Respond to Industrial Capitalism, 1867–1892* (Toronto: University of Toronto Press, 1980), 54.

12. Peter Kolchin, *Unfree Labor: American Slavery and Russian Serfdom* (Cambridge, MA: Harvard University Press, 1987).

13. As shown in the chapters in this volume of Chakraborty, Van Rossum, and Rupprecht.

14. Marcus Rediker, *Between the Devil and the Deep Blue Sea: Merchant Seamen, Pirates and the Anglo-American Maritime World, 1700–1750* (Cambridge: Cambridge University Press, 1989), 101–5; Rediker, *Outlaws of the Atlantic: Sailors, Pirates and Motley Crews in the Age of Sail* (Boston: Beacon Press, 2014).

15. Christian G. de Vito and Alex Lichtenstein, eds., *Global Convict Labour* (Leiden: Brill, 2015); O. Becerril, "Transnational Work and the Gendered Politics of Labour: A Study of Gender and Escape, or on the Racialization of Escape and Female Mexican Migrant Farm Workers in Canada," in *Organizing the Transnational: Labour, Politics and Social Change*, ed. L. Goldring and S. Krishnamurti (Vancouver and Toronto: UBC Press, 2007), 157–72.

16. R. P. Jackson, "From Profit-Sailing to Wage Sailing: Mediterranean Owner-Captains and Their Crews during the Medieval Commercial Revolution," *Journal of European Economic History* 18, no. 3 (1989): 605–28.

17. A. Corvisier, *L'armée francaise de la fin du XVIIIe siècle au ministère de Choiseul: Le soldat* (Paris: PUF, 1964), 55, 711–13, 725–47. See also Jan Lucassen and Leo Lucassen, *The Mobility Transition in Europe Revisited, 1500–1900: Sources and Methods* (Amsterdam: International Institute of Social History, IISH Research Papers, 2010), 74.

18. Patrick Manning, *Migration in World History* (New York: Routledge, 2013); Jan Lucassen and Leo Lucassen, "Theorizing Cross-Cultural Migrations: The Case of Eurasia since 1500," *Social Science History* 41, no. 3 (2017): 445–75.

19. Karin Hofmeester and Pim de Zwart, eds., *Colonialism, Institutional Change and Shifts in Global Labour Relations* (Amsterdam: Amsterdam University Press, 2018). See also Leo Lucassen, "Working Together: New Directions in Global Labour History," *Journal of Global History* 11, no. 1 (2016): 66–87.

20. See De Vito and Lichtenstein (*Global Convict Labour*, 1–4) on the place of convicts within the global labor relations typology, as both tributary and commodified labor. See also Marcel van der Linden, *Workers of the World; Essays toward a Global Labor History* (Leiden: Brill, 2008), 20.

21. Timothy J. Coates, *Convict Labor in the Portuguese Empire, 1740–1932: Redefining the Empire with Forced Labor and New Imperialism* (Leiden, Brill: 2014), chap. 6; Stephen A. Toth, *Beyond Papillon:*

The French Overseas Penal Colonies, 1854–1952 (Lincoln: University of Nebraska Press, 2006); De Vito and Lichtenstein, *Global Convict Labour;* Eric Richards, "Migration to Colonial Australia: Paradigms and Disjunction," in *Migration, Migration History, History: Old Paradigms and New Perspectives,* ed. Jan Lucassen and Leo Lucassen (Bern: Peter Lang, 1997), 151–76; Hamish Maxwell-Stewart, "Convict Labour Extraction and Transportation from Britain and Ireland, 1615–1870," in De Vito and Lichtenstein, *Global Convict Labour,* 168–96, 169.

22. Peter Kolchin, *American Slavery, 1619–1877* (New York: Hill and Wang, 1993), 279.

23. Ibid., 280.

24. Jan Lucassen and Erik-Jan Zürcher, "Conscription as Military Labour: The Historical Context," *International Review of Social History* 43, no. 3 (1998): 405–19.

25. Erik-Jan Zürcher, "Introduction: Understanding Changes in Military Recruitment and Employment Worldwide," in *Fighting for a Living: A Comparative History of Military Labour 1500–2000,* ed. Erik-Jan Zürcher (Amsterdam: Amsterdam University Press, 2013), 11–41, 20.

26. Alan Forrest, *Conscripts and Deserters: The Army and French Society during the Revolution and Empire* (New York and Oxford: Oxford University Press, 1989), 9–10.

27. Zürcher, "Introduction," 20.

28. Kaushik Roy, "From the Mamluks to the Mansabdars: A Social History of Military Service in South Asia, c. 1500 to c. 1650," in Zürcher, *Fighting for a Living,* 81–114, 87.

29. Peter Jackson, "Turkish Slaves on Islam's Indian Frontier," in *Slavery and South Asian History,* ed. I. Chatterjee and R. M. Eaton (Bloomington: Indiana University Press, 2006), 63–82, 70.

30. See the chapter by Terrien on French soldiers in Louisiana.

31. Forrest, *Conscripts and Deserters,* 70, 99.

32. Ibid., 63, 111.

33. John Komlos, *Nutrition and Economic Development in the Eighteenth-Century Habsburg Monarchy* (Princeton, NJ: Princeton University Press, 1989), 53.

34. See the chapters by Terrien, Ulrich, Chakraborty, Dator, and Van Rossum.

35. Robert J. Steinfeld, *The Invention of Free Labor: The Employment Relation in English and American Law and Culture, 1350–1870* (Chapel Hill: University of North Carolina Press, 1991), 35.

36. Alessandro Stanziani, *Sailors, Slaves, and Immigrants: Bondage in the Indian Ocean World, 1750–1914* (New York: Palgrave, 2014).

37. Kolchin, *American Slavery,* 241, 257, 278.

38. Matthew Harris, "'A Mean and Brutal Business': Indentured Servitude in Early Americas," in *British Colonial America: People and Perspectives,* ed. John A. Grigg (Santa Barbara: ABC Clio, 2008), 21–40, 30.

39. Marilyn C. Baseler, *"Asylum for Mankind": America, 1607–1800* (Ithaca, NY: Cornell University Press, 1998), 90; see also Steinfeld, *Invention of Free Labor,* 45–51.

40. Jeannette Kamp, "Between Agency and Force: The Dynamics of Desertion in a Military Labour Market, Frankfurt am Main 1650–1800," in Van Rossum and Kamp, *Desertion in the Early Modern World,* 49–72, 57.

41. Pepijn Brandon, "'The Privilege of Using Their Legs': Leaving the Dutch Army in the Eighteenth Century," in Van Rossum and Kamp, *Desertion in the Early Modern World,* 73–93, 85.

42. Forrest, *Conscripts and Deserters,* 7.

43. Gábor Ágoston, *Guns for the Sultan: Military Power and the Weapons Industry in the Ottoman Empire* (Cambridge: Cambridge University Press, 2005), 27.

44. Matthias van Rossum, "'Amok!': Mutinies and Slaves on Dutch East Indiamen in the 1780s," *International Review of Social History* 58, no. 21 (2013): 109–30, 127–28.

45. Richard Price, "Maroons and Their Communities," in *The Slavery Reader,* ed. Gad Heuman and James Walvin (New York and London: Routledge, 2003), 608–25; see also the chapter by Coates for an example of de facto but not formal recognition.

46. James Sidbury, "Resistance to Slavery," in *The Routledge History of Slavery*, ed. Gad Heuman and Trevor Burnard (New York and London: Routledge, 2011), 204–19.

47. Sarah E. Cornell, "Citizens of Nowhere: Fugitive Slaves and Free African Americans in Mexico, 1833–1857," *Journal of American History* 100, no. 2 (2013): 351–74.

48. Linda M. Rupert, "Marronage, Manumission and Maritime Trade in the Early Modern Caribbean," *Slavery and Abolition* 30, no. 3 (2009): 361–82.

49. Timothy James Lockley, "Race Relations in Slave Societies," in Heuman and Burnard, *Routledge History of Slavery*, 248–64.

50. Van Rossum, " 'Amok' ", and the chapter by Ulrich.

51. See the chapter by Oslavsky.

52. Eric Foner, *Gateway to Freedom: The Hidden History of the Underground Railroad* (New York: W. W. Norton, 2015) 4.

53. J. A. Banks and C. A. Banks, *March toward Freedom: A History of Black Americans* (New York: Fearon, 1970).

54. Kolchin, *American Slavery*, 158.

55. Damian Pargas, *Slavery and Forced Migration in the Antebellum South* (Cambridge: Cambridge University Press, 2014) 208, 249. See also the chapter by Mitchell.

56. Neville A. T. Hall, "Maritime Maroons: Grand Marronage from the Danish West Indies," in *Origins of the Black Atlantic*, ed. Laurent Dubois and Julius S. Scott (New York and London: Routledge, 2010), 47–68, 56–57.

57. James C. Scott, *The Art of Not Being Governed: An Anarchist History of Upland Southeast Asia* (New Haven, CT: Yale University Press, 2009).

58. Gareth Austin, "Factor Markets in Nieboer Conditions: Early Modern West Africa, c. 1500–c. 1900," *Continuity and Change* 24, no. 1 (2009): 23–53; Ibrahim Thiaw, "From the Senegal River to Siin: The Archaeology of Sereer Migrations in North-Western Senegambia," in *Migration and Membership Regimes in Global and Historical Perspective*, ed. Ulbe Bosma, Gijs Kessler, and Leo Lucassen (Leiden and Boston: Brill, 2012), 93–111.

59. Jan Lucassen and Leo Lucassen, "The Mobility Transition Revisited, 1500–1900: What the Case of Europe Can Offer to Global History," *Journal of Global History* 4, no. 4 (2009): 347–77; Robert C. Davis, "Counting Slaves on the Barbary Coast," *Past and Present* 172, (2001): 87–124; Davis, *Christian Slaves, Muslim Masters: White Slavery in the Mediterranean, the Barbary Coast, and Italy, 1500–1800* (New York: Palgrave Macmillan, 2003); Christian G. de Vito and Alex Lichtenstein, "Writing a Global History of Convict Labour," in De Vito and Lichtenstein, *Global Convict Labour*, 1–45, 11.

60. Leo Lucassen, *Zigeuner: Die Geschichte eines polizeilichen Ordnungsbegriffes in Deutschland 1700–1945* (Köln: Böhlau, 1996), 50.

61. Lucassen and Lucassen, *Mobility Transition in Europe Revisited*, 11, 17.

62. Dirk Hoerder, *Cultures in Contact: World Migrations in the Second Millennium* (Durham, NC: Duke University Press, 2002); Stanziani, *Sailors, Slaves, and Immigrants;* Jan Lucassen and Leo Lucassen, eds., *Globalising Migration History: The Eurasian Experience (16th–21st Centuries)* (Leiden: Brill, 2014); Jelle van Lottum, "The Necessity and Consequences of Internationalisation: Maritime Work in the Dutch Republic in the 17th and 18th Centuries," in *The Sea in History: The Early Modern World*, ed. Christian Buchet and Gérard le Bouëdec (Martlesham: Boydell Press, 2017), 839–51.

63. C. H. W. Johns, *Babylonian and Assyrian Laws, Contracts and Letters* (New York: Charles Scribner's Sons, 1904); H. W. F. Saggs, *Babylonians* (Berkeley: University of California Press, 2000), 56; see also Thomas Wiedemann, *Greek and Roman Slavery* (Baltimore: Johns Hopkins University Press, 1981), 11.

64. Carole A. Smith, *Guatemalan Indians and the State: 1540 to 1988* (Austin: University of Texas Press, 1990).

65. Rupert, "Marronage," 374–75.

66. Hall, "Maritime Maroons." Florida was part of the Spanish empire until 1763, when the British took over. Between 1783–1821, however, Spanish rule was reinstated. See also Jessica V. Roitman, "Land of Hope and Dreams: Slavery and Abolition in the Dutch Leeward Islands, 1825–1865," *Slavery and Abolition* 37, no. 2 (2016): 375–98, for similar runaways from Dutch to British Leeward Islands in the nineteenth century.

67. Only since the late 1990s has this been changing: Jan Lucassen and Leo Lucassen, eds., *Migration, Migration History, History: Old Paradigms and New Perspectives* (Bern: Peter Lang, 1997); Hoerder, *Cultures in Contact*; Manning, *Global Migration History*; Donna Gabaccia and Dirk Hoerder, eds., *Connecting Seas and Connected Ocean Rims: Indian, Atlantic and Pacific Oceans and China Seas Migrations from the 1830s to the 1930s* (Leiden and Boston: Brill, 2011).

68. As argued in Leo Lucassen and Aniek X. Smit, "The Repugnant Other: Soldiers, Missionaries and Aid Workers as Organizational Migrants," *Journal of World History* 25, no. 4 (2015): 1–39; Jan Lucassen, ed., *Global Labour History: A State of the Art* (Bern: Peter Lang, 2006); Clare Anderson, Niklas Frykman, et al., eds., *Mutiny and Maritime Radicalism in the Age of Revolution: A Global Survey*, special issue, *International Review of Social History* (Cambridge: Cambridge University Press, 2013).

69. Gerard Noiriel, *La Tyrannie du National: Le Droit d'Asile en Europe (1793–1993)* (Paris: Calmann-Lévy, 1991).

70. Pioneering is the work of Leslie Page Moch, *Paths to the City: Regional Migration in Nineteenth-Century France* (Beverly Hills: Sage, 1983) and Jan Lucassen, *Migrant Labour in Europe: The Drift to the North Sea* (London: Croom Helm, 1987).

71. Manning, *Global Migration History*; Leslie P. Moch, *Moving Europeans: Migration in Western Europe since 1650* (Bloomington: Indiana University Press, 2003); Jan Lucassen, Leo Lucassen, and Patrick Manning, eds., *Migration History in World History: Multidisciplinary Approaches* (Leiden: Brill, 2010); Lucassen and Lucassen, *Globalising Migration History*.

72. Rediker, *Devil and the Deep Blue Sea*; Peter Linebaugh and Marcus Rediker, *The Many-Headed Hydra: Sailors, Slaves, Commoners, and the Hidden History of the Revolutionary Atlantic* (New York: Verso, 2000).

73. On labor see Ulbe Bosma, Elise van Nederveen Meerkerk, et al., eds., *Mediating Labour: Worldwide Labour Intermediation in the Nineteenth and Twentieth Centuries*, special issue, *International Review of Social History* (Cambridge: Cambridge University Press, 2012). For migration see Drew Keeling, *The Business of Transatlantic Migration between Europe and the USA, 1900–1914* (Zürich: Chronos, 2012); Torsten Feys, *The Battle for the Migrants: The Introduction of Steamshipping on the North Atlantic and Its Impact on the European Exodus* (St. John's, Newfoundland: International Maritime Economic History Association, 2013); Christopher Rass, "Temporary Labour Migration and State-Run Recruitment of Foreign Workers in Europe, 1919–1975: A New Migration Regime?," *International Review of Social History* 57, no. 20 (2012): 191–224; John Salt and Jeremy Stein, "Migration as a Business: The Case of Trafficking," *International Migration* 35, no. 4 (1997): 467–94.

74. See the chapter by Maxwell-Stewart.

75. As Terrien notes in his chapter on French soldiers in Louisiana: "The Mississippi soldiers often deserted for the same reasons as their counterparts in France."

1

Runaways and Deserters in the Early Modern Portuguese Empire

The Examples of São Tomé Island, South Asia, and Southern Portugal

Timothy Coates

Portugal created an early modern empire that was extraordinary for its duration and global scope. It began in 1415 with the capture of the North African trading center of Ceuta. Stretching around the globe from Brazil, half the South American continent, to four Atlantic archipelagos, a series of coastal enclaves along the western, southern, and eastern African coastlines, it included a widely dispersed collection of outposts along the Indian Ocean littoral and ultimately Macau and Timor.

This empire was huge and equally porous. In spite of numerous edicts to the contrary, individuals entered and left the Portuguese World with great frequency. Selected convicts were deliberately abandoned along the African and Brazilian coasts as their punishments, with the idea that they would learn local languages and customs and facilitate future exchanges. Merchants and missionaries came and went throughout the empire. Runaways and deserters were also part of this picture, although their names and deeds are not always known.[1] Two of the first deserters who appear in the early modern Portuguese documentation were a pair of cabin boys who fled the famous expedition of Pedro Álvares Cabral when it landed in Brazil in 1500. We know very little about them, other than they fled their ship the last night it was in port and had not returned by the time the narrative was completed. They joined two convicts who were deliberately left in Brazil to live among the natives and learn their language and customs. The convicts were unwelcome guests and were forced by the natives to return to the ship several times, but the cabin boys were true deserters who fled the expedition of their own volition. By that time, they had several days to acquaint themselves with the nearby native village. They made the decision to abandon the arduous life aboard a small sailing ship and live among (what were to them) exotic peoples, with whom they could not communicate.[2] It is hard to know why they ran: was it powerful testimony to the hardships at sea for two young boys or the lure of life in the tropics?

This essay uses travelers' accounts and correspondence from the Catholic religious orders to focus on three distinct examples of runaways or deserters in three very different locales and circumstances in the Portuguese empire. Runaway slaves on São Tomé Island in the sixteenth and seventeenth centuries are frequently overlooked in the island's history. Portuguese in the early modern period who left various outposts in Portuguese Asia to reside outside it, chiefly along the Bay of Bengal, are a second group rarely mentioned in documentation. The third example is composed of criminals and sinners who escaped their sentences of internal exile within early modern Portugal itself. These three cases illustrate a diverse range of complexities and motivations of runaways and deserters in the early modern Portuguese World. They also exemplify differing responses from the crown to problems associated with creating the first global workforce.

RUNAWAY SLAVES ON SÃO TOMÉ ISLAND

The Island of São Tomé is located near the equator in the Gulf of Guinea, south of (modern-day) Nigeria and Cameroon and west of Gabon. By all written accounts, it was uninhabited at the time the Portuguese arrived around 1470–71.[3] With abundant water and fertile volcanic soil, the island quickly became an agricultural producer and exporter. It first supplied provisions to Portuguese outposts along the West African coast (e.g., São Jorge da Mina), but later, and more importantly, planters on the island turned to the cultivation, production, and export of sugar.

The island receives a great deal of rain, but it is not distributed evenly. The northern half of the island receives forty inches annually while the southern half receives four times that amount. The reduced rainfall and the relatively flat coastal areas in the north and northeast made these areas ideal for sugar cane plantations. According to historian Robert Garfield, "It is in this area that the vast majority of the island's inhabitants have lived and in which agricultural development, and the main events of the island's history, have occurred."[4] The interior and the south were covered with dense tropical rain forest. Sugar plantations were established along the narrow (northern and northeastern) coastal areas that could be cleared and planted with cane. This resulted in clusters of plantations in a small number of areas, each with large populations of enslaved Africans and few overseers, surrounded by rain forest.

Sugar production began in earnest on the island by 1510 and peaked in the period from 1580 to 1600. In that time, São Tomé sugar dominated global production, creating what many scholars consider the (original) model of the sugar plantation complex that would be employed in Brazil and later on many of the

Caribbean Islands. The enslaved were imported, four to five thousand annually, from the African mainland beginning around 1530.[5] The first slaves "originated from the Niger River delta," but the Portuguese then turned for more slaves "first to the Congo and slightly later to Angola."[6]

In addition to African slavery, a second form of forced labor was employed on the island. The bulk of the European population was exiled convicts, sent to the island for serious (and sometimes unpardonable) crimes.[7] At an early stage of colonization, some of these convicts were given land and slaves, but by the 1520s they were not paid by the state and thus had to survive by entering the local workforce. On São Tomé, those who lacked capital to become merchants or purchase land and slaves had three options: work on a plantation in a supervisory or technical role (e.g., overseer, cooper, sugar master); become a soldier; or act as agents in the slave trade, acquiring, detaining, selling, or transporting slaves. One of the unique characteristics of plantation slavery on the island was that many of the artisan and technical trades required on the plantation were filled by slaves.[8] This was probably due to the high mortality of Europeans new to the tropics and diseases on the island, chiefly malaria. Europeans widely believed the island to be a death trap, and for many it was.

Runaway ("maroon") slave communities went hand in hand with plantation slavery and were widespread in the Americas. The largest and most famous of these in Brazil was Palmares, but maroon communities appeared in places as diverse as Jamaica, Louisiana, and the Great Dismal Swamp in North Carolina. In spite of São Tomé's relatively small size, the rugged, mountainous, and densely forested interior offered refuge to runaways, who seized the ideal opportunity to escape the clustered plantations for the dense rain forest nearby. The numbers of slaves on the island—and in all likelihood the population of the runaway communities—rose in tandem with sugar production beginning in the 1520s and 1530s.[9] By the later 1500s, the sugar industry was in decline; the price of sugar from the island had plummeted by 1605 to 270 *réis* per *arroba*, half of its price only seventeen years earlier.[10] By 1614, fifty-nine of the sixty-two mills on the island had been abandoned. Sugar production revived briefly in the 1640s and 1650s, but soon declined again, the remaining farmers turning to subsistence agriculture.[11] The treatment of slaves during the crisis years (1580–1610) worsened and the number of runaways increased: "escapes decreased only when agriculture was refocused once again on foodstuffs."[12]

WHO WERE THE RUNAWAYS?

In 1536, King João III "had to send a special armed expedition to São Tomé under Paulo Nunez to suppress a negro revolt. Again, thirty-eight years later, a combined revolt of Angolares [see below] and [runaway] slaves contributed partly to the decline of the sugar plantations."[13] The first mention of the runaway slave community

("Blacks from Angola Peak") noted their attacks on sugar plantations and the city of São Tomé itself in 1574.[14] The largest revolt, in 1595, was led by a runaway named "Amador." At that time, "the rebels were practically masters of the island; they burned about 70 or more than half of the sugar mills and attacked the city on two separate occasions with about 2,000 men equipped with arrows and firearms."[15] Amador himself was captured the next year (1596) and killed. The Portuguese and their slaves on the island would carry out a "war of the bush" against the runaways for the next century. Runaways organized other major attacks on plantations in 1679 and 1693, but in the interim, plantation slaves rose up in 1617 and 1675. By the time Justice Lucas Pereira de Araújo e Azevedo filed his report in the early eighteenth century, the planters had made peace with the runaway community, who "cause no harm to anyone."

There is a great deal of scholarly uncertainty regarding the use of the term "Angolares." Understanding the term is critical since it reflects the identity and origins of this community. According to oral tradition, they are descendants of survivors from an Angolan slave ship that wrecked on the island around 1554. The survivors made their way into the interior of the island and formed a community. There are a number of problems with this oral history, as pointed out by Castro Henriques. The first and perhaps most serious question is how these slaves freed themselves from the chains on board ship and swam to shore. The second problem mentioned by Castro Henriques focuses on the physical geography of the island. How, she asks, given the dense topical vegetation on the island and its rugged terrain (the highest peak on the island reaches over 6,600 feet), did a group living in the southeast corner of the island attack plantations and the chief city located in the northeast? Finally, there is the problem of the term "Angolares" itself. At the time, these people were known as "Blacks from Angola Peak." "Angolares" appeared in the literature only in the middle of the nineteenth century.[16] Her conclusion, now shared by many, is that this was a runaway slave community or collection of small communities scattered throughout the interior of the island, which had been periodically reinforced by new escapees from the plantations.

Azevedo explained that in the first quarter of the eighteenth century most of the interior of the island was unpopulated, "except for some Blacks who used to cause a great deal of damage to the plantations, attacking them at night, stealing things and taking women, which was what they really needed." Addressing gender imbalance was a constant necessity of runaway communities, along with obtaining several of the critical items they could not produce, such as metal tools and salt. Azevedo observed that, "today they cause no harm to anyone." The runaways were able to survive by hunting and fishing, making their own clothes from tree bark, and raising a variety of crops.[17]

São Tomé sugar turned out to be of poor quality. The constantly high humidity on the island made it impossible for the planters to dry it sufficiently. In addition, after 1591, São Tomé sugar arrived in Europe with nests of tiny black ants buried within the loaves. Better-quality sugar from Brazil, made in much larger quantities, and the attacks from runaways, killed the sugar industry on the island.[18]

By 1600–10 sugar production had largely shifted away from São Tomé to Brazil. When it did, the model developed on the island went with it. Historian Arlindo Caldeira has made a convincing case that São Tomé was the origin for what would prove to be an international model. In his classic work on the Atlantic plantation, Philip Curtin also calls attention to the pivotal role of São Tomé in the development of the Atlantic plantation model before it arrived in Brazil.[19] An unintended part of the model included resistance to slavery, in this case, in the form of runaway communities. The struggle of slaves on São Tomé to live freely in the interior bush was a major cause of the shift to production in Brazil, and thus the beginnings of the transatlantic slave trade. After sugar production declined, the island became a hub for the Atlantic slave trade itself, collecting and transporting slaves to Brazil and elsewhere in the Americas. Another neglected aspect of this model is the concurrent use of European forced labor in conjunction with African slavery. The Portuguese, English, French, and Spanish all experimented with convict labor extracted from their own peoples, applying them at tasks in lieu of, in conjunction with, or in addition to slaves.[20] These tasks included the construction of Spanish forts in the Caribbean, so-called "public works" in Brazil transporting stone to building sites, and agricultural work in Barbados or Jamaica.[21] One form of forced labor coexisted with another.

Meanwhile, the runaways on early modern São Tomé ensured that the island was divided under the rule of two opposing groups: the Portuguese loosely controlled several coastal areas while runaway communities ruled the interior. The crown tolerated the presence of the runaway community as long as São Tomé produced and exported sugar and slaves. The profits made by the crown and individuals from sugar and the slave trade were sufficiently large that Lisbon could ignore the runaway community rather than attempt to suppress it, which was the norm later for such communities in the Americas.

SOUTH ASIA: HOME TO RUNAWAYS AND DESERTERS

Portuguese Asia (*Estado da Índia*) was a collection of outposts strung along the littorals of the Indian Ocean and South China Sea.[22] Their only connection each to the other was maritime, and local conditions largely determined the allure of leaving the Portuguese World. For example, on Mozambique Island, the gold of the Kingdom of Mutapa (modern Zimbabwe) attracted many adventurers and fortune seekers. On the Island of Hormuz at the entrance to the Persian Gulf (held by the Portuguese from 1515 to 1622), lucrative trade to the interior of Persia and further west to the Gulf was the draw. The heart of Portuguese Asia was the string of

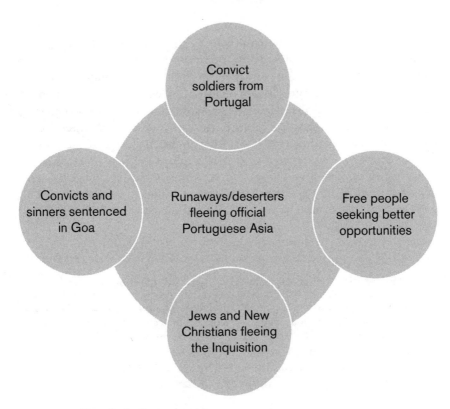

FIGURE 1.1. Those fleeing Portuguese Asia.

outposts along the western coast of India, stretching from Diu and Daman in the North, to Bombay Island and its immediate environs (Portuguese until 1665), to Goa and south to Cochin (1663). These areas, along with parts of Sri Lanka (until 1658), Mombasa (1593–1698), and to the east, Malacca (1511–1641), Timor, and Macau, were ruled by the viceroy in Goa.[23]

Creating the workforces for these outposts and the navy to support them was an unending task, and the authorities in Lisbon and Goa tried a variety of means to achieve it. Numerous single male fortune seekers freely left Portugal during the height of the *Estado da Índia* (probably to 1560). When the number of volunteers was insufficient, convicts were sent in annual batches from the prison in Lisbon. At other times, the local authorities impressed men from Goa (see below) and other regions in India or they used slaves, especially in the galleys. Unmarried Portuguese men were subject to military duty in Portuguese Asia; to be a single man was synonymous with "soldier." This was the main group that formed the runaways. Figure 1.1 depicts the overlapping relationships among those who deserted.

By 1510, the Portuguese had established their headquarters and capital city at Goa, in the middle of India's western shore. Goa had been an important trading center before their arrival and the Portuguese transformed the city into a European mold to be the largest and most prosperous city in all of Portuguese Asia. They also established two important judicial institutions in Goa, based on metropolitan models. The first of these was the High Court, established in 1544, and the second was a Tribunal of the Inquisition, established in 1560. Goa was also the destination for annual shipments of exiled convicts sent from Europe to fill the ranks of the military at various outposts. Those convicted before these two institutions, as well as their countrymen sent from Europe, formed a promising pool of potential runaways and deserters. They were joined by those avoiding prosecution or seeking more lucrative employment beyond the restricted limits of Portuguese Asia.

WHY DID THEY LEAVE?

The noted historian Malyn Newitt has considered this question and concluded:

> Merchants escaped royal monopolies and the greed of the fortress captains by setting up independent merchant communities under the protection of Asiatic rulers; soldiers deserted because of the low pay and hard life in the royal fortresses and ships and because they found their skills with firearms were much in demand; convicts fled the Portuguese settlements to escape from justice; New Christians had every incentive to get beyond the reach of the Inquisition.[24]

Let us examine these rationales one by one. Royal monopolies restricted merchants both in the trade of several of the most sought-after and profitable goods, especially pepper, and with respect to the extent of their participation in the most lucrative voyages, such as the annual fleet connecting Macau and Japan. In turn, local captains and other officials demanded a cut from the trade in their locality or attempted to force merchants to buy or sell goods exclusively to them, at prices they set. The author of *Dialog of a Veteran Soldier* (1617) explained: "The Captains ask [the viceroy] that they alone be allowed to send a ship to that port, as if the ocean and its navigation were not open to all. In this they hinder the commerce of the local people who supply the forts."[25]

Soldier and commentator Francisco Rodrigues Silveira explained that soldiers escaped from Portuguese India in the late sixteenth chiefly because of late wage payment—or no or payment at all. This forced them to "flee to Bengal, others to China, Malacca, Pegu, Diu, Hormuz, Sind, [and] Cambay." Others, he claimed, took employment on local ships or became mercenaries. The resulting manpower shortage made the viceroys request more men from Portugal, which then only fed the cycle of desertion.[26] We also have ample supporting evidence from many sources, including the *Dialog of a Veteran Soldier,* that soldiers ran because of late or unpaid wages.[27]

Convicts were an obvious group that would want to flee, as were sinners facing trial before the Inquisition. The pool created by such figures arriving from Portugal, as well as those convicted in Goa, was a never-ending source of runaways. New Christians (descendants of converted Jews) were another potential group of runaways. Some New Christians seized the opportunity to revert to the faith of their ancestors and joined the Jewish congregation in Cochin. Others fled because they feared persecution by the Holy Office.

WHERE DID THEY GO AND WHAT DID THEY DO?

Most of those who fled Portuguese Asia did so to become mercenaries / renegades working for another Asian power or to become merchants, as explained in contemporary Portuguese records as well as non-Portuguese travelers' accounts and missionary reports that discuss Indo-Portuguese communities outside the official *Estado da Índia*. Those who escaped to the center of Mughal power in Delhi / Agra in northern India in the seventeenth century did so to act as soldiers, in the same way other Portuguese had served the Hindu rulers of Vijayanagara a century earlier.[28] In both cases, the Portuguese were valued for their knowledge of firearms and cannons, specifically. There were a sufficient number of Portuguese serving the Mughal emperor to establish a Christian cemetery in Agra.[29] Portuguese mercenaries were also employed by the rulers of Bijapur, Ahmadnagar, and Golconda, the other Muslim states in central India.

Surat, in the Gulf of Cambay, was a center of trade for the western Indian Ocean. In the sixteenth and seventeenth centuries, the city was a cosmopolitan center, with many foreign residents, including a great many runaways. Father Manuel Godinho called Surat "the emporium of India," and noted the presence of a Portuguese community there on his travels in 1663: "the many Portuguese fugitives and exiles from our lands and their slaves [are] settled in the city."[30]

The Coromandel Coast of southeast India was another region with unofficial Portuguese communities established beyond the reach of Goa. São Tomé of Meliapur and Nagapattinam, in particular, south of modern-day Madras, both had a notable Portuguese presence.[31] A Jesuit report from 1579 stated that São Tomé town had "around 200 houses and that the townspeople had good business dealings with Malacca, Pegu, and Bengal, sending ships to those places each year with diverse goods."[32] Later reports by clergy claimed that in both cities combined there were "more than 1,000 Portuguese."[33] In such places, the Portuguese fugitive merchants traded in "rice, millet, pulse, and every other grain, butter and oil" and carried merchandise to Sri Lanka.[34]

Bengal was the favored region for independent Portuguese merchants, adventurers, deserters, and runaways. The cities and outposts where the Portuguese had a presence varied from an unofficial capital of Hughli, with a relatively large Portuguese population, to smaller coastal enclaves with a handful of Portuguese. According to Father Nicolas Espinola, who had lived in India for more than thirty years, Bengal in the early seventeenth century was home to "more than 2,000 Portuguese."[35] Such was the reputation of Bengal as a whole that Portuguese living there were synonymous with "traitors" to the authorities in Goa. The general view was that "many Portugals, decayed in their estates or questioned for their lives, resort hither, and live here plentifully, yet as banished men or outlaws, without government, practice, or almost profession, of religion."[36] It is not a coincidence that Bengal, more than any other specific region, was the target of a series of general pardons issued by the High Court in Goa beginning in 1596. Typically, these decrees stated that those who presented themselves for military duty in Goa would be pardoned, even those who had been sentenced to death.[37] There is no evidence that such men did indeed return in significant numbers; such pardons are, at best, simply an indication of where runaways were residing. Historian Anthony Disney states that "not more than one fifth of those who embarked at Lisbon actually served at Goa," and that "in 1627, an estimated 5,000 Portuguese renegades were in the employ of local Asian potentates between Bengal and Macassar [eastern Indonesia], 'with little hope of remedy for they are accustomed to the free life.'"[38] Additional Portuguese communities developed in Syriam when "two Portuguese traders turned soldiers-of-fortune, Salvador Ribeiro de Sousa and Felipe de Brito e Nicote, were awarded customs houses and a fort . . . Portuguese flocked to avail themselves of the new opportunities."[39]

Hughli was the largest settlement of the Portuguese in Bengal, established with the permission of the Mughal emperor Akbar in 1580 by Pedro Tavares, a wealthy merchant. This was, in many ways, a culmination of the unofficial presence of runaway and deserter Portuguese activities in Bengal as early as 1516. Father Manrique, who traveled throughout Asia from 1628 to 1643, states that Akbar gave the Portuguese permission to settle there because previously they had come and gone with their ships and this would allow them to trade without interruption. The Portuguese in Hughli, according to Manrique, brought goods from all over Asia and traded with numerous ports in Southeast Asia, including China, and Timor.[40] Hughli grew into a great commercial hub, which several travelers described as the richest and most prosperous of all the Portuguese outposts in the region. The only port that could rival that claim in Bengal was Chittagong, which the Portuguese called "Large Port" in contrast to the "Small Port" of Hughli. In Chittagong, the Portuguese maintained a "customs house, land, and houses . . . granted to them in 1537."[41] Across the Karnaphuli River from Chittagong was a third Portuguese enclave, Dianga. Of these three settlements, Dianga was clearly the most independent of any outside authority. By 1629 when it was visited by Father Manrique, Dianga had developed into a Portuguese community of 750 "pure or half-blood Portuguese," focused on slaving.[42] Sailors there routinely captured people on Sauger Island (and other islands in the Bay) and sold them into slavery. These three settlements entered into a loose confederation of sorts, trading and working together.

François Bernier, who also traveled in the region in the middle of the seventeenth century, said that in the Kingdom of Arakan, where Dianga is located, the local rulers encouraged many Portuguese deserters to settle there, Dianga being "the place of retreat for fugitives from Goa, Ceylon, Cochin, Malacca, and other settlements in the Indies, held formerly by the Portuguese." The king of Arakan, like the Mughal emperor, appreciated Portuguese expertise with weapons, keeping these runaways as "a species of advanced guards . . . it was not surprising that these renegades pursued no other trade than that of rapine and piracy."[43]

The Portuguese deserters had been attracted to the region because it had reached a critical point in its history. They inserted themselves into a volatile and lucrative struggle playing out between the expansionist plans of the Mughal emperors to the west and the defensive strategies of the king of Arakan to the east. These deserters and runaways were able to prosper by trading and offering their services as mercenaries to the rulers on both sides, a dangerous but profitable undertaking.

There were several notable Portuguese leaders, and since little is known about their backgrounds or why they were living in Bengal, it would be a safe guess that they were runaways or deserters from Goa. Chief among these would have to be Sebastian Gonçalves Tibau, "chief of the pirates and so celebrated and powerful that he married the king of Arakan's daughter." Tibau offered to turn the entire Kingdom of Arakan over to the viceroy in Goa, but the viceroy refused to deal with the man, according to Bernier, because Tibau's origins were too humble.[44] Tibau is not mentioned with any frequency in works on Portuguese history, but we know that he was born in Lisbon and left for India in 1605. He made money buying and selling salt, one of the most profitable trades in Bengal, especially Hughli. After he married the princess, he allied himself with the king of Arakan against the Mughals, only to betray the king and allow Mughal troops to enter Arakan.[45] Tibau became the master of the island of Sandwip, which he ruled from 1607 to 1616, conducting a delicate balance among the various powers near his shores. From his death in 1616 until the 1660s his remaining men inhabited "the vast rivers of Bengal and their banks became their homes. Schooled as they were not to recognize any law or authority, they sought the means of subsistence in plundering and piracy."[46] Tibau is the most famous of these men but there were others; unfortunately, we know even less about them. Damião Bernaldes is another, much earlier, example of a merchant turned pirate in the Bay of Bengal in 1531. Domingos Carvalho, a wealthy merchant adventurer/mercenary who ruled Sandwip Island before Tibau's conquest and Manuel de Matos, the captain of Diagna, are additional examples of figures who rose to prominence in the region.

Hughli, the virtual capital of Portuguese runaways in Bengal, was suppressed by the forces of Emperor Shah Jahan in 1632.[47] This was largely in retaliation for the illegal slaving activities in the region. The irony is that one of his advisors was Martin de Mello, a Portuguese renegade.[48]

At their inception in the sixteenth century, the Portuguese Asian settlements were established to make money for the state, its governing officials, and other fortunate enterprising individuals. As Portuguese power and influence in the region declined, so did profits. This heavily impacted those who lacked the influence and connections to obtain lucrative official positions in this shrinking empire (i.e., commoners); they were forced to depart and seek their fortunes elsewhere. An increasing number of Portuguese did just that in the period after 1600, if not well before then. This hard reality is at the heart of the complaints penned in *Dialog of a Veteran Soldier*, where the author (do Couto) repeatedly states that meritorious commoners were never awarded the lucrative positions reserved for the viceroy's friends and lackies, the nobility. A shrinking economic pie no longer offered that opportunity. Many would desert.

Runaways established themselves in a series of port cities (mostly) along the Bay of Bengal and entered into short- and long-distance trade. These Indo-Portuguese communities worked both independently and in tandem with the emerging new English and Dutch East India (VOC) companies, notably as soldiers for the English presidencies in Madras and Bombay, but they also traded with the VOC.[49] With each new generation, these communities became more Asian and less Portuguese, while the definition of "Portuguese" evolved into speaking (some) Portuguese, having Portuguese names, and being Catholic.

The Portuguese Asian state became a mechanism to enrich the Portuguese nobility and its friends and to simultaneously extract free or underpaid labor from the peasantry. The latter, in turn, were only able to better themselves by leaving the Portuguese sphere altogether. Thus, the impact of these runaways and their communities was to spread Portuguese cultural influences well beyond the official limits of the empire throughout the Bay of Bengal, Southeast Asia, and the Spice Islands. At the same time, the king profited by royal monopolies, the nobility prospered by their appointments, and runaways and deserters used their mobility as a "safety value" in this society. The judicial system was able to extract labor from offenders (in the form of military service); and if they deserted, they were replaced by newcomers. In the long run, everyone prospered or had the opportunity to do so. Portuguese communities founded or influenced by runaways developed well beyond the official limits of the *Estado da Índia* while its administration remained unchanged in the face of obvious decline after 1600.

RUNAWAYS FROM INTERNAL EXILE
WITHIN PORTUGAL

Those accused of crimes in early modern Portugal were collected in chain gangs and brought to a central jail in Lisbon. At the conclusion of their trials, they were normally sentenced to a set period of obligatory residence in a place determined by the court. The more serious the crime, the longer the sentence and the more distant (from the court) or challenging its location. This was the punishment of *degredo* or having one's legal status and mobility *degraded* by such restrictions. Those who violated the terms of their sentences by premature departure (i.e., runaways) were typically threatened with the death penalty. However, in sharp contrast to larger and more populous empires, capital punishment was rarely enforced by the state. Portugal had a small demographic base and a global empire with extensive manpower requirements. The empire needed labor, not death, which would have been counterproductive. While it is true that Portuguese courts were fond of *threatening* to call for the death penalty, the state rarely, if ever, implemented it. In his analysis of the state's legal records, the noted Portuguese historian A. M. Hespanha found an average of two executions annually in the period from 1601 to 1800.[50]

The attempt to make each criminal useful to the state becomes abundantly clear when we examine parallel uses of other marginal figures. Orphan boys were employed as cabin boys (like the two runaways cited at the beginning of this article) or placed in native villages in Brazil to become cultural intermediaries.[51] Orphan girls and "reformed" prostitutes were awarded dowries to relocate overseas and marry. The Roma were systematically collected and sent to Angola and Brazil as forced colonizers or employed as emergency troops in conflict.[52] All would swell the ranks of runaways.

The punishment of *degredo* simultaneously resolved several problems. By removing the offender from society, it demonstrated powerful social control over the population and had the potential to provide manpower where needed, either at home or overseas. Its sting was that it removed the offender from all that was familiar—home, family, friends, parish, town—and cast him or her into a new environment where he or she was forced to survive.[53]

One of the mildest forms of *degredo* for convicts and sinners in Portugal was to be exiled to the town of Castro Marim, in the extreme southeastern corner of the country, where Portugal, Spain, and the Atlantic Ocean meet.[54] Sentences of three to five years' obligatory residence were the norm for crimes and sins such as witchcraft / folk-healing, giving false testimony (to the Holy Office), and blasphemy.[55]

State courts and Inquisitorial Tribunals sentenced anywhere from fifteen to twenty-five individuals annually to *degredo* in Castro Marim; the beginning of their punishment was to walk the 190 miles from Lisbon to the town within the normal thirty-day grace period. There is no indication of any supervision or restraints used in this process; it appears they made their way individually with their legal papers for presentation to the local judge.

Once the guilty party arrived in Castro Marim, he or she faced years of hard work in the orchards, fisheries, and especially in the salt works surrounding the town, with possible compensation in the form of food and housing.[56] This is the hottest and driest region in Portugal, more similar to North Africa than Europe. The region is well suited for its principal industry of salt collection via evaporation of seawater from large shallow man-made ponds surrounding the town. The mounds at the edges of the salt pans have to be maintained and the seawater needs careful monitoring while being channeled into the ponds. Once the water has evaporated, the salt must be painstakingly collected and separated from the dry earth and then stored. This was the labor awaiting the guilty once they arrived in Castro Marim.

A critical document detailing runaways was drafted in 1771 by the secretary Diogo José de Andrade for local judge D. Francisco Luís Martin Veloso.[57] In an effort to update his (obviously out-of-date) records, the justice issued several public proclamations for all convicts and sinners sentenced to Castro Marim to present themselves and have their presence verified. This initial verification of arrival before a judge was obligatory and marked the beginning of the sentence. Failure to appear meant that the guilty had evaded his or her sentence by running away, which could result in secondary punishments. The original punishment ended in the same manner: once the individual had completed his or her sentence, a justice signed a certificate of completion and the individual was free to leave.[58]

The secretary then created a list of 152 people, sentenced from 1754 to 1771, who failed to verify their arrival in Castro Marim before a justice. The judge issued several public proclamations to provide ample time and warning; when the list was completed, it was posted in town. The register of 139 male and thirteen female runaways provides their crimes and lengths of sentences. An average of eight runaways annually had failed to appear in Castro Marim. Of course, some could have died on the way, but it is more likely that they made their way over the border to Sevilla or Madrid to find work and a new life in Spain. Others, like the folk-healer Domingos Álvares, may have run off after their initial arrival. Domingos complained that he was unable to make a living in Castro Marim and, in spite of his obligatory residence in the town, he left in 1745 for nearby Tavira. He ultimately traveled around the Algarve, Portugal's southernmost province, for two years before being rearrested in 1747.[59]

Given the paucity of pre-1755 records (destroyed by an earthquake), the crimes and sins of these runaways offer a rare window into social control and running away in early modern Portugal. The men were largely guilty of theft (11%), murder (10%), riot (9%), assault with a knife (9%), or lewd behavior (7%).[60] The women had been remanded to Castro Marim for riot (23%), theft (23%), infanticide (7.6%), influencing a slave woman (7.6%), and lewd behavior (7.6%); their crimes were not stated in 30% of the cases. For both men and women, only seven sentences were longer than five years; one was for ten years and another for life.

The state and the church combined their efforts to provide free labor for this small town in southern Portugal. The vast majority of the individuals were men

(91%) and the two main sources of employment in the town were salt production (a royal monopoly) and military service on the frontier—they would make money for the crown or protect the state. By 1771 when the list was created, the system of internal exile had been in operation for more than 300 years and was well known throughout Portugal. Indeed, in 1874, three generations *after* this punishment ended, the author of a descriptive dictionary of Portugal said this about the town:

> In all the places in Portugal where I have traveled (largely in Lisbon and to the north), when Castro Marim is mentioned, everyone becomes fearful, believing this town to be the end of the world, the most ugly and inhospitable land there is—the land of exiled convicts.[61]

Rather than take their chances for survival at "the end of the world" for five years, an average of eight people annually escaped from the clutches of the judicial system and disappeared from the records. This reduced the available pool of labor in the town and may have been one of the reasons the system declined by the 1820s.[62] For the crown and the townspeople, the system offered free labor. For the church, it created a purgatory where the sinner was redeemed through labor. For those who arrived in Castro Marim, it was years of unpaid work in demanding and sweltering conditions; for those who fled, it meant creating their own futures.[63]

This essay has examined three different types of runaways or deserters in the early modern Portuguese World. In each example, the imperial powers wanted labor and the runaways wanted their freedom, defined in various ways. Impoverished and exploited soldiers wanted better opportunities. Minor sinners and convicts wanted to avoid years of unpaid drudgery collecting salt. In all three cases, we can only make an educated guess as to how the escapees understood their intended fates and options.

Literacy was a hallmark of the nobility in early modern Portugal at a time when the vast majority of common people were illiterate. In two examples here, no written communications between runaway communities and the authorities have survived. This means information about these communities and the various opportunities they offered must have been circulated orally. On São Tomé Island, the runaway community would have received constant news from fresh arrivals; it is only logical to assume that information traveled the other direction as well. In South Asia, runaway travelers, religious figures, and merchants would have carried information about distant clusters of Portuguese to those remaining within the very porous *Estado da Índia*. In Portugal itself, the oral tradition clearly had identified Castro Marim as a purgatory built on hard labor, which would explain what the guilty expected and wanted to avoid. Runaways and deserters in the early modern

Portuguese World underline the words of Jesuit Father António Vieira, who wrote in the seventeenth century that "God gave the Portuguese a small country as cradle but all the world as their grave." Running away was truly global in Europe's first great transoceanic empire.

NOTES

1. The *Oxford English Dictionary* defines a runaway as "a fugitive or deserter" and a deserter as someone who "forsakes or abandons a person, place or cause, usually with implied breach of duty or allegiance." The critical difference is that the former is simply someone who flees (e.g., a runaway slave), while the latter is someone who by fleeing breaks a duty or oath (e.g., a soldier deserting his regiment).

2. This is mentioned in Pero Vaz da Caminha's letter to King Manuel. For an English translation, see *The Voyage of Pedro Álvares Cabral to Brazil and India,* trans. and ed. William Brooks Greelee (London: Hakluyt Society, 1938), 32. Unfortunately, Greelee mistranslated the original term, "grumetes," for "seamen" rather than the more accurate "cabin boys."

3. In regard to the exact date, Robert Garfield, *A History of São Tomé Island* (San Francisco: Mellen Research University Press, 1992), 5, says 1470; Isabel Castro Henriques, *Os Pilares da Diferença, Relações Portugal-África, Séculos XV–XX* (Lisboa: Centro de História, 2004), 248, claims 1471.

4. Garfield, *São Tomé Island,* 3.

5. Philip Curtin, *The Atlantic Slave Trade: A Census* (Madison: University of Wisconsin Press, 1969), 99.

6. Margarida Costa, et al. "Human Microevolution and the Atlantic Slave Trade: A Case Study from São Tomé," *Current Anthropology* 49, no. 1 (February 2008): 134. See also Joseph Miller, *Way of Death* (Madison: University of Wisconsin Press, 1988), 116.

7. Unpardonable crimes included heresy, sodomy, counterfeiting, and treason. See the author's *Convicts and Orphans: Forced and State-Sponsored Colonization in the Portuguese Empire, 1550–1755* (Stanford, CA: Stanford University Press, 2001), 61, 63–64. Banishment to São Tomé was reserved for the most serious criminal cases from Portugal and later from Brazil as well.

8. Arlindo Manuel Caldeira, "Learning the Ropes in the Tropics: Slavery and the Plantation System of the Island of São Tomé," *African Economic History* 39 (2011): 57.

9. Caldeira, "Learning the Ropes," 61.

10. Cristina Maria Seuanes Serafim, *As Ilhas de São Tomé no Século XVII* (Lisboa: Universidade Nova de Lisboa, 2000), chart 44 on 258. An *arroba* is approximately thirty-two pounds.

11. Serafim, *As Ilhas,* 258–59.

12. Caldeira, "Learning the Ropes," 60.

13. John W. Blake, *West Africa: Quest for God and Gold, 1454–1578* (London: Curzon Press, 1977), 140.

14. Isabel Castro Henriques, *São Tomé e Príncipe: A Invenção de Uma Sociedade* (Lisboa: Vega, 2000), 50–62.

15. Caldeira, "Learning the Ropes," 62.

16. Castro Henriques, *São Tomé e Príncipe,* 57–59.

17. Lucas Pereira de Araújo e Azevedo, "Memórias da Ilha de São Tomé" (manuscript written during the first quarter of the eighteenth century), extract published in Arlindo Manuel Caldeira, *Mulheres, Sexualidade e Casamento em São Tomé e Príncipe (séculos XV–XVIII)* (Lisboa: Cosmos, 1999), 236–37.

18. Stuart Schwartz, ed., *Tropical Babylons: Sugar and the Making of the Atlantic World, 1450–1680* (Chapel Hill: University of North Carolina Press, 2004), 10.

19. Philip Curtin, *The Rise and Fall of the Plantation Complex* (Cambridge: Cambridge University Press, 1990), 23–28.

20. For an overview of this process, see the author's "European Forced Labor in the Early Modern Period," in *The Cambridge World History of Slavery*, vol. 3, ed. David Eltis and Stanley L. Engerman (Cambridge: Cambridge University Press, 2011), 631–49 and the sources cited therein.

21. For the Spanish example, see Ruth Pike, *Penal Servitude in Early Modern Spain* (Madison: University of Wisconsin Press, 1983), 134–47; for the English colonies there is a wealth of publications starting with Abbot Emerson Smith, *Colonists in Bondage: White Servitude and Convict Labor in America, 1607–1776* (Chapel Hill: University of North Carolina Press, 1947).

22. Exploring Portuguese runaways and deserters in this region was initially spearheaded by Maria Augusta Lima Cruz, in "Exiles and Renegades in Early Sixteenth Century Portuguese India," *Indian Economic and Social History Review* 23, no. 3 (1986): 249–62. Her article is based on an examination of four of the major printed texts from the period. Her lead was followed by two other path-breaking studies on the subject by Sanjay Subrahmanyam and George Winius.

23. After the struggles with the Dutch and others in the 1660s, Portuguese Asia was reduced to Diu, Daman, and Goa, which the Portuguese retained until 1961. Timor was occupied by the Indonesian Army in 1975 and Macau was returned to the People's Republic of China in 1999. The small enclave of Dadra-Haveli (near Daman) was annexed by treaty in 1779 and captured by the Indian Army in 1954.

24. Malyn Newitt, *A History of Portuguese Overseas Expansion, 1400–1668* (London: Routledge, 2005), 190.

25. Diogo do Couto, *Dialog of a Veteran Soldier, Discussing the Frauds and Realities of Portuguese India*, trans. and ed. Timothy Coates (Dartmouth, MA: Tagus Press, 2016), 35, 58.

26. Francisco Rodrigues Silveira, *Memórias de um Soldado da Índia*, ed. A. de S.S. Costa Lobo (1877; repr., Lisboa: Imprensa Nacional, 1987), 185–86.

27. Do Couto, *Dialog*, 26. There are numerous examples of this process in the work.

28. Burton Stein, *The New Cambridge History of India*, vol. 1:2, *Vijayanagara* (Cambridge: Cambridge University Press, 1992), 143; Newitt, *Portuguese Overseas Expansion*, 192.

29. Alain Desoulieres, "La Communaute Portugaise d'Agra (1633–1739)," *Arquivo do Centro Cultural* (Fundação Calouste Gulbenkian) 22 (1986): 145–73.

30. Manuel Godinho, *Intrepid Itinerant: Manuel Godinho and His Journey from India to Portugal 1663* (Oxford: Bombay, 1990), 52.

31. Nagapattinam was outside the official empire until it was temporarily added in 1643. Captured by the Dutch in 1658, trade and the Portuguese presence there and in Porto Novo, to the north, continued into the seventeenth century. See the insightful articles in Sanjay Subramanyam, *Improvising Empire: Portuguese Trade and Settlement in the Bay of Bengal, 1500–1700* (Delhi: Oxford, 1990).

32. Father Alexandre Valignano, S.J., "Summary of Jesuit Activities in India," published in *Documentação para a História das Missões do Padroado Português do Oriente: India*, ed. António da Silva Rego (Lisboa: Fundação Oriente, 1996), 12:512.

33. Report of Father Nicolas Espinola, "Concerning the Things of India," Biblioteca Nacional, Madrid, manuscript 3015, published in *Documentação Ultramarina Portuguesa* (Lisboa: Centro de Estudos Históricos Ultramarinos, 1962), 2:45.

34. W.H. Moreland, *Relations of Golconda in the Early Seventeenth Century* (London: Hakluyt Society, 1931), 68–69.

35. Espinola, "Concerning the Things of India," 45.

36. Moreland, *Relations of Golconda*, 40–41.

37. On such general pardons, see Coates, *Convicts and Orphans*, 108–9 and the sources cited therein.

38. A.R. Disney, *Twilight of the Pepper Empire* (Cambridge, MA: Harvard University Press, 1978), 21; also cited in Sanjay Subramanyam, *The Portuguese Empire in Asia, 1500–1700* (New York: Longman, 1993), 256.

39. George D. Winius, "Portugal's 'Shadow Empire' in the Bay of Bengal," *Revista da Cultura* 13–14 (1991): 281.

40. Sebastian Manrique, *Itinerario delas Missiones del India Oriental* (Roma: A la instancia de Guillelmo Halle, 1653), 11–12.

41. J. J. A Campos, *History of the Portuguese in Bengal* (1919; repr., Delhi: Facsimile, 2018), 66.

42. Maurice Collis, *Land of the Great Image: Being Experiences of Friar Manrique in Arakan* (1843; repr., New York: New Directions, 1985), 109. This is an edited version of Manrique's *Travels*.

43. François Bernier, *Travels in the Mogul Empire AD 1656–1668*, 2nd ed. (1934; repr., Delhi: Low Price, 1989), 174–75. See also Collis, *Great Image*, 109.

44. Bernier, *Travels*, 178.

45. Elaine Sanceau, "Tibau" in *Dicionário de História de Portugal* (Porto: Figueirinhas, 1992), 6:168.

46. Campos, *Portuguese in Bengal*, 157.

47. John F. Richards, *The Mughal Empire: The New Cambridge History of India*, vol. 1.5 (New Delhi: Cambridge University Press, 1993), 202.

48. Newitt, *Portuguese Overseas Expansion*, 192. More Portuguese runaways scattered beyond the Bay of Bengal and operated in Cambodia and various islands of modern-day Indonesia.

49. In both Bombay and Madras, the British formed regiments of Portuguese runaways; see Coates, *Convicts and Orphans*, 90 and the sources cited therein. "Goan officials were already accusing the Indo-Portuguese population at Pulicat of doing business with the Dutch enemy in 1622 ... the V. O. C. rolls are full of Portuguese names in the eighteenth century"; Winius, "Portugal's 'Shadow Empire,'" 283.

50. António Manuel Hespanha, "da Justiça 'a 'Disciplina': Textos, Poder, e Política no Antigo Regime," *Boletim da Faculdade de Direito* (Coimbra), número especial (1986), 16. The Inquisitorial Courts, in contrast, were much more public and frequent with their use of capital punishment, and this may have been one of the major causes for the public fear of this institution.

51. More specifically, this applied to those orphan boys who broke the house rules or otherwise got in trouble in town. Those who followed the rules and who could learn to read were sent to seminaries to become priests. See Coates, *Convicts and Orphans*, 128.

52. Coates, *Convicts and Orphans*, 45–46, 109.

53. The system described was considerably more complex than this brief outline suggests and is described in greater detail in Coates, *Convicts and Orphans*, 21–64.

54. See also Coates, *Convicts and Orphans*, 50–53. Banishment to Castro Marim is the subject of Geraldo Pieroni and Timothy Coates, *Castro Marim: Da Vila do Couto à Vila do Sal* (Lisboa: Sa da Costa, 2002).

55. These four sins account for 57% of the cases sentenced to Castro Marim. The remainder were interfering with the work of the Holy Office (10%), Judaism (9%), bigamy (7%), false visions (5%), pretending to be a member of the Holy Office (3%), and revealing secrets of the Holy Office (3%). Other sins were 1% or less each. Source: Table 5 in Pieroni and Coates, *Castro Marim*.

56. There is no documentation indicating how they were fed or where exactly they lived, but the sheds next to the salt works were possible housing. These appear in drawings of the town dating from the Middle Ages. The women probably lived inside the walled town.

57. The collection in the municipal archives in Castro Marim begins around 1800, well after the earthquake. Unfortunately, the book the secretary was using in this process in 1771 is not in the municipal archives. This list is in the National Archives of the Torre do Tombo in Lisbon, *Desembargo do Paço, Repartição da Justiça do Alentejo e Algarve, maço 460*, document 23, dated August 25, 1771.

58. Other than one or two in galley registers in Lisbon, such certificates are exceedingly rare.

59. This was but a small part of his travels around the Atlantic. See James H. Sweet, *Domingos Álvares, African Healing, and the Intellectual History of the Atlantic World* (Chapel Hill: University of North Carolina Press, 2011), 191–218.

60. The remaining crimes (when stated) committed by the men were committing errors in office (4.3%), resisting authority (3.5%), escaping from jail or helping someone else escape (3.5%), fighting

(2.8%), kidnapping (2.8%), living in an unmarried union (1.4%), taking the virginity of a lady (1.4%), adultery (1.4%), petty theft (1.4%), public disorder (1.4%), and one case each of giving false statements, persuading a slave woman, possessing a razor knife, pandering, housebreaking, rape, incest with a sister-in-law, tobacco smuggling, copying a key, market fraud, and slander.

61. Augusto Soares d'Azevedo Barbosa de Pinho Leal, *Portugal Antigo e Moderno* (Lisboa: Mattos Moreira, 1874), 208.

62. Half or one-third depending on the estimate for the total sentenced. People were banished to Castro Marim with decreasing frequency after this report and the system ended with the judicial reform movements of the nineteenth century.

63. A frequent complaint of those working in the town was the intense heat.

2

Escaping St. Thomas

Class Relations and Convict Strategies in the Danish West Indies, 1672–1687

Johan Heinsen

On 19 November 1686, the Danish convict Peder Vognmand was forced to place a noose around the neck of his friend and fellow penal laborer, Jens Pedersen, and then to hang him from the gallows outside Christiansfort on St. Thomas.[1] He did so to save his own life. The two men had shared the experience of Atlantic displacement, exploitation, and destitution in the service of authorities tasked with building a small-scale Caribbean plantation colony. They also had shared dreams of escape that were articulated in whispers and expressed in the steady accumulation of knowledge and resources. Yet, despite careful planning, their repeated attempts at realizing such reveries had all failed. These attempts had involved several other workers who were also in the service of the Danish West India and Guinea Company, but the court had found that Vognmand and Pedersen were the ringleaders. Several of the soldiers and convicts in the crowd at the execution had taken part in the discussions leading up to these futile attempts. Despite covering for each other in court, both Vognmand and Pedersen had been sentenced to death after their last attempted escape earlier that November. Vognmand had only been pardoned on condition that he act as executioner. The coercive symbolism of the event echoed the practice of having workers everywhere in the Atlantic punish their peers. The implied moral was that solidarity was futile.

Vognmand and his friends had become part of a developing tradition of escape from the Danish colony in the Lesser Antilles—linked both to the general Caribbean tradition of maritime desertion as well as to a tradition of escape from the penal institutions in Denmark from which these convicts were transported. Toiling on St. Thomas's humid slopes and seeing their peers succumb to diseases in large numbers, lower-class subjects sought freedom via maritime routes to neighboring islands such as St. John and Puerto Rico. Those who ran away included all three groups of unfree laborers in the colony: the enslaved, the indentured, and the convicted. Such acts of resistance helped to unsettle the already precarious experiment in capitalism and empire-building undertaken by Danish merchants and heavily subsidized by the Danish state. In this way, they shaped Denmark's colonial aspirations at a time of intense imperial rivalry and the globalization of capital.

Pedersen and Vognmand's story allows us to grasp the social dynamics of the frustrated Danish colonial project, which echoed tensions found throughout the Atlantic economy. At the same time, it also allows detailed study of the very act of running away, revealing not only its difficulty but also the processes and the knowledge on which this act depended. The rich writings produced in the trials illustrate how lower-class subjects often depended on various contingencies as well as other acts of resistance in their quest for freedom. Thus, studying the minutiae of the antagonisms inherent to this key moment of European expansion reveals how attempts at escape often shared many traits.[2] Collective desertions therefore can often be broken down into a number of stages, all of which provided the possibility of failure. Vognmand and Pedersen had struggled at each one.

The first stage was the formation of the collective. A decision to run away had to be made and then communicated to everybody who needed to be involved. For instance, would-be escapees often needed accomplices to help operate or row the vessels that were crucial to attempts in maritime contexts. In other words, this step required solidarities that were often shaped in response to the exploitation and destitution that bonded workers suffered. However, often this stage also required the persuasion of those who were prone to fears or doubts. Consequently, this initial phase depended on the existence or creation of a space in which to talk safely.

The second phase of escape was preparation. This involved acquiring geographical knowledge about potential escape routes—a necessity that scholars have vividly demonstrated for other types of escapees elsewhere.[3] In maritime geographies, this type of desertion also demanded knowledge of where and how to obtain a vessel, the necessary provisions, and sometimes guns or tools. This often meant involving people with more extensive freedom. Then, prospective escapees needed to attain enough freedom to procure the necessary items without being caught. If escape did not immediately follow this step, one also needed somewhere to hide the items in the interim.

The third and final phase was actually to get away. This involved stealing a vessel or launching vessels crafted in secret. It also involved traveling far enough to avoid immediate recapture.

MAKING PLANS

During their labors in the salt ponds on the uninhabited islet called Salt Island, the small group of Danish convicts had moved out of earshot of the Dutch company skipper. On 30 July 1686, he had been ordered to use the large company canoe to sail from St. Thomas to this island located east of the abandoned St. John, where he was to harvest salt. Lying "on top of the water like ice in the fatherland in winter," the salt cost only "the pains of collecting it."[4] Those pains were the lot of a group of transported convicts. On August 3, they returned with six barrels full of salt, but also with a plan. According to several convicts, it was Jens Pedersen who was the instigator. Pedersen approached the others, detailing a plot for maritime escape. His plan involved stealing a spike from the company storehouse. Pedersen needed it because his wife (who was transported along with her convict husband, though she was formally free) had been locked up in the small jail at the fort for an unrelated case of petty theft.[5]

In the days following their return, the whispering continued. Several other convicts were approached by Pedersen, who was aided in his attempts at persuasion by Vognmand. Some turned the plan down, but a handful of the company's convict laborers agreed to it. They were joined by two soldiers, Søren Islænder and Niels Krog, who worked as guards at the fort that functioned as the company's headquarters. Reportedly, Islænder had complained that they "were young people, but were like convicts here," poignantly expressing the hardships of colonial servitude, which, for soldiers, meant being subjected to many different kinds of labor. The conclusion Islænder drew illustrates how such hardship created solidarities, even nascent class consciousness. The two soldiers came up with the plan of stealing guns from the room in which the constable slept. They assured their co-conspirators that he always slept so heavily "that you can take him in his hammock and carry him out, and he would still be sound asleep."[6] The intended use of the guns is unknown. The soldiers were central to the plan in another way as well. When approached by Pedersen, one of the convicts had doubted that the plan was feasible since the already starving convicts had no provisions for the escape. Pedersen explained that they planned to break into the company storehouse next to the fort at a time when the two soldiers were on guard. They did so during the night before August 12. They hoped to steal the company sloop one of the following nights and disappear into the Caribbean seascape that they had studied during their journeys harvesting salt.[7]

However, the plan had already suffered a major setback. Two days before, Jens Pedersen had been jailed at the fort with his wife. Rumors about the plan had leaked.[8] Then, on the thirteenth, the colony's governor Christopher Heins gathered his council and had all the convicts involved brought before the court. So many were interrogated that the court was forced to reconvene on the sixteenth. On the testimony of their fellow convicts, Pedersen and Vognmand were found to be the principal conspirators. The two had refused to give each other away, despite being tortured with thumbscrews. Both were sentenced to flogging and branding at the gallows. Pedersen had already been branded on the face before transportation, so he was branded on the back. After this dishonoring ritual, the two men were bolted together and sent to work among the enslaved workers on the company plantation. The rest of the convicts involved were sentenced to be "sold, to get the company the most and best profit, to some other nation, so that one can get rid of such roguish and loose people."[9]

Convicts in the Danish Atlantic were effectively the private property of the company, whose 1671 charter had granted them the right to transport men and women from Copenhagen's prisons. They used this right repeatedly during the 1670s and 1680s. In total, they received approximately 250 convicts for their minuscule colony—a number that might seem negligible in the context of unfree labor in the Atlantic, but which was considerable in the context of the size of the colony in particular and of the large but thinly populated Danish-Norwegian empire in general. In their instructions for their governors, the directors specified that the convicts were theirs to dispose of as they saw fit.[10]

Most transported prisoners came from the king's prison Trunken at the naval dockyard in Copenhagen. Male prisoners were sent there from all parts of Denmark, Norway, and even Iceland. They included soldiers, but also the rural and urban poor. Their transgressions often reflected attempts to maneuver within (or out of) other coercive labor relations, whether the long-term service and intense poverty of mercenary soldiers, the unfree state of conscripted maritime workers, or the serf-like status of tenant farmers bonded to their landlords and obligated to perform corvée labor. Between them, the convicts sent to St. Thomas numbered representatives of all these groups, each one selected from among the inmates with life sentences.[11] Before embarkation, they had carried out heavy labor in fetters, hauling building materials or producing naval stores in the dockyard workshops. Convicts from Trunken also contributed to the construction and maintenance of Copenhagen's military infrastructure—labor they often shared with conscript sailors and mercenary soldiers.[12] In many ways, convicts helped alleviate the constant labor deficit of a state that was caught up in the European race for power and expansion.

Despite being inexpensive, convicts were not the company's ideal laborers. From its beginning in 1672, the colony founded on the steep volcanic rock of St. Thomas was envisioned as a plantation economy. It was established to provide Denmark with colonial products such as cotton, tobacco, and sugar, but also to become a market for Danish exports. It rested on a dream of closed circulation, benefitting only the Danish state and the company's investors, including the royal family. To fulfill the dream, the company founded its own plantation. Among the leaders of the company were men who had firsthand knowledge of English plantation experiments in the region. The Danish plan seems to have been to mimic their rivals, relying heavily on indentured labor. However, the island also quickly attracted Dutch planters (along with some English and Irish), possibly on the run from the turbulence of the Anglo-Dutch wars. They brought their own enslaved workers with them and quickly turned the island into a highly heterogeneous community. Then, during the Scanian War from 1675 to 1679, the company became unable to provision the colony, which was suffering under French attacks. Previously, the company had relied heavily on support from the navy, which now became unavailable. Cut off from Copenhagen, St. Thomas became integrated in the regional economy instead.

Further weakening the company's ability to realize its colonial fantasies, the colony failed to attract sufficient numbers of indentured servants throughout the 1670s and '80s, in part because returning mariners circulated news about the brutality of colonial life to the effect that "among the common people our colony is so badly spoken of that they think that as they come to serve in the West Indies they are worse off than in serving in Barbary."[13] Slave labor was still a scarce commodity, in part due to the company's own repeated failures in the slave trade. While the governor managed to acquire some enslaved men and women through local trading, the numbers were far from sufficient. Thus, convicts were a last resort, substituting for other types of unfree laborers. In the colony, the convicts ranked somewhere between the indentured servants and the enslaved with whom they often worked side by side. At night, they were locked up in a small house by the fort. During the day, they fulfilled whatever labor needs the governor faced. Such tasks included clearing the forests and preparing St. Thomas's steep slopes for plantations, hauling building materials, producing limestone, doing construction work (especially in building the fort), herding cattle and fishing. Some undertook plantation work, but as the vast majority of them died within their first year in the colony, only few lived to see anything grow.[14] Their excessive death rates can partly be explained by starvation and the tropical disease climate of the colony, but also was linked to conditions in Trunken. This was an institution in which famine and disease were recurrent threats, especially in times of high food prices.[15]

This entire system was brutally coercive, but to seventeenth-century elites it made perfect sense. The key to this discontinuity is the stigma of dishonor. Honor and dishonor played a major part in the early modern Danes' understanding of punishment. As in northern Germany, any criminal whose punishment had involved the executioner (flogging, branding, etc.) was tainted by the dishonor surrounding this figure. This marked the person as a nonsubject for perpetuity. Dishonored convicts were considered unpardonable. The Danish term for dishonor ("uærlighed") also means "dishonest," and the dishonored were also seen as unable to tell the truth, enter into binding contracts, or take oaths.[16] They effectively had no legal rights, and could not bear testimony against honest people. It was a powerful ideology that legitimated coercion.

Most of the convicts in the colony had been convicted of crimes against property, signaled by the "thief's marks" that scarred their faces. Most had been pardoned from death sentences. The group included a burglar and several cattle thieves. Formerly an agricultural laborer on the small island of Falster, Pedersen had been convicted of stealing livestock. During his trial, it was found that he had committed "not only 1, 2, 3 or 4 but 10 accounts of theft" over a period of fifteen years.[17] Vognmand's background is unknown. "Vognmand" was only a nickname, meaning "carter," making him impossible to identify in the convict muster, which included four "Peders." Most likely, he was the one named "Peder Nelausen," which would mean that he had formerly been one of the rural poor, and had actually already broken out of prison once before embarkation.[18] Sentenced for conspiracy in the colony, the two arrived at the company plantation bolted together and with fresh wounds inflicted by the executioner on 20 August 1686. We can deduce the motivation behind this particular punishment. In a letter written in early October, the governor complained that because of droughts, he only had fourteen days of cassava left for his servants. However, due to recent showers, Heins was eager to put people to work planting.[19] Thus, Rusche and Kirchheimer's famous assertion that "every system of production tends to discover punishments which correspond to its productive relationships," holds true not only for the structural forces that propelled convicts into the Atlantic economy itself, but also for motivations on the miniature scale of the life of the colony.[20]

In contrast to the convicts, the two soldiers involved in the plans were not sentenced on August 16. The night before, the two (who were kept separate from the convicts) managed to break free of their bolts with a large knife.[21] Somebody probably turned a blind eye: the two succeeded in scaling the wall of the fort before heading into the colony's deep forests.

Their plan was to build a raft and head west to Puerto Rico. However, they had nothing with which to fell trees. A few days later, they sneaked up to the fort and broke into the house of the company cooper but found no appropriate tools. They managed to subsist on food stolen from plantations at night. At one point, they were spotted but got away.[22]

Failing to find a way off the island, they hatched a more radical plan. In the subsequent interrogation, Islænder explained "that some days after they had run away, Niels Krog had said to him that he should give himself over to the evil man and walk into the bushes, curse and swear, then the Devil would appear and help them [get] away from this country." Islænder claimed that he had not wanted to take part in the plan, but Krog argued that it had in fact been Islænder who had proposed it at a point when they "saw no other way out." Islænder had said that "by God I wish I had ink and paper. Then I would write a contract and leave it, and after that the evil spirit would come. He is such a crook that when you need him he will not be there, but when you don't want him there, he will come all the faster."[23] The belief was that the Devil personally needed to agree to the contract before it was valid. Such devil pacts were rare, but they appear in Denmark in the 1670s, principally among soldiers. They have been linked to circulating works about the popular figure of Doctor Faustus.[24]

The Devil never showed up. Islænder was caught on August 27. Krog remained free for another ten days. They were then sentenced to be bolted together and to join Pedersen and Vognmand at the company plantation. There they were to work in chains for three years as "indentured servants."[25]

However, Governor Heins had grown anxious about punishing the soldiers. Formerly the colony's lieutenant, Heins was newly appointed, having been chosen for the task by a naval commissioner who had arrived that spring along with the convicts in question. The commissioner's primary task was to reassert company dominion on the island. Having run a series of trials, he then left the colony in Heins's care in early June. However, Heins appears to have been unsure of his mandate to pardon. Therefore, he wrote to the company directors. The punishments of Pedersen and Vognmand had been "well-deserved," while the punishments of Krog and Islænder were more problematic, in spite of the fact that they had actually gotten away. Because both were "supposedly of good people," the inexperienced governor had wanted them to be pardoned but had not dared to do so himself as their actions constituted a capital offense.[26] Strategically, Heins failed to mention their Satanic flirtation.

He was being played. The day after Krog and Islænder's sentencing, Heins had sent his clerk to investigate who the two soldiers were, how they "had gotten here," and especially if they were "free or unfree."[27] These questions had arisen after the governor had heard the two soldiers tell their life stories in court. Islænder had explained that he was 25 years old and born in Rotterdam, while Krog had said that "his father was an official in the Meddelsom district court" in Jutland. Krog had added that he was only 18 years old.[28] It was this tale of youth and a background among honest people that had prompted the need for clarification—no such questions were asked of the convicts, whose branded faces told Heins everything he needed to know. Krog and Islænder called for more careful attention. The next day, Krog told the clerk that he had been a soldier and was innocent, but that his colonel had forced him to labor at the dockyard, "and because he would no longer serve him, he had given 20 Rix-dollars for his provisions going here with the ship Fortuna." Krog also claimed that one of the directors had "promised him that he would be brought back home with the ship and be given his free provisions at the fort." He emphasized that both he and Islænder were of an "honest" background. Islænder told a story of indenture turned into bondage: "he had been promised a spot on the plantation of the heirs of the former governor or to be employed in another good service, but upon arrival the commissioner had forced them to become soldiers and given them each a musket on their backs."[29] The phrase "to get a musket on your back" was commonly used when early modern Danes described forced military servitude.

Thus, we find Krog and Islænder telling stories about their lives as lower-class subjects facing unjust masters in a context of uncertainty about their status. Both hinted at narratives of subterfuge and arbitrariness in the Atlantic labor market—

stories that they knew to have a ring of veracity in the ears of the authorities. However, in articulating the deeply coercive nature of social relations in the early modern Atlantic, the two were also partly manipulating the truth. To Krog in particular, the situation presented an opportunity. Searching through the admiralty archives, I have found records of a sentence passed on Krog. As a soldier, he had stabbed another man and had been sentenced to death in a court martial. The sentence had then been commuted to transportation.[30] No branding or other defacing had been part of the sentence. Confronted by ignorant authorities and the telling question of whether he was free, Krog had seen and seized his chance to escape his past. His story about being tricked into Atlantic servitude played off the truths of labor relations in the Atlantic to hide a different story of bondage.

Thus, when the commissioner decided to use the convict Krog and the indentured servant Islænder as forced soldiers, he opened a loophole for Krog. Helped by a lack of visual markers of dishonor as well as a lack of documentation, which meant that Governor Heins had only spotty knowledge of the backgrounds of his workers, Krog effectively ran from his past. He styled himself not as a nonsubject bereft of social being but as a free man whose subject status was threatened by coercion and the threat of dishonor.[31] Had Heins been more certain of his mandate, this story would even have enabled Krog to lose his fetters altogether. Instead, he and Islænder would soon try their luck by fleeing again.

TRADITIONS OF SELF-EXCARCERATION

While the rudiments of the first plan might be traced back to the plotters' firsthand knowledge of Caribbean geography, Krog's and Islænder's Faustian plans and hopes of reaching Puerto Rico's shores were more complicated. In fact, they put us on the trail of what might be interpreted as intersecting traditions of illicit freedom in the face of authoritarian constraints.

In a sense, these practices of running preceded the empire itself. From its creation in the early seventeenth century, Trunken saw an almost constant series of escape attempts. The prison's first rebuilding in 1640 was undertaken because escapes were a "daily" occurrence, as the king himself phrased it.[32] It did not stop the flow of illicit exits. The sources allow a complete overview of all inmates (1,495 in total) in the period 1690 to 1740, during which 19.1 percent of them escaped.[33] This figure does not include the many failed attempts, but only those who actually managed to get away. Of those who escaped, one in four was eventually apprehended. Many of those then tried again. The group of inmates who were by far the most inclined to escape were the dishonored and unpardonable lifers—the same group selected for colonial transportation. They knew full well that their only route to freedom was flight—an act involving many steps. First, one had to get out of the prison itself, then, secondly, out of the sequestered and guarded territory that made up the naval wharf and docks (designed to regulate the movements of maritime workers), and then, thirdly, out of the gates of Copenhagen (guarded in part to keep the military workers in the garrisons from running). Finally, many appear to have wanted to leave Denmark altogether, following a maritime route to neighboring Sweden, which was also a favored destination for military and naval deserters. At some point in this process of escape, the convict had to get out of the fetters, which would otherwise make him easily identifiable.

A successful escape hinged on preparation. One common element was the forging of fake passports. Passes were crucial if a convict needed to exit Copenhagen's gates and if the convict was to enter other towns or cross the sound to Sweden by ferry. Such forgeries were common among other itinerant groups as well, and many convicts arrived with knowledge of how to produce fake papers. In one case in 1723, for instance, a former soldier sentenced for desertion and for having written a letter to the Devil later forged passes and sealed them with a stolen admiralty seal. The plot was only discovered after five of his fellow convicts had run away. Asked why he had helped them, he eloquently articulated the perceived unnaturalness of their unfree state by arguing that convicts were "like birds in cages, only longing to be free." He defiantly justified his assistance by referring to Solomon's proverb, "Rescue those being led to death."[34]

There were many ways to cross these concentric thresholds, and every thinkable way appears to have been tested. In 1732, for instance, the entire population of one of the two prison buildings planned to escape by digging themselves out, and the plot was only discovered after a six-meter-deep tunnel had been constructed. The digging had been going on for months. The plan was to head for a fishing village, steal a vessel, and go pirating.[35] Plans of stealing boats were common, mirroring aspirations in the colony as well as the practices of military deserters. Others conspired with the prison guards or used occasions when their superiors were drunk to run off.[36] The type of magic considered by Krog and Islænder was an option here as well, and at least one convict wrote to the Devil in hope of assistance, while others sought various magical remedies with which to make themselves invisible.[37] About half of all escapees teamed up with someone else. Not only were others a necessity if the plan was to steal a vessel, but inside the prison building, as in the colony, convicts lived together in large dormitories. Thus, large-scale preparations had to be collective. This could be problematic if convicts unwilling to run became witnesses to preparations. Silence made them complicit, and for the group of convicts with shorter sentences, there was a clear incentive to turn informer. Convicts revealing large plots such as the piracy plot of 1732 were given their freedom as a reward. Sometimes, convicts assaulted those suspected of informing.[38] Building trust was not an easy task.

However, labor itself created bonds, and as flight usually took place outside on the docks or in public works around Copenhagen, many ran from their worksites, where the members of small crews knew each other well. The fact that the labor was often monitored by sailors also offered opportunities; sometimes sailors and convicts would conspire to leave work to go drinking, which then provided opportunities for escape.[39] Moreover, convicts on the run often found accomplices. For instance, in crossing the Sound to Sweden, they would often be helped by fishermen who, for a fee, were also willing to assist deserters.[40]

Similar attempts at flight were made from other places of penal labor in the Danish empire, such as military fortresses. In fact, wherever we find lifetime convicts in the archives, they appear to have responded to exploitation by trying their best to escape it. For instance, an official at the fort of Kronborg, north of Copenhagen, described convicts as an indispensable source of labor. They carried out jobs that he could not have the soldiers take on, and it would be very costly if he should be forced to pay wages for others to do them. However, of the ten convicts under his command, three were missing and four others had tried to escape. One of them was a "daring bird" who had run away many times.[41] Even the isolated naval outpost on the tiny island of Christiansø in the Baltic Sea witnessed attempts at maritime escape when it came to house a contingent of convicts around 1730.[42] Even more remote, the similarly small contingent of convicts sent to labor in a failing colonial outpost in Greenland in 1728 made plans to run away and join Dutch fishing vessels.[43]

The convicts allotted to the company would use every opportunity to try their luck.[44] This had already happened during the first voyage from Copenhagen in 1671-72 when the ship was forced to stop in Bergen, Norway. Here, a group of convicts and indentured workers ran away, forcing the shipboard authorities to take on local convicts as replacements. This pattern repeated itself during subsequent voyages.[45] Consequently, the company leaders became increasingly anxious about their coerced workers. In the instructions for a captain who transported a large contingent to the colony in 1682—in an effort to reinvigorate an ailing project by finally finding enough workers to run the colony and the company plantation properly—the directors warned the captain that the convicts constituted a "multitude of indomitable people" and that the captain should be careful near foreign coasts as they might attempt to steal the boat and get away.[46]

The convicts in question did not have their eyes on the boat; instead they took the entire ship, dealing a massive blow to company aspirations. While in the English Channel, a group of them allied with a band of angry sailors. On 20 January 1683, they mutinied, killed the captain and his posse, and elected a convict their new captain. They had hatched a plot to take the ship and goods to Ireland, sell them, and share the spoils equally among all those involved in the takeover. Their plan combined piratical seizure of the ship with mass desertion. It was informed by the rumors about life in the colony that had been circulating in maritime Copenhagen. Unfortunately, contrary winds made its realization impossible. Instead of attaining riches and freedom, the mutineers lost trust in one another. Another mutiny split the coalition about a week later when four convicts were killed for conspiring to seize the ship because they had feared that they would not be taken to Ireland but would instead be marooned on some deserted island. Their deliberations were overheard, and the ringleaders were shot. As it turned out, they had been right: most of the convicts were abandoned in the Azores in mid-February. Hoping to be pardoned for saving the ship, the convict-captain then set course for Copenhagen but ended up wrecked on the Swedish coast. Nine ringleaders were executed outside Copenhagen's gates that summer.[47] The failed expedition was a severe blow to the already ailing company, which now presided over a colony spinning out of control yet lacked the means to intervene. Not until the 1686 expedition of the naval commissioner did they gain some measure of control of the island. That expedition also brought the last sizable contingent of convict workers to the colony.

Their unruliness in the colony also had a precedent. The convicts that the company managed to bring to the Caribbean in the 1670s had been far from docile. The first trial on St. Thomas involved a case of desertion. In June 1672, a few months after the arrival of the first ship, two Danish indentured servants and two Norwegian convicts ran away in a company boat with four guns, gunpowder, an axe, and a pot. The four went to St. Croix, but the two indentured servants were later apprehended. They had been gone for two and a half and four months respectively.[48] The time span was important. While they were gone, the governor had declared a law dictating the punishment of added time in servitude calculated on the basis of the length of absence. Masters were also allowed to put any servant who ran away in irons "until he gives up his evil habit," effectively blurring the already fine line between the indentured and the convicts. The escapee was explicitly defined as an "outlaw,"[49] and planters were allowed to "break the arms and legs" of runaway convicts found on plantations. This appears to have been an attempt to appease the dissatisfied planter class, who continued to challenge the company's hold on its colony.[50] Anyone housing an escapee of any rank was to be fined 1,000 pounds of sugar and all ships that left the harbor were to be searched.[51] Such anxious escalation of legal measures might indicate the vulnerability of the company, which simply could not afford to let people run away with large parts of its workforce dying.[52]

It is difficult to prove whether or not these escape practices were inspired by the practices of enslaved Africans, but we know that this group of subaltern workers provided ample examples of how to get away. Further, we know that the convicts and enslaved Africans learned from each other; in his writings, the first governor of the colony lamented how convicts would sometimes throw themselves on the ground and lie immobile when they were to be punished, a practice he claimed they had learned from the enslaved.[53] However, perhaps the clearest hint that convicts and the indentured could be inspired by slaves is simply how closely their practices of escape mimicked the practices of maritime marronage among the enslaved.

The pioneer historian of maritime marronage Neville Hall has described this tradition, which became so important in the Danish West Indies in the eighteenth century. The primary destination was Puerto Rico to the west.[54] He argues that maritime routes became crucial when, in the early eighteenth century, deforestation made marronage on the island itself impossible. However, the routes were used in the early years of the colony as well. Perhaps the first to test them was a group of three enslaved men who sought to go to Puerto Rico "to get fish and other things to eat" in October 1673. They might have known of this destination because one of them was of local descent. He was called Jan Indian and had been the author of the plot. Punishments were different for the enslaved; Jan Indian was the first of many to have a leg cut off for seeking his freedom.[55]

Rafts like the one Krog and Islænder had envisioned were the means of escape most widely used by enslaved workers. Various governors repeatedly sought to limit their laborers' access to vessels, as did authorities trying to hinder desertion to Sweden from the garrisons and penal labor sites in and around Copenhagen.[56] Such measures regularly accompanied coercive labor relationships in early modern maritime geographies. It was forbidden to own a canoe or vessel in the colony if the owner was unable to pay the damages it could cause. It was also forbidden to cut down trees that might be turned into rafts.[57] This edict did not successfully hinder such attempts. For instance, a group of enslaved Africans ran away from a plantation during a summer night in 1680. They had gathered materials for a raft, which they unfortunately had to abandon when their owner pursued them. With no way of getting off the island, they were recaptured.[58]

In other words, all segments of the subordinate classes on St. Thomas ran away: convicts, indentured servants, the enslaved, and even sailors and soldiers. In fact, mapping who took flight and who attempted to keep others from running away can provide a clear image of class relations in the colony: those who were in power or had property needed subjects to work and were bent on using coercion to extract such labor and to keep it in check; those who had nothing sought their freedom from this regime, and often did so together in ways that reflected solidarity.

Paradoxically, St. Thomas was also a destination for escapees from other colonies. Such foreigners probably provided would-be escapees with knowledge and inspiration. Early on, the Danish authorities paid close attention to such people and appear to have been eager to foster good relations with their neighbors by apprehending and returning them. When five sailors and two enslaved men arrived in a vessel in 1674 without passports, they were interrogated and found to have been in the service of a master from Barbados and to have run away after being badly treated. The vessel and the enslaved were then returned to the English at Nevis while the Danish governor sentenced the rest of the escapees to serve at Christiansfort.[59] However, after a change in governorship on St. Thomas, the Danes and the English came into conflict in 1680. One matter of dispute was that under pretense of St. Thomas having become a free port, the Danes allowed pirates to careen and trade. This appears to have been a response to the fact that the colony was completely severed from Denmark at the time. However, the situation also allowed the new governor to conduct private trade, and he appears to have encouraged piracy. The egalitarian pirate ships attracted lower-class subjects from the English colonies, and we know that one crew consisted almost entirely of English escapees.[60] This led the governor at Nevis to lament that St. Thomas housed "fugitive servants white and black" as well as "seamen and other personnes indebted who runaway to them and will never restore them alleadgeing the freedome of their ports to protect all."[61] These irregularities were stopped by 1686, but had persisted for so long that they enabled the circulation of knowledge about routes and destinations.

We cannot know from which of all these precedents the convicts in question drew inspiration, but while they had only been in the colony for a few months, we can establish with certainty that they had encountered other runaways. For instance, they had experienced an enslaved African being flogged at the fort on July 6 for marronage. He had been gone for six weeks. They had probably also heard that a group of eight soldiers had run away in August 1684, following a plot that seems almost identical to the initial plan hatched by the convicts in 1686. One of these soldiers was later returned to St. Thomas, where he was pardoned. He was still working at the fort when Krog and Islænder joined the small corps in the spring of 1686.[62]

Krog, Islænder, Pedersen, and Vognmand were determined to follow this tradition. When the four men went to rest in an old shed on the night of the two soldiers' arrival at the company plantation, Krog and Islænder saw something they might not have expected. Like Islænder and Krog, Pedersen and Vognmand had been bolted together, but now they took off their irons. It had only taken them a handful of days to break them in a way "so that at night they can be free, and again in the day put them back on."[63] Such manipulations of fetters were also common among convicts in Trunken, where such preparations allowed them to seize sudden opportunities to run away. Several cases in the admiralty court reveal how the convicts collaborated to file down the rivets and put in fake ones made of wood or lead to mask their tinkering.[64]

This practice benefited the convicts on St. Thomas in another way; when the convicts were chained together during the day, nobody appears to have suspected that they had complete freedom at night. Under an old canoe in the shed, they hid pork, bread, a pair of shoes, and various clothes, all stolen from the company stores. Pedersen's wife, Mette Nielsdatter, had been released in August and acted as their spy in preparation for these nightly expeditions into town. She gave them "knowledge about everything, when the time was right to steal, and where there was something to be had."[65] It may have been Nielsdatter who saw the opportunity to steal while the authorities were out of town to attend the clerk's wedding on a plantation on October 26. She also spotted the spikes that had been strewn in front of the storehouse. Unlike the others, Vognmand had shoes, so he broke into the storehouse and opened a window for the others to get in. It was also Nielsdatter who had spotted the old canoe that lay abandoned by the sergeant's house. This accelerated the plan. On November 5, the five broke into the smithy to steal tools.[66] The next night, Islænder took their stolen effects to a small bay on the southwestern side of the island. Meanwhile Vognmand, Pedersen, and Krog met up with Nielsdatter. They stole the canoe, picked up Islænder, and escaped into the night.[67]

Some days later, when Governor Heins sent the skipper and a group of his enslaved workers and convicts fishing, he ordered them to keep an eye out for the escapees.[68] He was in luck: they spotted the stolen canoe on the beach of one of the many small islands between St. Thomas and St. John. The escapees had headed for St. John but had stopped here, possibly because the canoe was too small to hold them all safely in open waters. Later, in court, it was said that they had intended to go from St. John to some Caribbean port and then return to Europe.[69]

On the sixteenth, they were brought to trial. There, they poignantly articulated their experiences. When asked why they had run, Islænder answered, "because he had suffered so much pain from prison, work and hunger." He had been given only a little cassava "which he could not possibly live on." Vognmand's explanation was "because they had endured much evil from prison and hunger." Krog agreed that it was "because of hard prison and hunger which he like the others had suffered." Jens Pedersen was the last to be questioned and he "answered like the rest of them because of hunger and the coercion of prison."[70] It appears that they had coordinated their answers, perhaps to present the strongest possible case. Yet, despite their strategic nature, these words powerfully evoke the conditions of convicts in the early modern Atlantic. They reveal a dialectic of incarceration and excarceration that brings to mind Rediker and Linebaugh's analysis of exploitation and lower-class agency.[71] If prison, work, and hunger were the lot of this class of workers, desertion was the response to being subjected to such conditions.

Once again, Governor Heins convicted Jens Pedersen of being the author of the plot. He and Vognmand were sentenced to death. Krog and Islænder received a milder sentence of flogging and banishment. However, Heins then spared them the flogging "because of others' intercession" so that "their honor was saved."[72] This must have been a result of Krog's subterfuge, as Nielsdatter was not spared the dishonor and was even sentenced to be branded as well. This extensive ritual of punishment and death was to be carried out on November 19, but the colony's executioner, an enslaved African, ran away the night before. In need of a hangman, Heins offered Vognmand his conditional pardon.[73] Besides hanging his closest friend in the colony, Vognmand also had to flog and brand Nielsdatter. The experience must have been harrowing.

Vognmand served as executioner without attracting any attention until August 1687. This is when, in a single note in a clerk's journal, we encounter what is the last trace of his actions. We should appreciate its concise character and the archival silence that followed to be his hard-earned victory:

> Tonight, the executioner Peder Vognmand, Svend Madsen who looks after the horses and Albrecht Olsen who was on the barque have run from the harbor in a boat belonging to the noble company. They went with each other and took the jib with them as a sail.[74]

Like most of the convicts, Islænder and Krog died during another epidemic in the first months of 1687.[75] They were not replaced. The company was entering hibernation, having failed to build a fruitful business based on coercion. Part of the island was leased to a group of foreign merchants, who turned it into a slave-trading entrepôt. The company's right to colonial trade was also transferred to private merchants. Over the next decade, the colony became increasingly involved in sugar cultivation and transitioned into a fully racialized labor regime. This change appears to have been inextricably tied to the company's difficulties in manning their colony with unfree Danes and in keeping what workers they had alive and in place. Ultimately, death and desertion (including the mutiny of 1683) were the causes of the demise of the company. Had it not been for the agency of convicts themselves, expressed most directly in the acts of desertion and mutiny discussed here, this experiment in exploitation would probably have lasted far longer; in this sense, the mobility of labor had a decisive impact on the Danish expansionist project.

The authorities learned from these struggles: when the company reemerged from its slumber in the late 1690s, it was with a heavy focus on slave trading and trade from the open harbor of St. Thomas, which had become the home of smugglers, interlopers, and privateers. Further, throughout the first half of the eighteenth century, the company repeatedly and explicitly rejected the use of convict labor because of the dangers that the agency of convicts would entail. At times, they referred to the mutiny of 1683 as concrete evidence, and emphasized that convicts would inevitably seek their freedom.[76] Such distrust reflected a paradox: the types of hard, extramural labor for which convicts were eminently useful often produced the conditions for escape. This is evident in the case studied here, but also in the thousands of instances of convicts running away from other penal labor sites in Denmark-Norway.

In fact, as this volume shows, analogous paradoxes are found throughout the history of imperialist and capitalist expansion. As elites everywhere sought to accumulate power and wealth through dispossession and violent coercion, their efforts hinged on creating circulations of not only goods but also labor. Capitalism was not forged from dreams of free markets, but from visions of chains. The forced movement of workers (whether enslaved, indentured, convicted, conscripted, or otherwise coerced) was a structural prerequisite in the building of the world economy. Seventeenth-century St. Thomas was like a miniature of this global dynamic. So are the developments of the myriad and sometimes entwined traditions of resistance expressed in Vognmand and Pedersen's struggles. Set in motion, the coerced laborers themselves moved in ways that looked ill conceived if not outright terrifying to their masters. The risks escape entailed should underline desertion's importance. Thus, the pathways forged by bonded workers themselves formed a powerful, though often desperate, response to life in the age of coercion.

NOTES

1. Journal, 13 July 1686, vol. 496, 496–98, West India and Guinea Company (WIGC), Rigsarkivet (RA).

2. Breaking desertion down into such stages reveals the extent of structural affinity that this act has with other perhaps more dramatic acts of collective resistance such as mutiny. Compare with Marcus Rediker, "The African Origins of the Amistad Rebellion, 1839," *International Review of Social History* 58, special issue (2013): 15–34.

3. For example, Hamish Maxwell-Stewart, *Closing Hell's Gates* (Sydney: Allen and Unwin, 2008), 169.

4. Court minutes, 13 August 1686, vol. 486, 486–87, WIGC; Journal, 30 July to 3 August 1686, vol. 496, 496–98, WIGC.

5. Court minutes, 13 August 1686, vol. 486, 486–87, WIGC; Journal, 13 July 1686, vol. 496, 496–98, WIGC.

6. Court minutes, 13 August 1686, vol. 486, 486–87, WIGC.

7. Journal, 9–13 August 1686, vol. 496, 496–98, WIGC.

8. Journal, 9 August 1686, vol. 496, 496–98, WIGC.

9. Court minutes, 13–16 August 1686, vol. 486, 486–87, WIGC; Journal, 19–20 August 1686, vol. 496, 496–98, WIGC.

10. Instruction for the governor of St. Thomas, 29 October 1682, 27, WIGC.

11. List of convicts, 29 August 1685, 181, WIGC.

12. On relations between convicts and labor markets, see Christian G. De Vito and Alex Lichtenstein, "Writing a Global History of Convict Labour," *International Review of Social History* 58 (2013): 285–325.

13. Copybook of letters, p. 328, 41, WIGC.

14. Memorandum, Fortegnelse huad det folck som döde paa henreysen til St Thomas hafuer kost Compagniet, 1682, 138, WIGC.

15. Johan Heinsen, *Det første fængsel* (Aarhus: Aarhus University Press, 2018).

16. Erling Sandmo, *Voldssamfunnets undergang: Om Disciplineringen av Norge på 1600-tallet* (Oslo: Universitetsforlaget, 2002), 136–43.

17. Jens Pedersen's sentence, 13 August 1685, 2, Holmens chef (Søetaten), RA.

18. Documents on Peder Nelausen, ibid.

19. Christopher Heins to the directors of WIGC, 5 October 1686, 89, WIGC.

20. Georg Rusche and Otto Kirchheimer, *Punishment and Social Structure* (1939; repr. New York: Russell and Russell, 1968), 5.

21. Court minutes, 22 September 1686, vol. 486, 486–87, WIGC.

22. Journal, 16 August to 7 September 1686, vol. 496, 496–98, WIGC.

23. Court minutes, 22 September 1686, vol. 486, 486–87, WIGC.

24. Tyge Krogh, *Oplysningstiden og det Magiske* (Copenhagen: Samleren 2000), 126.

25. Journal, 25 September 1686, vol. 496, 496–98, WIGC.

26. Christopher Heins to the directors of WIGC, 5 October 1686, 89, WIGC.

27. Journal, 23 September 1686, vol. 496, 496–98, WIGC.

28. Court minutes, 22 September 1686, vol. 486, 486–87, WIGC.

29. Journal, 23 September 1686, vol. 496, 496–498, WIGC.

30. Sentence of Niels Krog, 21 September 1686, 2, Holmens chef (Søetaten), RA.

31. Court minutes, 22 September 1686, vol. 486, 486–87, WIGC.

32. The King to Korfits Ulfeldt, 29 March 1640, printed in *Kong Christian den fjerdes egenhændige breve*, ed. C. F. Bricka and J. A. Fridericia (Copenhagen: Rudolph Klein, 1882), 4:319.

33. These figures are based on ongoing work in the prison registers in the admiralty archives, especially boxes 1, 15, and 16, Holmens chef (Søetaten), RA.

34. Court minutes, 5 June 1723, Overadmiralitetsretten, 20, Admiralitetet, RA.

35. Sentence, 27 September 1732, Justitsekstrakter, 11126, Generalauditøren, RA.

36. See, for instance, Court minutes, 15 May 1721, Domsbøger, Underadmiralitetsretten, 25, Admiralitetet, RA.

37. Convict register, 8 March 1729, Box 1, Holmens Chef (Søetaten), RA.

38. Court minutes, fol. 248–52, Standretsprotokoller, box 50, Overadmiralitetsretten, Admiralitetet, RA.

39. For example, Sentence of Abraham Andersen, 3 October 1730, Justitsekstrakter, 11126, Generalauditøren, RA.

40. For example, Documents concerning John Nielsen et al., 1729, Domme over fangerne på Bremerholmen, 12, Holmens chef, RA.

41. Litra B, Refererede sager oktober 1717, Krigskancelliet, RA.

42. Ingeborg Dalgas, *De Bremerholmske Jernfanger og Fangevogtere på Fæstningen Christiansø 1725–1735* (Aarhus, 2014), 51–53.

43. Finn Gad, *Grønlands Historie II: 1700–1782* (Copenhagen: Nyt Nordisk Forlag, 1969), 158.

44. On traditions of excarceration see Peter Linebaugh, *The London Hanged: Crime and Civil Society in the Eighteenth Century*, 2nd ed. (London: Verso, 2003), chap. 1.

45. Memorandum, Fortegnelse huad det folck som döde paa henreysen til St Thomas hafuer kost Compagniet, 138, WIGC.

46. Instructions for Johan Blom, 31 October 1682, 27, WIGC.

47. Johan Heinsen, "Dissonance in the Danish Atlantic," *Atlantic Studies* 13, no. 2 (2016): 187–205; Johan Heinsen, *Mutiny in the Danish Atlantic World: Convicts, Sailors and a Dissonant Empire* (London: Bloomsbury, 2017).

48. Court minutes, 9 September and 19 October 1672, vol. 484, 484–485, WIGC.

49. Ibid., 8 August 1672.

50. Journal, 11 October, 6 November and 26 November 1686, vol. 496, 496–98, WIGC.

51. Court minutes, 19 October 1672 and 9 September 1677, vol. 484, 484–85, WIGC. See also Neville A. T. Hall, *Slave Society in the Danish West Indies: St. Thomas, St. John and St. Croix* (Mona, Cave Hill and St. Augustine: University of the West Indies Press, 1992), 126. See also Jorge L. Chinea, "A Quest for Freedom: The Immigration of Maritime Maroons into Puerto Rico, 1656–1800," *Journal of Caribbean History* 31 (1997): 51–87; Hilary Beckles, "From Land to Sea: Runaway Slaves and Servants in Barbados, 1630–1720," *Slavery and Abolition* 6, no. 3 (1985): 79–94.

52. Several such attempts are listed in Jørgen Iversen to the directors of WIGC, 15 September 1681, 78, WIGC; Jørgen Iversen to the directors of WIGC, 12 October 1681, 78, WIGC.

53. Jørgen Iversen to the directors of WIGC, 15 September 1681, 78, WIGC.

54. Hall, *Slave Society*, 124–38.

55. Court minutes, 17 October 1673, vol. 484, 484–85, WIGC.

56. For example, Statute on Deserters, 13 October 1703, printed in Jacob Henric Schou, *Chronologisk Register over de Kongelige Forordninger* (Copenhagen, 1795), 2:81–83.

57. Ibid., 19 October 1672 and 1 November 1675.

58. Testimony of Simon van Ockeren, 3 July 1680, 77, WIGC.

59. Court minutes, 10 June 1674, vol. 484, 484–85, WIGC.

60. Deposition of Robert Richardson, 17 December 1683, CO 1/53, no. 98, Public Records Office, Kew.

61. Sir William Stapleton to Lords of Trade and Plantations, 11 November 1682, CO 1/49, no. 95, Public Records Office, Kew.

62. Journal, 19 August 1684, 495, WIGC.

63. Court minutes, 16 November 1686, vol. 486, 486–87, WIGC.

64. For example, Court minutes, fol. 135–37, Standretsprotokoller, 50, Overadmiralitetsretten, Admiralitetet, RA.

65. Court minutes, 16 November 1686, vol. 486, 486–87, WIGC.

66. Journal, 5–6 November 1686, vol. 496, 496–98, WIGC.

67. Court minutes, 16 November 1686, vol. 486, 486–87, WIGC.

68. Journal, 8 November 1686, vol. 496, 496–98, WIGC.

69. Court minutes, 16 November 1686, vol. 486, 486–87, WIGC; Journal, 9–11 November 1686, vol. 496, 496–98, WIGC.

70. Court minutes, 16 November 1686, vol. 486, 486–87, WIGC.

71. Peter Linebaugh and Marcus Rediker, *The Many-Headed Hydra: The Hidden History of the Revolutionary Atlantic* (London: Verso, 2000).

72. Journal, 19 November 1686, vol. 496, 496–98, WIGC.

73. Ibid.

74. Journal, 6 August 1687, vol. 496, 496–98, WIGC.

75. Journal, 22 January, 7 February, 8 February, and 8 March 1687, vol. 496, 496–98, WIGC.

76. The WIGC directors to Copenhagen's chief of police, 4 June 1701, 181, WIGC; The WIGC directors to J. L. v Holstein, 21 September 1737, 181, WIGC, RA; The WIGC directors to J. L. v Holstein, 28 November 1747, 181, WIGC. See also Johan Heinsen, *Mutiny in the Danish Atlantic World* (London: Bloomsbury, 2017).

3

Between the Mountains and the Sea

Knowledge, Networks, and Transimperial Desertion in the Leeward Archipelago, 1627–1727

James F. Dator

Between late June and mid-July of 1689, a multi-ethnic rebellion gripped the divided colony of Saint Kitts, which was at the time shared between the English and French. A large group of Irish islanders, likely a mix of servants and poor island-born settlers, rebelled against the English government after it declared William III King of England. Deserting the new monarchy, they torched the colony's English plantations, leveling estates and ripping apart sugar mills as they went. As they marched, the rebellion drew in other dispossessed islanders. A group of the "King's soldiers" stationed in the colony deserted their officers and joined with the Irish band, eager to fight against a government that had left them without pay, decent food, and clothing for six years. Around the same time, a mysterious group of "Negroes," some French-speaking islanders of African descent, also joined the rebellion.[1]

Working together and using their knowledge of Saint Kitts's unique physical and imperial geography, the group quickly attacked—and bested—the English crown's defenses. Starting their rebellion with a surprise attack on the weaker windward side of the island, they overwhelmed the king's settler militia and soldiers, triggering a mass exodus of English settler families to nearby Nevis. The few hundred settlers who remained with lieutenant governor Thomas Hill followed him to Fort Charles, a leeward coastal retreat within view of the French border town of Pointe de Sable. The rebels penned in the fort on three sides, cutting Hill's crew off from food, fresh water, and gunpowder. With the English colonial government cornered, the insurgents symbolized their moment of collective power, stitching together a new flag, a red "standard" decorated with "four white balls," emblazoned with the initials "J. R.," or Jacobus Rex, the Latin inscription for recently overthrown James II. They declared their new flag "King James's Colours."

Raised above the divided colonial landscape, the flag sent a message to all oppressive despots like Hill.[2]

Although they had the upper hand, the deserters faced difficult choices. Hill still had access to the sea, which abutted the fort. The sea route enabled him to communicate with his ally, lieutenant governor Jonathan Netheway at Nevis, who smuggled a small group of armed men to the fort. He also contacted the English governor Edwin Stede at Barbados, who began preparing a fleet of ships for Hill's defense. The rebels had seized the day, but they were only about two hundred in number and lacked the military firepower on its way from other English colonies. Luckily for them, Louis XIV's ministry had already directed French governors to offer sanctuary to Irish Catholic deserters after James II fled London by sea for Paris the previous December.[3] In Saint Kitts, however, deserting to French lines simply meant walking down the roadway shared by the two nations for the past sixty-odd years. Long open to laborers and elites alike—regardless of nationality—the road passed right by Fort Charles. Weighing their options and drawing on a long history of transimperial desertion in the Leewards, the rebels repurposed French sovereignty to their advantage. Their knowledge of borders gave them power.

Gaining sanctuary in French Saint Kitts, the rebels allied with a French commander named Deandmare. It seems that the deserters provided the French colonial government with valuable intelligence, especially about Hill's situation in the fort. After news arrived that Louis XIV had declared war against England in defense of James II, the French governor general from Martinique, Blénac, launched a massive invasion of the English part of Saint Kitts on July 17, 1689. Aware that Hill was stuck in Fort Charles, Blénac's fleet bombarded the fort from the sea. Meanwhile, the rebels, strengthened by French forces, finished what they had started weeks earlier. They destroyed the means of production essential to the established hierarchy in English Saint Kitts, targeting the "Coppers, Mills, Stills, and whatsoever they could lay their hands on."[4]

The little-analyzed Saint Kitts rebellion of 1689 is usually treated by historians as a spasmodic episode of Irish Catholic violence motivated by the group's loyalty to the ousted James II. But when considered from a broader Atlantic perspective the uprising illuminates a larger set of issues about slavery, resistance, empire, and capitalism. The circulation of Atlantic news and rumor, the contingent processes of group formation and radical organization, and the relationship between war and slavery all come to the fore when the rebels' story is read from the bottom up.[5]

This article focuses on a theme that connects these issues: the historical accumulation and strategic use of knowledge by rebels like those who made the uprising of 1689. Building on a long history of interisland mobility and desertion in the Leeward Islands, they combined several different strands of knowledge as they mobilized against Hill and his new government. They knew about Saint Kitts's topography, which they would have to navigate if they were to overtake the English colonial militia. They knew who to trust and where to find their allies—a social knowledge about the ways in which class, nation, and religion interacted with power and hier-archy in the colonies. Like the Maroons of Jamaica and Haiti, they developed a tactical, martial knowledge to turn their small size to their advantage. Perhaps most importantly of all, the rebels employed a powerful political knowledge about empire and the class domination on which it depended.[6] These rebels used their bottom-up knowledge of imperial rivalry to alter the history of the Leeward Islands.

GEOGRAPHIC KNOWLEDGE AND THE TOPOGRAPHY OF POWER

By 1689, the well of knowledge from which the rebels drew was deep, stretching back to a culture of mobility first crafted by Amerindian islanders. Archaeological studies have revealed that early Amerindian groups in the Leewards used their canoes and large *periaguas* to create impressive networks of exchange across the Caribbean as early as 400 BCE.[7] Waves of human settlement washed through the region over the course of the next two thousand years, establishing new patterns of trade, interaction, and exchange that would continue to inform the region's long history of mobility. Knowledge of the region depended on knowledge of the sea— and how to travel across it.

When Europeans invaded what they called a "New World" in the 1500s, groups of Amerindians had already begun to settle in the Lesser Antilles in order to escape violence between warring groups on the South American coast. As they fled, they brought with them a many-sided knowledge of the natural environment. They knew how to produce edible cassava from the poisonous manioc plant. They fash-ioned subsistence strategies from the skill of fishing with bow and arrow. Amerin-dians introduced these skills to places like Saint Kitts, Guadeloupe, and Dominica. Citing the myths first created by Columbus about these highly mobile, "war-like" islanders, Europeans called the diverse groups of the Lesser Antilles "Caribs."[8]

According to the Dominican missionary Raymond Breton, however, Amerin-dian islanders in the Leewards preferred to call themselves Kalinago and viewed the term "Carib" as a hostile European invention.[9] Breton lived in Dominica at a Kalinago *carbet,* or village, for more than a decade, during which time he studied their language, religious customs, and social organization closely. Eventually he published several works, including two Carib–French dictionaries, which provide considerable insight into how Amerindians in the Eastern Caribbean defined their collective identity. Breton's informants told him that they distinguished them-selves as "Oubao-bonon"—or "islanders"—as opposed to "Batoüe-bonon," or peo-ple of the "firm land."[10] As Breton and other contemporaries noted, interisland waterways were central to Kalinago understandings of the cosmos. The Kalinago *boyez,* or shaman, captured this spirit when he painted water deities on canoes, symbols of the ambiguous power of the sea as both a creative force for life and a destructive power of death.[11]

Kalinagos used their defensive skills and their knowledge of the environment to turn the Eastern Caribbean into a place of refuge in the late sixteenth and early seventeenth centuries. Africans and Europeans were sometimes incorporated into *carbets*. Enslaved in Seville, Lewis ran away from his master by getting aboard a ship bound for the Caribbean via Cadiz sometime in the early 1610s. But the ship captain ended up beating him severely during the journey, and when the ship anchored at yet-to-be-invaded Guadeloupe, Lewis decided to escape. Kalinagos on the island adopted him into their village. He learned their language, worshipped spirits with them, and had three children with an Indian "wife." When Spanish and French ships anchored offshore, his fellow islanders hid Lewis from view to prevent him from being re-enslaved.[12] Similarly, Amerindian islanders at Saint Kitts incorporated runaway and wayward outsiders into their communities before Europeans invaded the island in 1624. One of the first English settlers to arrive, John Hilton, recalled that a European child from a shipwreck and at least three French men were living with the Indians on the island when he arrived. Using local resources, Kalinagos at Saint Kitts kept Hilton's camp alive by sharing their provisions.[13] It was an act of generosity they would soon regret.

In 1627, after receiving several shipments of arms and people, French and English colonists jointly seized Saint Kitts. Following a surprise massacre of villagers at a *carbet*, French and English authorities divided the island into three parts—the middle would be English, the ends of the island, French—thereby introducing European-style boundaries to the Eastern Caribbean.[14] This act of enclosure—called the *Partage*—made Saint Kitts the first English *and* the first French colony in the West Indies.

The *Partage* established internal boundaries and defined rules governing where laborers from the two nations could travel within the colony. It required that French and English settlers share, in "common," the salt ponds at the southern end of the island, woods "of any value," and the island's freshwater streams.[15] Laborers from the two nations quickly learned how to use these common areas to their advantage. French and English servants, for example, traded stories about their brutal masters. Servants, in turn, used these stories to improve their condition. In one case, a group of French *engagés* protested against their bosses after they began to mimic the ways of English masters, who illicitly kept their servants in bondage beyond their seven-year contracts. In response to the protest, French authorities shortened contracts of *engagés* to thirty-six months. Memorializing the incident, English servants enviously called fellow French workers "thirty-six-month men."[16] Shared woodlands and watering holes, so crucial in the early years of settlement, served as spaces for French and English servants to learn about each other's experience and exploitation.

Saint Kitts, like many of the islands nearby, has a remarkable volcanic mountain range that stretches down its center like the ridged backbone of a fish. Laborers learned how to escape the brutal tobacco regime in the colony by escaping into this mountain range. Knowledge of the terrain proved crucial when the Spanish admiral Toledo bombarded the colony in 1629. Hundreds of servants, slaves, and some tobacco planters hid in the mountainous woodlands for protection. Within a decade, large groups of runaway Africans began to use their knowledge of the upcountry to withdraw from the tobacco lowlands. In 1639, a group of slaves deserted the tobacco camps and formed a band in the highlands above French Capisterre, terrifying settlers by their independence and their nocturnal raids on plantations. One report suggested that they were overtaken by a French expedition, but a legend indicated that at least one runaway survived the onslaught and continued at large, striking fear in colonists of retribution.[17] With its steep ascent, dense forest, and remarkable vistas of the surrounding islands, Saint Kitts's mountains would continue to be a refuge for deserters and rebels into the next century.

Runaways in the mountains saw another route to escape all around them: the sea. When Toledo's fleet reached the island in 1629, hundreds of servants and slaves weighed their options and sided with the Spanish instead of risking a dangerous trek up Mount Misery. Upwards of seven hundred desperate settlers, servants, and slaves escaped on Spanish ships. The loss of labor was so staggering that French authorities nearly abandoned the colony.[18] Instead of fighting, laborers in Nevis jumped into the sea and swam to the Spanish, yelling out "Liberty, joyful liberty!"[19] Hearing about the events in Nevis, authorities at Saint Kitts captured and tortured those who tried to run away by sea. The English governor, anxious about the subversive Nevis example, ordered maritime deserters to ride a "wooden horse"—a mock saddle with a sharp point that cut into the rider's genitals.[20] Planters and imperial authorities feared the contagious quality of autonomous mobility in the islands, where news from one colony easily crossed borders and inspired resistance nearby.

IMPERIAL EXPANSION AND CATHOLIC SOCIAL NETWORKS

Together, these early types of desertion—to the mountains and to the sea—established the foundation of what would become a regional pattern. By the 1640s, England claimed Nevis, Antigua, Montserrat, and the middle third of Saint Kitts; France possessed Guadeloupe, Martinique, and the ends of Saint Kitts; and the Netherlands asserted control over Saint Eustatius and Saba. The expropriation of Kalinago land produced new contradictions. As settlement expanded, tobacco production accelerated regional interdependency for resources like salt, water, and wood. Laborers, in turn, developed wider social ties that reached across island boundaries. At the center of this transformation stood divided Saint Kitts, which possessed all of these precious resources. Within fifteen years of settlement, Saint Kitts—only thirteen miles long but divided into thirds by two empires—was the most densely populated colony in the region. The island also became a center for communication, for both rulers and rebels.[21]

In the first two decades of Leeward colonization, most servants shared the nationality of their masters. By the 1650s, however, visitors remarked that the Leewards were settled by people "shuffled together from diverse places."[22] Indentured Europeans from Nantes, Dublin, and London labored alongside indigenous enslaved Amerindians and Africans shipped from West African ports such as Ardra, Elmina, and Loango.[23] A small number of European families and royally appointed authorities dominated each island's planter class. Tobacco was the key crop in most of the islands, but Africans grew sugar cane on the slopes of Nevis and the rolling hills of French Basseterre Quarter, Saint Kitts.[24] Indentured and poor white settlers, mostly Irish, comprised the laboring majority in Antigua, Montserrat, and parts of English Saint Kitts by the late 1660s.[25]

Itinerant Catholic missionaries and laboring Irish servants created interisland and transimperial social networks in the Leewards. In Montserrat—often described as an "Irish colony"—French priests secretly ministered in the island's woodlands by dressing as commoners.[26] In Saint Kitts, mobile laborers used their feet to cross borders and practice their faith. Irish settlers traveled to the nearby French town of Pointe de Sable to take communion, baptize their children, and be married by Catholic missionaries.[27] These ritual acts reaffirmed a collective consciousness as Irish workers and priests created alliances. These everyday acts of mobility informed broader political alliances that led to collective desertion.

Indeed, Irish workers deserted in droves when war aggravated religious tensions and presented new opportunities. The outbreak of the Second Anglo-Dutch War in 1666 was a case in point. Actions taken by disaffected Irish servants and settlers proved decisive in English losses to the French. Irish and African laborers found moments of solidarity. In late 1666 and early 1667, Irish deserters joined with armed black islanders, Kalinago fighters, and *flibustiers* to help the French take Antigua, Montserrat, and English Saint Kitts.[28]

In one battle, Irish runaways and black allies joined with a "French General," who encouraged them to destroy the Protestant church at Nichola Town.[29] The Irish could protest their religious persecution and their exploitation by Protestant masters in one fell swoop. Several witnesses claimed that two priests marched into Saint Kitts's English quarter with the French captains and successfully recruited Irish colonists to join the battle against their English masters.[30] On the south side of Saint Kitts, Irish men deserted English captains in the middle of a firefight. According to one witness, a group of rearguard Irish conscripts opened fire on the front lines, killing the English governor of the colony. For English planters, such acts underscored that the Irish were a "perfidious people"—and a powerful one.[31] As a result of the coalition, England lost three islands. The French left Antigua and Montserrat in the hands of governors who accepted French commissions, but the French crown refused to return Saint Kitts until 1671—four years after the Treaty of Breda ended the war.

The coalition of Irish and African deserters, Kalinago warriors, and French troops forced colonial elites to reassess how the English Leewards would be governed. Prior to the war, decisions about naval protection had been taken in Barbados. After their devastating loss, a self-professed group of "loyal" English petitioners convinced Whitehall that "His Majesty's Leeward Caribees" should be a separate colonial federation.[32] The plan united English Saint Kitts, Antigua, Montserrat, and Nevis under a single governor general and, in 1674, a general assembly.

The crown's choice for their first governor general, William Stapleton, underscored how Irish desertion shaped metropolitan policy in the Leewards. Whitehall most emphatically did not want to lose Saint Kitts, Antigua, and Montserrat again. The Ireland-born Stapleton spoke French, supported the Restoration, and had served as lieutenant governor in Irish-dominated Montserrat. Under his governorship, poor white laborers obtained new protections and Irish Catholics gained greater religious freedom. At the same time, Stapleton led anti-Kalinago raids and expanded planter access to enslaved labor by establishing a Royal African Company entrepôt at Nevis.[33] The imperial strategy implemented by Stapleton was to drive a wedge between English and French settlers and another, simultaneously, between Irish and African laborers.[34]

One law passed in the Leewards after the war illustrates how Stapleton exploited racism to stifle dissent. In 1670, while he still served as Montserrat's lieutenant governor, Stapleton helped to pass one of the first laws in the English Leewards dealing with mobility of servants and slaves. According to Montserrat's government proclamation, "Many Freemen and Christian Servants" were "accustomed to combine with Negroes in running away from the said Island." The new law targeted these interracial alliances in several ways. First, it ordered all overseers and masters to disperse "strange Negroes" and "any other slaves" who visited plantations without permission. If mobile visitors still "loitered," or if "Negro or Negroes" or any "other slaves" were found to be hiding runaways, the law ordered the justice of the peace to give them forty lashes. Second, the law punished masters or overseers who refused to discipline wayward workers with a fine of £500 in muscavado sugar. Finally, the law penalized freemen and servants who colluded with runaway slaves. Free people who "combined" with "any Slave or Slaves" to escape were fined £1,000 of muscavado. Defendants who could not pay were forced into a year's servitude. Servants caught running away with slaves had their time doubled. However, servants who ran away *without* slaves suffered less than islanders of African or Indian descent. "Negroes or any other slave or slaves" would be whipped in public, but white servants who ran away served an extra week for every day they absented themselves, an extra month for every week, and extra year for every month.[35] The Montserrat law thus helped to create the category of "white" by its differential punishments to maintain labor discipline after the war. This dynamic demonstrates how, in the postwar Leeward context, the colonial English ruling class responded to collective Irish dissent by racializing the division of labor.[36]

Poor whites who worked for wages also gained new rights in the 1670s and '80s.[37] These changes accelerated with James II's coronation in 1685. King James appointed a new governor general, Nathaniel Johnson, to administer English Saint Kitts, Montserrat, Nevis, and Antigua.[38] During his brief tenure Johnson expanded civic protections for Irish Catholics in Saint Kitts and Montserrat by offering them permission to build churches. Johnson even freed them from paying tithes to the Church of England. The search for a base of political loyalty continued, but not without resistance.[39] In May 1688, against the backdrop of revolution in England, islanders from Saint Kitts testified that Johnson's lieutenant governor there, Thomas Hill, refused to implement the general's orders on Catholic liberties.[40] Hill—who also commanded the "distressed" troops at English Saint Kitts—used the physical distance between the islands to stall for time.[41] For Hill, as for many others, the prospect of Catholic liberty appeared dangerous in a colony where Irish and French Catholics had long intermingled across the island's internal boundaries.

As the account of the rebellion that opened this essay highlights, Hill's repression backfired. Building on a long history of knowledge accumulated from years of laboring in Saint Kitts and the surrounding islands, Irish servants, poor settlers, and Hill's unpaid soldiers combined and rose up. In their view, Hill was defending a coup that seemed more like a counterrevolution. News about the Saint Kitts uprising encouraged other Irish islanders to take action. Soon, colonists in Nevis heard that Irish inhabitants in Montserrat were rising up to support a French invasion. "The Irish in Montserrat, who are three to one English," Nevis's deputy governor explained, "say openly that they will desert their allegiance and give up the island to the French."[42] English authorities cracked down on Irish residents in Montserrat and Antigua, but by September French authorities had captured Saint Kitts. Irish desertion proved decisive in French victories in 1666 and again in 1689. It would be the last time.

THE ERADICATION OF IRISH DISSENT AND THE RISE OF THE "MOUNTAIN NEGROES"

War engulfed the Leewards for two decades after the uprising in Saint Kitts, breaking out from 1689 to 1697 and again from 1702 to 1713. The uprising triggered a Protestant backlash. English authorities in the Leewards believed that as long as they depended on servant labor—especially Irish labor—the problems of archipelagic desertion and subversion would persist. Militant Protestant planters like Christopher Codrington despised Stuart policy in the Leewards because it had privileged "servants" over "settlers." In his view, slave-owning landowners were "more carefull & vigorous in the defence of their Country" because, unlike servants, they had "something to lose."[43] Codrington, who helped orchestrate Johnson's departure, seized the role of governor general. He moved to rid the islands of Irish laborers in order to purge the English colonies of deserters. His government seized the arms of more than a thousand Irish islanders across the region, from Anguilla to Montserrat, and exiled hundreds more. Sixteen conspirators from Montserrat were transferred to jail in Nevis, where they were likely executed; Codrington ordered three from Anguilla tried for treason at Antigua and executed, and another five Irish sailors hanged for aiding the French.[44] Hanging from the public gallows, their bodies were meant to strike terror into any prospective Irish deserter.

This violence aimed to crush Irish dissent as it accelerated the shift toward African labor. English Leeward planters imported more African workers for their plantations during wartime than ever before. A decade before the Irish deserted to the French in 1689, white workers in the English colonies outnumbered black. But by 1708, each island had a majority "Negro" population (see Table 3.1). Protestant anxieties about Irish colonists began to fade. Those Irish laborers who were not executed or deported became overseers, small-scale slave owners, and maroon-catchers. In time, the subsequent racial contract between big planters, small farmers, and landless white laborers offered a psychological wage large enough to reinforce the ideology of white supremacy. By the early eighteenth century, census takers no longer bothered to identify the number of French, Dutch, or even Irish colonists living in the Leewards. Instead, officials counted these settlers as white (in contrast to "slave" or "Negro," terms colonists used interchangeably).[45] The "plantation revolution" in the English Leewards was not simply the result of changes in labor supply, demand, and new "efficiencies" in the Atlantic slave trade; it was a product of resistance from below as waged by mostly Irish workers in the context of war.

As Irish desertion waned, Africans continued to draw on the knowledge of archipelagic desertion and escape. They had, after all, cooperated with the Irish in the early history of the region, which allowed knowledge of desertion to be preserved and passed on as the social composition of the plantation workforce changed. This knowledge proved as crucial as ever, for the rapid expansion of sugar plantations decimated the natural landscape and gobbled the region's woodland hiding places.

The mountains, a refuge for runaway Africans and other laborers for decades, remained an important site of resistance. Imperial conflict continued to create moments of interracial alliance in the mountains. Black runaways fled up the steep volcanic slopes of Saint Kitts soon after the Irish rebellion erupted in the summer of

TABLE 3.1 Leeward populations.

Colony	ca. 1671/72		ca. 1678		ca. 1708		ca. 1720	
	Black	White	Black	White	Black	White	Black	White
Antigua	570	1,052	2,172	2,308	12,943	2,892	19,186	2,954
Nevis	1,739	1,411	3,849	3,521	3,676	1,104	5,689	1,275
Montserrat	570	1,171	992	2,783	3,574	1,545	3,772	1,593
English Saint Kitts	952	886	1,898	1,436	2,861	1,669	7,321	2,540
English Totals	*3,831*	*4,520*	*8,911*	*10,048*	*23,054*	*7,210*	*35,968*	*8,362*
French Saint Kitts	4,468	3,333	4,301	2,885	934	901		
Guadeloupe	4,267	3,331	4,109	2,998	9,706	4,689	17,184	6,238
French Totals	*8,735*	*6,664*	*8,410*	*5,883*	*10,640*	*5,590*	*17,184*	*6,238*
Regional Totals	*12,566*	*11,184*	*17,321*	*15,931*	*33,694*	*12,800*	*53,152*	*14,600*

SOURCES: Governor Stapleton to the Board of Trade, July 17, 1672, CO 1/29; English Leewards Census, 1678, CO 1/42/337–381; List of Inhabitants by Island, 1708, CO 152/7/L54, L58–61; List of Inhabitants of the Leeward Islands, July 18, 1720, CO 152/13; Pritchard, *Search for Empire*, 50, 54–55.

1689. When Codrington launched a counteroffensive to retake the island from the French a year later, so-called "mountain Negroes" formed camps near Mount Misery. After French authorities evacuated the island in 1690, rumors circulated that "some French" islanders had joined the "mountain Negroes." In 1691, the group descended into the lowlands and launched an attack that killed seventeen English volunteers. A devastating surprise, the assault ended when sailors from the English ships *Hampshire* and *Jersey* drove the group back into the mountains.[46] The raid became a part of islander memory, but colonists remembered its African rather than its interracial character. While facing a similar crisis in 1706, authorities in Nevis recalled what happened in Saint Kitts over a decade earlier. "When the island of St. Xtopher's was in the year sixteen hundred and ninety reduced to the Subjection of the Crown of England," planters Richard Abbot and William Burt noted, "the Negroes kept out in the Mountains more than a Twelve month and never could be brought in." A motley tradition was slowing becoming an African one.[47]

Much as Irish laborers used their knowledge of imperial politics to maintain religiously defined kin ties, Africans and other slaves also fled to the mountains to maintain their families. When French forces and *flibustiers* appeared at Nevis in 1706, enslaved islanders took up arms and led their communities up Mount Nevis. The runaways may have acted to save themselves from French capture, as claimed by a large group that fled Russell's Rest plantation on the northeast side of Nevis. They promised their white overseers that they would "come home the next day after the French went off."[48] French-led troops spent two weeks trying to capture the runaways before withdrawing in defeat. After the French ships departed, runaways stayed in the mountains as maroons. For several weeks in 1706 Nevis was thus a colony turned upside down after armed slaves repulsed the French onslaught, then claimed their own freedom. Free but hungry, Nevis's black mountain rebels began to attack, kill, and eat their masters' plantation livestock—an act that would have been unthinkable just weeks earlier.[49]

British writers attributed the rebels' actions to French rumor and manipulation. In his history *The British Empire in America* (1708), John Oldmixon related how the "Blacks" of Mount Nevis were lured down from the mountains by a French commander who offered them "Hopes of Liberty" and "very pleasant and easy servitude" if they surrendered and traveled back with them to the French Islands. They were promised that they would "live with ease." According to Oldmixon, some of the mountain rebels agreed to the terms, but once on board the ships they discovered that d'Iberville intended to sell them to the Spanish. One re-enslaved man escaped a French ship, swam to Nevis's shoreline, and informed the mountain rebels that the promise of "easy servitude" in the French Leewards was treachery. According to Oldmixon, after hearing the news the remaining "Blacks took Arms," attacked the remaining French troops on Nevis, and "cut their throats."[50]

Oldmixon's account highlights how slaves used their knowledge of French and English competition to improve their condition. The ruling classes on both sides understood and played the game: English and French officials put out rumors to encourage slaves to desert and gain freedom if they fought against their masters. In 1666, French officials in Saint Kitts armed slaves "with bills, hoes, and fire-brands" to drive the English out of Cayon Division.[51] Hearing rumors that French authorities across the channel armed their slaves and "promised each man a white wife and freedom," slaveholders in Nevis also decided to arm their slaves and issued a "proclamation of freedom if they fight" against the pending French attack.[52] Much like French officials did when d'Iberville invaded Nevis in 1706, English captains also stirred up Africans on French islands by spreading rumors of liberty to "French Negroes" who picked up arms against their masters. In 1703, when English ships descended on Guadeloupe, British captains spread freedom rumors to encourage mass desertion.[53] Once in British territory, however, black runaways faced the prospect of re-enslavement at the hands of duplicitous officers.

Deserters had no rights in local courts unless they could prove that they had gained their freedom in a way that imperial authorities considered legitimate. Some runaways who fell prey to false offers of freedom *did* manage to bring their claims before local governments. In 1707, a Mulatto man named Ardra testified to the Antigua legislature that he had been promised freedom and liberty during the failed English invasion of French Guadeloupe. Ardra—who appears to have taken his name from the great Fon capital in Benin—argued that he deserted to the English and "by their consent he was to have been freed, & sett at Liberty." Arda argued that he "was never sold, or accounted for to the said Army," but that the leader of the expedition, Christopher Codrington, illegally kept "him as a slave." The legislature subsequently declared Ardra free, but reserved the right to retry his case should Codrington return from England and testify.[54]

Ardra's case emerged as each of the English Leewards began passing comprehensive slave codes. These laws were responses to wartime black mobility and resistance. One clause in an Antigua law of 1702 illustrated white fears about freed Africans who fled from the French. "An Act for the better Government of Slaves and free Negroes" stipulated that all "Free Negroes, Mulattoes, or Indians, not having Land" had to "choose some Master or Mistress to live with, who shall be owned by them."[55] In other words, the law enslaved all landless free people of color in Antigua, taking aim at black islanders who arrived in Antigua, like Ardra, with promises of freedom. The law also signaled fears of slave mobility, as it became a template for anxious planters on nearby islands.[56] By the middle of the 1720s, Nevis, Antigua, Saint Kitts, and Montserrat had all passed slave codes that governed black mobility, targeted "mountain Negroes," and rewarded white islanders who captured runaways—themes that first appeared in Leeward laws between 1697 and 1702. Running away drove the legal development of the region.[57]

WARTIME KNOWLEDGE, PEACETIME RESISTANCE

Desertion and marronage always required knowledge: runaways had to know where to go, who could help, and how to escape. War enhanced opportunities because it heightened claims of sovereignty between competing empires and, for those knowledgeable about imperial conflict, created space for initiative from below. By the early 1700s, more enslaved islanders drew on this knowledge as they stole boats and canoes to escape from one empire to another. Their motivations were similar to those of other deserters in the archipelago: some sought better treatment, some claimed religious freedoms, and some desired to reconnect with kin. But these acts also illuminate African understanding of how rival empires sought to disrupt each other's labor regimes. Sea-based peacetime desertion thus speaks to the ways slaves knowledgeably used imperial boundaries to their advantage.

These escapes are impressive but not surprising. Not only did sloping mountains offer laborers vistas of the surrounding islands, but the plantations in these small islands were never far from the sea. Sugar production required an island infrastructure that included access to the shoreline so that slaves could haul the sugar hogsheads to the "droggers," or small boats, which they rowed to offshore merchant vessels.[58] As white labor declined, more Africans worked the interisland and coastal trade in the region, too. In Antigua in 1720, black seamen outnumbered whites on boats and comprised a significant number of the sailors working sloops.[59] Enslaved runaways hoping to get off the island tapped into these networks, but not without risk. Slaves who conspired to help others escape were tortured in public, as happened to a man named Stephen in Antigua in 1738.[60]

Despite the risk, Africans frequently deserted by boat during peacetime. Soon after peace came to the Leewards in 1697, some twenty slaves seized a boat on Antigua's coast and escaped to French Guadeloupe, more than sixty kilometers away. One report indicated they had originally arrived in Antigua via French Saint Kitts, where they had slaved prior to the war. Members of the group claimed that they were Catholic and that they had been baptized into the church by a French missionary while there. When they reached Guadeloupe, the runaways found the missionary, who tried to protect them by arguing they were denied Catholic rites while in Protestant Antigua.[61]

News of the escape reached Nevis, where slaveholders feared their slaves would follow suit. "We daily fear that this practice of running away of our French Negroes taken in the late war," the councilmen related in February of 1699. "If special care be not taken," they insisted, "it will prove of very pernicious consequence to many of His Majesty's subjects." For Nevis's planters, sea-based escape to the French was a "growing evil," one that would prove detrimental to plantation discipline by inspiring other slaves and possibly free white laborers to run.[62] A year later, the Nevis government passed a law that anyone who stole a boat or canoe—whether they be "bond or free"—was to be put to death, proving that maritime runaways had commanded the full attention of the island's rulers.[63]

Similar fears of black escape by boat spread across Saint Kitts during Queen Anne's war. In 1711, the Saint Kitts government passed sweeping legislation aimed for the "better Government of Negroes, and other Slaves." Article 16 focused on people of color trying to get to French territory by hiding out near the salt ponds. "Lately sundry Negroes, and other slaves, have deserted their Masters and Owners," the article began, "and have withdrawn themselves into the late French Quarter and there absconded themselves in the Grounds called the Salt Ponds, and in other Grounds lying to windward of Frigatt Bay." Their "design and intent," the law continued, was "not only to go over themselves to the Enemy, when opportunity shall present, but also to persuade and entice other Negroes and Slaves to go with them." African workers gravitated to the very place—the salt ponds—where vessels of various nations presented the best opportunities for escape.[64]

Perhaps no case better highlights African political knowledge of empire than the one involving runaways who fled from French Guadeloupe to Montserrat, briefly returned to their former island to gather more kin, and escaped again in 1713. Three men, Joseph, Thomas, and Jean-Louis, vanished from the plantation of Guillaume Garet in Les Abymes, Guadeloupe. Garet had no idea where the runaways had gone until a visiting English sailor informed him that he had witnessed a canoe full of black islanders land at Montserrat. Rumor had it that a planter named Molineux was keeping them on his plantation. A year later, when fourteen more slaves stole a canoe and escaped, Garet suspected that they, too, fled to Montserrat. The runaways drew on their common history as captives of war and plantation workers. At least one of the runaways was an African man who went by the name "Congo." Another key figure was George, whom Garet identified as being "from Montserrat."[65]

Three years later, several of the maritime runaways returned to Guadeloupe. In 1717, Garet testified in court again, eager to get officials abroad to intervene. The deserters who returned to Garet's plantation hatched another escape for six more people.[66] By 1724, more than ten years after the initial escape, Garet had had enough and wanted his slaves back. He hired a man named Courtois to travel to Montserrat, find Molineux, and order him to return all of Garet's runaways. By the time Courtois arrived, Molineux had fled by boat for Saint Kitts, leaving Governor Paul George to handle the complaint. The governor informed Garet's messenger that he would not pay for the losses, for Molineux had informed the governor that the slaves Garet claimed had in fact been seized from him during the previous war, and that Garet thus had no legal title to them.[67]

The French planter, frustrated by the runaways who had by now outwitted him three times, pushed on. Eventually, both the English board of trade and secretary of state weighed in. They suggested that the Leeward governor general restore any slaves that Garet could prove a title to, but they pointed out that Garet was not alone in this dilemma. They noted that his adversary, Montserrat's Molineux, recently lost a far greater number of enslaved runaways who fled from the English colony to a French one. His maritime deserters escaped in the opposite direction, from Montserrat to French Marie-Galante. The vicissitudes of war and the practices of running away were deeply intertwined.[68]

The broad patterns of collective desertion in the imperially crowded Leeward archipelago illuminate the global history of capitalism. Like workers around the world between 1600 and 1850, laboring islanders were people who had been violently uprooted, displaced, and relocated; they were "people shuffled together from diverse places."[69] And like workers everywhere, they faced enormous top-down efforts to contain and control their mobility through the law, violence, and other forms of brutal coercion. They challenged this violence by turning to friends, kin, and fellow workers who helped them figure out where to go and how to get there. They resisted by creating new solidarities and new kinds of knowledge derived from their immediate experience, forms of resistance that authorities and state actors would try their best to dissolve and destroy. In this sense, the story of desertion in the Leeward archipelago offers a window onto much larger dialectical processes in the history of global capitalism.

Two great historical themes run from the earliest days of Kalinago "Carib" settlement, through the Irish-led resistance of the late seventeenth century, to the transimperial escapes of Africans in the eighteenth century. The first is the central role that violence and war played in the development of desertion, running away, and escape. Whether we consider how Amerindians used the archipelago to escape war in the sixteenth century, how Irish servants crossed French borders to fight against English tobacco lords in the seventeenth century, or how Africans like Congo and Jean-Louis used the environment to escape brutality in Guadeloupe in the eighteenth century, it is crucial to note that all were responses to large-scale violence.

The invasion of the Leeward Islands by European settlers, however, transformed the dynamics of violence. Whereas Kalinago islanders used the seaways and mountains to keep out Spanish slave raiders and Indian war parties, European settlers used violence to exploit and contain laborers for the purpose of producing tobacco and sugar. In Saint Kitts, French and English officials subdivided the transnational colony into distinct sovereign zones of government and established treaty guidelines that required runaways who fled across borders be returned, all to assure their respective planters that bond labor would remain fixed and under their control. Labor discipline and physical containment went hand in hand as class struggle took on a spatial dimension in the Leeward archipelago.

The second theme in Leeward history is that even though the social composition of labor changed, workers of all kinds responded to top-down violence and war with fast feet and sharp minds. All runaways, beginning with Amerindian islanders, used the natural boundaries of sea, land, and mountains to establish or protect their autonomy, but Catholic servants and enslaved Africans added something new to the arsenal of resistance: how to use man-made imperial boundaries. The long view of desertion in the Leewards highlights an intellectual history from below.

Island bond laborers relied on four different kinds of knowledge to challenge top-down violence and exploitation when they deserted and ran away. Drawing on an Amerindian heritage, they developed natural knowledge about the physical environment. This entailed learning about local plant life and sources of food and where to find fresh water for sustenance. This environmental folk knowledge was intimately bound up with a second, geographic, knowledge or shared understandings about where one could find refuge, distant from the reach of authority, in mountains or at sea. Knowing of a hidden path up Mount Nevis or Mount Misery in Saint Kitts could mean the difference between life and death. Understanding how to navigate, by canoe, the winds and currents of the forty-mile seaway connecting the southern coast of Antigua to the northern shoreline of Grande-Terre, Guadeloupe, required precious expertise. Social knowledge was a third requirement: Irish Catholic servants who sought to have their children baptized in French territory and enslaved Africans in French Guadeloupe seeking a canoe to carry their family to Montserrat needed to know who to trust as they planned their escapes and who could help them on their way.[70]

Leeward runaways relied on a fourth kind of knowledge: a political understanding of empire. In their effort to maintain labor discipline and contain mobility, English and French imperial authorities subdivided the natural environment into competing sovereign regimes of labor and accumulation, which savvy servants and slaves could manipulate to their own advantage. The origins of this kind of deserter knowledge appeared in the *Partage* treaty signed in Saint Kitts in 1627, which recognized that runaway laborers would pit masters from the two nations against each other. Workers understood the importance of their own labor power, which they could transfer to their master's enemy by crossing a border. Political knowledge of empire proved exceptionally important during wartime, as deserters like Ardra could use their know-how to leverage freedom from authorities by fighting and serving as spies. This kind of knowledge and action sometimes triggered the transfer of entire colonies from one imperial power to the other.

War planted the seeds of its colonial subversion and, in crucial moments, even destruction. As C. L. R. James noted of the Caribbean, African knowledge of competition among the Spanish, English, and French in Saint-Domingue was central to the victory of the Haitian Revolution. Perhaps some of the revolutionaries drew on knowledge from the thousands of enslaved Africans transplanted to Saint-Domingue from the war-torn Leewards in the 1690s and early 1700s. Slaves' knowledge of the rivalry between the Union and the cotton empire of the Confederacy led to what W. E. B. Du Bois called the "general strike," when thousands of African Americans deserted to the Union army, giving fresh and decisive power to the Northern military effort. When examined in the context of a long global history of desertion, events like the uprising in Saint Kitts in 1689 illuminate a common theme in the history of slavery and capitalism. Dispossessed people learned from the contradictions of imperial violence and used them to transform their own world.[71]

NOTES

1. Petition of the Governor and Council of the island of St. Christophers, July 11, 1689, CO 152/37/17i, f. 294; Governor Stede to the Earl of Shrewsbury, July 16, 1689, CO 28/37/16.

2. Jonathan Netheway, Nevis, June 27, CO 153/3, pp. 429–30; Deposition of Darby Considine, Fort Charles, Saint Kitts, June 29, 1689, CO 153/3, pp. 432–33.

3. Netheway to Colonel Bastian Bayer, Nevis, June 27, CO 152/37, No. 14, ff. 304–5; Netheway to the King and Queen, Nevis, June 27, 1689, CO 152/37, No. 13, ff. 300–301.

4. Present State of St. Christophers, Fort Charles, Saint Kitts, July 11, 1689, CO 152/37, No. 17ii, ff. 298–298v; Netheway, Nevis, June 27, CO 153/3, pp. 429–30; Journal of the Siege of the Fort at St. Christophers by the French, 1689, CO 152/37, No. 33iii; Copie d'une letter escrite à Monsieur Hinselin par Monsieur de Blenac, Guadeloupe, June 4, 1689, FR ANOM COL C8A/5, ff. 217–18; Blénac à la Guadeloupe, Martinique, April 20, 1689, FR ANOM C7A/3, F° 173.

5. Most accounts of the uprising have not improved upon the pioneering work of Richard Dunn, *Sugar and Slaves* (New York: Norton, 1972), 134. See also Natalie Zacek, *Settler Society in the English Leeward Islands, 1670–1776* (New York: Cambridge University Press, 2010). For a recent exception, see Jenny Shaw, *Everyday Life in the Early English Caribbean* (Athens: University of Georgia Press, 2013), 146–47.

6. This framework is inspired by Marcus Rediker, *Outlaws of the Atlantic* (Boston: Beacon Press, 2014), 47.

7. George Harlow, Reg Murphy, David J. Hozjan, Christy N. De Mille, and Alfred A. Levinson, "Pre-Columbian Jadeite Axes from Antigua, West Indies: Description and Possible Sources," *Canadian Mineralogist* 44, no. 2 (2006): 305–21.

8. Neil Whitehead, "Carib Ethnic Soldiering in Venezuela, the Guianas, and the Antilles, 1492–1820," *Ethnohistory* 37, no. 4 (1990): 357–85.

9. Stephan Lenik, "Carib as a Colonial Category," *Ethnohistory* 59, no. 1 (2012); Doris Garraway, *The Libertine Colony: Creolization in the Early French Caribbean* (Durham, NC: Duke University Press, 2005), 39–42; Peter Hulme and Neil Whitehead, eds., *Wild Majesty: Encounters with Caribs from Columbus to the Present Day* (Oxford: Oxford University Press, 1992), 67–73.

10. Charles Rochefort, *The History of the Caribby-Islands,* trans. John Davies (London: Printed for John Starkey, 1666), 205, 306; Anonymous, *Histoire Naturelle & Morale des îles Antilles de l'Amerique* (Rotterdam: Chez Arnout Leers, 1658), 509.

11. Ibid.

12. Thomas Gage, *A New Survey of the West Indies* (London: Printed by E. Cotes, 1655), 18–19.

13. Reprinted in Vincent Harlow, ed., *Colonising Expeditions to the West Indies and Guiana* (London: Hakluyt Society, 1925), 3. On Carib slaveholding, see Hulme and Whitehead, *Wild Majesty*, 38.

14. Dunn, *Sugar and Slaves,* 119.

15. Partage made between ye governours, April 28, 1627, British Library, Egerton Manuscripts 2395.

16. Philip Boucher, *France and the American Tropics to 1700* (Baltimore: Johns Hopkins University Press, 2008), 147; Anonymous, *Histoire Naturelle & Morale,* 320.

17. Jean-Baptiste Du Tertre, *Histoire Generale des Antilles* (Paris: T. Iolly, 1667–71), 1:153; Nellis Crouse, *French Pioneers in the West Indies* (New York: Columbia University Press, 1940), 100–101.

18. Stewart Mims, *Colbert's West India Policy* (New Haven, CT: Yale University Press, 1912), 18–19; Dunn, *Sugar and Slaves,* 119–20; Rochefort, *History of the Caribby-Islands,* 165–68; John Appleby, "English Settlement in the Lesser Antilles during War and Peace, 1603–1660," in *The Lesser Antilles in the Age of European Expansion,* ed. Stanley Engerman and Robert Paquette (Gainesville: University of Florida, 1996), 90–92.

19. Appleby, "English Settlment"; Harlow, *Colonising Expeditions,* 11.

20. Harlow, *Colonising Expeditions,* 54–102; Appleby, "English Settlement," 93.

21. Carla Pestana, *The English Atlantic in an Age of Revolution* (Cambridge, MA: Harvard University Press, 2004), 229, 32; Carl Bridenbaugh and Roberta Bridenbaugh, *No Peace beyond the Line* (New York: Oxford University Press, 1972), 20.

22. Rochefort, *History of the Caribby-Islands,* 174.

23. Boucher, *France and the American Tropics,* 144–46; Dunn, *Sugar and Slaves,* 122; Zacek, *Settler Society,* 5–11, 49–56; Voyages: Trans-Atlantic Slave Trade Database, http://slavevoyages.org/voyages/KkTFJYbe (accessed January 10, 2017).

24. Appleby, "English Settlement"; Anonymous, *Histoire Naturelle & Morale,* 35; Jean-Baptiste Labat, *Nouveau Voyage aux îles de l'Amérique* (Paris: Chez P. F. Giffart, 1722), 5:37.

25. Bridenbaugh and Bridenbaugh, *No Peace,* 102–3; Donald Akenson, *If the Irish Ran the World: Montserrat, 1630–1730* (Montreal: McGill-Queen's University Press, 1997), 51–53; Boucher, *France and the American Tropics,* 147; Zacek, *Settler Society,* chap. 1.

26. Akenson, *Irish Ran the World,* 44–45; Kristen Block and Jenny Shaw, "Subjects without an Empire: The Irish in the Early Modern Carribean," *Past & Present* 210, no. 1 (2011) 33–60.

27. Du Tertre, *Histoire Generale,* 3:300; Gwynn, "Documents," 195–96, 208–14; Akenson, *Irish Ran the World,* 44–45; Societé de Jesuits, *Mission de Cayenne et de la Guyane Française* (Paris: Julien, Lanier, Cosnard, 1857).

28. James S. Pritchard, *In Search of Empire: The French in the Americas, 1670–1730* (New York: Cambridge University Press, 2004), 105; Mark Hanna, *Pirate Nests and the Rise of the English Empire, 1570–1740* (Chapel Hill: University of North Carolina Press, 2017), 106–7.

29. Joseph Browne to Williamson, June 24, 1666, CO 1/20/103.

30. Sir Charles Wheler to the Secretary of the Council, September 2, 1675, CO 1/35/14.

31. Francis Sampson to his brother John Sampson, June 6, 1666, CO 1/20/97; Shaw, *Everyday Life.*

32. Petition of Clement Everard, November 13, 1667, CO 1/21/145.

33. Governor Stapleton to the Council, August 7, 1672, CO 1/29/19; C. S. S. Higham, *The Development of the Leeward Islands under the Restoration* (Cambridge: Cambridge University Press, 1921).

34. Governor Stapleton to the Council, August 7, 1672, CO 1/29/19.

35. An Act for the Restraining the Liberty of Negroes, and to Prevent the Running Way of Christian Servants, no. 17, 1670, *Acts of the Assembly Passed in the Island of Montserrat* (London: John Baskett, 1740), 9.

36. Theodore Allen, *The Invention of the White Race* (New York: Verso, 1993), 1:21; David Eltis, "Seventeenth-Century Migration and the Slave Trade: The English Case in Comparative Perspective," in *Migration, Migration History, History: Old Paradigms and New Perspectives*, ed. Jan Lucassen and Leo Lucassen (Bern: Peter Lang, 2005), 107.

37. An Act impowering Justice of the Peace to order Labourers Wages; and restraining Persons going on board Ships or other Vessels, no. 24, 1673, *Acts of Montserrat*, 31; An Act Enabling Artificers, Labourers, and Servants to Recover their Wages from their Master, Antigua, no. 70, October 28, 1684, *Acts of Assembly Passed in the Charibbee Leeward Islands* (London: John Baskett, 1740), 73.

38. C. S. S. Higham, "The General Assembly of the Leeward Islands," *English Historical Review* 41, no. 162 (1926).

39. Instructions to Sir Nathaniel Johnson, November 28, 1686, CO 153/3/213–229; Nathaniel Johnson to the Lords, March 3, 1688, CO 1/64/28.

40. Deposition of John Barry, May 22, 1688, CO 1/64/71iii; Deposition of John Martin, May 22, 1688, CO 1/64/71iv.

41. Nathaniel Johnson to the Lords, August 10, 1687, CO 1/64/7.

42. John Netheway to the King and Queen, June 27, 1689, CO 152/37/13.

43. Some Propositions and Observations Relating to the Thorough Settlement of St. Christophers, September 8, 1691, CO 152/1/B.A. No.3/1.

44. Henry Carpenter to Thomas Belchamber, August 19, 1689, CO 152/37/35; Codrington to the Lords, July 31, 1689, CO 152/37/22; Codrington to the Lords, August 15, 1689, CO 152/37/30; Codrington to the Lords, September 19, 1689, CO 152/37/41.

45. Antigua, March 5, 1708, CO 152/7/L53; Saint Kitts, January 1708, CO 152/7/L58; Trinity Palmato Point, February 8, 1708, CO 152/7/L59; Nevis, 1708, CO 152/7/L60; Montserrat, January 29, 1708, CO 152/7/L61.

46. Captain Lawrence Wright to Governor Kendall, March 19, 1691, CO 28/1/60iii.

47. Richard Abbott and William Burt to D'Iberville, March 30, 1706, CO 184/1/black 20–21; An Account of the Taking of the Island, June 3, 1706, CO 184/1/Red6i.

48. Thomas Easom to Lady Stapleton, April 22, 1706, Stapleton MSS. 6/13.

49. Extrait des Negres prouenants[?] de La Prise de Nieve, April 21, CO 184/1/32.

50. John Oldmixon, *The British Empire in America* (London: 1708), 2:217–18.

51. Jo. Browne to Williamson, June 24, 1666, CO 1/20/No. 103.

52. Francis Sampson to his brother Joseph Sampson, June 6, 1666, CO 1/20/No. 97.

53. David Marley, *Wars of the Americas* (Santa Barbara: ABC-CLIO, 1998), 225.

54. David Barry Gaspar, *Bondmen and Rebels: A Study of Master-Slave Relations in Antigua* (Durham, NC: Duke University Press, 1993), 163.

55. An Act for the Better Government of Slaves and Free Negroes, Antigua, no. 130, Passed June 28, 1702, Confirmed May 8, 1703, *Acts of the Charibee Leeward Islands*, 138.

56. David Barry Gaspar, "With a Rod of Iron: Barbados Slave Laws as a Model for Jamaica, South Carolina, and Antigua, 1661–1697," in *Crossing Boundaries: Comparative History of Black People in Diaspora*, ed. Darlene Clark Hine and Jacqueline McLeod (Bloomington: Indiana University Press, 1999).

57. An Act for the Insolence of Slaves, no. 36, 1693, *Acts of Montserrat*, 43–45; An Act for the Government of Negroes and other Slaves, no. 81, 1717, *Acts of the Assembly Passed in the Island of Nevis* (London: John Baskett, 1740), 75–78; An Act for Attainting several Negroes therein Mentioned, 1722, *Acts of Assembly Passed in the Island of St. Christopher* (London: John Baskett, 1739), 69–70; An Act for attainting several Slaves now run away from their Master's Service, no. 176, 1723, *Acts of the Charibee Leeward Islands*, 206–17.

58. Governor General Hamilton to the Board, August 22, 1720, CO152/13/Q51.

59. Gaspar, *Bondmen and Rebels*, 110.

60. Trustees of Maine Swete, 1738–1739, Swete Papers, Devon Record Office, 388M/E4.

61. [Guillaume Moreau (?)], "Mémoires concernant la mission des pères de la compagnie de Jésus dans les isles françoises de l'Amérique," reprinted in *Annales de la Société d'Histoire de la Martinique* 27 (1988–91): 74–75; Peabody, "Dangerous Zeal," 53–54.

62. Letter from the President and Council of Nevis to the Board, February 4, 1699, CO 152/3/C16.

63. An Act against Running Away with Boats or Canoes, no. 27, 1700, *Acts of Nevis*, 21–22.

64. An Act for the Better Government of Negroes, and other Slaves, Saint Kitts, 1711, *Acts of St. Christopher*, 12.

65. Copie de Plusieurs pieces concernant les Negres sauvés du Monsieur Guillaume Garet, habitant de la Guadeloupe, December 22, 1714, CO 152/14/R107.

66. Requeste à Messieurs De Frequiere and Blondel, June 16, 1724, CO 152/14/R107.

67. Lettre du Monsieur Courtois à Monsieur Garet, April 10, 1724, CO 152/14/R107.

68. Letter from the Board of Trade to the King, March 29, 1728, CO 152/40/Red23i.

69. Rochefort, *History of the Caribby-Islands*, 174.

70. Rediker, *Outlaws of the Atlantic*, 47.

71. Pritchard, *Search for Empire*, 379–83; C. L. R. James, *The Black Jacobins* (New York: Vintage, 1989); W. E. B. Du Bois, *Black Reconstruction* (New York: Harcourt, Brace, 1935), 55–83, especially 57; Stephanie Camp, *Closer to Freedom: Enslaved Women and Everyday Resistance in the Plantation South* (Chapel Hill: University of North Carolina Press, 2004).

4

Desertion of European Sailors and Soldiers in Early Eighteenth-Century Bengal

Titas Chakraborty

In November 1734, eight sailors of the Dutch East India Company (VOC) hatched a conspiracy to desert their ship, the *Wendela*. Leendert van den Burg, "an ageing sluggard" in the eyes of VOC officials, led the gang of seven "young careless whelps" in escaping to Calcutta, the headquarters of the British East India Company (EIC), located fifty kilometers upstream on the Hugli River from Falta, the anchoring place of the VOC in Bengal. The sailors unanimously claimed that the ship officials, especially the first mate, treated them "not as company servants but as slaves,"[1] which induced them to run away to EIC grounds in search of better opportunities for work. When VOC guards in Falta intercepted the deserters as they silently made their way to Calcutta on a boat in the dead of night, they surrendered without a fight. Within a few days one of the arrested deserters died in chains and "escaped the hands of justice." The VOC *fiscaal* (judge) found Leendert van den Burg and his two most trusted assistants, Pieter Janzen and Christian Houvle, guilty of the grievous crime of "seduction of young ones," and sentenced them to death. After the executions were carried out on VOC grounds in Chinsurah, the remaining three sailors were "again employed and distributed on ships." Reflecting on the severity of the punishment, the *fiscaal*'s office in Bengal concluded that they had shown "compassion" in their judgment as only half the convicted deserters went to the gallows.[2]

The deserters of *Wendela* committed the most widely practiced crime by European workers in the early East India Company settlements in Bengal. In fact, unlike Leendert van den Burg and seven other sailors, most deserters successfully ran away from work. Holden Furber, a pioneering historian of European trade in seventeenth- and eighteenth-century Bengal, observed that Europeans of the "lower order served the English, Dutch, French, Danes or 'Ostenders' with a *catholicity* which is astonishing."[3] This "catholicity" was best expressed in European sailors' and soldiers' propensity to switch employers by running away from work. Desertion rates in Bengal, compared to other settlements, remained exceptionally high. Indeed, in Bengal the companies lost more workers to desertion than to death—in a quite deadly place.[4] In certain years, the VOC directorate in Bengal reported that desertion involved between one third and half of the total number of European servants.[5] The bulk of the deserters were sailors, and the rates of desertion ranged from 1.1 to 45.2 percent of the crew of VOC vessels (see Table 4.1).[6]

This article explores desertion as a weapon used by European workers to leverage their position in the labor market of precolonial Bengal. As lower-class members of the European East India companies, their interests were never aligned with the mercantile corporate interests of the companies. Historians have variously interpreted the recalcitrance among European sailors and soldiers in early European settlements in India as adventurism or renegadism, demonstrating the weakness of imperial reach of early European enterprises.[7] More recently, Elizabeth Kolsky, considering the various acts of insubordination perpetrated by lower-level company servants, has called them "the third face of colonialism."[8] Yet none of these studies conceptualizes European sailors and soldiers as workers, nor do they study desertion, which was the most common form of resistance, primarily to negotiate their positions within the Bengal labor market. For the companies, desertion of their lower-level servants undermined their economic and political ambitions in foreign lands. Desertion not only fostered a competitive market for European labor in Bengal leading to higher wage levels, it also challenged the sovereignty of the companies. Since the seventeenth century, East India companies overseas had conceived of themselves as settling a growing population and thereby developing the state's economic strength and expanding its sovereignty.[9] Desertion violated this sovereignty. The first section briefly sketches the social world of European workers in Bengal, with special emphasis on deserters, their motives, and their social relations. Hardships of work and debt encouraged desertion, but they were not the primary reasons for absconding. The following two sections show that European sailors and soldiers who reached Bengal discovered that their labor was much in demand in the armies and ships of rival European companies and indigenous elites. Desertion was thus a weapon that European sailors and soldiers used to ramp up the competition among their prospective employers and ultimately to bring better wages and working conditions. The first of these sections also explains how indigenous elites sought out European workers for their armies and how European workers found their place in the social milieu of precolonial Bengal in opposition to the interests of their European masters. The third and final

TABLE 4.1 Desertion rate by VOC ship, 1712–1740

Ship	Year	Deserters	Closest Year for which Information Is Found	Crew Size for Closest Year	Tonnage	Desertion Rate for Closest Year (%)
Duivenvoorde	1712	33	1711	73	620	45.2
Rijssel	1712	3	1711	83	858	3.6
Brug	1712	2	1712	74	600	2.7
Schuitwijk	1726	7	1726	132	650	5.3
Sleewijk	1726	7	1726	64	520	10.9
Opperdoes	1727	8	1727	80	600	10.0
Wendela	1734	3	1734	86	600	3.5
Duifje	1734	2	1734	117	450	1.7
Sutama	1734	8				
Cats	1734	2	1734	92	580	2.2
Goudriaan	1734	3	1733	119	630	2.5
Aldegonde	1734	1	1734	88	580	1.1
Hartenlust	1735	2	1735	80	650	2.5
Spiering	1735	2	1735	77	810	2.6
Loenderveen	1735	4	1735	113		3.5
Sleewijk	1735	4	1734	87		4.6
Groenswaart	1735	2	1735	112		1.8
Groenswaart	1736	3	1736	118		2.5
Hof niet altijd	1736	1	1735	79		1.3
Land van beloft	1736	1	1738	68		1.5
Loenderveen	1736	5	1737	98		5.1
Purmerlust	1737	2	1737	74		2.7
Meerlust	1738	10	1738	52		19.2
Dishoek	1738	3	1738	50		6.0
Opperdoes	1738	1	1737	76	600	1.3
Constantia	1738	2	1736	31		25.8
Batavia	1738	1				
Steenhoven	1738	1	1736	74		1.4
Schonauwen	1740	2	1740	70		2.9
Zorgwijk	1740	2	1740	57		3.5
Lis	1740	2	1740	50		4.0

SOURCES: For the number of deserters: VOC 8744, fols. 386, 472, VOC 8789, fols. 1055–57, VOC 8755, fol. 450, VOC 8756, fol. 113. For the crew numbers of the vessels in their intra-Asiatic voyages: Matthias van Rossum, "Generale Zeemonsterrollen, Verenigde Oost-Indische Compagnie, 1691–1791," Dutch Ships and Sailors, www.dutchshipsand-sailors.nl (link is external) (April 2014).

section discusses the climate of intercompany competition in the early eighteenth century, which induced desertion among European sailors and soldiers. Companies perceived and articulated this uncontrolled mobility of their European workers as insubordination and subversion that undermined their profits and sovereignty in foreign lands.

THE OPEN ROAD

European workers constituted an important segment of the East India companies' workforce in Bengal. From the seventeenth century, European workers came to Bengal as crew members on deep-sea vessels. When in Bengal, European sailors and soldiers were usually bound to their respective ships. From the early eighteenth century, as European companies gained the political right to maintain their own standing armies in Bengal, they frequently employed the European crew members of their vessels as military personnel on land whenever there was a manpower shortage as a result of sickness, death, and desertion. The primary task of the standing army of both companies throughout the early eighteenth century was to escort people and commodities up and down the riverine highway of the Ganga.

The hardships of shipboard life in the age of sail is a much-discussed topic.[10] Even the best ship was "a prison for the poor sailor."[11] The ship captain or commander played the role of the jailer. As the despot of the sea, he could "earn the poor sailors both heaven and hell on earth."[12] One VOC report on desertion from 1711—a year with an unprecedented number of desertions—identified "the fear of discipline for the misdeeds committed on board" as a primary cause.[13] Shipboard discipline was certainly harsh and abusive. Oftentimes, it was not just the ship captains but also other higher-ranking officials on board—as is evident from the *Wendela* incident—who meted out abusive punishment to the sailors. Both the boatswain and the captain noticed the excessive abusive behavior of the first mate and asked him to reduce his harsh methods.[14] All witnesses who were sailors on the *Wendela* complained that they did not get enough rest in the journey from Batavia to Bengal. The boatswain admitted that the lack of skilled men on board during seastorms required that the sailors work harder than usual. Cristiaan Onfreij, a nineteen-year-old sailor, complained that he had "no free time" once the Batavia–Bengal voyage started. He had "no interest" in running away, but the overwork and abuse compelled him to desert.[15] The conditions of work were no better on English ships, where seafaring was perpetual work. As the seventeenth-century English East India sailor Edward Barlow noted, seamen "were not to lie still above four hours."[16] As Barlow lamented, his occupation was "one of the hardest and dangerousest callings I could have entered upon."[17] Prolonged work in unhygienic conditions resulted in illnesses of various sorts, which led to sickness and sometimes death. "Death and desertion" were almost always uttered in the same breath by ship captains, requiring them to look for fresh recruits.[18] The perils of life at sea often brought forth mass desertions immediately after the arrival of ships at Bengal.

Although the working conditions of soldiers within the Bengal directorate were much better than those of the sailors on deep-sea vessels, death haunted the many soldiers who worked on inland shipping. European soldiers were quick to succumb to the diseases of the tropics. In 1728, seven of the 333 soldiers of the Patna fleet of the VOC died within three months.[19] The next year the fleet was manned by 307 soldiers, thirteen soldiers of whom were so sick that they were unable to work; another eleven died soon.[20] Moreover, combat situations always put life at peril. Three EIC soldiers were killed in an armed conflict with the Chakwars in 1719.[21]

Quotidian hardships were often inscribed on the flesh of soldiers and sailors, who might be identified by a scar running "from above his left until under his right breast" or "signs of injury on the left side of his head and one under his calf" or "crooked posture." Experience of collective misery, in turn, gave rise to collective sociability. The collective experience of working together created a common language and culture among seamen.[22] Similarly, in Bengal the Christian names of sailors and soldiers often gave way to endearing monikers: Piet Janszoon Stael was known to his mates as "Piet the Pendulum"; Dirck Reijers was nicknamed the "Castle Durendael"; the shy Guijljam van Beveren was called the "Housekeeper"; Arent Arentzoon's pet name was "The Baptist"; Elias Corneliszoon was known to all as "Man Elephant"; Johannes Abrahamzoon was called "Jan Ding Ding" by the crew. This alternative sociability of workers arising out of the zones of cooperation during the workday was critical to the acts of desertion.[23]

As the *Wendela* incident demonstrates, such cooperation often made desertion a collective act. Groups of twelve, thirteen, thirty-three, or fifty-three workers escaped from company grounds. As shipboard life created bonds of camaraderie, waterfront areas were sites of working-class socialization. The taverns in European settlements were an especially important part of the sailors' and soldiers' lives in Bengal. People missing from the daily attendance call could often be found in the taverns. In 1686, in the midst of the Anglo-Mughal war, the taverns in Hugli became the places where VOC workers deserted to the EIC side.[24] In 1733, the EIC found it necessary to involve punch house owners in their desperate efforts to stop desertion from intercontinental ships. Both punch house owners and home owners were strictly ordered to report to the officer of the guard if they "entertain in their house any stranger." If punch house owners failed to notify the EIC, and if the guards apprehended deserters from these establishments, especially those belonging to the company's shipping, the owner of the house "will not be suffered to remain here but will be sent directly to Europe."[25] Such orders thus marked punch houses as a critical space for socialization among potential deserters.

The sailors of *Wendela* did not put up a fight against the VOC forces, but most successful cases of desertion involved arms. Taking control over arms was of strategic importance to the eleven soldiers and two sailors who fled the VOC *panchallang 't Weroname*, a small one-masted vessel stationed at Falta in the early hours of April 10, 1733. The desertion of *'t Weroname* was a well-planned effort as shown in the lightning speed of its execution. At 2:00 a.m. on April 10, right after a new guard had taken over his shift patrolling the lower deck, the thirteen rebels launched a two-pronged attack—one group tackled the guard and lowered the ship boat, while the other group stormed the cabin of the quartermaster on the upper deck, where all the arms of the ship were stored. Even though the quartermaster was present in his cabin with two sergeants and two corporals, the suddenness of the attack prevented any defense. Within an hour, after confiscating the arms, the rebels from the upper deck joined the rest in the lowered boat and made their way to Calcutta.[26]

Communication with "partners" (*mackers*) was essential to the designs of the eight sailors of the *Wendela*. The leader of the deserters, Leendert van den Burg, had been to Bengal on multiple voyages. As a thirty-seven-year-old sailor, Leendert van den Burg's experience came in handy as he led the group of young deserters, all under twenty-five years of age. Van den Burg individually spoke to all the deserters after they were physically abused by the first mate and convinced them that they could all find better work with the English in Calcutta. The entire group waited for Van den Burg to give them the signal to lower the boat, as he had knowledge of the movement of the VOC patrol at Falta. When arrested by a group of native guards of the VOC, Van den Burg, knowing that the guards did not understand Dutch, communicated to the rest, "we should stick to the same story." Except for the Christiaan Houvle, everyone else told the identical story in the *fiscaal*'s office, down to the curse word allegedly used by the first mate. Veteran deserters like Van den Burg were always a menace to company authorities. Such "faithless vagabonds" never remained in service for long. They would "pinch not only the weapons but also money" from their "lawful masters" but most importantly they "seduced others" to run away with them.[27] Free communication among workers, which the companies desperately tried to limit, was essential to the act of running away.

More often than not, desertion entailed harsh punishments. Authorities executed several captured runaways. According to my calculation, twenty-one death penalties were given for desertion by the *fiscaal* in the Bengal directorate, of which seventeen were carried out in Chinsurah.[28] Certain deserters were given the punishment of walking the gauntlet, which sometimes entailed suffering the harsh physical abuse of a battalion of two hundred soldiers.[29] Those "repenting" deserters taken back by the company resumed labor at the lowest salary level. European sailors and soldiers nonetheless continued to desert despite the harsh punishments and the "strong currents and crocodiles" in the river and the deltaic lands around Falta, which sometimes claimed the lives of deserters as they surreptitiously swam to shore in the dead of night.[30] What could explain such strong desire to run away?

Bad working conditions, legal persecution, and indebtedness encouraged but did not cause most desertions. Among the deserters were a few servants convicted for their crimes in Bengal and awaiting deportation as convicts to Batavia. Although it is impossible to determine the percentage of the deserters who were convicts, one can safely conclude that they formed at least a significant minority.

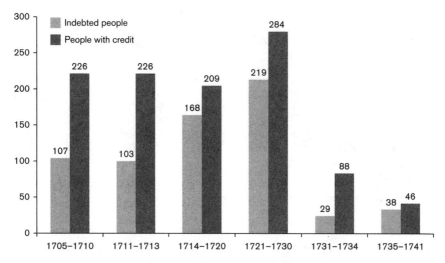

FIGURE 4.1. Proportion of indebted deserters to deserters with credit.

Indebtedness was endemic to lower-level company servants, especially sailors and soldiers. Some of them had debts of over 100 Dutch guilders, which would take years or many months of wages to repay. Owing money to creditors was a strong impulse, but indebted workers were still a minority among the recorded number of deserters (see Figure 4.1).[31]

Many workers ran away even though the company owed them wages, in some cases as much as 50 Dutch guilders. What then spurred the workers who were not in any financial bondage with the company to escape? The answer must be sought in the unique employment opportunities that Bengal presented to European workers, indebted or otherwise.

EUROPEAN DESERTERS AND INDIGENOUS ARMIES

The VOC in Bengal suffered the highest number of desertions between 1711 and 1713—the years marking intense political turmoil in the region (see Figure 4.2).[32]

The reasons for the spike in desertion lay in the political turmoil that engulfed the entire subcontinent of India, including the province of Bengal, after the death of Aurangzeb in 1707. The emperor's son, Bahadur Shah, acceded to power. The governor of Bengal—the grandson of Aurangzeb and the son of Bahadur Shah, Prince Azim (also called Azim-us-shan)—began to quarrel with the *diwan* (provincial head of revenue collection) of Bengal, Murshid Quli Khan, who had been a long-trusted imperial officer. In 1708, Azim successfully persuaded his father to transfer Murshid Quli from Bengal to Daccan. But the emperor, Bahadur Shah

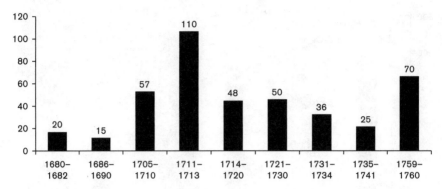

FIGURE 4.2. Average number of deserters by year.

soon changed his mind and reappointed Murshid Quli as *diwan* of Bengal in 1710. In 1711, the emperor granted him the collectorship of customs at Hugli port and made him the *faujdar* (military leader) of Midnapur district, a position occupied by Zia-ud-din Khan, a trusted subordinate of Azim. Zia-ud-din refused to relinquish his post, which caused great strife that would last two years. In the meantime, Bahadur Shah died and the Mughal throne passed to a different son of Bahadur Shah, Jahandar Shah, in 1712. The same year Azim's son (and Jahandar's nephew) Farukhsiyar launched another round of succession war. When he sought support for a campaign in Delhi against Jahandar, he asked Murshid Quli for help but was refused. Farukhsiyar then sent troops against Murshid Quili and finally became emperor in 1713. This dynastic and bureaucratic warfare provided extraordinary opportunities to European soldiers and sailors.[33]

During these political upheavals the common seamen of the VOC got "desertion in their head" and jumped from their ships, sailed to the shores with small boats, and took up service in the armies of the "Moors."[34] The political climate even gave them the audacity to attack the company factory and village, which they did in groups of a dozen or more, armed "to commit various insolences."[35] After 1711 Dutch authorities were at their wit's end trying to stop the exodus of sailors and soldiers to the warring armies. The situation was similar for other companies, including the EIC. Statutes against desertion were being read out on the decks of the incoming ships and were also proclaimed in Dutch villages accompanied by drumroll. The "loitering" of common seamen was severely checked, but extramilitary patrols failed to stem the tide of desertion. In July 1711, the VOC hired a troop of indigenous soldiers to guard the boundaries of the Dutch settlement, but dismissed them again within less than a year as "in Bengal they [deserters] can always get away despite all serious means."[36]

What advantages did the competing indigenous armies offer? European sailors and soldiers were especially prized as superior handlers of cannon. During times

of military strife, all sides aggressively recruited cannoneers from among the soldiers and sailors in the East India company settlements. Better wages were the
biggest incentive for this mass desertion. The usual wage for a VOC sailor or soldier in early 1700s was 9 guilders. Indigenous armies offered the deserters four
times as much money: 40 rupees or 36 guilders per month.[37] Skilled common seamen could only dream of such wages. In Mir Jumla's Assam expedition in 1661–62
not only Dutch and English sailors and soldiers but also a surgeon and carpenters
were recruited from Bengal. Among the recruits were fifteen survivors of the ship
Ter Schelling wreckage. They observed that ships laden with cannon moving
against the stream on the Ganges were being operated only by English, Dutch, and
Portuguese (both black and white) sailors and soldiers. The wages, though varied,
were far better than what they could have earned in the service of the company: at
the end of twenty-eight days, each member of *Ter Schelling* got a wage of 20 rupees
or 18 guilders. The sailors observed that Portuguese and English "volunteers" got
even better wages.[38]

Although better pay was probably the most important inducement to desertion, the promise of a different life lured many deserters. Companies complained
that the lower orders found the "short pleasurable life amongst the Moors" attractive.[39] Reckless living with small concern for the future was a trademark of the
sailors. East India seaman Edward Barlow's stints at home, though short, were
always joyous occasions—but as soon as his earnings were spent, he went off looking for a ship. A seventeenth-century account of the shipwreck of *Ter Schelling*
mentioned how the steersmen of the sinking ship, faced with a severe storm at the
sand banks of Bengal delta, "knew no calm." With glasses of arak in their hands he
and his fellow sailors made sure that the rising water could not touch their buoying
spirit. Faced with death, "their last escape being their drink," they defied death.[40]
Thus, in 1711–12, the VOC resented the promise of a "lazy and unconstrained life"
in indigenous armies that had seduced the deserters, despite the dangerous nature
of the work. Even though quite a few of them had perished in war, the VOC officials alleged that there were many more who died of their "drunkenness and fool-
hardiness," as their excesses "knew no measure."[41]

Various regional potentates, Mughal or otherwise, saw the company grounds as
a reliable source for their gunners. In times of crisis, the companies were regularly
solicited for manpower. In 1677 the VOC had to send a boat and a sloop with
twenty sailors to assist Shaista Khan's campaign against a rebellious chief in Orissa.
In 1711, Zia-ud-din Khan constantly pressed the VOC for skilled manpower, until
they were forced to lend out a hundred men. In the event of the second Maratha
attack in 1743, the Nawab Nazim Ali Vardi Khan called in the company *wakils*
(court mediators of local authorities) of three companies, Dutch, English and
French, and requested that each lend out two hundred men who would be put on
the payroll of the army of the Nawab.[42] European soldiers also served in the

Maratha army.[43] Some even found places in very local indigenous polities. Bharatchandra Ray, a late eighteenth-century court poet of the *zamindar* (major landowner) of Nadia, mentioned that English, Dutch, Portuguese, French, Danish, and Germans filled the ranks of gunners at an unnamed fort in Annadamangal.[44]

When the recruitment of European sailors and soldiers failed to take the course of mutual agreement, indigenous armies depended on desertion. Alexander Hamilton met two Dutch deserters whom he called *"renagadoes"* (renegades) while he was in Cattack, the capital city of Orissa, the neighboring province of Bengal. Although Hamilton stated very clearly that the place "is not frequented by Europeans," these two deserters made their way into the army of the Nawab Nazim of Orissa as gunners.[45] Thus, the EIC at Kassimbazaar, ever "cautious to prevent desertion," sent to Calcutta all extra European sailors and soldiers, when, at the hour of the first Maratha invasion in 1740, the Nawab Nazim of Bengal had asked for a hundred men.[46] Both the VOC and the EIC denied any knowledge of or responsibility for the seventeen European prisoners of war that the Nawab Alivardi Khan had captured from the retreating Maratha army in 1743. In the battle of Plassey of 1757, as many as fifty-six Dutch soldiers defected to the Siraj-ud-daulah's army.[47] As late as 1766, two soldiers of the EIC were lured by a "black man in the bazaar, who offered [them] fifty rupees a month for [their] service."[48]

Conversion to Islam was not uncommon among Dutch and English soldiers and sailors.[49] At Dacca, when the shipwrecked sailors of the *Ter Schelling* met a Dutch man "from head to foot clad in Moorish" clothes they "thought inevitably that he was circumcised."[50] Conversion was sometimes used as a strategy by deserters to garner protection of indigenous authorities against the companies. The *faujdar* of Hugli shielded a deserting VOC sailor who had converted to Islam in 1685. The company tried to cajole him into handing over the deserter, but he refused, saying that handing over a Muslim "will cost his head" if the higher authorities came to know about it.[51] The company then appealed to Governor Shaista Khan for his intervention, but to no avail. The next year VOC officials captured the deserter in Balasore and hauled him back, only to lose him again to the forces of *faujdar* Malik Barkhordar, specifically sent to rescue the converted deserter. A French soldier in the service of the EIC at Patna deserted to the "Moors and complained that [even though he was] a Musselman," the company had obliged him to "eat their victuals."[52] Local rulers sometimes handed over deserters to the companies, though the practice was rare and could be achieved only by paying a fat bribe in any case.[53]

The importance of Europeans in the indigenous armies resulted in their settlement in Bengal outside the bounds of the East India company settlements. Europeans were known in the entire Mughal world as *firingi*, a term originally used to describe the Portuguese in the Mughal empire in the sixteenth century, then extended to all Europeans or European descendants residing in the realm. As Aniruddha Ray has shown, the development of *zamindaris* of Eastern deltaic lands involved the use of European military labor as well as Christian missionary activities.[54] Augustinian and Jesuit churches cemented together the communities of the rowdy groups of *firingis,* who served as mercenaries in the armies of various *zamindars.* Such settlements became part of the social geography of seventeenth- and eighteenth-century Bengal. In the *Dharmamangal* of the seventeenth-century poet Rupram Chakraborty, a *"firingipara"* or *"firingi"* colony was mentioned alongside various place-names or settlement types during Ranjhabati's journey from the city of Maina to the abode of Dharma, Champa.[55] Many of these colonies were composed of gunners. It is quite likely that the settlements had been built through desertion.

Even if they had not settled in these colonies, *firingis* certainly joined the inner circle of military indigenous armies and courts. These Europeans—and their descendants—had a wide variety of origins, including indigenous roots. But as Sanjay Subrahmanyam has argued, *firingis* were never fully natives just as they were never fully Europeans.[56] Thus, gunner colonies of *firingis* in Eastern Bengal also had Portuguese-speaking Africans. Runaway European sailors and soldiers were thus incorporated into indigenous society as *firingis.* The unique social space that Europeans occupied in Mughal Bengal suspended their "European-ness" and expanded their opportunities in indigenous societies.

The socioeconomic hinterland of Bengal was not alien to the common seamen and soldiers of East India companies. It did not take long for a newcomer to find his niche in indigenous society—one that was always prejudicial to the interests of the company. Not only were the interests of the indigenous state and that of the companies diametrically opposed to each other, their regard of waged work was completely different. Disgorged by enclosures of land, wars, and religious strife in Europe, sailors and soldiers were part of a large pool of mobile casual workers, often considered unskilled. In fact, this trend was intensified during the second half of the seventeenth century in Europe.[57] The social degradation that the rank and file of the armies of the Dutch Republic or English fiscal military states experienced in Europe could be dramatically reversed in the indigenous armies. "Who merely carries a Christian name is here acknowledged as a full-fledged soldier," the sailors of *Ter Schelling* observed. In certain places, as among the *zamindari* of Bhulua, they were "honored as lords and counts."[58] The Jesuit priest Padre Godinho complained that the Mughal army was infested with inexperienced gunners of European origins, but the demand by leaders of indigenous armies indicate that they were seen as highly skilled workers.

EUROPEAN DESERTERS AND INTERCOMPANY COMPETITION

By the middle of the seventeenth century the two largest trading corporations, the VOC and EIC, had established their trade on a more or less firm footing in Bengal.

Yet intercompany rivalry in Bengal continued and indeed grew stronger in the early eighteenth century as the French East India Company and the Ostend Company established their trading posts. Bengal became a fiercely competitive labor market, which strengthened the power of European workers and drove their wages through their autonomous mobility. Companies had to either work in unison to regulate this uncontrolled mobility or co-opt it into their recruitment practices. Mobile European workers severely challenged the East India companies' capacity to assert themselves as sovereign entities in Bengal.

The Ostend Company, based in Flanders and trading under the Habsburg flag, made their presence felt in Bengal from 1722–30. The VOC and EIC joined hands to drive out the new competitor from Bengal, yet the Ostenders managed to survive. They were housed in the abandoned grounds of the erstwhile Danish factory until 1727, after which Alexander Hume, the governor and commander of the Ostend Company, obtained Nawab Murshid Quli Khan's permission to set up a factory at Banquibazaar. Even though the Ostend Company itself was abolished in 1730, former officials of the company, along with some private merchants from the English and Dutch companies, used the Banquibazaar factory for their intra-Asiatic trade until 1745. Hume openly announced that it was prudent to replenish personnel shortages of the Ostend Company by engaging deserters. The "foundation for wanton desertion" of workers from VOC and EIC grounds had been laid.[59]

Because the Ostend Company paid better wages, desertion erupted on a huge scale, shaking the foundations of the VOC and EIC. In 1726 the Ostend Company offered soldiers and sailors a wage of 14 guilders per month, significantly great than the 9 guilders offered by the VOC.[60] The EIC admitted that this "extraordinary pay" led to desertion of their workers too.[61] In June 1724 the VOC reported that the abandoned Danish factory, which was then occupied by the Ostend Company, sheltered a hundred deserters, a good number of *toepassen* (soldiers of mixed origins), and indigenous sailors.[62] Desertion to the Ostend Company remained a constant concern for the VOC and EIC until 1727 and shot up in 1744. Around three hundred sailors of the EIC deserted to Bankibazaar in this period and joined the army of Francois Schonamille, commander of the Ostend factory.[63] The EIC strictly prohibited any "intercourse with the Ostenders or to furnish them with powder or any sort of ammunition." They posted military guards at Perrius Garden in Calcutta, and along the banks of the river in numerous boats. Notices in several languages prohibiting desertion were "affixed at the factory gates and other publick places about town."[64] None of the measures worked. Leaders of the EIC and VOC appealed directly to the governor of the Ostend Company to return their deserters, but to no avail. The EIC even tried to plead with their own seamen, asking them not to run away to the Ostend grounds.[65] Only when Schonamille gave up his post and escaped to Pegu in 1745—with a hundred VOC and EIC sailors and soldiers—did the epidemic desertion of EIC workers finally decline.[66]

The EIC was eventually reduced to encouraging the desertion of European workers of rival companies as a strategy to stock its own army. Losing men to the EIC was a constant source of concern for the VOC from the late seventeenth century.[67] The VOC reported in 1732 that the EIC, "getting no or very few soldiers from Europe or Madras," was forced to build its military with the runaways of the VOC.[68] As we have seen, access to ready money was a big reason behind desertion. Both the VOC and EIC paid the common soldier 9 guilders, but the VOC paid the wages at the end of 3–5-year contracts, while the EIC paid wages at the end of each month. The EIC thus used more casual labor for their army, turning Bengal into a recruitment grounds for soldiers. Such an arrangement was preferred by European workers as they gained quicker access to their wages. In 1711, the EIC induced large-scale desertion by paying a bonus of 10 rupees cash to each runaway as a reward for deserting to Fort William.[69] The EIC was forced to recognize the power of the mobility of the workers and to tap into their quest for "ready money."[70]

Intercompany negotiations over deserting workers reflected anxiety about their sovereignty in Asian lands. The French East India Company's strategy to curb the autonomous mobility of the workers was to put forward a united front of company interests with the VOC and EIC. They were particularly cooperative in recovering runaways from the VOC who had taken shelter on their grounds. On two different occasions the French helped the VOC to hunt down armed fugitives in the precincts of Chandernagore.[71] In 1732 the VOC signed a contract with the French for the mutual return of sailors, soldiers, sergeants, corporals, quartermasters, and young apprentices. The French could keep the deserter only if the nationality of the deserter was French; the same rule applied for the Dutch. Moreover, neither side could condemn the returnees to capital punishment. Such a contract applied to Chandernagore, Chinsurah, and Kassimbazaar. In 1734, officials extended the same contract to Patna.[72] The EIC had entered into a similar contract with the French in 1728. The French ended up with a tripartite policy with the VOC and EIC. Runaways thus forced highly competitive, even antagonistic, European powers to cooperate.

Control over deserters, like the war against interlopers in trade, required the exertion of state power.[73] Endless letters about the violation of "colours" and "flags" and the retrieving of deserters were a centerpiece of intercompany diplomatic relations in Bengal. In 1724, when the EIC impressed a few sailors and soldiers from the boats of the VOC on the river near Calcutta, the VOC complained of "public violence done to our colours." They further warned the EIC that such violence "would certainly open the door to great many larger misdemeanors, which may be a ground of misunderstanding between the two Nations."[74] In a letter to the EIC in May 1706, asking for the return of deserters in Calcutta, the VOC reminded the former of the "good harmony and concord" that had existed between the Republic and the English crown.[75] Deserters could not be returned by the Ostend Company to the Dutch as every single worker in the Ostend factory was "bound with oath in the service of the Kaiser."[76] Deserters challenged and undermined the authority of sovereign state companies.

Desertion, an autonomous practice of European workers, was antithetical to legal subjecthood defined by the sovereign corporate entities. Sometimes this contradiction became painfully transparent as in the tragic case of Jan Striker. A VOC soldier, Striker had escaped to the EIC army stationed at the Kassimbazar factory in 1734. On hearing that his old friend Harmanus van Tomputten had come to Bengal as a soldier of the VOC, he visited him in the Dutch village in Chinsurah. Another soldier, Hendrik Tuske, joined them for drinks. Striker and Tomputten soon got drunk, "lost their senses," and then "got into a fight with the natives." In a bid to escape the brawl Striker started running, too drunk to realize that he was running onto the VOC grounds. Striker was arrested and condemned to death. On May 6, 1734, he was hanged on a sailing ship anchored close to the VOC headquarters at Chinsurah, after which his corpse was "cut into pieces and fed to the fish." His friend Tomputten was forced to walk the gauntlet.[77] The VOC asserted its sovereignty by executing its mutinous soldier. The comradely conviviality of Striker and Tomputten came to a fatal end on the sovereign grounds of the VOC.

European workers posed the ultimate challenge to corporate sovereignty when they completely rejected the world of waged work. The companies were always suspicious of the "great many stragling seamen both of Dutch and English which belongs to no shipping lye sculking in the back parts of the town."[78] In 1715, the EIC reported armed robbery carried out by a group of Europeans just off the coast of Chittagong. They were especially concerned about the luxury textile items coming out from Dacca. The robbers, they reported, were "deserters from us because they have red coats." The EIC officials also identified some as "the Dutch soldiers discharged from our service."[79] The trajectory of the Dutch deserters thus finally took them to the limits of waged work in Bengal. Having served the EIC they finally left it for high-seas robbery. Displaying the red coats, the military symbol of sovereign EIC state, they usurped the property of the company, violating the very foundation of its sovereignty.

Historians have long assumed that European workers in Asia were part of a separate labor market, located in Europe, where their service contracts with various overseas enterprises were sealed. One result of this assumption is that very few historians have studied these workers as part of the maritime labor market in Asia.[80] Not only were European workers deeply embedded in the labor market of precolonial Bengal, they shaped the contours of this market through their autonomous mobility. Whether in Europe or in its East India companies, common soldiers, as the lowest-paid members of the army, were seen as unskilled workers. But in the indigenous armies of Bengal they were considered the very opposite—

highly skilled workers. By moving in and out of different companies, they shaped the wages, the payment structure, and the recruitment procedures in Bengal. A close reading of reports and interrogations on cases of desertion show that the companies adopted different strategies to circumvent the "problem" of desertion. While the VOC continued to contract workers from the Republic and hoped to stall the leakage of the workforce to rival companies, the EIC and the Ostend Company set up mechanisms to recruit European workers in Bengal. In fact, the EIC and the Ostend Company depended on desertion for the supply of their European sailors and soldiers. But such a strategy could only be sustained through higher wages. The worker's strategy of running repeatedly drove wages up.

Following in their wayward footsteps, we see the many different meanings of "European worker" in precolonial Bengal. By running away to the Mughal empire, these workers slipped in and out of their European identities. Their escapes reveal clearly that European-ness was largely confined to the bounds of company settlements in the region. As soon as they crossed over to the other side of the company settlements they became *"firingis,"* a social existence that offered them various places in indigenous society—in the colonies of gunners or as honorable members of the close circles of the *zamindars* and provincial or imperial bureaucrats. Moreover, some European deserters chose to convert to Islam, thereby denying their European and Christian pasts.

Brought together by their work for the companies, runaways transformed their laboring ties into new solidarities and new resistance that went beyond the workplace. Desertion in Bengal was usually a collective act. To exercise the power of autonomous mobility these workers had to plan carefully, for getting caught might mean hanging on the gallows of Chinsurah or Calcutta. The practice of desertion drew on the knowledge soldiers and sailors had gained in previous experience in Bengal but also generated new knowledge—of people, place, and power. The return of deserters to their own companies often meant the diffusion of such knowledge, as the companies knew and feared.

The desertion of European workers was, in sum, a form of class conflict that precipitated a crisis of corporate sovereignty for the East India companies in foreign lands. Running away repeatedly challenged the companies' efforts to assert their respective statehood. The defiance of the sovereignty of the companies was the most powerful element in what Holden Furber called the "catholicity" of worker action in Bengal. The logic of survival for waged workers was antithetical to the logic of capital accumulation, which underwrote the sovereignty of these companies. In discussing the Atlantic sailors in the eighteenth century Marcus Rediker has argued that desertion affirmed the "free" in free wage labor, contradicting the conception of controlled wage labor as endorsed by the merchant capitalist.[81] In England, the legal prosecution of desertion generated a contradiction between the conception of the "free individual" and "free wage labor." According to the Statute of Labourers and Statute of Artificers, the desertion or breach of contract was a penal offense. By the late eighteenth century, the merchant capitalist idea of the inviolable free "possessive individualism"[82]—i.e., each individual was his or her own master by virtue of birthright and self-ownership— undergirded the legal theory of contract. Through labor contracts, workers exchanged the power of their bodies—that is, labor—for money. By making desertion a criminal/penal offense, the English state effectively denied waged workers their individuality. This contradiction was not resolved, as the state continued to uphold the interests of merchant capitalists in disciplining workers, enabling increased accumulation through exploitative, unequal contracts. Only with the repeal of the Statutes of Labourers and Artificers in 1863 was the free personhood of the waged worker restored.[83] Until then, desertion allowed workers to realize their own "free" personhood as they engaged in communication with each other, formed collectives, and moved autonomously, against the grain of exploitation, accumulation, and corporate sovereignty.

NOTES

1. Tamil Nadu State Archive (digitized by Nationaal Archief, Den Haag) (hereafter 1.11.06.11), 1677B, fols. 332–33.

2. Archives of the Dutch East India Company kept in Nationaal Archief, Den Haag (hereafter VOC) 8777, fols. 269–71; "meededogenhijt plaats gegeeven is," VOC 8777, fol. 270.

3. Holden Furber, "Glimpses of Life and Trade on the Hughli 1720–1770," in *Private Fortunes and Company Profits in the India Trade in the 18th Century* (Hampshire: Variorum, 1997), 13–23; my emphasis.

4. Matthias van Rossum, *Werkers van de Wereld: Globalisering, Arbeid en Interculturele Ontmoetingen Tussen Aziatische en Europese Zeelieden in dienst van de VOC, 1600–1800* (Hilversum: Verloren, 2013), 111–12.

5. W. P. Coolhaas, *Generale Missiven der V. O. C. van Governeurs-Generaal en Raden aan Here XVII (deel 6, 1698–1713)* ('s Gravenhage: Martinus Nijhoff, 1968–76), 773.

6. The VOC archive provides better and denser information for the period, although important information from the EIC archive has also been used. The Bengal directorate of the VOC maintained "desertion lists" for certain years from which numbers and debts of deserters can be reconstructed. Even for years for which desertion lists exist, it is very difficult to determine the rates of desertion due to gaps in archival information. For Bengal, VOC maintained only land muster rolls, which recorded employees on land and did not include the crew on various intra-Asiatic vessels. However, the bulk of deserters were running away from various intra-Asiatic vessels. The desertion lists mention the ships with which the runaways came to Bengal. I have reconstructed rates of desertion based on the available data on crew size of VOC's intra-Asiatic vessels for thirty-one ships. These cases are representative of the range of percentage of crew members from VOC vessels lost to the practice of desertion in Bengal.

7. Maria Augusta Lima Cruz, "Exile and Renegades in Early Sixteenth-Century Portuguese India," *Indian Economic and Social History Review* 23 (1986): 249–62; George Winius, "The 'Shadow Empire' of Goa in the Bay of Bengal," *Itinerario* 7 (1983): 83–101; G. V. Scammell, "European Exiles, Renegades and Outlaws and the Maritime Economy of Asia, c. 1500–1700," *Modern Asian Studies* 26 (1992): 641–61.

8. Elizabeth Kolsky, *Colonial Justice in British India: White Violence and the Rule of Law* (New Delhi: Cambridge University Press, 2010), 8–9, 37–38.

9. Philip J. Stern, *The Company-State: Corporate Sovereignty and the Early Modern Foundations of the British Empire in India* (Oxford: Oxford University Press, 2011), 83–99; Philip Stern, "From the Fringes of History: Tracing the Roots of the English East India Company-State," in *Fringes of Empire: People, Places, and Spaces in Colonial India,* ed. Sameerah Agha and Elizabeth Kolsky (New Delhi: Oxford University Press, 2009), 19–44.

10. Marcus Rediker, *Between the Devil and the Deep Blue Sea: Merchant Seamen, Pirates and the Anglo American Maritime World, 1700–1750* (New York: Cambridge University Press, 1989), 77–115.

11. Isaac Sunderman, *Isaac Sundermans: Zyn Geschriften* (Amsterdam, 1712), 66.

12. Ibid., 68.

13. VOC 8744, part II, fol. 15.

14. 1.11.06.11, 1677B, fols. 340–43.

15. 1.11.06.11, 1677B, fol. 338.

16. Edward Barlow, *Barlow's Journal of His Life at Sea in King's Ships, East & West Indiamen, & Other Merchant Men from 1659 to 1703,* vols. I and II, ed. Basil Lubbock (London: Hurst and Blackett, 1934).

17. Barlow, *Barlow's Journal,* 339.

18. "There being severall dead and deserted," P/1/1, fol. 407r; "Mortality and deserters having lessened my ships company seventeen men," P/1/11,177v; "Having had the misfortune since I came from England of burying seven of my men . . . have had seven more runaway," P/1/11, fol. 338r.

19. VOC 8760, fols. 33–35.

20. VOC 8762, Part II, fol. 25.

21. P/1/4, fol. 124v.

22. Rediker, *Devil and the Deep Blue Sea,* 77–115, 153–204.

23. VOC 1422, fols. 1510–15.

24. VOC 1422, fols. 1450r–1451v.

25. P/1/10, fol. 126r.

26. VOC 8774, fols. 752–63. Confiscation of arms was integral to the mass desertions of November 1727 and May 1730, VOC 8757, fol. 396; VOC 8763, fol. 312.

27. VOC 8774, fol. 765.

28. Coolhaas, *Generale Missiven (deel 7, 1713–1725),* 1968–76, 146; Frank Lequin, "Het Personeel van de Verenigde Oost-Indische Compagne in de Achttiende Eeuw, Meer in Het Bijzonder in de Vestiging Bengalen," Deel I (PhD diss., Leiden University, 1982), 136; VOC 8745, Part I, fols. 32–33, VOC 8745, Part II, fols. 74–75, VOC 8752, Part II, fols. 276–77, VOC 8754, fols. 73–274, VOC 8756, fols. 107–8, VOC 8769, fol. 312.

29. VOC 8757, fols. 140–43.

30. VOC 8744, part II, fols. 15–17.

31. Sources for Figure 4.1: VOC 1361, 1378, 1422, 1470, 8737–8800 (all files).

32. Sources for Figure 4.2: Ibid.

33. Jadunath Sarkar, "Bengal under Murshid Quli Khan," in *History of Bengal,* vol. 2, *Muslim Period 1200–1757,* ed. Jadunath Sarkar (Dacca: BRPC, 1943), 397–421.

34. VOC 8743, part I, fols. 512–13.

35. VOC 8743, part II, fol. 40.

36. VOC 8743, part I, fol. 513.

37. VOC 8743, part II, fol. 40.

38. Frans Janszoon van der Heiden and Willem Kunst, *Vervarelycke Schip-breuk van 't Oost-Indisch Jacht ter Schelling onder het landt van Bengale* (Amsterdam, 1675), 111.

39. VOC 8743, part I, fol. 513.

40. Van der Heiden and Kunst, *Vervarelycke Schip-breuk,* 30.

41. VOC 8743, part I, fols. 512–13, VOC 8743, Part II, fols. 39–40.

42. P/1/15, fol. 212r.

43. P/1/15, fols. 317r–v.

44. Bharatchandra Raygunakar, "Annadamangal," in *Bharatchandra Granthabali,* ed. Brajendranath Bandopadhyay and Sajanikanta Das, vol. 2 (Kolkata: Bangiya Sahitya Parishat, 1944), 9.

45. Alexander Hamilton, *A new account of the East Indies, being the observations and remarks of Capt. Alexander Hamilton, who spent his time there from the year 1688, to 1723, trading and travelling, by sea and land, to most of the countries and islands of commerce and navigation, between the Cape of Goodhope, and the Island of Japon* (Edinburgh, 1727), 389–91.

46. P/1/14, fol. 129r.

47. Lequin, "Het Personeel," 135.

48. Factory Records (hereafter G) 37/1/2, fols.13–15.

49. Van der Heiden and Kunst, *Vervarelycke Schip-breuk,* 102; Scammell, "European Exiles," 658.

50. Van der Heiden and Kunst, *Vervarelycke Schip-breuk,* 102.

51. VOC 7530, fol. 799.

52. P/1/15, fol. 332r.

53. Five soldiers were returned by the "moors" to the VOC after paying an expensive present to them. VOC 8756, fol. 107.

54. Aniruddha Ray, *Adventurers, Landowners and Rebels, c. 1575–c. 1715* (New Delhi: Munshiram Manoharlal, 1998), 55–75.

55. Akshyaykumar Kayal, ed., *Rupram Chakraborty birachita Dharmamangal* (Kolkata: Bharabi, 1992), 54–55.

56. Sanjay Subrahmanyam, *The Portuguese Empire in Asia* (New York: Longman 1993), 261–83.

57. Jelle van Lottum, "Labour Migration and Economic Performance: London and the Randstad, c. 1600–1800," *Economic History Review* 64 (2011): 531–70; Page Moch, *Moving Europeans: Migration in Western Europe since 1650* (Bloomington: Indiana University Press, 1992), 31–60; Peter Way, " 'The scum of every county, the refuse of mankind': Recruiting the British Army in the Eighteenth Century," *Fighting for a Living: A Comparative Study for Military Labor,* ed. Eric-Jan Zurcher (Amsterdam: Amsterdam University Press, 2014), 291–330.

58. Van der Heiden and Kunst, *Vervarelycke Schip-breuk,* 101.

59. VOC 8753, fol. 222

60. VOC 8755, fols. 343–44.

61. P/1/17, fol. 239v.

62. VOC 8753, fol. 224.

63. Jan Parmentier, *"De Holle Compagnie": Smokkel en Legale Handel onder Zuidnederlandse Vlag in Bengalen, ca. 1720–1744* (Hilversum: Verleron, 1992), 86.

64. P/1/17, fol. 239v.

65. P/1/17, fol. 340v.

66. P/1/17, fols. 588r–589v.

67. There are examples of mass desertion of sailors and soldiers of the VOC to the EIC from 1675, 1706, 1711, 1732, 1760, VOC 8737, VOC 8742, Part I, fols. 65–66, VOC 1320, fol. 548r, P/1/9, fol. 415v.

68. VOC 8770, fol. 255.

69. VOC 8742, Part II, fol. 106.

70. Barnaby Slush, *The Navy Royal: Or a Sea-Cook Turn'd Projector* (London, 1709), 92, quoted in Rediker, *Devil and the Deep Blue Sea,* 116.

71. VOC 8761, fols. 108–9; VOC 8763, fols. 312–13.

72. VOC 8771, fols. 1610–1615, VOC 1877, fols. 274–75.

73. Stern, *Company-State,* 61–82.

74. P/1/5, fol. 516v.

75. VOC 8737, fol. 351

76. VOC 8753, fol. 221.

77. VOC 8777, fols. 266–67.

78. P/1/11, fol. 338r.

79. P/1/3, fols. 53v–54r.

80. There has been effort to study Asian workers of the VOC as part of the Dutch maritime labor market, but not Europeans as part of the Asian labor market. Jelle van Lottum and Jan Lucassen, "Six Cross-Sections of the Dutch Maritime Labour Market: A Preliminary Reconstruction and Its Implications (1610–1850)," in *Maritime Labour: Contributions of Work at Sea, 1500–2000*, ed. Richard Gorski (Amsterdam: Amsterdam University Press, 2007), 5–35.

81. Marcus Rediker, *Devil and the Deep Blue Sea*, 105.

82. C. B. Macpherson, *The Political Theory of Possessive Individualism* (Oxford: Oxford University Press, 1962).

83. Robert Steinfeld, *The Invention of Free Labor: The Employment Relation in English and America Law and Culture, 1350–1870* (Chapel Hill: University of North Carolina Press, 1991), 55–93.

5

"More of a Danger to the Colony Than the Enemy Himself"

Military Labor, Desertion, and Imperial Rule in French Louisiana (ca. 1715–1760)

Yevan Terrien

From 1682 to 1762, France claimed the North American colony of Louisiana, the last addition to its empire under the *ancien régime*, named after the Sun King Louis XIV. Yet most of this vast territory, which stretched over a fourth of today's contiguous United States along the Mississippi Valley, from the Illinois Country south of the Great Lakes to New Orleans and Mobile on the Gulf Coast, was Indian country. By 1715, when the crown and commercial proprietors first attempted to populate the colony, this area counted about 77,000 Natives but hardly more than 300 Europeans, most of whom belonged to the military, and 100 Africans.[1] Despite the arrival of thousands of European migrants and African captives in subsequent years, Louisiana remained much less populated than England's North American colonies or France's own settlements in Canada and the Caribbean. The Lower Mississippi's fledgling plantation economy exported commodity crops produced by enslaved labor, chiefly tobacco, indigo, and rice, but its transatlantic commerce paled in comparison with sugar islands like Martinique and Saint-Domingue, which Louisianans supplied with timber and foodstuff. As an entrepôt for the French West Indies, a buffer between English and Spanish colonies, and a protection for New France, Louisiana's peripheral settlement was of strategic value to the French empire. A dozen forts materialized the Gallic presence in the region, yet their chronically shorthanded garrisons represented a poor defense for the colony and its Indigenous allies, who often had to guard them against enemy raids.[2] The meager troops sent overseas by the *Marine* ("Navy department") in charge of the colonies were dwarfed by the French army, the largest state institution in Europe at the time: from 1700 to 1763, when two million men went through the ranks of the army, Louisiana received less than five thousand soldiers.[3]

FIGURE 5.1. Detail from "Veuë du camp de la concession de Monseigneur Law, au Nouveaux Biloxy, coste de la Louisianne," 1720, by Jean-Baptiste Michel Le Bouteux.

In spite of their small numbers, soldiers were instrumental in plans to colonize Louisiana. Beyond their military duties, much of the labor required in the colony fell on the troops, whose service involved patrolling settlements and policing slaves in the absence of formal militias; performing hard labor on public works like levees and fortifications; loading and rowing boats on various voyages; compensating the chronic shortage in craftsmen by providing skilled trades like carpentry; trading food, clothes, and other basic goods with other lower-class whites, Africans, and especially Native Americans through the informal networks of a "frontier exchange economy"; and becoming *habitants* ("settlers") as farmers or artisans. Controlling the mobility of this limited yet critical manpower was therefore an imperative for colonial administrators (see Figure 5.1).[4] Desertion was a social as well as a military problem, and French Louisiana could hardly afford the massive defections that plagued European armies.

Colonial troops often proved unwilling to serve imperial ambitions. Mutinies were exceptional but desertions occurred in every garrison. As in Europe, soldiers primarily deserted to escape their poor living and working conditions, although the consequences could be significantly more life-threatening on a colonial frontier; runaways relied on skills acquired during their military service to navigate their physical and political environment. While local authorities sought to retrieve defectors, punish them, and limit future losses of manpower, such assertions of

French sovereignty paradoxically depended on the cooperation of European and Indigenous neighbors. Focusing on the impact of military desertion therefore highlights how power was negotiated on the ground when soldiers—designated agents of imperialism—frustrated imperial designs by reclaiming their mobility.

FREQUENCY AND SIGNIFICANCE OF DESERTION IN FRENCH COLONIAL LOUISIANA

A recent article analyzing a 1752 desertion trial in the Illinois Country claims that military officers exploited such affairs to advance their career, yet "the phenomenon was not that important, involving about 1 percent of colonial troops." According to Éric Wenzel, "soldiers of New France were thieves, smugglers, and brawlers much more often than [they were] guilty of a crime against the state that was akin to treason."[5] This assertion misrepresents the reality of desertion and its significance, which are admittedly difficult to assess given the limits of the available documentation. Both quantitative and qualitative evidence about Louisiana's deserters is limited: muster rolls are incomplete and uneven, and very few court martial records from the colonies have survived. Information must therefore be supplemented from multiple and fragmentary sources, including colonial correspondence, official memos, and personal files.

Carl Brasseaux's biographical database of military personnel in French Louisiana lists 4,239 soldiers who served between 1715 and 1771, of whom 170 or 4 percent were either tried or simply reported as deserters.[6] My own calculation, which relies on a more comprehensive approach, more than doubles the number of runaways. Most deserters were never condemned or even prosecuted, much of the documentary evidence fails to mention them by name, and their reported numbers are often approximate, so that repeat offenders in particular are difficult to estimate. But by incorporating unnamed runaways discussed in various sources, I have identified 54 desertion plots or incidents involving 400 to 500 individuals.[7] These findings indicate that 9–11 percent of all soldiers absconded, or attempted to, during their service in the colony. Other recruits deserted en route to or before sailing to the New World.[8] Back in Europe, early modern armies frequently experienced even higher desertion rates. France lost up to 25 percent of its troops to defection each year, and over 100,000 soldiers from 1718 to 1763.[9] The significance of military defection, however, was very different in the Mississippi Valley, where soldiers were prized commodities.

In 1751, Louisiana governor Pierre Rigaud de Vaudreuil informed the French Court at Versailles that he barely possessed enough forces to protect New Orleans after manning the colony's other posts. The capital's garrison was so small that he resolved to drill soldiers inside the barracks, "daring not inform the public, the Savages [i.e., Native Americans], and the Negroes of our weakness."[10] A few years later, his successor reported that, despite recent reinforcements, only 1,216 troops were available instead of the 1,850 projected by the French state.[11] The crown continued to increase the number of companies stationed in the colony, each of which was to include 50 men. Yet disease, mortality, and desertion in America, combined with the difficulties of recruitment in Europe, rendered all companies permanently incomplete.

The *compagnies franches de la Marine* detached in the colonies alongside a company of Swiss auxiliaries were freestanding units, independent of any regiment, and devoid of territorial bases. Whereas army captains recruited their troops themselves within single regions, the *Marine* relied on recruiting agents to raise men across the kingdom as the need arose. The majority of soldiers came from Atlantic provinces and the Paris area, yet the nicknames used by many testified to the diversity of their origins (e.g., "Champagne," "Picard," "Provençal"). In the *Marine* as in the army, French authorities insisted that recruitment be free and voluntary; they even released and compensated some soldiers who had been tricked or forced into service while reprimanding their officers.[12] While it is impossible to know how frequent those cases were, they reveal that the realities of recruitment differed markedly from the official doctrine of voluntary enlistment.[13] Although France never adopted a systematic policy of impressment, the *Marine*'s limited budget and the particular constraints of its recruitment made its agents even more likely than army officers to enlist young and surplus labor via dubious methods involving drink, debt, and deception. One favorite strategy was to send recruiters on the sites of demobilized units to try and reenlist seasoned soldiers with limited prospects outside the military.

Officials identified several obstacles to the enlistment of soldiers and workers for the colonies.[14] The *Marine* had to compete for a limited pool of laborers against other employers who offered better rewards or conditions. Seamen were excluded from military service by the elaborate maritime conscription known as the *classes* and preferred to join fishing trips. Times of harvest and military campaigns, when labor was in high demand, further limited the number of available candidates. Finally, potential recruits proved reluctant to emigrate toward "the islands of America" and Louisiana in particular.[15] In 1716, the Marine Council secretly ordered the intendant at the arsenal of Rochefort not to send any recruits to Louisiana against their will.[16] Three years later, a commissary at Antibes, on the Mediterranean coast, reported the mass desertion of an entire crew. "The very word of Mississippi," he explained, "where those people believe they are bound to, and which they imagine to be a much more distant and savage land than Peru or Japan, scared them away."[17] To persuade more men to enlist, recruiters highlighted the benefits of military service overseas, notably the prospect of earning additional wages and a tract of land at the end of their term, as did *engagés* (indentured servants).[18]

Although most troops enlisted for three to six years, a significant number of soldiers were condemned to lifetime service overseas as commutation of a death or galley sentence, mostly for desertion. Their numbers can only be estimated, but various samples studied by Boris Lesueur suggest that 5–15 percent of colonial recruits were in fact convicted deserters, exiled overseas "by order of the King."[19] Lesueur argues both that such decisions were made on an individual basis and that enlisting deserters was costly, troublesome, and exceptional. Rather than a desperate method of forced labor recruitment, he views this policy as a disciplinary and largely symbolic strategy. Yet military authorities on both sides of the Atlantic explicitly acknowledged that no punishment served as a deterrent against desertion. Because the companies detached in the colonies were perpetually incomplete, reinforcements of 5–15 percent were all but negligible, especially since those exiles were sent overseas to stay. The *Marine* also supplemented the small numbers of its recruits by transferring prisoners, including smugglers and vagabonds from the interior to Rochefort and other port cities.[20]

Successive governors denounced the troops sent to the Mississippi as insufficient, physically unfit, and morally deficient. These poor reinforcements had sometimes hardly disembarked before colonial officers dismissed some individuals as unable to serve. Sick, crippled, epileptic, insane, or simply too young or too weak, numerous soldiers were thus immediately released, admitted to the hospital, or sent directly back to France. Governor Vaudreuil described the most improbable case in 1748, after finding on the ship *Le Parham* "fifteen newly enlisted soldiers who are unfit to bear arms, being only children, some of whom are deaf and blind."[21] Better not to send any, argued some officers, who repeatedly demanded that the recruits be carefully selected and inspected before their departure.[22] The staggering number of recruits deemed unfit is remarkable since the *Marine* had considerably relaxed its standards regarding the minimal height and age of soldiers by the early eighteenth century. Although military leaders struggling to rule an immense territory with limited resources may have inflated such reports, numerous testimonies confirm that recruiters often resorted to enlisting only the men who acquiesced or were forced to serve in Louisiana.

The language employed in the governors' correspondence reflected their frustration with soldiers depicted as "vagabonds," "dusty feet," and "professional deserters, of the most vicious kind."[23] Such complaints were not just rhetorical, as numerous recruits went to serve in the colonies as a punishment for previous acts of desertion in Europe, some of whom would become repeat offenders and leaders of mutinies in the New World. Local administrators blamed defections in Louisiana on the pernicious influence of convict workers and those soldiers already condemned for desertion in the metropole.[24] Vaudreuil went as far as to argue that all colonial recruits possessed a "spirit of desertion" that motivated them to emigrate in the first place.[25] He and other officials lamented in similar terms the wandering habits that seemingly affected every group in the colony, from settlers and traders to slaves, sailors, and *engagés*.[26]

Elite obsession with social control and the management of working-class mobility was nothing neither new nor specific to Louisiana. European precedents such as vagrancy laws and anti-smuggling legislation, for instance, informed colonial efforts to curb the movements of the troublesome Indian traders known as *coureurs des bois* ("wood runners"). Yet these preoccupations took a different meaning in the colonial context, where they intersected with new racial and legal categories. Desertion was such a ubiquitous concern that Louisiana officials liberally applied the term beyond military parlance. Along with runaway slaves, defecting indigenous allies and their families were occasionally referred to as deserters.[27] There was little reason for Native inhabitants and enslaved Africans to display loyalty to their self-proclaimed rulers. Forbidding bondspeople to run away obviously served the interests of Louisiana's slaveholding class, yet petty, temporary *marronage* was far more common than outright and permanent desertion.[28] As for Indigenous warriors, their notions of warfare and authority were hardly compatible with French expectations of military discipline.

By contrast, soldiers who chose to desert knew perfectly well that they committed a capital offense. A 1717 ordinance reinstituted the death penalty for the desertion of *Marine* troops regardless of circumstances.[29] Running away from military duty in Louisiana was also much more difficult and dangerous than it would have been in Europe. The landscape of the Gulf Coast and the Mississippi Valley offered plenty of opportunities to hide and escape, but American swamps and woods remained largely unfamiliar to European soldiers, not to mention inhabited by Indian nations who were as likely to capture as to assist them. While some fugitives managed to escape as stowaways with the complicity of sailors and ship captains, most recruits lacked the local connections and community support they would have found in their home country. Unlike their European counterparts, colonial troops were stationed in forts or barracks and found themselves very far from home in a most isolated colony. Even the larger and better-connected settlements along the coast like Mobile and New Orleans only received a handful of ships from France every year.

CAUSES AND MEANS OF DESERTION

Why then did hundreds of men commit such a seemingly desperate act? What means and routes did they rely on as they attempted to run away? Given the fragmentary nature of extant sources, reconstituting the trajectories of Louisiana's fugitive soldiers requires some speculation regarding their numbers, motives, destinations, and even fate. Although the term desertion applied to a wide variety of acts ranging from individual flight to mutiny, most incidents were collective affairs, a few of which mobilized entire garrisons. Most deserters ran away in small groups of seven men on average: 28% of incidents involved two or three soldiers,

35% four to ten, and 26% ten or more. Except for the few who defected on their own, soldiers rarely sought the assistance of other types of workers, probably because they found enough trust and resources among themselves. Even in the rare cases where enslaved Africans and Native Americans joined military desert-ers, it is unclear whether they acted as coerced servants, hired hands, or fellow conspirators.[30] Large-scale, outright mutinies remained exceptional, but local authorities investigated six alleged desertion plots in Natchitoches (1720), Mobile (1723, 1744), New Orleans (1728), and Fort Tombecbé (1736, 1745).[31] The reality of these conspiracies is difficult to demonstrate with certainty, and the administrative correspondence from the colony mentions only the last one. Successive governors may have been tempted to silence such events in order to avoid blame.

The largest mutiny in the history of French Louisiana took place in 1721 at Fort Toulouse (near today's Montgomery, Alabama), where at least a dozen troops tied up their officers and joined eight defectors from the Mobile garrison on their way to the English colony of Carolina. The French officers claimed to have enlisted 250 warriors of the Alabama nation in chasing the runaways, with whom they caught up less than three miles from the fort. Eighteen deserters died in the resulting skirmish, the largest number of soldiers killed by Natives outside of the Natchez and Chickasaw wars. The survivors were court-martialed and sentenced to hard labor for life, except for a sergeant who was executed by firing squad.[32] The troops' collective flight at Fort Toulouse garrison occurred only two years after another mass desertion during the War of the Quadruple Alliance (1718–20). In this unique episode of interimperial warfare in the region, French troops captured the Spanish fortress of Pensacola in western Florida, but the entire garrison quickly surren-dered and defected en masse at the sight of the enemy's counteroffensive. When French reinforcements retook the citadel, they captured over fifty fugitives from their own ranks among the Spaniards: thirty of them were condemned to death, the remainder to a life sentence in the king's galleys.[33] In the wake of this affair, Vaudreuil's predecessor, Governor Jean-Baptiste Le Moyne de Bienville, lamented having nothing to defend the colony

> but a gang of deserters, smugglers, and rascals who are always ready not only to abandon you, but also to turn against you. How indeed could such people be attached to this country, where they are sent here by force, with no hope left to go back to their homeland? Can one believe that they will not make their efforts to leave it, especially in such an open country where they can go to the Spaniards or to the English?[34]

Bienville understood why colonial troops defected. Despite official decrees against impressment, many soldiers were indeed coerced or tricked into service, while others were condemned to serve overseas for the rest of their life. Even a standard term of six years could mean a life sentence, due to the high mortality rates in Louisiana's frontier conditions and the habitual policy of reenlisting soldiers. Commanders reserved military discharges for sick and aging soldiers or those ready to settle in the colony, so that flight was the only hope to go back home for many recruits. Officials in Canada confirmed that Frenchmen were reluctant to enlist for the colonies due to the widespread notion that their service could only end in death, infirmity, or desertion. Writing from the Louisbourg fortress on Cape Breton Island in 1752, a few years after the local garrison mutinied and occupied the town for several months, a civil administrator urged that all soldiers be dismissed when their terms expired. Colonial troops were so frequently denied their discharge papers and forced to serve indefinitely, he argued, that they had come to believe "they will only leave from here to go to the *Invalides*," the Paris hospital for aged and disabled veterans.[35] Direct statements from runaways are extremely rare, but their actions demonstrated that desertion was a powerful form of collective protest and mobilization. In 1716, Louisiana's governor reported that a large group of soldiers from the Mobile garrison walked up to him

> saying they were skilled artisans, that they did not enlist to serve the King, but only to settle in this colony where they were told and promised they would find a lot of work, that it was a land of gold and silver where they would make a fortune; that having found nothing of the sort, and seeing themselves reduced to carrying the musket, almost naked, and poorly paid, they decided to go to the Spaniards.[36]

This early incident offers rare evidence of the struggles involved in the recruitment of military labor. Not only did these disgruntled soldiers brazenly announce to the highest-ranking officer in the colony their intention to desert, they also claimed to be skilled workers who had been deceived into emigrating to Louisiana, without realizing that they would be serving as troops. Their other complaints echoed the motives invoked in most desertion cases. Running away to foreign colonies or indigenous settlements allowed some criminals to escape the reach of French jurisdiction, yet the vast majority of fugitives defected at least in part for material reasons.[37]

From the soldier's perspective, desertion was a radical but often convenient option in a spectrum of collective acts aimed at seeking what they regarded as fair treatment from their officers. In defense of this moral economy of the military, the troops protested in speech and in writing, plundered warehouses to appropriate supplies, threatened and occasionally manhandled their superiors, and mutinied.[38] Correspondingly, their motivations for absconding largely revolved around the poor quality of their pay, living conditions, and nourishment. In 1751, eight soldiers including four Swiss ran away from Fort Tombecbé, two hundred miles north of Mobile in Choctaw country, leaving behind a note to explain their motives. Due to high prices and their long overdue pay, they could not afford decent clothes and food, especially flour.[39] Colonial authorities repeatedly warned that the insufficient and erratic delivery of supplies to Louisiana posts was a major cause of desertion. More surprisingly, they acknowledged that many soldiers also defected to escape abuse and beatings from their superiors. Unrestrained, wrote a governor, "most officers . . . would treat soldiers like slaves."[40]

Local realities encouraged or facilitated desertion. Slow communications between France, New Orleans, and the various settlements spread across the interior and the Gulf Coast compounded the logistical difficulties of transporting and accounting for all recruits. In 1752, the new civil administrator Honoré-Gabriel Michel described a troubling discovery made by his predecessor. While inspecting the New Orleans garrison during the governor's absence, the commissary inquired about an allegedly sick soldier, only to realize that he had deserted a month earlier but had not yet been reported. Michel added that such incidents were common, because most captains kept no muster of their companies and hardly knew their men.[41] A few weeks later, twenty-one soldiers ran away from Kaskakia Fort in the Illinois Country and headed east toward English colonies. The commandant of the post launched a party of volunteers after them, but he could not describe the defectors because neither he nor their captains possessed any knowledge of them, in blatant violation of military policy.[42]

Louisiana deserters acted on their knowledge of local geography to run away. During their time in the colony, soldiers learned to navigate a foreign environment as they were assigned to or hired themselves out on military and commercial expeditions. The skills they gained as hunters, fishermen, and rowers on these voyages proved invaluable to those who defected. Like the twenty-one fugitives from the Illinois Country, most of them stole boats and canoes to escape along maritime or riverine routes. In 1722, for instance, another large group of French and Swiss troops absconded from New Biloxi, between New Orleans and Mobile, aboard two brigs they had captured with the assistance of sailors and convict laborers. Spanish authorities arrested twelve of the French defectors in Saint Joseph Bay, 150 miles east of Pensacola, and returned them to Louisiana. Others found refuge in Carolina, while the Swiss fugitives offered their services in Havana.[43] The proximity of other Spanish and English settlements in Texas, Florida, and the Caribbean offered more potential havens to runaways.

Most deserters did not set off on an unknown adventure, but rather followed well-known paths. In short, they knew where and when to run away. In 1735, six Swiss deserters followed the well-established route from Mobile to Pensacola, where the Spanish commandant in turn sent them to Mexico. Governor Bienville demanded the fugitives' extradition, which was denied on the grounds that the Swiss, as foreign and auxiliary troops, were not included in Franco-Spanish agreements for the return of deserters. Mexican monks had even offered asylum to the runaways and threatened to excommunicate those attempting to arrest them. Bienville tried to keep the news from the troops for fear it would encourage further defections, yet the word got out and three more Swiss soldiers absconded soon afterwards.[44] Historian Julius Scott shows how, during the era of the Haitian Revolution, black populations of the

Caribbean developed informal networks of communication to keep each other informed of events that Europeans sought to hide from them, like slave revolts and abolitionist movements.[45] Such a "common wind" appears to have carried the news among laborers of the Gulf Coast and the Mississippi Valley.

The deserters of French Louisiana were also quick to adopt new routes when an opportunity arose. In 1743, the newly arrived commandant of the Illinois Country reported the recent defection of ten soldiers headed toward New Mexico, a march into unknown territory that the officer judged foolhardy, especially given the threat of Chickasaw raids against the French. Those men, who were more familiar with the area and their Native neighbors than their superior, had enlisted Missouri Indian guides to accompany them. The commandant also seems to have ignored that another, official expedition had left the Illinois Country eighteen months earlier "to discover the Western Sea and the unknown countries that border this province." Its leader, André Fabry de la Bruyère, carried a letter of introduction from Louisiana's administrators to the Spanish governor of Santa Fe. By a remarkable coincidence, the message requested that any potential fugitive be returned, as "we follow the same usage with the neighboring Spanish garrisons, with which we have cartels for the mutual restitution of deserters."[46] Most members of Fabry's expedition failed to reach New Mexico, but the defecting soldiers had plenty of time to gather information from their experience before escaping in their footsteps, just as colonial authorities had anticipated.

Louisiana's deserters mobilized geographical and geopolitical knowledge to navigate between different worlds and competing authorities, Indigenous as well as European. Some fugitives even managed to make themselves indispensable as cultural brokers and go-betweens. Such was the case of Jolicœur, a soldier from the Illinois garrison who went missing for six years to live with a Shawnee band, whose métis chieftain Pierre Chartier adopted him and asked for clemency on his behalf. In 1746, when a Shawnee party visited the post and asked for a military escort on a diplomatic trip to the Cherokees, the local commandant obliged and recommended Jolicœur for his linguistic skills and personal connections.[47] Chartier was well aware that such individuals were indispensable to Natives and Europeans alike: his own father, Martin Chartier, was a French soldier who deserted from the 1682 expedition of Robert de La Salle down the Mississippi River to the territory that would become Louisiana. More than sixty years after Martin abandoned La Salle to find refuge among the Shawnees, it was his son's turn to shelter colonial deserters and help them become "white Indians."[48]

IMPACT OF DESERTION ON THE COLONY

The most immediate impact of military desertion in the Mississippi colony was numerical. Added to the losses caused by death and sickness, desertion limited the number of available troops and crippled French imperial ambitions in the region. The threat of further defections also disrupted military service. Following the mutiny and desertion of at least seven soldiers at Cat Island along the Gulf Coast in 1757, governor Louis Billouart de Kerlérec declared his own recruits "more of a danger to the colony than the enemy himself."[49] Several officers even disarmed their own men to prevent such incidents.[50] The risk of desertion was enough of a strategic concern to justify locating forts and trading posts where they could halt potential fugitives.[51] Defections were so common in certain areas like Mobile and Natchitoches, on the Red River, that colonial administrators were reluctant to send them supplies or new recruits, despite official recommendations to rotate garrisons regularly.[52] Vaudreuil asked for the removal of Spanish recruits and the stationing of Swiss soldiers alongside French troops because he considered them less likely to run away together.[53]

Desertion was as much a labor problem as a military one. Fugitive soldiers aggravated the chronic labor shortage that plagued the colony. Given the lingering scarcity of slaves and artisans, colonial troops provided much needed additional labor, to be used in construction, transportation, and the skilled trades. Metropolitan and local authorities logically sought to enlist artisans among the troops as *ouvriers-soldats* (working soldiers), and regularly listed the trades most needed in the Mississippi. This was most evident in the Swiss company, which was to be made up of 210 Catholic men, including 159 "*soldats-ouvriers gens de métier*" (craftsmen) such as carpenters, sawyers, stonecutters, and brickmakers. Military duties could only be required of them if no other troops were available, and the Swiss could only be drilled on Sundays and holidays so as not to disturb their work.[54] Yet recruiting, transporting, and retaining European soldiers were such challenges that Louisiana's administrators increasingly sought alternative sources of labor. Free and enslaved Africans were trained to replace white artisans and, in times of crisis, some even served on military expeditions alongside the local militia to remedy troop shortages. Most importantly, France's indigenous allies constituted its military arm in the colony rather than mere auxiliaries.[55]

Still more problematic were the judicial and diplomatic issues posed by efforts to suppress desertion. Officers and administrators preached the most severe application of martial law for this capital offense. In practice, though, executions remained exceptional and mostly limited to specific events involving other crimes such as murder, mutiny, or treason.[56] Deserters from Louisiana could be found from New Mexico to Carolina and from Cuba to the Yucatan. French authorities negotiated their return by offering individual pardons and collective amnesties, and by seeking the cooperation of their indigenous and European neighbors. At the end of the war of Austrian succession in 1748, when Governor Vaudreuil declared a royal amnesty for all deserters who would return within a year, he made sure to send a copy to Havana. He claimed that many hoped for an opportunity to come back from Spanish or Indigenous settlements where they had found refuge, and he argued that their return would curb desertion by dispelling the notion that they were welcome there.[57] This amnesty was neither the first nor the last, but few defectors seemed to have embraced the opportunity: only during the Seven Years' War did military rolls mention significant numbers of pardoned soldiers among the troops.[58]

The risk of desertion was especially high in certain posts within reach of *terres de franchise* ("free lands"), namely foreign colonies.[59] At Natchitoches and Mobile, in particular, French officials frequently accused their Spanish neighbors of harboring fugitives and encouraging soldiers to run away.[60] For several decades, Louisiana's officers therefore demanded the adoption of local cartels or agreements for the reciprocal restitution of deserters. European states had long exchanged prisoners and fugitives as part of peace settlements, but to turn this practice into a permanent policy was a novelty that rapidly spread to the colonies, perhaps because the restitution of runaway slaves posed similar issues of sovereignty and international law.[61]

Louisiana's Indigenous allies played a major role in these negotiations as they pursued, returned, and frequently protected European deserters. French officials relied on Native warriors not only to defend the colony but also to arrest fugitive soldiers and runaway slaves. This reliance on local *sauvages* ("savages") to enforce discipline in the king's army laid bare the fiction of French sovereignty in the Mississippi Valley. What made matters worse was that Indigenous leaders routinely demanded that the fugitives be pardoned in exchange for their return, effectively thwarting their superiors' power to punish.[62] In promising to spare the life of deserting soldiers, French officers bowed to the will of their Indian allies and acknowledged a dependence that they struggled to rationalize, just like they insisted that the yearly presents delivered to the Natives were not a tribute.

Indigenous appeals for the life of deserting soldiers intrigued French observers, but contemporary testimonies provide a few clues about their significance. Frenchmen and Indians shared some symbols and taboos, as Governor Kerlérec explained by comparing the asylum given in Christian churches with the protection granted to fugitives and criminals who entered the Natives' *cabanes de valeur* (sacred "valor cabins").[63] Back in France, the king regarded the right to pardon as a royal privilege, and his ministers condemned officers who absolved deserters without the monarch's explicit permission.[64] While their Indigenous allies grew familiar with European ideas of sovereignty, colonial personnel learned to negotiate with their leaders and to recognize their own political principles. In 1755, the commander of the Alabama post informed Governor Kérlerec that local Abeka Indians had captured two deserters and returned them under the condition that they would not be harmed, which he was forced to agree to. Kerlérec judged "this sort of cartel detrimental to the good of the service" but admitted that the officer had no other choice, "since my predecessors have conceded this usage long ago, and the red men (who are no longer savages nowadays but for their color) guard anything resembling a privilege jealously."[65] Remarkably, the governor designated an agreement between Natives and colonists by the same word (cartel) used between Europeans; other officers similarly noted that Indian petitions differed little from the provisions for the restitution of deserters between Mobile and Spanish Pensacola, which also proscribed afflictive punishments.[66]

While some defectors sought asylum in foreign colonies, others like Pierre Chartier's protégé Jolicœur took advantage of Louisiana's dependence on its Indigenous allies to ask influential chiefs to lobby for their pardon and reinstatement. Colonial officials may have regarded this behavior as an admission of guilt or an aggravating circumstance, but it paid off, as each level in the chain of command (local officer, governor, minister of the *Marine,* king) opted to absolve fugitives rather than jeopardize Native support. Through the intercession of leaders like the Shawnee Chartier and the Offougoula Toubamingo, alias *Perruquier* ("Wigmaker"), soldiers who occupied the lowest rank in French society forced the hand of their supposedly absolute, God-chosen monarch.[67]

Beyond cultural exchanges and "creative misunderstandings" between Frenchmen and Indians, both sides understood that competing authorities and jurisdictions were at stake in such interactions.[68] Native leaders made their appeals on solemn occasions, and their forceful rhetoric invoked the fictive kinship and common interests that united them to the French, as well as the sacrifices they made for them. Such arguments were especially powerful when coming from the Choctaws, Louisiana's long-lasting military and commercial partners and its strongest allies. In 1751, a Choctaw delegation of fifty visited Fort Tombecbé to return seven deserters and request their pardons in eloquent harangues. Chief Alibamon Mingo notably declared that they would be "sorry to see [French authorities] spill the blood of the persons who bring their daily needs . . . moreover are those Frenchmen not like our brothers, do we not live as in a same cabin?"[69] The Choctaw leader may have been moved by a sense of duty toward fugitives whom he had caught but also rescued, which in turn made him responsible for their safety.[70] Yet his words also had a more literal meaning. The deserters had complained of being poorly fed and clothed due to dwindling supplies, which also affected the Choctaws who obtained most of their French trading goods from the military personnel at the forts. For the soldiers of those frontier posts, joining the ranks of fur traders and *coureurs de bois* in Indian country must have been seemed as a relatively easy transition toward a desirable alternative to garrison life, and a powerful motive to run away. It was no coincidence that the report of the Choctaws' speeches at Fort Tombecbé came from the *garde-magasin* ("warehouse keeper"), who stressed the visitors' anger that the governor was late in delivering their annual presents. French officers could not ignore their many debts to Indigenous allies like Alibamon Mingo and other Eastern Choctaw warriors who had just waged a brutal civil war against pro-British Choctaw factions.[71] The Natives' support of defecting soldiers resulted from their own notions of justice, hospitality, and solidarity, as both groups shared material grievances against colonial authorities, but Indigenous leaders also recognized that this situation offered them precious political leverage.

As they chased, returned, and protected deserters, Indigenous communities asserted their power over the land and challenged the sovereignty claimed by Louisiana officials, forcing them to reconsider European norms and practices of justice and diplomacy. Governor Vaudreuil offered the most dramatic response to the dilemma of Indian demands. Faced with Native threats to no longer arrest runaways and instead to guide them to English colonies, Vaudreuil informed Choctaw warriors that he would hear no more petitions on their behalf. Instead, he offered to pay the same rewards for their scalps as for those of Indigenous enemies.[72] In the eyes of the governor, this policy would have the additional benefit of breeding hostility and preventing interracial cooperation between Indians and soldiers.[73] Vaudreuil's successor chose to acknowledge the influence of Native leaders through an equally spectacular gesture: he invited Choctaw, Arkansas, and Offogoula leaders to seat in the *conseils de guerre* ("war councils" or court martials) that decided the fate of deserters, a privilege military officers often refused to share with the colony's civilian personnel.[74] In addition to its impact on defense and labor needs, military desertion forced the authorities to adapt French judicial norms to the colonial situation in ways that would have been unimaginable in Versailles.

"The soldier was an anomalous type of laborer," writes historian Peter Way of eighteenth-century British troops, "both free in that he received a wage and unfree as many rights were stripped away from him as a result of the military labor contract."[75] The men who served in French Louisiana shared this ambiguous status. As in other early modern armies, however, many recruits were forced into service without contract, the onerous labor extracted from them went well beyond military duties, and their low wages like their mediocre supplies were often late, diminished, or not delivered at all. The other essays in this volume demonstrate that soldiers but also sailors and indentured workers around the world faced similarly oppressive conditions, which motivated them to run away.

The French military presence in the Mississippi Valley was designed to serve the inseparable goals of imperial and capitalist expansion. As soldiers protected the emergence of a plantation economy based on the exploitation of slave labor and the occupation of Native lands, they facilitated the production and circulation of global commodities: furs from Indian country, locally grown cash crops like tobacco and indigo, and even West Indian sugar, whose fabrication partly relied on wood and food exports from Louisiana. Those veterans who settled in the colony may have hoped to reap some of the profits generated by global capitalist circuits, but most enlisted men either deserted, died during their service, or returned to France without having received any.

The Mississippi soldiers often deserted for the same reasons as their counterparts in France, and in fact many of them had already served there and were transported overseas as a punishment for previous defections. While Louisiana troops did not desert at the same staggering rate as contemporary European armies did, running away in the New World was an even more radical decision that required determination, organization, and skill. Rather than individual acts of desperation, the vast majority of defections were collective forms of resistance and at times explicit protests against the conditions of military life and labor. Even in a colonial setting otherwise more fluid and less hierarchical than *ancien régime* France, soldiers occupied a low socioeconomic position alongside other unfree workers like convicts and slaves.[76] From an administrative perspective, military desertion posed quite similar issues as *marronage,* but soldiers certainly resented being treated like bonded laborers in a slave society.[77] Their actions and their voices (when we can hear them) reveal a sense of community, cooperation, and solidarity that allowed poor workers to reclaim their autonomy and their mobility. Those runaways had a profound impact on French efforts to colonize the Mississippi. As they deprived the colony of valuable troops and labor, defections increased its demographic weakness and stunted its development. Desertion and the threat thereof thwarted ambitious plans and remained a thorn in the side of military officers and administrators. Eager to catch and punish runaways, as well as to prevent further losses, colonial authorities had no choice but to revise metropolitan judicial and diplomatic norms.

Nowhere did the French, or perhaps any early modern empire, rely on so few forces to claim so much territory as in Louisiana, and that they did so successfully until the end of the Seven Years' War appears even more remarkable given the constant problems caused by desertion. One explanation is that colonial troops did very little fighting in the Mississippi Valley, where warfare was episodic, limited, and mostly waged by Native Americans. Another is that the king's sovereignty over Louisiana was in fact entirely relative and relied on various forms of negotiation. Royal officers routinely pardoned defectors, altered strategic operations to prevent desertion, and negotiated the terms of the fugitives' capture and punishment with foreign and Indigenous powers. Accommodation was the rule on the margins of the French empire, where runaways showed that the monarch was less absolute than in his home kingdom.[78]

NOTES

1. James S. Pritchard, *In Search of Empire: The French in the Americas, 1670–1730* (New York: Cambridge University Press, 2004), 99, 423.

2. Arnaud Balvay, *L'épée et la plume: Amérindiens et soldats des troupes de la marine en Louisiane et au Pays d'en haut (1683–1763)* (Québec: Presses de l'Université Laval, 2006), 88.

3. T. A. Crowley, "The Forgotten Soldiers of New France: The Louisbourg Example," in *Proceedings of the Third Meeting of the French Colonial Historical Society* (1977), 52–69; John A. Lynn, *Giant of the Grand Siècle: The French Army, 1610–1715* (Cambridge: Cambridge University Press, 2006), 32–66.

4. Daniel H. Usner, *Indians, Settlers and Slaves in a Frontier Exchange Economy: The Lower Mississippi Valley before 1783* (Chapel Hill: University of North Carolina Press, 1992), 198, 220–27.

5. Éric Wenzel, "Justice et culture militaires dans le Pays des Illinois au XVIII siècle à travers une affaire de désertion (1752)," *Revue d'histoire de l'Amérique française* 68, nos. 1–2 (2014): 90.

6. Carl A. Brasseaux, *France's Forgotten Legion Service: Records of French Military and Administrative Personnel Stationed in the Mississippi Valley and Gulf Coast Region, 1699–1769* (Baton Rouge: Louisiana State University Press, 2000).

7. The evidence for those 54 desertion incidents comes from the following narratives and archival collections: Jean-Philippe Goujon de Grondel, *Lettre d'un officier de la Louisiane à M *** commissaire de la marine a *** à la Nouvelle-Orléans* (La Rochelle?, 1764); Louis Narcisse Baudry des Lozières, *Second voyage à la Louisiane faisant suite au premier de l'auteur de 1794 à 1798* (Paris: Chez Charles, 1803); Secrétariat d'État à la Marine, Archives Nationales d'Outre Mer, Aix en Provence [hereafter ANOM]: Correspondance au départ, B ; Correspondance à l'arrivée en provenance de Louisiane, C13A and C13C; Personnel colonial ancien, E; Collection Moreau de Saint-Méry, F3; Vaudreuil Papers, Huntington Library [hereafter VP]; Records of the Superior Council of Louisiana, Louisiana State Museum, New Orleans [hereafter RSC].

8. In 1733, one-fourth of 60 recently enlisted soldiers deserted before embarking for the colonies. Minister to La Croix, 13 July 1733, ANOM, B, 58:167.

9. Albert Babeau, *La vie militaire sous l'ancien Régime* (Firmin Didot, 1890), 328–29; André Corvisier, *L'armée française de la fin du XVIIe siècle au ministère de Choiseul: Le soldat* (Paris: Presses universitaires de France, 1964), 2:693–748; Louis XIV's minister of war Vauban estimated that half a million soldiers deserted between 1666 and 1690. Sébastien Le Prestre de Vauban and Michèle Virol, *Les oisivetés de monsieur de Vauban, ou ramas de plusieurs mémoires de sa façon sur différents sujets* (Ceyzérieu, France: Editions Champ Vallon, 2007), 1028.

10. Vaudreuil to Court, 4 April 1751, VP, LO 9, Letterbook II:106.

11. Report on the Louisiana Troops, 10 September 1754, ANOM, C13A, 38:213.

12. "Second registre des délibérations du Conseil de la Guerre," 10 November 1716, Service Historique de la Défense, Vincennes, Archives anciennes, Correspondance A1, 2534: 95. See cases of forced enrollment in the same register, folios 16, 246, and 260.

13. Minister to Bigot de la Mothe, 4 February 1737, ANOM, B, 65:10.

14. Minister to Macarty, 21 January 1737, ANOM, B, 65:494; Macarty to Minister, 5 February 1737, ANOM, C13A, 22: 246; Bienville and Salmon, 15 April 1736, ANOM, C13A, 21:7.

15. See for instance Minister to Robert, 23 August 1713, ANOM, B, 35:147.

16. Conseil de la Marine to Beauharnais, 20 March 1716, ANOM, B, 40:92.

17. La Coeurtière to Conseil de la Marine, 13 December 1719, Archives Nationales, Fonds Marine, Lettres reçues: B3, 260:57.

18. Salmon to Minister, 1 December 1731, ANOM, C13A 39:108. *Engagement* could describe either the physical document or the contractual obligation that defined the terms of service of both soldiers and indentured workers.

19. Boris Lesueur, "Les Troupes Coloniales Sous l'Ancien Régime" (PhD diss., Tours, 2007), 398–99, 471–72.

20. Conseil de la Marine to La Galissonière, 29 March 1716, Service Historique de la Défense, Rochefort [hereafter SHDR], Correspondance du Commandant de la Marine, 1A, 2: 253; Conseil de la Marine to Beauharnais, 19 June 1720, SHDR, Correspondance de l'intendant de la marine, 1E, 94:719, 723.

21. Vaudreuil to Minister, 17 June 1748, ANOM, C13A, 32:106.

22. Bienville and Salmon to Minister, 28 February 1734, ANOM, C13A, 18:8; Kerlérec to Minister, 22 June 1754, ibid., 38:74.

23. Périer to Minister, 7 December 1731, ANOM, C13A, 14:158; Vaudreuil and Michel to Minister, 20 May 1751, ibid., 35:13; Kerlérec to Minister, 20 October 1757, ANOM, F3, 25:17.

24. Superior Council to Company Directors, 27 February 1725, ANOM, C13A, 9:64.

25. Vaudreuil to Court, 20 March 1748, VP, LO 9, Letterbook II:44.

26. Louboey to Minister, 20 May 1733, C13A, 17:226; Vaudreuil to Maurepas, 30 August 1744, VP, LO 9, Letterbook I:28; Bienville and Salmon to Minister, 14 May 1737, ANOM, C13A, 22:28; Vaudreuil to Minister, 20 March 1748, ibid., 32:31.

27. See for instance Crémont to Minister, 24 February 1734, ANOM, C13A, 19:121; Vaudreuil to Louboey, 6 November 1743, VP, LO 9, Letterbook III:20; D'Orgon to Vaudreuil, 7 October 1752, VP, LO 399.

28. Thomas N. Ingersoll, *Mammon and Manon in Early New Orleans: The First Slave Society in the Deep South, 1718–1819* (Knoxville: University of Tennessee Press, 1999), 85–87.

29. "Ordonnance du roi qui accorde l'amnistie générale aux soldats déserteurs . . . ", 2 January 1717, ANOM, Actes du pouvoir souverain, A, 25:117; Conseil de la Marine to Intendant, 3 May 1717, SHDR, 1A, 3:187. In the *Marine* as in the army, which reestablished the death penalty for desertion in 1716, it replaced a life sentence to the galleys accompanied by the cropping of the ears and nose and the branding with a *fleur de lys,* a punishment increasingly reserved to runaway slaves.

30. "Déclaration des nègres fugitifs appartenant à Monsieur de Benac," RSC, 1748–03–22/1; Macarty to Vaudreuil, Kaskakia, 2 September 1752, VP, LO 376.

31. Dossier Maret Dupuy, ANOM, Personnel colonial ancien (XVIIe-XVIIIe), E, 301; Louboey to Bienville, RSC, 1723–07–29/1; Vaudreuil to Maurepas, 30 August 1744, LO 9, Letterbook I:30–31; Interrogation of Langlois, RSC, 1728–06–04/2; Baudry des Lozières, *Second voyage à la Louisiane,* 57–61; Vaudreuil to Minister, 30 October 1745, ANOM, C13A, 29:57–58, 60; Louboey to Minister, 6 November 1745, ibid.:199.

32. Bienville to Minister, 15 December 1721, ANOM, C13A, 6: 181.

33. Serigny to Conseil, 20 June 1719, ANOM, F3, 24:109; Serigny to Conseil, 26 October 1719, ibid.: 112.

34. Bienville to Conseil, 20 October 1719, ANOM, F3, 24:130

35. Prevost to Minister, 9 October 1752, ANOM, C11B, 32:173.

36. La Mothe Cadillac to Conseil, 7 February 1716, ANOM, C13A, 4:575.

37. See, for instance, two cases involving noncommissioned officers from the Natchitoches garrison in Bienville and Salmon to Minister, 26 March 1734, ANOM, C13A, 18:8; Bienville and Salmon to Minister, 1 April 1734, ibid., 18:20.

38. "Délibération du Conseil sur le payment des troupes," 26 May–5 June 1723, ANOM, C13A, 7:162–65. The classic examination of a moral economy based on customary rights is E. P. Thompson, "The Moral Economy of the English Crowd in the 18th Century," *Past & Present* 50 (1971): 76–136.

39. Vaudreuil to Minister, 20 July 1751, ANOM, C13A, 35:158; Dupumeu to Vaudreuil, 18 June 1751, ibid., 35:354. Bread was a mainstay of the French diet in the eighteenth century. While the colony imported wheat from Europe and the Illinois Country, flour was so often spoiled or lacking that settlers and soldiers reluctantly turned to rice and corn.

40. Summary of letter from La Mothe-Cadillac 7 February 1716, ANOM, C13A, 4:203 (quote); Vaudreuil to Court, 22 March 1748, VP, LO 9, Letterbook II:44.

41. Michel to Minister, 15 January 1752, ANOM, C13A, 36:220.

42. Macarty to Vaudreuil, 27 March 1752, VP, LO 339.

43. Le Blond de la Tour to Minister, 30 August 1722, ANOM, C13A, 6:330–31; Analysis of letters to the council no. 2, 24 January 1723, ibid., 6:392.

44. Bienville and Salmon, 13 April 1735, ibid., 20: 29; Analysis of a letter from Bienville, 18 March 1738, ibid., 23:41.

45. See the long-awaited publication of Scott's groundbreaking 1986 dissertation: Julius Scott, *Common Wind: Afro-American Organization in the Revolution against Slavery* (New York: Verso, 2018).

46. Bienville to Minister, 4 February 1743, ANOM, C13A, 28:31; Letter to the Governor of Sante Fe, 1 June 1741, ANOM, F3, 242:320.

47. Vaudreuil to Minister, 20 November 1746, C13A, 30:75.

48. Stephen Warren, *The Worlds the Shawnees Made: Migration and Violence in Early America* (Chapel Hill: University of North Carolina Press, 2014), 112–13, 224.

49. Kerlérec to Minister, 20 October 1757, ANOM, F3, 25:17.

50. Analysis of a letter from Louboey, 30 November 1722, ANOM, C13A, 6: 390; Decision of the Conseil de la Marine on three letters from La Mothe-Cadillac, 2 January–7 February 1716, ibid., 4:185.

51. Diron D'Artaguiette to Minister, 24 October 1737, ANOM, C13A, 22:233; Vaudreuil to Minister, 6 December 1744, ibid., 28:245.

52. Vaudreuil to Minister, 28 April 1751, C13A, 35:78; Kerlérec, 22 October 1757, ibid., 39:284.

53. Vaudreuil to Court, 20 March 1748, VP, LO 9, Letterbook II:44. That Swiss and French soldiers could in fact desert together was demonstrated at Fort Tombecbé in 1745 and again in 1751. See Louboey to Minister, 6 November 1745, ANOM, C13A, 29:199; Vaudreuil to Minister, 20 July 1751, ibid., 35:158.

54. "Capitulation avec le Sr Bugnot pour une compagnie suisse," 27 February 1720, ANOM, Troupes et personnel civil, Louisiane, D2C, 51:21–29.

55. See for instance Salmon to Beauharnais, 4 May 1738, ANOM, C13A, 23:72.

56. Many fugitives were condemned *in absentia*, while others were spared after drawing lots with their comrades.

57. Vaudreuil to Minister, 18 March 1747, ANOM, C13A, 31:30.

58. See "Rôle des soldats et matelots déserteurs . . . ," 1 January 1759, ANOM, D2C, 52:73.

59. Vaudreuil to Minister, 28 April 1751, ANOM, C13A, 35:78; 20 July 1751, ibid., 35:158.

60. Decision of the Council on two letters from Duclos, 8 September 1715, and 25 January 1716, C13A, 4:267; Le Blond de la Tour to Minister, 30 August 1722, ibid., 6:330; Bienville to Minister, 27 August 1734, ibid., 18:188.

61. The term *cartel* first appeared in French dictionaries with this meaning in the 1690s. From 1718 to 1763, French authorities in the metropole signed at least fifty conventions for the mutual return of deserters. See Corvisier, *L'armée française*, 723.

62. Bienville to Minister, 5 September 1736, ANOM, C13A, 21:218; Beauchamps to Minister, 1 May 1737, ibid., 22:249; Dupumeu to Minister, 18 June 1751, ibid., 35:354; Kérlerec to Minister, 5 October 1755, ibid., 39:52. See Michael James Foret, "Red over White: Indians, Deserters, and French Colonial Louisiana," in *Proceedings of the Seventeenth Meeting of the French Colonial Historical Society* (Chicago, 1991), 79–89.

63. Kerlérec to Minister, 20 June 1756, ANOM, F3, 25:11.

64. Minister to Vaudreuil, 25 April 1746, VP, LO 62.

65. Kerlérec to Minister, 5 October 1755, ANOM, C13A, 39:52; Same to same, 12 September 1756, ibid., D2C, 52:46.

66. Louboey to Minister, Mobile, 6 November 1745, ibid., 29:196. When the French commandant of the Alabama post hired Indigenous warriors to chase a group of deserters headed to Carolina in 1737, the Natives, perhaps aware of the Franco-Spanish cartel, advised the officer to make a similar agreement with the British. Bienville to Minister, 28 February 1737, ibid., 22:85.

67. Vaudreuil to Minister, 18 March 1747, ANOM, C13A, 31: 30; Dunbar Rowland, A. G. Sanders, and Patricia Galloway, eds., *Mississippi Provincial Archives: French Dominion* (Baton Rouge: Louisiana State University Press, 1984), 5:177n8.

68. Richard White, "Creative Misunderstandings and New Understandings," *William and Mary Quarterly* 63, no. 1 (2006): 9–14.

69. Dupumeu to Minister, 18 June 1751, ANOM, C13A, 35: 354.

70. Michelene E. Pesantubbee, *Choctaw Women in a Chaotic World: The Clash of Cultures in the Colonial Southeast* (Albuquerque: University of New Mexico Press, 2005), 51.

71. Patricia Galloway, "Choctaw Factionalism and Civil War, 1746–1750," in *Pre-removal Choctaw History: Exploring New Paths,* ed. Greg O'Brien (Norman: University of Oklahoma Press, 2008), 70–102.

72. Vaudreuil to Minister, 28 January 1752, ibid., 36:55.

73. Alan Taylor, *American Colonies* (New York: Viking, 2001), 386.

74. "Procès-verbal du conseil de guerre tenu à La Mobile . . .," 12 June 1753, ANOM, C13A, 37:62; "Procès-verbal du conseil de guerre tenu à La Nouvelle-Orléans . . .," 20 June 1756, ANOM, C13A, 39:177. Following this latter council, Kerlérec issued a general pardon for all deserters, unauthorized by the king yet posted in every post and village of Louisiana. Kerlérec to Minister, 2 September 1756, ibid., 185.

75. Peter Way, "Class and the Common Soldier in the Seven Years' War," *Labor History* 44, no. 4 (2003): 458.

76. Shannon Lee Dawdy, *Building the Devil's Empire: French Colonial New Orleans* (Chicago: University of Chicago Press, 2008), 200.

77. Tensions between soldiers and slaves are analyzed in Cécile Vidal, "Caribbean New Orleans: Urban Genesis, Empire, and Race in the Eighteenth-Century French Atlantic" (Habilitation à diriger des recherches, original manuscript, Université Paris-Sorbonne, 2014), 300–301, 203–6, 208–9.

78. For an overview of revisionist perspectives on the French absolute monarchy, see William Beik, "The Absolutism of Louis XIV as Social Collaboration," *Past & Present* 188 (2005): 195–224.

6

"Journeying into Freedom"

Traditions of Desertion at the Cape of Good Hope, 1652–1795

Nicole Ulrich

BALLAD OF A MUTINY

Long is the tale of a prisoner,
Thomas van Bengalen lived a life of toil.
Slave to a master, he yearned to be free.
Accomplices he made of Titus, Tromp, and Hannibal,
In twelve was all, his company, who mutinied with speak

A bond against the Dutch, they with blood would seal,
Drinking it with promise never to slave-hood to return.
Boldly they fled to the mountain of Picketberg.
Wearing muskets filled with powder, escaping to the wild.

In twelve was all, his company, conspiracy would heed.
Journeying into freedom, food became rare to meat,
The band of runaway slaves made for to steal the masters' beasts.
Being discovered by commandos, slaves and soldiers faced each other,
Steel!
Bodies falling down, at the water's edge.
In twelve was all, his company, who mutiny would seek,

These are the harms of Batavia, these are the harms of Batavia.

Thomas van Bengalen, captured, he faced his choice,
Taking hold of a blade he pulled it along his throat.
He began to bleed,
his capturers retreated, they were pleased.
But Thomas didn't die, he became a story tellers' keep.

These are the harms of Batavia, these are the harms of Batavia.

Neo Muyanga composed this ballad as part of the theatre production *Cargo* on slavery that was performed in South Africa in 2007. It is based on a criminal trial in 1714 at the Cape of Good Hope (southern Africa) that was ruled by Dutch East India Company (*Verenigde Oost-Indische Compagnie*, or VOC) at this time. The records indicate that Thomas from Bengalen, the main protagonist of the ballad, was part of a band of slaves who aimed to make their way to "the land of Portuguese" (probably Angola).[1] They were armed, having stolen guns and ammunition, and carried clothes and food, including rusks baked by Thomas from Bengalen himself.[2] A notable aspect of this group was that they took an oath, marked by eating bread soaked in their own blood, and swore allegiance to each other.

Through the efforts of storytellers such as Muyanga, Thomas from Bengalen's tale of desertion is relatively well known. Yet his experience of running away was not unique and the vast majority of the other runaways linger in obscurity. Stories of desertion—undertaken by slaves, sailors, soldiers, convicts, and servants—litter the archive, suggesting that running away was one of the most common forms of labor resistance in the colony. This chapter explores desertion across labor type and pieces together archival fragments to discern distinct traditions of desertion, especially collective desertion. The conclusions oppose an established literature that juxtaposes desertion and rebellion, as well as histories that fail to locate desertion within the armory of forms of collective resistance repeatedly undertaken by slaves and other laborers. Desertion was often a *social* act enabled by connections and networks and one that, when practiced collectively, gave rise to new, dissident communities. Given the prevalence and social nature of desertion, the stories of runaways provide a powerful lens through which to view class formation in the colonial context of the Cape.

"STORY TELLERS' KEEP": TOWARD A COMMON HISTORY OF DESERTION

Historians have long commented on desertion at the Cape, although narrowly: most scholarship on desertion has been "single category" histories[3] (of "slaves," "Khoesan," or "free-burghers") that usually present the Cape as a plural society of racially and ethnically distinct "population" categories / groups. Shula Marks's important work on Khoesan resistance drew attention to the slaves, sailors, and soldiers who joined remnant Khoesan bands on the colonial borderland.[4] Yet the "single category" analytical frames have led to discrete and partial histories of resistance, including desertion. For instance, there is a literature that specifically deals with runaway slaves.

Single-category histories reveal deep assumptions among historians about class formation (or the lack thereof) and the possibility (or impossibility) of collective revolt at the Cape. This is especially true of Robert Ross's influential work on slavery and resistance in South Africa.[5] Ross argues that slaves in the Cape were atomized, with "no sense of slave community" and no identification with other laborers or subalterns. This, he argues, led them to "fight as individuals, not to form a culture of resistance that could encompass them all."[6] Ross insists that slave resistance was "almost always an individual act."[7]

What then of collective slave desertions such as that of Thomas from Bengalen and his comrades? Ross is quick to dismiss any signs of sociality or solidarity among slaves under VOC rule as dysfunctional, violent, and even predatory. For instance, he dismisses the Hanglip (or Hangklip) "maroon" community under the leadership of Leander from Boegis (also Bugis / Sulawesi) in the 1720s and 1730s. He claims that Khoesan laborers were far too concerned about protecting their own status as free workers and did not assist slave deserters. In addition, he argues, that the "Hanglip maroons behaved brutally towards each other and were no kinder to those farm slaves they encountered . . . maroons lived, not as fish in the water of the local population, but as sharks amongst fish."[8]

Historians also question the political nature and threat posed by slave desertion. Muyanga's ballad portrays the slave runaways as resistance in motion. But slave historians tend to view running away narrowly as a mode of escape. For instance, Nigel Worden and Gerald Groenewald argue that while Bengalen's group may have been unique in terms of scale and organization, they were typical slave deserters in that they "did not mount a rebellion against their owners, but rather sought to escape from them and the colony."[9]

These views are now subject to critique. In a recent synthesis of slave desertion at the Cape, Kate Ekama questions the extent to which slaves operated in isolation. She argues that the "ethnic heterogeneity of the Cape slave population did not stop slaves from running away together. Slaves interacted with fellow slaves, convicts, soldiers and sailors in locations where they worked and socialized together which provided and created opportunities to make escape plans."[10] Slaves frequently established connections with each other and with other laborers in order to assert their autonomy.

Ekama also claims that desertion was overwhelmingly undertaken by slave men. This she attributes to skewed sex ratios (the rural slave population was predominantly male) and to the difficulty for mothers to desert with young children in tow.[11] She echoes an older argument that slave women were less inclined to desert, or contest their bondage, because they were integrated into their masters' households as child minders and concubines and therefore formed intimate bonds with their masters.[12] While this may be true of some slave women, we cannot generalize this identification with elites to all slave women at the Cape. There is ample evidence to suggest that many slave women were integrated into subaltern families and social networks, suggesting that scholars should be careful of assuming that women slaves were politically passive and easily misled.[13] Such assumptions reinforce the misinterpretation of women's agency by masters and authorities in the archival records and at the same time render slave women invisible in modern histories. While it is true that certain occupations were male-dominated—among, for example, slaves, sailors, and soldiers—it is also true that large numbers of Khoesan women were drawn into the colony as laborers. It was, after all, primarily women and children who were captured in borderland raids by commandos and forced into labor. These women in turn socialized with and were connected to laboring men, and, as will be shown below, they too deserted their masters.

This chapter (and my broader work on the early colonial Cape) argues that the connections among slaves as well as between slaves and other laborers were significant.[14] These bonds created a basis for an alternative, class-based community and provided the social foundation for political solidarity. Within this context of social connection and political solidarity lies a common history of desertion. Here Marcus Rediker's work on Atlantic sailors provides a good model for analysis.[15] He shows how sailors—physically separated from other proletarians on land for long periods of time—created unique traditions, beliefs, and even a distinctive language based on the ship and the sea. Nevertheless, sailors' rough culture was still primarily proletarian, and recognized as such by themselves and others. Rediker's approach acknowledges the diversity of proletarian experience and cultural expression, but does not assume that this diversity automatically resulted in discord and separation. Indeed, desertion at the Cape was rooted in social connections that emerged from common experiences that could, and did, transcend ethnicity, nation, race, and even gender.

The political threat posed by desertion was contingent and contextual. Many deserters chose to escape rather than challenge their masters and colonial authorities openly and directly. Yet, those deserters who committed arson, joined enemy forces, attacked masters and mistresses or the colony spread panic among elites who feared the breakdown of the existing order. Anders Sparrman, a Swedish scientist who visited the Cape in the 1770s, noted that deserters were regarded as a public threat in the colony and argued that the colonists feared "runaway and rebel slaves" who continually wandered about "in order to plunder houses for victuals and fire-arms, or else to draw others to their party."[16]

Revealing evidence of desertion abounds in the archival records. Heese's list of *sententiën*, a set of records summarizing the sentences of cases deemed significant by the court, for example, provides valuable data.[17] Yet these records document only the most serious cases of desertion, and do not include all those prosecuted. This source can be supplemented by the fragmented stories of individuals that emerge from the testimonies of the accused, to shed light on actual practices of desertion, the operation and extent of social networks, and the making of new communities.[18] These sources detail a rich history of desertion as a multifaceted, class-based response to dispossession and exploitation by different laborers and the poor at the Cape, rather than represent desertion as merely a sign of the social atomization of enslaved men.

"THE HARMS OF BATAVIA": IMPERIAL POLITICAL ECONOMY AND LABOR

The Cape of Good Hope was colonized by the VOC in 1652 until it was drawn into the British imperial orbit from 1795. This African territory, which was initially inhabited by indigenous San hunter-gathers and Khoe pastoralists, was plugged into imperial circuits of trade and labor migration that spanned the Atlantic and Indian Oceans. Through empire, the Cape was drawn into a broader global economic context of profound change: traditional political and social relations were disrupted by enclosure, slavery, and European colonialism; laborers and the poor from various parts of the world were uprooted and moved across oceans and continents in unprecedented numbers; and new relations of production and forms of work emerged in a number of different geographical sites.[19]

The Cape was not a significant port of trade or a key commodity producer.[20] However, the strategically located colony played a vital role in replenishing sailors and soldiers traveling between Europe and Indian Ocean ports by providing them with water, food, and medical convalescence. Thus, the Cape played an important part in reproducing the military and commercial forces that would ultimately facilitate the global ascendancy of capitalism. The colony's reproductive role as a "refreshment station" did not give rise to benign forms of colonialism. On the contrary, imperial rule was based on conquest, expropriation, the entrenchment of private property, and violent forms of labor exploitation.[21]

Indeed, it was due to this reproductive role that the Cape became a settler colony. In 1657 the VOC introduced a unique and somewhat limited form of citizenship: respectable servants were released from their contracts and awarded the status of "free-burgher" to take up farming in order to stimulate agricultural production.[22] This did not apply to the largest section of inhabitants, slaves and laborers, who were governed through harsh labor codes and subject to a criminal justice system that used violent physical punishments (mutilation, hanging, breaking on the wheel) to uphold social and political inequalities.

As the colony grew and diversified, three regionally based, yet interdependent, economic sectors emerged.[23] These consisted of, firstly, an urban-centered port economy dominated by the VOC, which relied on the labor of low-ranking Company servants (sailors, soldiers, and a small number of artisans) as well as slaves. This sector also included retail and small-scale manufacture run by free-burghers and "free blacks," who drew on family labor as well as the labor of urban slaves and the free poor.[24] The second sector consisted of the agricultural production of wheat and grapes (wine) in the more fertile hinterland, on farms owned by wealthy free-burghers.[25] This sector mainly relied on slaves. In addition, these farmers also made use of a small number of other laborers, often drawn from Khoesan communities, as well as low-ranking Company servants (sailors and soldiers) permitted to take up private work as wig makers, carpenters, farm overseers, or teachers for free-burgher children.[26] Thirdly, from the 1700s, a stock-farming sector emerged on the colonial borderlands.[27] Stock farmers owned slaves, but most relied on family labor supplemented by the labor of poorer free-burghers or of men and women from Khoesan communities. Toward the end of the 1700s, Khoesan were increasingly forced into labor, with many women and children kidnapped during cattle raids on the borderland and "'indentured" or "apprenticed."[28]

The Cape is often classified by historians as a rural slave society because of its large number of slaves, mostly men, required for the wheat and wine farms of the hinterland. Company-owned slaves never increased beyond 1,000 at one time.[29] However, the total number of slaves (including "private" slaves) was 14,747 in 1793.[30] Slaves came from Indonesia, India, Madagascar, and East Africa. Toward the late 1700s, increasing numbers of slaves were born in the Cape and were imported from Mozambique. Yet the Cape was not strictly a "slave society," for slavery existed alongside other systems of labor, including other forms of bonded work. By the late eighteenth century the number of Company servants—mainly sailors and soldiers recruited from across Europe—stationed at the Cape had grown to about 3,000–4,000.[31] No systematic records were kept of the numbers of Khoesan in the colony until the 1800s, but it is estimated that approximately 23,000 Khoesan were still living (with a large portion of them working) in the colony by the 1780s.[32] Khoesan therefore outnumbered the enslaved and other Company workers combined.

"MUTINIED WITH SPEAK": PRACTICES OF DESERTION

There is a long tradition of desertion at the Cape, dating back to 1652, the very year of the founding of the colony under the command of Jan van Riebeeck.[33] The records indicate that those men and women who deserted between 1652 and 1795 were a complex dissident group, whose history cannot be reduced to a simple typology. Slaves, sailors, Khoesan laborers, convicts, and soldiers all ran away. Deserters took temporary absences from work without permission, often repeatedly. Some deserters returned of their own volition; others were caught after a few years, or even a couple of decades after they ran away. There were even those who managed to run away, never to return, some of whom became masterless wanderers (or vagabonds) in the colony. Some deserters ran across land, others across the seas. Some ran to avoid punishment, some ran to improve their conditions or wages, some wanted to reconnect with their loved ones momentarily. Others wanted their freedom, or ran away as an act of anticolonial resistance. Some ran as individuals, many were supported by their fellows, and many deserters ran in small groups. Some groups were heterogeneous, transcending labor type, ethnicity, race, or gender; other groups were families; still others mobilized along occupational lines. Many deserters created new dissident communities in remote spaces of the colony. Others ran to join up with communities on the colonial borderland and beyond. Some wanted to return to faraway homes. Desertions could be well planned and well provisioned, or spontaneous.

Armstrong, Worden, and more recently Ekama have identified individual spontaneous escape, sparked by a moment of crisis, from which a slave fled to avoid punishment as a key—and most common—form of desertion at the Cape.[34] There were certainly many such cases, involving not only slaves. For instance, in 1777, Jan de Boer, a sailor, deserted and joined a French ship traveling to Mauritius after he was involved in a brawl.[35] He deserted to escape punishment, but gave himself up when he later returned.

Yet spontaneous running away motivated by fear of imminent punishment was not the only form of desertion undertaken by individuals. Many desertions suggest forethought and social cooperation, as in the case of those slaves who deserted via the VOC's shipping system disguised as sailors. In 1750, Jan from the Cape fled on the ship *Hof d'Uno* to the Netherlands.[36] He made his way to Zeeland where he apparently married. He returned to the Cape in 1751 as a sailor under the pseudonym of Jan Harmensz Grutter of St. Helena, but, unhappily, was recognized and caught. Jacob from the Cape also changed his name, to Jacobus Claasz, after he managed to flee to the Netherlands on a ship, and subsequently signed up as a ship's "boy."[37] He was also discovered and captured when he returned to the Cape. A recent study by Linda Mbeki and Matthias van Rossum on the intercontinental private slave trade suggests that such desertions were made possible because the distinction between slaves and seafarers on VOC ships was often blurred as private traders sought to hide their cargo by disguising them as sailors.[38] Even so, it is unlikely that individual slaves would be able to escape in this way without connections to sailors or soldiers.

In many instances, desertion was never a final act of resistance. Many individual laborers were habitual deserters who ran away repeatedly. For instance in 1741, Fortuijn from Bengal deserted repeatedly to be with his beloved Christijn.[39] He was usually sent back to his master, after some rough handling, and in at least one instance, a beating with a broom. When Christijn decided to end the relationship, because her "*baas* [master] and *juffrow* [mistress] do not understand it," Fortuijn retaliated by setting Christijn's master's home alight. Fortuijn's case indicates maintaining contact with loved ones and families could be a powerful motivation for repeated desertion.

For many who ran away on their own, desertion would not have been possible without the assistance of others. For instance, in 1706 Ari from Bengalen appeared before the Council of Justice on a charge of arson.[40] In his testimony, Ari explained that after he deserted his master and mistress, he made his way to a farm across the Berg River where two slaves, still in service, gave him tobacco and bread. From there he moved to a nearby vineyard, where he met three other runaways and "where upon they all formed an alliance."[41] Ari remained true to the alliance after capture, refusing to give the court information about his comrades. He was placed on Robben Island until he was more forthcoming.[42] In another case in 1742, Adam, a Khoesan laborer who was tasked to escort a runaway slave called Fortuijn from Bengalen, let his prisoner go. When Adam reached the Paardeberg, he told Fortuijn: "I shall sleep, if you want to get away, you could do so."[43] These cases show that deserters relied on the solidarity of laborers still in service for help, whether with provisions or by looking the other way and letting them go free. Desertion was embedded in social connections forged between laborers.

"ACCOMPLICES HE MADE": COLLECTIVE DESERTION

Desertion of groups was especially complex. Two very broad forms of collective desertion can be identified, although it is important to keep in mind that these often intersected or overlapped. The first type of collective desertion includes groups of deserters, of varying size, who attempted to leave the colony. The second type was made up of runaways who remained within or close to the colony (on the borderland), as deserters joined existing fugitive communities or built new ones.

The groups that deserted with the aim of leaving the colony ran away across land and sea. Some made a dash for African communities in the interior or fled to distant lands. Many Malagasy slaves believed that they could reach home by traveling overland.[44] Like Thomas from Bengalen's group, the "land of the Portuguese" (presumably Mozambique or Angola) emerges as a popular possible destination. Others, especially those who traveled via ship, aimed to leave the continent entirely, for Europe, especially Turkey, Indonesia, and South America.

Groups could be small, consisting of just a few runaways at a time. But there are also cases in which large groups deserted together. In 1712 Joudan Tappa (known as "Paap"), a political exile who resided on the Groot Constantia wine farm, led a group of twenty-three deserters.[45] They planned to travel to the eastern interior and then to Indonesia.[46] Perhaps one of the most ambitious desertions was undertaken in 1728 by Company soldiers stationed in Rio de Lagoa (Mozambique), then under VOC control. A third (sixty-two) of the 186 men planned to ransack the Company store, and march overland to the Portuguese station at Inhambane.[47] Unfortunately for them, their plot was discovered before they could escape.

Sometimes laborers deserted in smaller groups, in quick succession over a short period of time. In July 1795, for example, VOC authorities noted with alarm that over a three-week period, as many as twenty-seven soldiers had deserted, often taking their weapons and rations with them.[48] Since an attack on the Cape by the British was imminent at the time, soldiers caught deserting to the English were accused of treason. In addition, the military set up armed patrols and stations specifically for the purpose of stopping deserters who intended to go to False Bay, where the English were based.[49] The court did not speculate on the motivations of the twenty-seven soldiers who defected to the enemy. Those soldiers tracked down and captured were "hanged by the neck upon the Gallows with ropes until death ensues and thereafter their dead bodies to be dragged to the outskirts of the town."[50] Another remarkable case, similar to that of Thomas from Bengalen's group, came to trial in 1786. It involved six slave deserters: August from the Cape, Andries from Calcutta, Jonas from Batavia, Damon from Bougies, Sapripa from Mandaar, and Welkom from Ternate.[51] They sought to escape to African communities in the interior. To enable their smooth passage, they had organized false passes (unwittingly forged by a young schoolboy) that stated they were traveling with permission of their masters. They also secured charms from a "Mohammedan" priest (banished to the Cape from Batavia) for protection, as well as guns and weapons, a file and machete (used to break the chains of Jonas from Bengalen), and clothes and money. Like Thomas and his comrades from Bengalen, these runaways "made a mutual alliance" never to leave one another but to die together.[52] They stopped at several farms and, in one case, a Khoesan *kraal* (livestock and homestead), buying bread and wine along the way. However, after a brutal attack on the homestead of a free-burgher rumored to "have many goods and cash," they were apprehended by the authorities, tried, convicted, and broken and beheaded.

Maritime desertion could also be collective in nature. Most notable was the "piratical seizure" of ships by groups who aimed to desert to distant places.[53] The earliest such seizure took place in 1659 when soldiers of the garrison (mostly English, Scots, and Irish) plotted to commandeer the provision ship, the *Erasmus,* ransack the fort, and then travel to "the land of the Portuguese."[54] The rebel group included not only soldiers but "a black convict," "two servants of freemen," and some slaves.[55] Another notable incident took place in 1751, when a small group of Asian convicts and slaves on Robben Island planned to capture the provision ship and sail to their homelands.[56] They did not know how to sail and agreed to spare the lives of a couple of sailors to help them guide the ship. Their plot was finally betrayed. Fifteen of the would-be deserter-pirates were convicted and sentenced to be broken on the wheel.

The social composition of runaway groups varied as those who sought to escape mobilized different networks to facilitate plans. Some runaway groups drew on occupational solidarities, such as the Company soldiers mentioned above. Others reached beyond specific workplaces. For instance, the twenty-three deserters who escaped with Paap included convicts, private slaves owned by free-burghers, and slaves owned by the Company. Obviously, members of this group drew on preexisting connections that spanned the convict-slave and private-VOC divide. Others were bonded by common ethnic origins, as demonstrated by a case in 1760 in which a group of runaways killed a free-burgher family, frightening authorities.[57] Most of these runaways were executed when captured, but the court also tried those who provided these runaways with shelter and food. Their testimony points to an ethnic network that centered on a slave named September who "acted as a doctor amongst the slaves of the Bugis [Sulawesi] nation" and was regularly visited by slaves from his homeland for advice and medicine.[58] Indeed, September indicated that it was custom for Sulawesi men to refer to each other as "brother." Families sometimes deserted together. For instance in 1793 the slave Adam deserted with Jannetje, a Khoesan woman whom he regarded as his wife, and their son, named April.[59] Family desertions were probably most prevalent in the stock-farming sector on the borderland where masters often indentured children like April, or held family members of their laborers hostage to force them into longer service after their contracts had expired.[60] The final destination of this particular family is not clear, although it is unlikely the runaways intended to leave the region.

This leads to the second type of collective desertion, which included those groups who either remained within remote regions of the colony or deserted to join bands on the colonial borderland. A key aspect of this kind of desertion is the creation of alternative fugitive communities that were dependent on, but not entirely integrated into, the colony. Again, it is difficult to provide a full typology of fugitive communities—largely because they took a variety of forms. A rough distinction can be made, however, between *droster* bands and borderland bands. These fugitive communities sometimes occupied the same spaces and overlapped.

The best-known *droster* bands—or "maroons"—fled to Hanglip, a remote and difficult-to-reach area near False Bay. Led by Leander from Boegis in the 1720s and 1730s, this marron community almost succeeded in burning down Cape Town in March 1736.[61] Several other groups occupied the area up until the end of slavery in 1838.[62] Ross has traced fifty names in the archives associated with this community over the eighteenth century (they did not all live at Hanglip at the same time). He maintains that all fifty were deserted slaves: forty-two men and eight women. Even though Ross argues that the *droster* bands that occupied Hanglip were fractious and predatory, he notes that these bands had regular contact with slaves and other runaways on Table Mountain and participated in the illicit economy of the urban underground, which included barter and trade in stolen goods. These transactions were often facilitated by laborers still in service. Ross does not examine the Hanglip maroon community on its own terms, but rather compares it, unfavorably, to larger and more durable maroons in the New World. Some of the key characteristics of *droster* bands emerge in the comparison of the Hanglip maroons to other similar groups.

In 1780 a group of eleven runaways appeared before the court for the murder of one of their comrades, a runaway slave by the name of Solomon.[63] A notable feature of this *droster* band was that it had been in existence for a relatively long period—almost a decade before the accused were captured. The *droster* band was initially organized by a group of twelve slaves, including a locally born slave woman, Sara. They "roamed in the Goudini, on Paarde Berg, in the Hottentots Holland mountains and elsewhere and had, according to their claim, during that time lived on fruit and whatever else they could find in the veldt."[64] Sara's band remained hidden within the colony and maintained coherence over a long period.

It is unclear if the trial records provide a full account of all those who were part of Sara's band. Most members of the group were slaves, drawn from different parts of the world. Based on the personal details of the eleven accused, the groups consisted of creolized Cape-born slaves, as well as slaves from Bengal, Malabar, and Mozambique. In addition, the records indicate that the group included a Khoesan woman named Betje. Most of the group were men, but also included were at least two women. The group varied a great deal in terms of age: the youngest, February from the Cape, was 12; the oldest, Domingo from Mozambique, was 50.

The *droster* band itself was also relatively mobile. Around 1779 it moved to "Helderenberg which forms part of the Hottentots Holland mountain range, where they took shelter in a ravine above the farms of Pieter Roux and Pieter Heijnkes."[65] Here this *droster* band was joined by two additional runaways, one of whom had previously known Solomon and Sara. Sara's band became acquainted with the slaves on Heijnkes's farm, and developed "a close association and fellowship" with them.[66] The runaways visited the slave lodge and ate with the slaves when Heijnkes had gone to sleep. In turn, Heijnkes's slaves visited the *droster* combination when given the slightest opportunity—on Sundays when they were sent to gather bark in the mountains, and when they were sent to look for missing horses or cattle. Not surprisingly, eight of Heijnkes's slaves decided to join the *droster* band. *Droster* bands were usually based on established social connections and networks.

The enlarged group returned to the Goudini mountains. Along the way, they were joined by four more slaves—Apollos and Ram from Bengalen, December and Toppi whose origins the court did not note. Having been in the Goudini mountains for about three weeks, the maroon community was discovered and its members taken captive. According to the court, the "other absconders, having scattered," were not apprehended.[67] We do not know what happened to those who managed to escape capture, but it is possible that they rebuilt their dissident community in some form, although significantly depleted.

Other *droster* bands to be found in the archive were much smaller—for instance, Pero from Mauritius and fellow deserters, who appeared in court in 1781.[68] When

Pero initially absconded, he joined a *droster* band of about six members who roamed the "Cape Dunes." For reasons unknown he decided to leave this group and made his way to Table Mountain, where he joined another *droster* band, consisting of twelve men and one woman. Together they robbed a cottage situated on Leeukop, taking bedding, clothes, and cash. They then traveled to Cape Town, where they successfully sold the stolen goods, dividing the money between them.

Court records reveal that *droster* bands were variable in composition and tactics. For instance, the Hanglip maroon under Leander did not include Khoesan, while Sara's band did. Ross claims that Leander's band was violent toward slaves on farms, but Sara's band formed a close association with other farm slaves in service and enticed them to join. In spite of such differences, *droster* bands also shared a number of common characteristics. They were relatively small and fluid—members came and went, some were captured, others decided to go their own way, and new deserters joined. These *droster* combinations moved around and were quite mobile. Sara's combination appeared to move about in a particular area while other runaways, such as Pero, traveled longer distances and joined *droster* bands in different locales, raising the question of whether groups communicated over distance.

Ross argues that from the 1800s a more stable maroon community took root at Hanglip.[69] These deserters were apparently anglers who were able to sustain and reproduce themselves based on fishing and selling their catch. This was perhaps an important departure as other *droster* combinations relied on hunter-gathering, the support of slaves and servants still in service, and pilfering from the colony for subsistence. The runaway fishermen were probably a smaller, more flexible, more mobile group, but they were also necessarily connected to outsiders on whom they depended to buy and sell their catch. Once a *droster* band was able to establish a reliable and independent mode of subsistence, it could grow into a more stable and larger community.

Droster bands were mainly slaves but they did include other kinds of workers. For instance, in response to the March 1736 fire set by Leander's band in Cape Town, the council ordered a commando to round up deserters—both slaves and Europeans—hiding in the mountains.[70] In the early 1800s a mixed *droster* band may have hid out at Green Point, near Cape Town. It was here that James Hooper, deserted sailor, Michael Kelly, deserted soldier, and Abraham from the Cape, deserted slave, appear to have taken refuge before they plotted the 1808 revolt against slavery.[71]

A second type of fugitive community in the history of runaways was the borderland band. Unlike *droster* bands, these bands were preexisting communities that included—sometimes actively welcomed or recruited—runaways and vagabonds. Borderland bands can be further divided into commando-type bands and dissident raider bands, all situated in what has been called the "frontier zone." Marxist historian Martin Legassick argues that this zone was "a fluid region of social transition, relatively autonomous from both the colonial base and indigenous social systems, but dependent on both."[72] The frontier zone was characterized by the emergence of new social formations—and a great deal of violence.

The violence can mainly be attributed to the commando bands, which Legassick identifies as the major institution of the frontier. Commandos were military groups usually considered to be the preserve of white, free-burgher men. Yet, there were frontier commandos that were made up almost entirely of free-burghers' black dependents, *Oorlam* and *Bastaards*.[73] Unscrupulous free-burghers also hired runaways of different races and ethnicities to seize livestock and land.[74] These commando bands served as militarized hunting and trading parties involved in coercive trade, raiding the cattle of surrounding Khoesan communities, and extending the colony north and east by occupying new land. Jan Bloem, a runaway sailor, and Klaas Afrikaaner, an *Oorlam,* established the best known of these bands.[75] For a time, they supplied the wealthy free-burgher Petrus Pienaar with the cattle they raided in return for guns and ammunition. Both bands soon evolved into independent communities in their own right. Bloem became a powerful force in the Orange River region and acquired a following of disparate Khoe and San groupings, including the Kora, Kats, and Springbok clans. In the 1790s Afrikaaner established a new community on an island on the Orange River peopled by Khoesan and displaced (fugitive) Xhosa from the east. Afrikaaner and his sons continued to raid and hunt and ended up leading a social configuration that resembled a commando team of a frontier free-burgher. Yet Afrikaaners symbolized something more: "disaffected *Oorlam,* Khoikhoi and *Bastaards* joined the [their] ranks or attempted to emulate their attitude of aggressive independence."[76] No longer directly linked to free-burghers such as Pienaar or the colony, these commando bands evolved into significant new actors in the region.

The dissident-raider type of borderland band emerged from the 1690s onwards. These were bandits who attacked colonial free-burgher homesteads, VOC cattle stations, and Khoesan loyal to the colony, primarily in retaliation for earlier incidents of colonial plundering.[77] Marks notes that from an early stage, these bands of raiders were joined by runaway slaves and other runaway sailors and soldiers.[78] Indeed, deserted slaves who had stolen ammunition and guns were particularly important new recruits.

Raider bands had a similar motley social base—although it is difficult to draw any conclusions about the place and role of women without more research. Yet they also differed from commando-type bands in important ways. First, the conflict between indigenous groups on the borderland should not be read as a primordial battle over resources. Rather, the contestation between wealthier Khoe, many of whom were loyal to the free-burghers or the colony and formed the core of colonial commando-type bands like that of Bloem and Afrikaaner, and rebellious Khoesan bandits must be considered as a class-based response to social differentiation, accumulation of wealth, and political control, within the colonial Cape

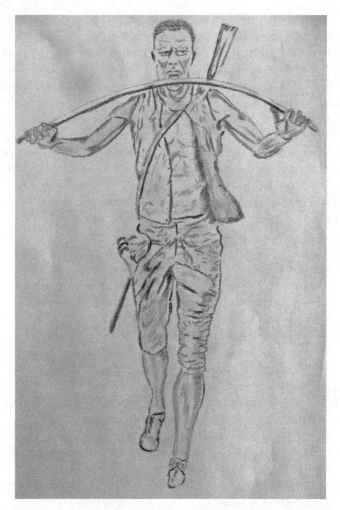

FIGURE 6.1. Bronze statue of Klaas Stuurman, "Long March to
Freedom," National Heritage Project Company, as drawn by Azile Cibi.

and the increasingly stratified Khoesan and African agrarian polities of the interior. Second, Marks argues that these raids were informed by an anticolonial
motive. For instance, in 1739 more than 100 raiders, some of them armed, attacked
Piquetberg, the Bokkeveld and Lange Valley and stole 400 head of cattle and 2,400
sheep.[79] An interpreter explained that the aim of the raid was "to chase the Dutch
out of their land as long as they lived in their land."[80]

Marks also notes that raids increased again in the 1770s, just as free-burghers
gained new ground and Khoesan communities faced additional pressure from

Xhosa moving west to establish Kora and Tswana groups on the Orange River.[81] Raider bands increased in size; some were several hundred strong. Little is known about how these raiders organized themselves and operated internally. It is known that their growing size can partly be attributed to the "escape[d] slaves, white deserters and Khoi servants" who joined and swelled their ranks.[82]

Droster bands and borderland bands sometimes intersected. For instance, Thomas from Bengalen baked 260 rusks as a gift for "Class Cok," who historians believe was the progenitor of Adam Kok, a manumitted slave who acquired land at Piketburg and provided a safe haven for runaway laborers, including slaves, Khoesan laborers, sailors, and soldiers.[83] Indeed, the records indicate that this group of runaways briefly joined what seems to have been a borderland band, and, in this way, was drawn into the hunter-raiding economy, attacking and robbing other communities in the region. Borderland bands remained a popular destination for deserters into the nineteenth century. When Governor Jan Willem Janssen journeyed across the Cape between 1803 and 1806, he "met in different places with six other English deserters. Some were concealed amongst the savages [presumably Khoesan], some among the colonists".[84]

"BUT THOMAS DIDN'T DIE"

Desertion had a common history across race, ethnicity, and labor type at the Cape under VOC rule. Running away was widespread, in both its individual and collective incarnation. Many runaways deserted in groups with the aim of leaving the Cape. Others remained within the colony, creating new social formations or joining fugitive communities on the borderland. The latter consisted of commando bands and new dissident raider communities. These bands contested colonial rule, especially its practices of dispossession and land enclosure.

The British empire occupied the Cape (1795–1803 and again from 1806–13) to protect its political and commercial interests in the Indian Ocean region during the Revolutionary and Napoleonic Wars. In 1814, the Dutch officially ceded the Cape to the British. This moment marked the start of a new, more intensive phase of imperialism and global capitalism. The new colonial officials in the Cape were keen to ameliorate some of the more violent excesses related to labor control and discipline, to curb movement of laborers, and to bind them more firmly to their masters and mistresses. Yet unfree forms of labor persisted. Slavery would not be officially abolished until 1838.

Within this context, laborers at the Cape developed new repertoires of resistance and a new language of rights. Desertion continued as a common form of protest and indeed soon took on a profound "national" form. Just north of the Cape colony, *Bastaards,* runaways slaves, sailors and soldiers, and indigenous Khoesan formed their own nation and adopted the name "*Griqua*" to claim a common ancestor and heritage.[85] The Kok family had long incorporated runaways and played a key role in the creation of the *Griqua*. On the eastern reaches of the colony we see a more proletarian response. Mainly Khoesan laborers and some slaves deserted their masters in large numbers and joined large raider bands massing on the borderland. These laborers believed that their class and colonial oppression were intimately linked. The best remedy to indenture and violent abuse was, in the words of one of the rebel captains, Klaas Stuurman, to reclaim "the country of which our fathers were despoiled by the Dutch," and to fight for their independence from their Boer masters.[86] By the end of July 1799 raider bands were in control of the whole southeastern portion of the Graaf-Reinet district. Although this rebellion dissipated in 1803, the "Servants" Rebellion was a major anticolonial revolt that emerged from a long history of desertion. For a brief moment it succeeded not only in halting the latest colonial encroachments, it also managed to push back the colonial border.

NOTES

EPIGRAPH: "Ballad of a Mutiny," from the *Cargo* soundtrack, can be found on Neo Muyanga's 2007 album *Fire, Famine, Plague and Earthquake.*

1. Western Cape Provincial Archives [hereafter WCPA], Council of Justice [hereafter CJ], 318 Criminele Process Stukken, 1714, ff. 90–97, translated in Nigel Worden and Gerald Groenewald, *Trials of Slavery: Selected Documents Concerning Slaves from the Criminal Records of the Council of Justice at the Cape of Good Hope, 1705 1794* (Cape Town: Van Riebeeck Society, Second Series, No. 36, 2005), 21–22.

2. Ibid.

3. The term "single-category history" comes from Nigel Worden (see Introduction in *Contingent Lives: Social Identity and Material Culture in the VOC World* (Cape Town, Pretoria: Historical Studies Department, University of Cape Town and Royal Netherlands Embassy, 2007).

4. Shula Marks, "Khoisan Resistance to the Dutch in the Seventeenth and Eighteenth Centuries," *Journal of African History* 13, no. 1 (1972): 55–80; Richard Elphick and Vertrees C. Malherbe, "The Khoisan to 1828," in *The Shaping of South African Society, 1652–1840*, ed. Richard Elphick and Herman Giliomee, 2nd ed., 3–65 (Cape Town: Maskew, Miller and Longman, 1989). An important set of qualifiers need to be entered here relating to the terms used to refer to indigenous Khoesan laborers. The use in recent decades of "San" (in place of "Bushman") and "Khoe"/"Khoi" (for "Hottentot") was meant to contest the derogatory colonial terminology used for the nonagricultural indigenous African peoples of the Cape, dating back to Company rule. From the 1970s, both revisionist-Marxist and liberal scholars have contested the idea that "Khoe" and "San" were racially separate—each at a different level of "civilization"—and argued that these groups should rather be distinguished on the basis of their way of life. The Khoe were, in this reading, pastoralists and owned cattle, while the San were hunter-gatherers, who did not. These historians also noted that the groups were not static: whether due to environmental crisis, or colonial expansion and violent competition over the control of the meat/cattle trade, some San were able to acquire cattle (becoming "Khoe"), while increasing numbers of Khoe lost their stock (becoming "San"). Thus the distinction between the "Khoe" and "San" broke down, leading to a preference for the term "Khoesan" as a way of grouping the two. While revealing, and an important advance, such revisions still beg the question of what constituted "Khoe" or "San" or indeed "Khoesan" as these groups were integrated into the colony's labor systems during the 1700s, and, in so doing, became

increasingly connected to other laborers and the poor in the colony. The complexity of the "Khoesan"' category clearly goes well beyond the fact that the "Khoe" and "San" distinction is blurred.

5. Robert Ross, *Cape of Torments: Slavery and Resistance in South Africa* (London: Routledge and Kegan Paul, 1983).

6. Ross, *Cape of Torments,* 6.

7. Ross, *Cape of Torments,* 10.

8. Ross, *Cape of Torments,* 61.

9. Worden and Groenewald, *Trials of Slavery,* 21.

10. Kate Ekama, "Just Deserters: Runaway Slaves from the VOC Cape, c. 1700–1800," in *Desertion in the Early Modern World: A Comparative History,* ed. Matthias van Rossum and Jeanette Kamp (London: Bloomsbury, 2016), 161–86, 161.

11. Ekama, "Just Deserters," 167.

12. See Robert Shell, *Children of Bondage: A Social History of the Slave Society at the Cape of Good Hope, 1652–1838* (Johannesburg: University of the Witwatersrand Press, 2001), 285–330.

13. For discussions on gender and slavery in the Cape see Pumla Gqola, "Like Three Tongues in One Mouth: Tracing the Elusive Lives of Slave Women in (Slavocratic) South Africa," in *Women in South African History: Basus'iimbokodo, Bawel'imilambo / They Remove Boulders and Cross Rivers,* ed. Nomboniso Gasa (Cape Town and Pretoria: HSRC, 2007); Pamela Scully, *Liberating the Family? Gender and British Slave Emancipation in the Rural Western Cape, South Africa, 1823–1853* (Cape Town: David Philip, 1997); Carla Tsampiras, " 'Stubborn Masculine Women,' Violence, Slavery, the State, and Constructions of Gender in Graaf-Reinet, 1830–1834," *Radical History Review* 126 (2016); Patricia van der Spuy, "What Then Was the Sexual Outlet for Black Males? A Feminist Critique of Quantitative Representations of Women Slaves at the Cape of Good Hope in the Eighteenth Century," *Kronos* 23, no. 1 (1996): 43–56; Patricia van der Spuy, " 'Making Himself Master': Galant's Rebellion Revisited," *South African Historical Journal* 34 (1996): 1–28.

14. See for instance Nicole Ulrich, "Cape of Storms: Rethinking Popular Protest in Eighteenth-Century South Africa," *New Contree* 73 (2015): 16–39; and "Popular-Community in Eighteenth-Century Southern Africa: Family, Fellowship, Alternative Networks, and Mutual Aid at the Cape of Good Hope, 1652–1795," *Journal of Southern African Studies* 40, no. 6 (2015): 1139–57.

15. Marcus Rediker, *Between the Devil and the Deep Blue Sea: Merchant Seamen, Pirates and the Anglo-American Maritime World, 1700–1750* (Cambridge: Cambridge University Press, 1993).

16. A. Sparrman, *A Voyage to the Cape of Good Hope, towards the Antarctic Polar Circle, around the World and to the Country of the Hottentots and the Caffers from the Year 1772 -1776,* vols. I and II, ed. V. S. Forbes (Cape Town: Van Riebeeck Society, Reprint Series, 2007), I:102.

17. H. F. Heese, *Reg en Onreg: Kaapse Regspraak in die Agtiende Eeu,* C-Reeks: Narvorsingspublikasies, No. 6 (Bellville: Insituut vir Histories Narvorsing, Universiteit van Wes-Kaapland, 1994).

18. These records provide a stable, and more manageable, base of analysis. Nevertheless, court records are limited by significant gaps. They do not include temporary absences or desertions punished directly by masters and commanders. This means that the scale of desertion is vastly *underestimated.* In addition, fugitive communities (created or composed by deserters) operated beyond the reach of colonial authority and are not well documented. Our view of fugitive communities remains opaque.

19. See Peter Linebaugh and Marcus Rediker, *Many-Headed Hydra: Sailors, Slaves, Commoners and the Hidden History of the Revolutionary Atlantic* (Boston: Beacon Press, 2001).

20. This point about linking the reproductive role of the Cape to capitalism was drawn to my attention by Calvin Jordan. See "The English East India Company and the British Crown: c. 1795–1803, the First British Occupation at the Cape of Good Hope" (master's thesis, Rhodes University, 2018).

21. Wayne Dooling, "Social Identities and the Making of Private Property: The Cape and Lagos Colony Compared," in *Contingent Lives: Social Identity and Material Culture in the VOC World,* ed.

Nigel Worden (Cape Town and Pretoria: Historical Studies Department, University of Cape Town and Royal Netherlands Embassy, 2007), 266–78.

22. On free-burghers see Gerald Groenewald, "Kinship, Entrepreneurship and Social Capital: Alcohol Pachters and the Making of a Free-Burgher Society in Cape Town, 1652–1795" (PhD diss., University of Cape Town, 2009); Lenard Guelke, "Freehold Farmers and Frontier Settlers, 1657–1780," in Elphick and Giliomee, *Shaping of South African Society*, 66–108; Laura Mitchell, *Belongings: Property, Family, and Identity in Colonial South Africa* (New York: Columbia University Press, 2009)

23. Richard Elphick and Herman Giliomee, "The Origins and Entrenchment of European Dominance at the Cape, 1652–c. 1840," in Elphick and Giliomee, *Shaping of South African Society*, 534.

24. For more detail on the urban economy see Nigel Worden, Elizabeth van Heyningen, and Vivian Bickford-Smith, *Cape Town: The Making of a City: An Illustrated History* (Cape Town: David Philips, 2004).

25. The most comprehensive studies of slavery and this sector include Nigel Worden, *Slavery in Dutch South Africa* (Cambridge: Cambridge University Press, 1985) and Shell, *Children of Bondage*.

26. Low-ranking Company servants were permitted to become *pasgangers*, which meant that they were allowed to pay others to take over their usual duties while they earned extra money by engaging in a wide range of activities ranging from wig-making to carpentry. Many were also employed to teach burghers' children or serve as *knechten* (farm supervisors / overseers).

27. See Guelke, "Freehold Farmers and Frontier Settlers," 66–108.

28. Elphick and Malherbe, "Khoisan to 1828," 27.

29. James Armstrong and Nigel Worden, "The Slaves, 1652–1834," in Elphick and Giliomee, *Shaping of South African Society*, 123.

30. Ekama, "Just Deserters," 164.

31. Worden et al., *Cape Town*, 49.

32. Worden, *Slavery in Dutch South Africa*, 11.

33. Adrien Delmas, "The Role of Writing in the First Steps of the Cape Colony: A Short Enquiry into the Journal of Jan van Riebeeck (1652–1662)," in Worden, *Contingent Lives*, 500–512, 500.

34. Armstrong and Worden, "Slaves," 158; Ekama, "Just Deserters," 163.

35. Resolutions of the Council of Policy of the Cape, 1752–1795 [hereafter C], transcribed and digitized by Towards a New Age of Partnership, Nationaal Archief, The Hague [hereafter TANAP], C. 155, 90–139, 18 March 177 (TANAP, C151–160, 339).

36. WCPA, CJ 33, *Criminele Regtsrolle*, 1751, ff. 3–3, translated in Worden and Groenewald, *Trials of Slavery*, 287.

37. WCPA, CJ 34, *Criminele Regtsrolle*, 1752, ff. 28–30, translated in Worden and Groenewald, *Trials of Slavery*, 303–4.

38. Linda Mbeki and Matthias van Rossum, "Private Slave Trade in the Dutch Indian Ocean World: A Study into the Networks and Backgrounds of the Slavers and Enslaved in South Asia and South Africa," *Slavery and Abolition* 38, no. 1 (2017): 95–116.

39. WCPA, CJ 347 *Criminele Process Stukken*, 1742, ff. 18–19v, translated in Worden and Groenewald, *Trials of Slavery*, 213.

40. WCPA, CJ 2961 *Minuut Justitieële Attestatiën, Actens* etc., 1706, ff. 73–76, translated in Worden and Groenewald, *Trials of Slavery*, 7–9.

41. WCPA, CJ 2961 *Minuut Justitieële Attestatiën, Actens* etc., 1706, ff. 73–76, translated in Worden and Groenewald, *Trials of Slavery*, 8.

42. Worden and Groenewald, *Trials of Slavery*, 5.

43. WCPA, CJ 786, *Sententiën*, 1736 -1743, ff. 377–83, translated in Worden and Groenewald, *Trials of Slavery*, 210.

44. Worden, *Slavery in Dutch South Africa*, 132–33.

45. CJ 782, 53 in Heese, *"Reg en Onreg,"* 224 and M. Paulse, "Escape from Constantia," UWC, South African Contemporary Society and Humanities Seminar, Paper No. 21 (African Studies Library, University of Cape Town, 2004), published as "'We are free, you are slaves. Come on, let's run away': Escape from Constantia, 1712," *New Contree* 69 (2014): 26–44.

46. Paulse, "Escape from Constantia," 34–35.

47. Nigel Penn, "Great Escapes: Deserting Soldiers during Noodt's Cape Governorship," in Worden, *Contingent Lives*, 573, 574.

48. WCPA, CJ 797.6, *Sententiën* (translated by Maureen Rall).

49. Ibid.

50. Ibid.

51. WCPA CJ 795, *Sententiën*, 1782–1789, ff. 376–406, translated in Worden and Groenewald, *Trials of Slavery*, 547.

52. WCPA CJ 795, *Sententiën*, 1782–1789, ff. 376–406, translated in Worden and Groenewald, *Trials of Slavery*, 550.

53. For more on the concept of piratical seizures see Ian Duffield, "Cutting Out and Taking Liberties: Australia's Convict Pirates," *International Review of Social History* 21, no. 58 (2013): 197–228.

54. For an account see Johan Jacob Saar in R. Raven-Hart, *Cape Good Hope / 1652–1702 / The First 50 Years of Dutch Colonisation as Seen by Callers* (Cape Town: A. A. Balkema, 1971), 58–67.

55. Saar, *Cape Good Hope / 1652–1702*, 64.

56. Kerry Ward, "'The Bounds of Bondage': Forced Migration from Batavia to the Cape of Good Hope during the Dutch East India Company Era, c. 1652–1795" (PhD diss., University of Michigan, 2002), 261–69.

57. Groenewald and Worden, *Trials of Slavery*, 355 (summary of case: 1760 Achilles van de West Cust); see also M. Cairns, "The Smuts Family Murders," *CARBO* 2, no. 3 (1980): 13–16.

58. WCPA, CJ 789, 1756–70, ff. 268–93, translated in Worden and Groenewald, *Trials of Slavery*, 371.

59. Penn, *Rogues, Rebels and Runaways*, 150–51.

60. Elphick and Malherbe, "Khoisan to 1828," 10.

61. Ross, *Cape of Torments*, 54.

62. Ross, *Cape of Torments*, 54–72.

63. Western Cape Provincial Archive [WCPA], South Africa, Council of Justice [CJ], *Sententiën*, 794.17 (translated by Maureen Rall).

64. WCPA, CJ, *Sententiën*, 794.17 (translated by Maureen Rall).

65. Ibid.

66. Ibid.

67. Ibid.

68. WCPA, CJ, *Sententiën* 794.22 (translated by Maureen Rall).

69. Ross, *Cape of Torments*, 69.

70. Ross, *Cape of Torments*, 54.

71. WCPA, CJ 516, first examination of Michael Kelly; first examination of Abraham.

72. Martin Legassick, "The Northern Frontier to c. 1840: The Rise and Decline of the Griqua People," in Elphick and Giliomee, *Shaping of South African Society*, 358–420, 360.

73. As explained by Legassick, "Northern Frontier," 369–70, the *Oorlam* were Khoesan who had lost their cattle and attached themselves to frontier free-burgher families as dependents in return for cattle, a horse, and a gun. *Bastaards* were usually Khoesan of mixed parentage (European or slave) or trusted servants and overseers (including slaves and Khoesan) who occupied a higher status than other laborers and who were able to secure some autonomy by occupying (but not necessarily owning) some land. *Bastaards,* who were Christian and spoke Dutch, gravitated to less menial jobs and established themselves as transport riders or small farmers.

74. Legassick, "Northern Frontier," 368.

75. See Legassick, "Northern Frontier," 369, 374, and Penn, *Forgotten Frontier,* 72, 175, 187–201.

76. Penn, *Forgotten Frontier,* 201

77. Marks, "Khoisan Resistance," 70.

78. Ibid.

79. Ibid.

80. Ibid.

81. Marks, "Khoisan Resistance," 73.

82. Ibid.

83. Worden and Groenewald, *Trials of Slavery,* 34. And for Kok see Legassick, "Northern Frontier," 372.

84. Henry Lichtenstein, *Travels in Southern Africa, in the years 1803,1804,1805,1806,* vols. I and II (British and Foreign Public Library, 1815), I:391.

85. Legassick, "Northern Frontier," 382.

86. Susan Newton King, "Part I The Rebellion of the Khoi in Graaf-Reinet: 1799–1803," in Susan Newton King and Vertrees C. Malherbe, *The Khoikhoi Rebellion in the Eastern Cape (1977–1803)* (Cape Town: Centre for African Studies, 1981), 20.

7

Running Together or Running Apart?

Diversity, Desertion, and Resistance in the Dutch East India Company Empire, 1650–1800

Matthias van Rossum[1]

"BIRDS OF EQUAL FEATHERS"

"In that way [they] had come together as four birds of equal feathers and settled on the mountain of Oenewatte."[2] Describing the group of men accused of desertion and theft in May 1777, Gerrit Joan de Moor, *fiscaal* of Galle, one of the key settlements of the Dutch East India Company (VOC) on Ceylon (Sri Lanka), explicitly referred to the diversity of these runaways who nevertheless acted as if they were "of equal feathers." The runaways differed not only in their geographical origins, but also in their place in society.

The first of the runaways, the Sinhalese Haberelege Babe, was a convict from Ceylon, who had "broken out of prison and ran away." The second, Alie from Maccassar, was not native, but had been sent as a convict to Trinconomale in 1774. He "had fled from there together with three other exiled convicts and returned to here [Galle] via Matura."[3] Alie seems to have been the only one of this group who went to Galle; the other convicts remained in the "Maturese lands." The third member of the group, Kupido from Ternaten, had been a slave to the assistant Jakob Pietersz. By his own account, he had fled "because his master did not provide sufficient food, but did not want to sell him either."[4] The fourth runaway was also from Southeast Asia. Fortuijn from Samarang, however, had previously been a *caffer*. Although *caffers* were often themselves slaves or (former) convicts, they occupied a very distinct position, serving as early modern (urban) police forces under the authority of the *fiscaal*.[5]

This group was joined by at least three other runaways. Rejap from Samarang (roughly 25 years old) and Simon from Batavia (30–35 years) had been employed as convicts in the public works of Galle. Kahar from Ankien, however, had been a *moquadon* or overseer at public works. There he supervised and controlled convicts like Rejap and Simon, but also local corvée workers such as Haberelege, who were put to work by the VOC for not living up to their corvée labor obligations. The differences in the social origins of the runaways are telling. Although some of the runaways may have known each other from the streets and workplaces of Galle, they certainly did not have "equal feathers" before they decided to run. They came from different places throughout South and Southeast Asia, and lived and worked in the different and often conflicting condition of slave, convict, watchman, and overseer. After their escape, however, they lived as runaways on the mountain of Oenewatte and cooperated as a highly diverse group of runaways, transgressing earlier boundaries of social position, hierarchy, and ethnicity.

This essay explores the dynamics of labor conflict, desertion, and diversity among a VOC workforce of sailors, soldiers, corvée workers, and slaves from different parts of the globe. It studies patterns of cooperation and exclusion through the lenses of the lines of differentiation drawn during individual and collective acts of desertion and related deviant strategies. It does so based on the use of court records to study (everyday) interactions through a kind of global subaltern social history as proposed in my study of Asian and European VOC sailors and the ongoing project "Resilient Diversity."[6] In their classic study, Linebaugh and Rediker situated early "labor radicalism" in a proto-proletarian "multi-ethnic class" of sailors, port workers, slaves, and runaways in the Atlantic of the seventeenth and eighteenth centuries.[7] In response to this, a new historiography has turned the Atlantic region into the main area of investigation for maritime and labor radicalism. The effect of such studies on the Indian Ocean region has been more limited, resulting in a (perceived) dichotomy between a "peaceful Indian Ocean world" and a "revolutionary Atlantic."[8] The historiography of the VOC and its labor relations fits this pattern: the world of labor in the VOC is portrayed as relatively tranquil with low levels of both individual and collective conflict.[9]

Jan Lucassen, for example, has pointed out that among European and Asian workers under the VOC "collective actions were rare."[10] Herman Ketting argued that life among VOC sailors was not marked by a class or oppositional culture, nor by radical collective actions.[11] According to Ketting, only "once in the four weeks an incident occurred, and only once every eight weeks labor conditions and authority were challenged" during intercontinental voyages of the VOC.[12] Individual strategies such as patronage and career-making to improve labor conditions were more important as "crews acted less often as a collective" in labor conflicts.[13] Similar perspectives appear in the Dutch history of slavery in Asia, where the level of slave resistance is said to be low and that "large or even . . . medium-scale" slave

FIGURE 7.1. Crew of a Dutch East
Indiamen, Jan Brandes, 1778–1787.

revolts were nearly absent. This situation is explained by strong relationships of power and the high degrees of diversity of the slave populations.[14]

More recently, however, several studies have stressed the importance of the inherently violent character of the operations of the VOC with regard to other states, local populations, and everyday life, for example in the context of slavery or shipboard life.[15] Other studies have begun to discover a previously understudied world of resistance among workers of the VOC: uprisings, collective labor conflicts, and desertion.[16] This challenges existing arguments about the lack of labor conflicts, but also questions the dynamics of ethnic, linguistic, and occupational boundaries. This chapter focuses on individual and collective acts of desertion within VOC labor regimes that combined contract, corvée, convict, and slave labor. As strategies of desertion were intimately related to the wider range of collective strategies, this begs the question how lines of solidarity were drawn. This chapter, therefore, explores how workers related to each other during moments of revolt and desertion, contributing to the writing of a global history of desertion, as well as to the revision of the history of diversity, desertion, and labor under the VOC.

DIVERSITY, COERCION, AND LABOR IN THE DUTCH
EAST INDIA COMPANY EMPIRE

Throughout its Eurasian empire, the VOC employed large numbers of sailors, soldiers, and other workers engaged in construction, maintenance, warfare, control, and the production and transport of goods.[17] At its height in the middle of the eighteenth century, the Company directly employed some 57,000 workers.[18] Casual wage workers, such as the *coolies* of Batavia and the shipwrights of Amsterdam, worked together on a daily basis without penal sanctions to enforce their labor contract.[19] Yet these workers in casual wage labor relations formed a small part of the Company's workforce. The VOC exercised stricter control over contract wage workers, slaves, corvée, or tributary laborers.[20] Convict labor was a smaller part of the overall workforce, but played a crucial role in enforcing discipline and control.[21] Convicts labored in the public works of the various settlements and on convicts' islands in the rope factory of Edam, the wharves of Onrust and Allelande, and the shores of Robben Island and Rosingain where they collected shells, stone, and wood.[22]

The VOC recruited most Asian sailors and soldiers and almost all European workers through wage labor contracts.[23] They also bought slaves and used them mainly for transportation and other work in and around the settlements.[24] They employed corvée workers primarily in agricultural production, transportation, and military work in and around settlements on Ceylon and later increasingly in rural Java. Thousands of local Asian corvée workers were obligated to labor for the VOC for part of each year, sometimes for as much as four months.[25] Such workers included *coelies* (carriers, general workers), *chalias* (cinnamon peelers), and *lascorins* (soldiers).

Despite important differences in position, treatment, opportunities, and (self-) perception, contract, slave, convict, and corvée workers under the VOC shared one crucial characteristic. All were obligated to work for the Company by a variety of laws that restricted their mobility and dictated their work—its duration, conditions, and compensation. Legal arrangements varied from contract, to conviction, to obligated labor services, to slavery. Constraints were obvious for the slave, corvée worker, and convict, but less so for workers who engaged in contractual labor. Yet even these workers were not free *during* the contract period.[26] This was true for both hundreds of thousands of European sailors and soldiers shipped from Europe to Asia and for the thousands of Asian sailors and soldiers recruited in Asia.[27] The legal and physical constraints that resulted from the different coercive labor regimes of the VOC show remarkable similarities across labor types. Contract, enslaved, and corvée workers could all be sentenced to convict labor for labor offenses, ranging from absence, desertion, theft, revolt, and other criminalized acts. As the runaways of Oenwatta demonstrated, workers from very different backgrounds could end up together as convicts.

FIGURE 7.2. Drawing of workers (presumably convicts) at work in Batavia, Cornelis de Bruyn, ca. 1701–1711.

LABOR, RESISTANCE, AND DESERTION IN
GLOBAL HISTORY

The expansion of the VOC was part of the complex and interrelated dynamics of global capitalism: expanding (labor) markets, intensifying mobility, and multiplying mechanisms of coercion. Runaways figure prominently in these histories and are key to understanding the processes at work. Although often less visible than the turbulent moments of outright resistance, running away was one of the crucial and widespread strategies of workers throughout history. The act of desertion has close connections to other strategies of resistance. And although seemingly less heroic than outright confrontation, desertion could at times have similar undermining effects, for example when flows of (small-scale or individual) desertion swelled to mass exits.

The connection between desertion and other forms of resistance is not only in the impact of such acts, but also in how different strategies were used by workers. In addition to running away, as temporary or permanent *exit,* workers could also opt for strategies in which workers stood up for themselves—*voice* (Hirschman)—or accommodated existing situations— *acquiescence* (in later reformulations of the trilogy).[28] Such strategies could be employed *individually* or *collectively.* Within this framework, desertion served not only as an act of defiance in which workers, either individually or collectively, rejected working conditions and power relations, but as a strategic act, variously aimed at the improvement of individual circumstances through social mobility and finding better jobs.[29] Desertion must, therefore, be studied both as *running from* as well as *running toward.*[30] One common pattern among soldiers was to collect the advances promised at recruitment and disappear before they had taken their oath. In the context of competing trading companies and armies, contract workers would desert to enlist with competing employers offering higher wages, better treatment, or career opportunities. Skilled workers, such as sailors, artisans, and even administrators or merchants, could gain by playing employers off each other despite the legal restrictions.[31] Some of these acts of desertion sometimes seem closer to the strategy of *voice* than that of *exit,* for example strategies that involved temporary absence that aimed to strengthen a protest or a bargaining position. At the same time, temporary absence could again be close to the strategy *acquiescence*; for example, instances in which workers stay away during drinking tours.

Authorities and employers defined unpermitted absence from work as a breach of law or labor obligation, creating a wide range of concepts of desertion, such as *desertie* (desertion), *absentie* (absence), and *fugie* (fleeing). There are commonalities in the different forms of running away, however, that argue for a broad and inclusive definition of desertion across restrictions and labor type. It is important to see desertion within a global and long-term history, not least because in most places across the world withdrawing oneself from the work process was a punishable offense well into the twentieth century.

Such an open definition should include labor relations in which the coercive and binding elements are highlighted (slave labor, corvée labor, convict labor), but also those in which the mobility of workers was constrained in other ways— through binding labor contracts (military, maritime, and colonial labor), domestic regimes and laws (servants in households), and apprenticeship systems.[32] Deser-

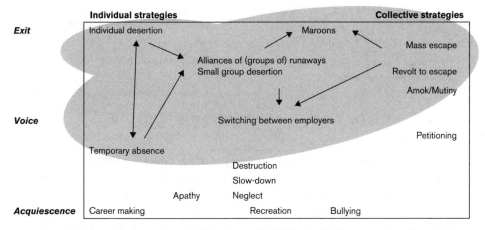

FIGURE 7.3. Forms of desertion (gray) and the range of individual and collective workers' strategies.

tion involved not only a large variety of workers, but the many regimes and actors seeking to control them, such as corporations, heads of household, urban and state governments. It is crucial to look at the refined mechanisms of the formal and informal regulatory regimes affecting peoples' mobility in both working and living environments.

Although authorities were preoccupied with preventing and punishing running away, definitions were not always as clear-cut as one might expect. The lines between temporary absence and more permanent forms of desertion were often fuzzy. Some degree of absence was tolerated, especially for contract workers.[33] Absence could turn into desertion if one remained away too long.[34] For slaves similar distinctions were employed, such as *petit marronage* (temporary absenteeism) and the permanent *grand marronage*.[35] Under the VOC, temporary absence by slaves was punished under domestic law, desertion by criminal courts.[36] Authorities actively struggled with such definitions and legal distinctions.[37]

The attempts of authorities and employers to counter or reduce desertion ranged from extreme punishments to refined mechanisms of control. Depending on the need for manpower or the need to strike fear among the remaining workforce, recaptured runaways could be sentenced to death or pardoned. More often, however, rulers inflicted severe painful physical punishment, but avoided lasting injuries that diminished work capacities. The VOC often sentenced captured runaways to years of convict labor. The prevention of desertion also relied on financial and administrative mechanisms created to entice the loyalty of workers via the regulation of payment, explicit forms of public social control (shaming deserters, branding convicts), the closure of working environments (forts, ships, plantations, mines) and the regulation of mobility and access to public and corporate spaces, through the use of passes, guards, and even "hunting systems."[38] These dynamics seem to have had a strong (segregating) impact on social, intercultural, and racial relations, especially in the context of European colonial expansion into non-European worlds.[39]

REVOLT AND RUNNING UNDER A "PEACEFUL" COMPANY

In contrast to existing claims on the peaceful relations under the Dutch East India Company, labor conflicts and collective acts of organized resistance occurred regularly, as indicated by the recently updated list of maritime mutinies on board ships of the VOC.[40] During the two centuries of its existence, the Company faced at least 53 maritime mutinies. On average, therefore, yearly about one out of the two hundred VOC ships was confronted with an outright mutiny. Mutinies occurred most often in intercontinental shipping, with peaks of yearly mutiny rates of almost 2 to 4 percent. Most of these mutinies occurred in the first half of the seventeenth century, reaching a level of unrest that would remain unparalleled throughout the history of the VOC. Unrest declined to an all-time low in the first half of the eighteenth century, and slowly rose in the middle of the eighteenth century to peak again in the 1780s and 1790s.

The diversity of the workforce of the VOC compels scholars to move beyond the study of mutinies and uprisings by sailors and soldiers, and to take into account individual and collective actions of Asian slaves, corvée, and convict workers as well. As all of these workers functioned under coercive labor regimes that restrained and criminalized behavior that conflicted with obligations and hierarchies, acts of revolts not only occurred frequently, but also indicate the close relation between desertion and strategies of collective resistance.

On Ceylon, corvée workers organized collective actions to back up their petitions and claims to the VOC in 1736–37, 1744–47, 1757–58, and 1783–90.[41] By collectively threatening to abandon cinnamon plantations or even to defect to the king of Kandy, the local competing power holding sovereignty over the inner parts of the island, Ceylon workers used desertion as a key strategy. Collective absence was also practiced on the Coromandel coast, where in September 1699 "part of the *patnams*" (villages) "had withdrawn themselves from the service of the Honourable Company and had hidden themselves here and there in the outer city" of Nagapatnam. The villagers disappeared from their (obligated) work in loading and unloading Company ships after four locals had been convicted of theft and exiled to the Cape of Good Hope. The leaders of local communities, as well as "several women, had very compellingly requested" to overturn the sentence of exile. The combination of worker holdout and negotiation was successful as the VOC gave in to the demands, because "it should be feared that the rest of the patnams would also disappear."[42]

For slaves, resistance was always tied closely to the possibility and need to escape. Slaves revolted—or plotted to revolt—on a range of VOC ships during the eighteenth century. Illegally transported slaves from South Sulawesi revolted just before the ship *Delfland* arrived at the Banda Islands in 1743. They managed to take over the ship, run it ashore, and disappear.[43] In 1766, slaves transported for the VOC from Madagascar to the Cape of Good Hope revolted on the *Meermin* and forced the crew to bring the ship to land, where they battled until ambushed by VOC militias. Balinese slaves being trained as sailors and soldiers revolted and hijacked the *Mercuur* in 1782. It took an armed VOC ship several days and multiple attacks to defeat the slaves, most of whom seem to have managed to escape after burning the ship in the Sunda Strait.[44] After this massive rebellion, the Company authorities were frightened by conspiracies of slaves to "run amok" on the ship *Slot ter Hoge* (1783). A violent uprising of Chinese sailors erupted on the *Java* in 1783, possibly planned in cooperation with the slaves on board. Another slave conspiracy jolted the *Haasje* in 1790.[45]

Uprisings and conspiracies were even more common on land. A slave conspiracy was uncovered on the island of Mauritius in 1706.[46] Shortly after, in 1710, a suspected slave uprising was prevented on the island of Banda Neira.[47] In 1715, a group of Balinese slaves revolted and fled from the work island Edam, used mainly as a detention island where convicts were employed in the rope factory. The history of Batavia is filled with slaves running amok, alone or collectively.[48] Some slaves ran amok while on the run, chased by masters, bystanders and soldiers.[49] Asian convicts plotted a revolt on Robben Island in 1751.[50] In 1772, Asian convicts revolted successfully on Edam, running away with one of the island's vessels. In 1781, Edam was again confronted with an uprising by Asian convicts.[51] Slaves and convicts tried to run away collectively from the farm Constantia at the Cape of Good Hope in 1712.[52] Runaway slaves, in turn, used violence to sustain themselves. In 1725–26, a gang of more than twenty slaves raided farms in the agrarian hinterland of Cape Town. A group of slaves who ran in 1713 was later captured during a raid in which they tried to steal cattle from Khoikoi.[53] Similar actions took place in Batavia, where slave runaways fled in groups and remained in hiding in the outer city or in the hills.[54] At Ambon, runaways engaged in robbery, while slaves who had not (yet) ran away planned acts of arson.

Runaways organized maroon communities, consisting mainly of former slaves, although occasionally other runaways (convicts, sailors, soldiers) seem to have joined. Such communities dotted the VOC empire. At Ambon, maroons established a community in the late seventeenth century and maintained themselves by robbery. In Batavia it was reported in 1677 that a group of three hundred deserters had attacked several villages near Crawang. The Company regularly sent out military expeditions to try to recapture bands of runaway slaves. At the Cape, a group of maroons existed at least from the 1720s until 1737 and perhaps later into the eighteenth century. A group of maroons also thrived in Mauritius during the early eighteenth century.[55]

WAVES OF DESERTION

Strategies of running were a major part of the resistance and negotiation under-taken by workers in the VOC world. Desertion rates could be high. During the eighteenth century, European workers ran from the VOC throughout Asia. The total number of Europeans who had originally been recruited in the Dutch Repub-lic deserting in different parts of the VOC empire rose to several hundred employ-ees per year in the 1740s to 1760s, and again in the 1780s and 1790s.[56] Thousands of newly recruited VOC workers in the Dutch Republic went absent at the moment of their departure to Asia, especially after 1745, rising to almost 4 percent of all recruits in the 1750s, and 6–8 percent in the 1780s and 1790s. Similarly, Asian con-tract workers, especially sailors and soldiers, were not hesitant to run during their work for the VOC, especially in South and Southeast Asia.[57] In 1741, governor Van Gollenesse recounted that "some 300 of [the *Lascorins*] deserted during the last campaign, and many of them took the Company's muskets with them."[58]

Thriving economic regions were prone to higher desertion rates. Surat, for example, was an important port city, where the VOC employed only a dozen of merchants and other VOC personnel in a small trading factory. Between April 1757 and May 1758, nevertheless, a total of thirty-two employees deserted from the VOC factory and ships. Reportedly, they all found employment with "foreign nations," "except for the sailor Pieter Davidsz, who went to the Moors," most likely to work in the service of local merchants or rulers.[59] By April 1759, another thirty-two VOC employees, mostly soldiers, some sailors and petty officers, had deserted from the factory and four anchored VOC ships.[60] From April 1759 until the end of April 1760, 103 VOC workers deserted at Surat, consisting of eighty soldiers, twenty sailors, a trumpeter, an artisan, and the petty officer in charge of provi-sions.[61] The year after, only nine employees deserted.[62] Between 1757 to 1759, around 5 percent of VOC employees absconded.[63] The following year the number rose to somewhere between 15 and 30 percent.[64]

European trading companies faced waves of desertion throughout their empires, especially in regions where a great demand for labor made it easy for workers to find employment outside the European settlements. In response European trading companies hired deserters from their competitors, making matters worse. For the VOC, Bengal—as well as Surat—was one of the main places where the Company lost its contract workers. Between 1754 and 1780, workers arriving on ships from Europe were much more likely to desert in Bengal than the workers arriving in Batavia and Ceylon, the two main destinations for VOC ships sailing from the

Dutch Republic. Desertion rates in Bengal within the first six months after arrival varied from 1 to 10 percent. In regions where the VOC exercised stronger control, such as Batavia and Ceylon, desertion rates among newly arriving workers within their first half year in Asia were much lower, ranging from 0.2 to 1 percent.[65]

Desertion was not restricted to the world of contract wage labor. Rates of desertion were often comparable or even higher among other groups of workers. On Ceylon, for example, corvée workers such as the "Moors" and "Chittijs" of Galle, Matura, and Belligam regularly absented themselves, individually and in small groups, from their obligated labor duties. In the 1750s, this resulted in desertion rates of 4 to 5 percent and at times as high as 7 percent. The scarce data on convicts suggests desertion rates were comparable, as 6.5 percent escaped from the public works of Galle in 1750. Slaves ran away much less, with fragmented data suggesting desertion rates of only 1 to 2 percent in this period. These rates are remarkable especially in relation to the different death rates for these groups: the scarce data indicates death rates of 6 percent for convicts, 2–3 percent for slaves, and only 1 percent for corvée workers. These differences seem to reflect the tough labor conditions of convicts and slaves, but also the differences in regimes of labor and control of slaves and convicts compared to corvée workers.[66]

COLLECTIVE AND INDIVIDUAL STRATEGIES

Running away was never a completely individualized act. Although individual desertions occurred everywhere, runaways almost always depended on the help of friends, relatives, intermediaries, or strangers and on temporary alliances with locals or, more often, other runaways. Running together did provide specific advantages over escaping alone.[67] Two important distinctions must be made here. First, the size of the group was important, varying from individuals, to pairs, to small groups and, finally, large groups. Second, desertions varied by the degree of planning: some were carefully worked out in advance while others were spontaneous or accidental. Desertion in small numbers—from pairs to roughly four to six runaways—seems to have provided sufficient support while still minimizing the risks of plans leaking out. Planned desertions by groups were more common where breaking out proved more challenging, for example in the case of slaves trying to get out of a city or soldiers running from forts.[68] Individual and paired desertions could quickly succeed each other, gradually turning small escapes into a wave of desertion. This in turn could lead to another type of desertion in which groups organized themselves afterwards.

The registers of deserters from VOC settlements in the southern parts of South Asia illuminate the patterns of desertion on the Coromandel and Malabar coasts of India and in Ceylon. In 1759, twenty-nine European and Asian workers escaped the settlements on the Coromandel coast. Most of them ran from the ship *Lycochton* while it was anchored near Bimilipatnam. The ten workers who left the ship made up roughly 15 percent of the crew.[69] The other runaways fled from forts and settlements along the coast: Bimilipatnam (three), Nagapatnam (eight), Pulicat (four), Sadraspatnam (two), and Jaggernaijkpoeram (two). Soldiers, eleven European and three Malayan or Javanese, led the way. Seven sailors joined in, followed by two tambours, a cook's mate, a corporal, and a quartermaster.[70] The *Oosterlingen* or Asian soldiers stationed at Bimilipatnam deserted together or shortly after one another: Laban from Malacca deserted on May 10, Samat from Batavia and Madi from Malacca deserted on June 10.

Company workers frequently deserted individually, or in small groups of two to five. Desertion by larger groups was less frequent. VOC personnel fled from urban working environments in significant numbers, while the military posts outside urban settlements provided even better opportunities to desert, especially for larger groups. From the post at Cape Comorin, for example, nine of the ten deserters in 1741 seem to have deserted with someone else. Others escaped the post in two pairs and a group of five.[71] From "the camp at Climanoer," two Dutch gunners deserted in late March. The camp "at Totocatte" was hit by an even larger wave of desertion. First, the soldier Jan Roedolf Goedknegt absconded from "Hogerswe" on April 3. The next day, three soldiers followed him: Jan Christiaan Schoghart from Lunenburg, Fredrik Lots from Coblenz, and Judocus van Mellefilloost from Gent. On April 8, the deserters were joined by a group of five German and Dutch soldiers. In early May, a group of six German, Dutch, and French soldiers fled from the "pagger [post] Zeeburg at Paroe."[72]

RESISTANCE AND INTERCULTURAL RELATIONS

If the success of running away depended on collaboration, what then was the influence of the large diversity of social and ethnic composition that marked the global and multicultural workforce of the VOC world? Were the "four birds of equal feathers" on the mountain of Oenewatte exceptional? How did different groups of workers relate to each other in individual and collective acts of desertion and related defiant strategies? Under what circumstances could boundaries of occupational, ethnic, and linguistic differences be transgressed? When was cooperation possible? The story of the motley group of runaways on Oenewatte mountain shows that workers from different occupations, positions, and groups could form alliances after their escape. What were the dynamics and limitations of workplace acts of resistance?

The impact of occupational and regional background on the dynamics of desertion seems to have been mixed. Boundaries could be transgressed and deserters did run in quite diverse coalitions. The waves of desertion from VOC posts in South Asia, as discussed earlier in this chapter, have provided various examples of groups escaping in various alliances. Europeans of various national backgrounds, from Northwest to South or Central Europe, deserted together. Non-European workers of different backgrounds also cooperated. The multiple escapes from the regiments at Bimilipatnam by soldiers from Malacca and Batavia seem to have been linked to each other. This was not exceptional as workplace or occupational commonalities could be stronger than differences in regional background. Sometimes other commonalities were at play. In 1739, for example, the Court of Justice of Cochin tried Hendrik Willemse from Ceylon, Sebastiaan Rosairo from Bengal, and Domingo de Cruz from Cochin, who had attempted to escape and "defect to the French." The men came from different parts of South Asia, but all were "Toepassen," meaning that they were Catholics of Portuguese-Eurasian descent. Before their escape, they assembled in "Bhaijpin" (Vypin, just opposite Cochin) and performed the rituals of Holy Communion at the house of the "Christen Coelij" (Christian coolie) Anthonij.[73]

The patterns of desertion among the diverse workers also indicate some limitations to the inclusiveness of groups of runaways. Non-Dutch laborers seem to have been more inclined to run with other non-Dutch, while Dutch (and European) workers ran more often with others like themselves. Likewise, sailors were inclined to run with other sailors, while soldiers usually ran with other soldiers. The runaways from the post at Cape Comorin in 1741 illustrate the pattern. On July 19, a group of five German and French soldiers deserted together. On September 27, the Dutch sailor Evert van der Heijden from Hoorn and quartermaster Willem Terwel from Zutphen escaped. On August 2, the soldiers Ustasitus Benedictus de Lanoij from "Annas" and Jan Jacob Christiaansz from Gelhausen fled.[74]

Mixed groups ran together regularly, but deserters with both European and Asian workers seem to have been exceptional. This in part reflected social and regional differences among workers, but also the way the VOC employed Europeans and Asians in distinct regiments of soldiers. Asian and European sailors worked together on board the same ships, but were employed in different crews. When multiple lines of differentiation corresponded, this increased the difficulty to transgress the boundaries of origin, language, free-unfree status, or labor category. Regional differences combined with social status (free-unfree) created a divide between European contract workers and Asian slaves that proved too big to bridge in acts of desertion or resistance.

The reverse, however, was also true, as specific commonalities could ease the creation of alliances across boundaries. In November 1758, the "Malleijts" (Malay) soldier Lambo Fortuijn was tried in Colombo for an attempt to escape with seven slaves. The slaves declared that Lambo had "asked them if they would not be inclined to run away to the King's territory [Kandy], as he was assured of a better and easier life there . . . and he offered to bring them there." The slaves were young, ranging from eight to sixteen years in age. The youngest slave, the Buginese Alexander, declared that Lambo had "promised him to raise him as his own child." The slaves agreed and ran with the soldier. They were a highly diverse group—Buginese, Madurese, and Amboinese—but all were from the Indonesian archipelago.[75]

Recent research on runaway slaves in Asia indicates that environment had an important impact on the dynamics of desertion. In smaller communities, slaves of different origins could work together in running away or sustaining a maroon community; this was much less common among those from larger urban communities. In densely populated Batavia, the ethnic origins remained much more important for runaway slaves. In 1760, for example, runaway slaves from various Indian and Chinese owners living in different parts of Batavia—ranging from the "southern outer city," the quarters outside the *Utrechtse Poort* and the Chinese campong—joined each other in a group that appears to have been organized around their common Butonese background.[76]

The information available on instances of individual or small-group desertions provides an interesting insight into the dynamics of differentiation and transgression, but such relations seem to have come under more pression during moments of collective action, ranging from attempts at collective escape, revolt, bargaining, or combinations of these. This was especially the case when occupational and ethnic lines overlapped (between slaves and contract workers, for example), but was also the case between for example European sailors and soldiers, as the case of the mutiny by the soldiers of the *Barbestein* (1786) seems to indicates. Such differences did not make cooperation completely impossible. Differences in ethnicity and nationality among European workers seem to have become less important in Asia, but divisions between Dutch and non-Dutch, especially German, workers could at times still remain to play a role. The mutiny on the *Nijenborg*, for example, was led by the "zwavelbende" (the "sulfur gang"), consisting of eleven German and three French crew members. During the uprising the rebels mobilized "ethnic" claims to rally comrades, shouting "Allons, Duytsche broeders valt aen, hout, smijt en steekt" ("Come, German brothers, attack, hold, strike and stab!"). The *Barbestein* soldiers employed "Luxembourg en haut" as a battle cry. Such Dutch-German divisions may have been strengthened by the hierarchical structures that stimulated patronage as a way to organize social mobility in VOC working environments. The patronage dynamics through which shipboard hierarchy was reproduced favored workers' assimilation to a common Dutch language and work culture. Workers who remained outside such circuits of patronage and career could face negative consequences through the closing of opportunities at social mobility and more importantly to increased exposure to the violence, abuse, and harsh discipline that characterized shipboard working life.[77]

During moments of collective desertion and revolt that involved mixed European and Asian crews, the most common strategy of such crews would be to aim to adopt a *neutral* stance toward the collective action taken by the "other" group— they tried to remain outside the conflict by not choosing sides for either the rebels or the authorities. In the case of the *Windhond* in 1733, for example, the Balinese soldiers on board stood back as European mutineers took over the ship in the Gulf of Persia. Some of the Balinese deserted the ship some days after the mutiny, but most stayed on board, reaffirming their loyalty only after all mutineers had abandoned the ship.[78] At the start of a mutiny of Balinese slave-sailors on the *Mercuur* in 1782, the Javanese and many of the European sailors and soldiers on board the vessel opted to stay out of the conflict and flee the ship to the nearby islands in the Bay of Batavia.[79]

The dynamics of cooperation and conflict among convicts and slaves differed from those of contract workers as the convict uprisings on the island of Edam in 1772 and 1779 demonstrate. Convicts who rose in the revolt of 1772 came from all over South and Southeast Asia: eleven came from Mandaar, seven from Ceram, three from Bali, two from Maccassar, two from Palembang, two from Malacca, and several others from Bantam, Calemongo, Indrapura, Sulthan Anam, Sumbauwa, Surat, and Tangerang.[80] Court documents identified thirteen convicts—three "Javanese," three "Moors," three "Buginese," two "Chinese," and two "peranakan Chinese" (of mixed Chinese and Southeast Asian descent).[81] These Asian convicts operated as a group, indicating that their life and experience as "Asian convicts" was stronger than their extreme diversity in social, geographical, and ethnic backgrounds. Their transethnic cooperation resulted in victory: 87 Asian convicts escaped with the *tanjongpoura* (small vessel) of the island.

There were, however, limits to convict solidarity in these revolts. Europeans convicts did not participate in either rebellion. On the contrary, in 1772 Asian convicts actively distrusted the European convicts, locking them in their sleeping quarters before they initiated their uprising.[82] Similarly, in cases involving slave revolt, some European contract workers (sailors, soldiers, and artisans) remained loyal to the VOC, refusing neutrality and helping to suppress the uprising. In the case of the *Meermin* in 1766, the European sailors repeatedly attacked the mutinous slaves. When in October 1779 the slave Singana of Mandaar protested by confining himself on the attic of a VOC building on the island Onrust, European artisans broke the bars from the window, attacked and confined Singana, and brought him before the court, to prevent him from running amok.[83]

The Dutch East India Company was not a peaceful bureaucratic merchant enterprise that met little resistance but rather a violent amphibious beast. The VOC created an empire that combined a range of coercive labor regimes, mobilizing Asian and European workers through labor contracts, convict sentences, enslavement, and corvée labor obligations. The coercive elements that figured prominently in these instruments were not a blunt tool, but rather refined mechanisms to control soldiers and sailors on multiannual contracts, local populations on corvée duties, and slaves and convicts in urban and rural environments. As a merchant imperialist in an increasing globalized arena, the VOC learned to play different categories of workers off of each other in its global search for both skilled and unskilled workers. European and Asian workers in different labor relations (contract, enslaved, corvée, and convict workers) worked alongside each other. Early modern capitalism thrived, therefore, not only on warfare, violent expansion, and coercive labor regimes, but also on the more refined interplay of the regulation of diversity and disciplining mechanisms of control.

Workers responded to their plight with uprisings and revolts, as well as by voting with their feet. All of these strategies aiming at *voice* or *exit* were marked by complex and pervasive dynamics of both solidarity and differentiation. The highly diverse workforce of the Dutch East India Company was not primarily preoccupied with racial or ethnic conflicts. This did not mean, however, that such differences did not play a role in resistance. Occupational, ethnic, and hierarchical boundaries shaped the individual and collective strategies employed by VOC workers. Such boundaries could be transgressed by individuals and small groups, but at the same time commonalities in terms of origin, occupation, or religion played a role in the formation of alliances as well as in the transgression of other boundaries. Small-group escape was often segmented according to the line of occupation (in the case of contract and corvée workers) or social status (slave, convict). Once workers had escaped, their differences melted away more easily, turning coalitions of runaways into "motley," open groups.

Boundaries between different groups played a more important role in collective actions, but here too some important distinctions can be observed between different kinds of workers and the situations they faced. Contract workers mainly formed alliances based on broad regional backgrounds. More specific boundaries could fade, but European sailors, Indian sailors, Javanese sailors, and Chinese sailors would mostly initiate collective actions on their own. European sailors could at times cooperate with European soldiers, but occupational lines could also cause tensions and conflict, especially when intersecting with ethnic divides. In situations where different groups of contract workers worked side by side, European and Asian sailors and soldiers tried to respect the collective actions of other groups by refusing to help the VOC authorities and remaining *neutral*. In situations where elements of coercion pressed more strongly on working and living conditions, acts of violence or escape were more often collective, and boundaries of social and ethnic categories tended to be overcome more easily. This was especially true for convicts and slaves. The uprisings of Asian convicts show how ethnic, linguistic, and regional boundaries could fade under circumstances of increased (work) pressures and coercion. The relation between Asian and European convicts in such moments of revolt was, in return, much more antagonistic. This closed down the neutral space that might otherwise have been occupied on VOC ships.

This chapter has shown that the imperial and capitalist expansion of the Dutch East India Company was met with ongoing resistance by diverse groups of workers who tried to escape, strike, bargain, mutiny, or run amok. All of these actions required collaboration or support, but underlying solidarities needed to emerge within a highly global and multicultural workforce. These acts suggest that differences among workers did not obstruct solidarity across group boundaries, but that the way solidarities and resistance played out were shaped by how lines of differentiation were transgressed, challenged, or sometimes deepened during specific moments of resistance. The profiteers of early modern imperial and capitalist expansion—such as the Dutch East India Company—responded by refining their strategies of division and control. The history of runaways is crucial to understanding a global contest between worker solidarity and resistance and the divisiveness of disciplinary techniques and racializing strategies. Runaways enable us to trace both the changing times as well as the alternatives that remained.

NOTES

1. This chapter was presented at the international workshops "Runaways: Desertion and Mobility in Global Labor History, c. 1650–1850" (Amsterdam, 22–23 October 2015; Pittsburgh, 4–5 May 2016) and builds upon an earlier historical-comparative initiative in the conference session, "Leaving Work across the World: Comparing Desertion in Early Modern Globalization, 1600–1800," at the European Conference of Global History (ENIUGH, Paris, September 2014). This chapter is therefore heavily indebted to the participants of these meetings and to the contributors to the book Matthias van Rossum and Jeannette Kamp, eds., *Desertion in the Early Modern World* (London: Bloomsbury, 2016).

2. Sri Lanka National Archives [SLNA], VOC Archives, Record Group 1, inv.nr. 6470.

3. SLNA 1/6470. Alie was roughly 30 years old.

4. SLNA 1/6470. Fiscal De Moor believed this to be a lie, adding "quasie" before this statement. Kupido was estimated at 40 years.

5. See G. Groenewald, "Panaij van Boegies: Slave—*Bandiet – Caffer*," *Quarterly Bulletin of the National Library of South Africa* 59 (2006): 591–609; H. E. Niemeijer, *Batavia: Een koloniale samenleving in de 17de eeuw* (Amsterdam: Uitgeverij Balans, 2005).

6. The research for this chapter is related to the projects *Between Local Debts and Global Markets: Explaining Slavery in South and Southeast Asia, 1600–1800* (Matthias van Rossum, International Institute of Social History, NWO Veni Grant, 2016–19) and *Resilient Diversity: The Governance of Racial and Religious Plurality in the Dutch Empire, 1600–1800* (Cátia Antunes, Ulbe Bosma, Karwan Fatah-Black and Matthias van Rossum, Leiden University and International Institute of Social History, NWO Vrije Competitie Grant, 2017–22). Many of the cases of this chapter have been found during my PhD research (*Werkers van de wereld*, 2014), indexing one-third of the court records of the *Raad van Justitie* (Court of Justice) of Batavia. This index will be completed in the *Resilient Diversity* project.

7. Peter Linebaugh and Marcus Rediker, *The Many-Headed Hydra: Sailors, Slaves, Commoners, and the Hidden History of the Revolutionary Atlantic* (New York: Verso 2000); Emma Christopher, *Slave Ship Sailors and Their Captive Cargoes, 1720–1807* (Cambridge: Cambridge University Press, 2006); Marcel van der Linden, "Labour History as the History of Multitudes," *Labour/Le Travail* 52 (2003): 235–44.

8. For sailors, the notion of a more cooperative (in contrast to European conflictive) atmosphere is prominent in M. Pearson, "Class, Authority and Gender on Early-Modern Indian Ocean Ships: European

and Asian Comparisons," *South African Historical Journal* 61, no. 4 (2009): 680–701. For enslaved, see note 14 below. There are, of course, important exceptions, for example in the work of Clare Anderson and in earlier collaborative projects on mutinies; see Niklas Frykman, Lex Heerma van Voss, and Marcus Rediker eds., *Mutiny and Maritime Radicalism in the Age of Revolution: A Global Survey* (Cambridge: Cambridge University Press, 2014). Recent studies into maritime radicalism include Aaron Jaffer, *Lascars and Indian Ocean Seafaring, 1780–1860: Shipboard Life, Unrest and Mutiny* (Rochester: Boydell Press, 2015).

9. An exception is the argument that mutinies and shipwrecks were the cause of the demise of the VOC in the second half of the eighteenth century; C. R. Boxer, *Jan Compagnie in oorlog en vrede* (Houten: De Boer Maritiem, 1977), especially the chapter "V(ergaan) O(nder) C(orruptie)?" Translated in English as C. R. Boxer, *Jan Compagnie in War and Peace, 1602–1799* (Hong Kong: Heinemann Asia, 1979). See also C. R. Boxer, *The Dutch Seaborne Empire* (London: Hutchinson, 1965).

10. Jan Lucassen, "A Multinational and Its Labor Force: The Dutch East India Company, 1595–1795," *International Labor and Working-Class History* 66, no. 2 (2004): 12–39, 31.

11. Herman Ketting, *Leven, werk en rebellie aan boord van Oost-Indiëvaarders (1595–1650)* (Amsterdam: Aksant, 2002). This argument is in line with Pablo E. Pérez-Mallaína, *Spain's Men of the Sea: Daily Life on the Indies Fleets in the Sixteenth Century* (Baltimore: Johns Hopkins University Press, 1998) and Lucassen, "Multinational."

12. Ketting, *Leven*, 203–4. Original: "eens in de vier weken een incident voordeed en dat ongeveer eens in de acht weken arbeid en autoriteit ter discussie werden gesteld."

13. Ketting, *Leven*, 295.

14. Kate Ekama points out the dominant character of this line of argument in the literature in her chapter "Just Deserters: Runaway Slaves from the VOC Cape, c. 1700–1800" in Van Rossum and Kamp, *Desertion*, 161–84; Markus Vink, "'The World's Oldest Trade': Dutch Slavery and Slave Trade in the Indian Ocean," *Journal of World History* 14, no. 2 (2003): 131–77; Robert Ross, *Cape of Torments: Slavery and Resistance in South Africa* (London: Routledge, 1983), 3–5.

15. Especially the work of Ewald Vanvugt has been dedicated to Dutch colonial atrocities: E. Vanvugt, *Nieuw Zwartboek van Nederland Overzee* (Amsterdam: Aspekt, 2011); Vink, "World's Oldest Trade"; Niemeijer, *Batavia*; Reggie Baay, *Daar werd iets gruwelijks verricht: Slavernij in Nederlands-Indië* (Amsterdam: Athenaeum, 2015); Matthias van Rossum, *Kleurrijke Tragiek: De geschiedenis van slavernij in Azië onder de VOC* (Hilversum: Verloren, 2015).

16. Ekama, "Just Deserters" and other chapters in Van Rossum and Kamp, *Desertion*. See also Matthias van Rossum, "'Amok!' Mutinies and Slaves on Dutch East Indiamen in the 1780's," *International Review of Social History* 58 (2013): 109–30; R. J. Guy, "First Spaces of Colonialism: The Architecture of Dutch East India Company Ships" (PhD diss., Cornell University, 2012); Van Rossum, *Werkers van de wereld* (Hilversum: Verloren, 2014); Van Rossum, "Chasing the Delfland: Slave Revolts, Enslavement, and (Private) VOC Networks in Early Modern Asia," in *Navigating History: Economy, Society, Science and Nature: Essays in Honor of Prof. Dr. C. A. Davids*, ed. P. Brandon (Leiden: Brill, 2018), 201–27.

17. Derived from Matthias van Rossum, "'Working for the Devil': Desertion in the Eurasian Empire of the VOC," Van Rossum and Kamp, *Desertion*, 127–60, 132–34.

18. Ibid., 133, for the most recent revised estimates, based on Jan Lucassen. Note that this number only refers to the workers directly employed by the VOC (slaves, contract and convict workers) and does not include the workers engaged via obligated corvée labor services.

19. In Batavia and Malacca, workers performing casual wage labor called *coeliewerk* could be free persons as well as slaves. On Ceylon, *coelie* services were often performed by corvée laborers. Elaborated in Matthias van Rossum, "Coolie Transformations: Uncovering the Changing Meaning and Labour Relations of Coolie Labour in the Dutch Empire (18th and 19th century)," in *Bonded Labour, Global and Comparative Perspectives (18th–21st Century)*, ed. S. Damir-Geilsdorf et al. (Bielefeld: Transcript, 2016), 83–102. For the Dutch Republic, see F. S. Gaastra, *De geschiedenis van de VOC* (Zutphen: Walburg Pers, 1991); Pepijn Brandon, *War, Capital, and the Dutch State (1588–1795)* (Leiden: Brill, 2015).

20. Van Rossum, *Werkers van der wereld.*

21. For more on this argument, see Matthias van Rossum, "The Dutch East India Company in Asia, 1595–1811," in *A Global History of Convicts and Penal Colonies,* ed. C. Anderson, 157–82 (Bloomsbury: London 2018).

22. Ibid.

23. This was not unusual in comparison to the Asian maritime labor market, following Van Rossum, *Werkers van der wereld,* and "The Rise of the Asian Sailor? Inter-Asiatic Shipping, the Dutch East India Company and Maritime Labour Markets (1500–1800)," in *Towards a New History of Work,* ed. S. Bhattacharya (New Delhi: Tulika, 2014), 180–213.

24. Vink, "World's Oldest Trade"; Nigel Worden, *Slavery in Dutch South Africa* (Cambridge: Cambridge University Press, 1985); Van Rossum, *Kleurrijke tragiek.*

25. SLNA, 1, 2758, nr. 22; 5906.

26. Jairus Banaji, *Theory as History: Essays on Modes of Production and Exploitation* (Chicago: Haymarket Books, 2011).

27. Van Rossum, *Werkers van der wereld.*

28. M. van der Linden, "Mass Exits: Who, Why, How?" in Van Rossum and Kamp, *Desertion,* 31–48.

29. This point has also been raised in Jeannette M. Kamp and Matthias van Rossum, "Introduction: Leaving Work across the World," in Van Rossum and Kamp, *Desertion,* 3–14.

30. Kamp and Van Rossum, "Introduction: Leaving Work"; J. M. Kamp, "Between Agency and Force: The Dynamics of Desertion in a Military Labour Market, Frankfurt am Main 1650–1800," in Van Rossum and Kamp, *Desertion,* 49–72.

31. Ibid.

32. See, for example, Alessandro Stanziani, *Bondage: Labor and Rights in Eurasia from the Sixteenth to the Early Twentieth Centuries* (New York: Berghahn Books, 2014); Stanziani, "Runaways: A Global History," in Van Rossum and Kamp, *Desertion,* 15–30.

33. Karwan Fatah-Black, "Desertion by Sailors, Slaves and Soldiers in the Dutch Atlantic, c. 1600–1800," in Van Rossum and Kamp, *Desertion,* 97–126; Pepijn Brandon, "'The Privilege of Using Their Legs': Leaving the Dutch Army in the Eighteenth Century," in Van Rossum and Kamp, *Desertion,* 73–96; Van Rossum, "Working for the Devil."

34. Kamp, "Agency and Force."

35. Fatah-Black, "Desertion."

36. Ekama, "Just Deserters."

37. This stems from Kamp and Van Rossum, "Introduction: Leaving Work," 8. For difficulties of employing definitions and legal distinctions by authorities, see Van Rossum, "Working for the Devil," 135–37.

38. Ibid. See also Fatah-Black, "Desertion"; Van der Linden, "Mass Exits"; Matthias van Rossum, "From Contracts to Labour Camps? Desertion and Control in South Asia," in Van Rossum and Kamp, *Desertion,* 187–202.

39. Multiple contributions indicate this: Fatah-Black, "Desertion"; Van Rossum, "Contracts to Labour Camps"; Stanziani, "Runaways."

40. Van Rossum, *Werkers van der wereld,* 346–70, 390–91. This is an update of an earlier reconstruction made by Bruijn et al. in J. R. Bruijn and E. S. Eyck van Heslinga, *Muiterij: Oproer en berechting op schepen van de VOC* (Haarlem: De Boer Maritiem 1980). More mutinies and uprisings are likely to be found through the completion of the indexation of the Court of Justice of Batavia in the *Resilient Diversity* project.

41. L. Hovy, *Ceylonees Plakkaatboek* (Hilversum: Verloren, 1991), LXIII.

42. Nationaal Archief [NA], Archief van de VOC [VOC], inv.nr. 8313, Coromandel, 176–81. See also Van Rossum, "Contracts to Labour Camps," 192–93.

43. Van Rossum, *Kleurrijke tragiek.*

44. Ibid.; see also Dan Sleigh and Piet Westra, *De Opstand op het Slavenschip Meermin* (Amsterdam: Cossee, 2012).

45. Van Rossum, "Amok!"

46. J. Edouard, "The 1706 Slave Conspiracy in Dutch Mauritius: A Case of Collective Resistance" (BA thesis: Leiden University, 2014).

47. Vink, "World's Oldest Trade."

48. See Van Rossum, *Kleurrijke tragiek*; M. van Rossum and M. Guldemond, "Slavernij, geweld en recht onder de VOC: Een inleiding op nieuwe verkenningen," *Acta Historica* 3, no. 4 (2014): 5–10; M. van Oostende, "Amok in Batavia: Over Amok in Nederlands-Indische rechtszaken," *Acta Historica* 3, no. 4 (2014): 11–15; W. Schmidt, "'Maar zig alleen in dien toestand gedragen heeft als een mensch': Slavenrechtzaken en de VOC," *Acta Historica* 3, no. 4 (2014); L. Koppenrade, "'Heb jij geen medelijden': Het verzet van Ontong Kitjil en de relatie met zijn mannelijke medeslaven," *Acta Historica* 3, no. 4 (2014): 23–30; A. Bos and J. Calkhoven, "Januarij van Babian: Een familietragedie als ingang op het slavernijverleden," *Acta Historica* 3, no. 4 (2014): 31–39.

49. Van Oostende, "Amok!"; Koppenrade, "Ontong Kitjil."

50. Paul Truter, "The Robben Island Rebellion of 1751: A Study of Convict Experience at the Cape of Good Hope," *Kronos* 31 (2005): 34–49.

51. Matthias van Rossum, "Radjas, Sailors and Slaves: Convict Workers and Resistance," paper and presentation at *Labour History: A Return to Politics? Tenth AILH Conference* (Delhi, 23 March 2014).

52. Michele Paulse, "'We are free, you are slaves. Come on, let's run away': Escape from Constantia, 1712," *New Contree* 69 (2014): 26–44.

53. Ekama, "Just Deserters."

54. Van Rossum, "Working for the Devil".

55. Ekama, "Just Deserters"; Van Rossum, "Working for the Devil"; Edouard, "Slave Conspiracy"; G. J. Knaap, *Kruidnagelen en Christenen: De Verenigde Oost-Indische Compagnie en de bevolking van Ambon 1656–1696* (Dordrecht: Foris, 1987), 133–35.

56. Van Rossum, *Werkers van der wereld*, 343.

57. Van Rossum, "Working for the Devil."

58. Van Rossum, "Contracts to Labour Camps," 192.

59. NA, VOC, 11327.

60. NA, VOC, 2966.

61. NA, VOC, 3025.

62. NA. VOC, 11330.

63. The number of ships visiting Surat can be derived from the Boekhouder Generaal-Batavia Database (http://bgb.huygens.knaw.nl/bgb/). From the Generale Zeemonsterrollen Database (http://dutchshipsandsailors.nl/) it can be estimated on average eighty-five workers were on board ships sailing (from Batavia) to destinations such as Surat, Bengal, Ceylon, and Persia. The exact average derived from 342 ships in the database is 83.1—excluding small local vessels referred to as *pantjalang, hoeker,* or *chialoup.* The number of local personnel in Surat is estimated at forty workers.

64. Only four ships can be traced to have visited Surat, leading to an estimate of 27 percent; calculating the desertion rate with the yearly average of eight ships would lead to 14 percent. Barendse mentioned that "the Dutch complained in 1760 they lost their entire garrison"; R. J. Barendse, *Arabian Seas, 1700–1763* (Leiden: Brill, 2009), 578.

65. Van Rossum, "Working for the Devil."

66. SLNA, 1, 2758, 2766 and 5906.

67. This stems from Kamp and Van Rossum, "Introduction: Leaving Work." See also Van der Linden, "Mass Exits"; Ekama, "Just Deserters."

68. Ekama, "Just Deserters"; Fatah-Black, "Desertion"; Van Rossum, "Contracts to Labour Camps."

69. Matthias van Rossum, "Generale Zeemonsterrollen, Verenigde Oost-Indische Compagnie, 1691–1791" database, April 2014, at www.dutchshipsandsailors.nl. The crew of the ship *Lycochton* was 67 sailors in June 1759.

70. NA, VOC, 9733.

71. NA, VOC, 2580, Malabar, 740.

72. NA, VOC, 2580, Malabar, 740.

73. NA, VOC, 1.11.06.11, 284.

74. NA, VOC, 2580, Malabar, 740.

75. NA, VOC, 1.11.06.08 [Duplicates from SLNA 1], 4628, fols. 63–67.

76. Van Rossum, "Working for the Devil," 149.

77. See Van Rossum, *Werkers van der wereld*. Important studies in this respect are Guy, "First Spaces"; Nigel Worden, "'Below the Line the Devil Reigns': Death and Dissent aboard a VOC Vessel," *South African Historical Journal* 61, no. 4 (2009): 702–30; Nigel Penn, "Soldiers and Cape Town Society," in *Cape Town between East and West: Social Identities in a Dutch Colonial Town*, ed. Nigel Worden (Hilversum: Verloren, 2012), 176–93.

78. D. L. M. Weijers, "'Dappere waterleeuwen versus schelmen': Een muiterij in Perzische wateren, 1733," in Bruijn, *Muiterij*, 44–57.

79. Van Rossum, "Amok!"

80. Of the Balinese, two were mentioned as coming from Bali, one from Balimboeang.

81. NA, VOC, 9499, case F.

82. NA, VOC, 9499, case F.

83. Schmidt, "Slavenrechtzaken en de VOC."

8

Voting with Their Feet

Absconding and Labor Exploitation in Convict Australia

Hamish Maxwell-Stewart and Michael Quinlan

The rise of global capital was catalyzed by access to the colonial commons and the yoking of the labor necessary to exploit these overseas assets. In the case of colonial Australia, that labor force largely consisted of convicts sentenced to transportation in British, Irish, or other imperial courts. While convict laborers were among the best documented of all British colonial workforces, they are not a group of workers who have historically been associated with organized labor resistance. This reflects the management strategies used to extract labor from the bodies of prisoners. Conviction in a court of law was used both to justify exploitative work practices and to blunt any attempt to challenge the day-to-day circumstances faced by the tens of thousands of convicts transported to Britain's overseas penal colonies. Any attempt to resist confirmed that convicts were deviants who could only be controlled through the use of coercion.[1] Yet analysis of the day-to-day paperwork used to manage the 73,000 convicts transported to Van Diemen's Land reveals plenty of evidence of labor withdrawal.

One important method convicts used to withdraw labor was to abscond from their allotted place of work. Between 1824 and 1860 over 22,000 reward notices for runaway convicts were placed in the *Government Gazette*. In this chapter we first explore the strategies the colonial administration adopted to try and keep its convict charges in place. We then link the identifying details contained in runaway notices to the records used to manage convicts in order to reconstruct convict attempts to steal away at a colony-wide level. By exploring the desertion rates for both male and female convicts across different sectors of the colonial capitalist economy we seek to illuminate the relationship between the operation of colonial labor markets and the factors that motivated attempts to run. We conclude by arguing that convicts were not a distinct and largely apolitical form of colonial labor. Instead both the processes used to manage them and the manner in which they resisted attempts to reduce labor mobility were similar to those utilized by free workers, especially those employed in the maritime sector.

PUNISHMENT AND WORK IN
THE PRISON WITHOUT WALLS

Between 1803 and 1853 around 13,500 female and 59,500 male convicts were dispatched to the British penal colony of Van Diemen's Land. Although sentenced by civil and military courts to terms of transportation ranging from seven years to life, few bricks or bars were used to hold these prisoners in place. The majority of convicts were either lent or hired out to the private sector as cheap labor. Many worked as farm laborers or domestic servants, others as shophands or artisans in colonial workshops.

Until 1839 newly arrived convicts were "assigned" to private-sector masters. Although assigned convicts were prohibited from earning wages, masters were obliged to clothe, feed, and accommodate them at a standard that at least matched the level of provisions supplied to prisoners in government service. In return assigned convicts were required to work for their masters during "government hours." These varied from ten hours per day in summer to nine in winter.[2] While convicts were not required to work on Saturday afternoons and on Sundays, masters frequently provided small monetary incentives (although these were technically illegal) and other perks as an inducement to work longer hours. This was a particularly common practice during the harvest.[3]

From 1840 male convicts who had passed through a stage of probationary labor were permitted to sign a contract with an employer for a minimal wage, which was less than a third of the rate at which free workers were remunerated. A similar system was introduced for women in 1844.[4] Convicts close to the completion of their sentence could also apply for a ticket of leave. This provided the right to seek employment in the private sector, although ticket holders had to remain within a specified police district until they were fully emancipated.

Unlike prisoners who were retained for government duties and wore uniforms, convicts in the private sector were clothed by their masters. As a result, it was often difficult to distinguish them from other members of the colonial lower orders. This was a crucial issue in a society where the unfree were largely drawn from the same ethnic groups as the free. Unlike skin color, conviction history was not a trait that could be discerned with a glance.

Absconding convicts used this to their advantage, melting into colonial lower-class communities.[5] The manner in which some masters hired their servants out to work for others for wages, or turned a blind eye to such practices, further complicated the issue of who was illegally at large and who was not. Although legislation was introduced to prosecute those who harbored convicts in 1825, the practice persisted.[6] Free men and women were regularly fined by magistrates for harboring or employing convicts.[7]

Convicts wore uniforms but rarely suffered physical restraint. Many "government hands" were housed in barracks at night but were deployed during the day in government-run workshops like the lumberyard where furniture, tools, and other fittings required for official use were manufactured. Others labored as clerks in various government offices or as boat crews and carters distributing supplies to more isolated workstations. Even the police force, an ancillary service crucial for the maintenance of convict discipline, was staffed by serving prisoners.[8]

Discipline was largely maintained through a system of magistrates' benches. Prisoners could be tried at civil law or in a lower court for breaking the rules and regulations of the convict department. This included a variety of mobility offenses. Convicts could be arraigned for being absent from their place of work or absconding—a more serious charge that implied an attempt to desert their place of employment. Each magistrate's bench was empowered to recommend a range of punishments including flogging and solitary confinement. They could also order a convict to be removed to a site of punishment.

The convict system was multilayered. While the majority of prisoners labored for private individuals or in government offices under little restraint, others worked on or in road parties, chain gangs, penal stations, and houses of correction at hard labor as a result of a court appearance. These varied in severity. Male convicts sentenced to road parties were billeted in a stockade or other temporary station at night and worked in gangs under the supervision of an overseer during the day. Convicts in chain gangs were tasked with similar work, but were encumbered with leg irons. While they were not chained one to another (a common misconception), their movements were restricted by iron basils riveted to each leg and joined by a short length of chain. A bench consisting of two or more magistrates was empowered to order male convicts to be sent to a penal station. These isolated labor camps contained their own hierarchy of gangs and chain gangs.

A similar hierarchy of labor experiences existed for female convicts. They could be sent to labor in a house of correction (commonly referred to as a female factory) as a punishment. These frequently overcrowded buildings were divided into yards where work was graded according to the severity of the convict's sentence. Most of the work in factories involved the processing of laundry, but inmates were sometimes employed in spinning and picking oakum. The most onerous duties were reserved for the "crime class."[9]

Each convict was provided with a police number on arrival in the colony. This, along with details of their sentence and the ship that had brought them to Van Diemen's Land, was used to keep track of individuals, enabling references held in multiple record groups to be efficiently cross-referenced. Such record-keeping ensured that convicts in Van Diemen's Land were rendered "legible" in ways that were unusual elsewhere in the first half of the nineteenth century.[10] There were few attempts to introduce comparable criminal record-keeping systems in Britain until mid-century.[11]

Partnership with the private sector necessitated greater levels of documentation than those generated by British and Irish early nineteenth-century correctional institutions. Convict labor in Van Diemen's Land was highly mobile. Convicted workers were routinely transferred among private properties, government gangs, prison barracks, houses of correction, and other institutions. These legitimate movements needed to be documented. In order to ensure that the wicked were chastised and the dutiful appropriately rewarded, it was also necessary to create a centralized system where details of the indiscretions of all prisoners could be stored and retrieved. Record-keeping had other uses too. The process of stripping convicts to the waist and interrogating them was an effective way of psychologically intimidating new arrivals.[12] The knowledge that so many details of a convict's life were committed to paper was designed to reinforce the extent to which each prisoner was subject to state power. The aim was to use words, as opposed to bricks and mortar, to mentally incarcerate the colony's bonded workforce. Above all, however, descriptive details were required to ensure that information about runaways could be efficiently circulated.[13]

TRACKING THE CONVICT DEPARTMENT'S LOST PROPERTY

The "black books," a 226-volume series, lay at the heart of the convict system. These records contain summaries of over 450,000 separate charges brought against the 73,000 convicts transported to Van Diemen's Land. As the entry for each convict also listed their police number, place and date of trial, sentence, and ship of arrival, entries have been efficiently cross-referenced with other record series. This included the physical descriptions of prisoners, information on next of kin, and the Convict Savings Bank ledgers. Information about prisoners was routinely circulated via the *Government Gazette,* a weekly publication that carried notices of licenses, new orders and regulations, and other administrative business. Routine notices included details of the transfer of convicts between masters, appointments to the police as well as the issue and cancellation of tickets of leave, pardons, and certificates of freedom. The *Government Gazette* also carried information on prisoners who had deserted their place of work.[14]

While this paperwork system of surveillance was a successful means of controlling the social movements of convicts, such archival restraints were not particularly effective when it came to restricting physical mobility. Analysis of the *Gazette* notices reveal that between 1824 and 1860 a staggering 17,633 descriptions for

POLICE DEPARTMENT.

10th January, 1844.

THE under-mentioned Convicts having escaped from their authorised places of residence, all constables and others are hereby required to use their utmost exertions to apprehend and lodge them in safe custody.

FRANCIS BURGESS, *Chief Police Magistrate.*

ABSCONDED.

From Deloraine Probation Station, on the 1st instant.

9535 William Carter (2nd), per Cressy, tried at Southampton, Winchester Q. S., 28th June 1842, 10 years, farm labourer and ploughman, 5 feet 1½, complexion sallow, hair dark brown, eyes brown, age 20, native place South Wamby, Hampshire, scar on little finger left hand, mole on chest, mole on neck, mole on left arm, several moles on right arm. Reward 2*l.*, or such lesser sum as may be determined upon by the convicting Magistrate.

10,590 James Skinner, per Forfarshire, tried at Montreal, Canada Court Martial, 11th October 1841, 14 years, labourer, 5 feet 7, complexion ruddy, hair brown, eyes blue, age 23, native place Clapham, pockpitted, heart and darts 2 wreaths angel C. G. mermaid on right arm, scar inside right hand, S. O. S. 2 wreaths R. S. C. + G. man holding bottle 5 dots cross part of a bracelet woman rose and thistle on left arm, scar on chin. Reward 2*l.*, or such lesser sum as may be determined upon by the convicting Magistrate.

10,250 William Fletcher, per Emerald Isle, tried at Warwick Q. S., 18th October 1842, 7 years, labourer and carter, 5 feet 4½, complexion fresh, hair brown, eyes blue, age 19, native place Leicester, slightly pockpitted, scar on left cheek, 2 moles on right jaw, stout made, scar on back of right hand, small scar on forefinger left hand. Reward 2*l.*, or such lesser sum as may be determined upon by the convicting Magistrate.

FIGURE 8.1. Excerpt from absconding notice, *Hobart Town Gazette*, Friday, January 12, 1844.

absconding male prisoners were advertised and 4,855 for female. As some individuals ran many times over the course of their sentence the actual number of unique absconders is slightly less. In all, 14,626 male and 3,924 female convicts appeared as absconders in the pages of the *Government Gazette* on at least one occasion. This represents over a quarter of the convict population.

Yet this is only part of the story—the many convicts who absconded but were apprehended before the weekly publication of the *Gazette* were not advertised as missing. On the other hand, even when notified promptly by the employer there could be significant delays in the notice being placed in the *Gazette*. Thus, Samuel Hall complained bitterly that by the time three probationers who had absconded from him were notified in the *Gazette* the men had five weeks to make good their escape.[15]

In addition to efforts to leave their employer permanently, many convicts absented themselves for short periods of time before returning to their place of work. Such absences were frequently not advertised although masters who did not report absconding servants risked losing all access to convict labor.[16] Given the advantage of employing unfree workers over free, this was a powerful inducement to promptly notify the colonial administration of any prolonged absence. Colonial newspapers reported thousands of cases where convict workers were brought before the courts and tried for temporary absence of a few hours to two or three days (reasons given include recreational and social activities or simply the desire to get away from their employer). A significant minority of these involved collective absence, which could be deemed a strike because they essentially amounted to a temporary withdrawal of labor. For example, in 1836 three bootmakers assigned to Charles Flegg in Hobart were sentenced to seven nights in the cells, but to do their work during the day for being absent without leave.[17]

In order to place the *Gazette* notices within a wider context of convict labor management, a longitudinal four percent sample of entries in the various "black book" series for male convicts was transcribed. This consisted of all entries for convicts with police numbers ending in 06, 33, 56, and 83. These were coded in order to identify the number of movement offenses over time and identify the manner in which convicts deserting from different locations were punished.

THE POLITICAL ECONOMY OF ABSCONDING

In his otherwise pioneering assessment of convict protest Atkinson did not include the withdrawal of labor by running away since magistrates' bench cases where convicts were tried for absconding rarely included the convicts' motives.[18] As Roberts argued, these could vary from a desire to affect a permanent escape to a temporary leave of absence designed to gain relief from the monotony of convict life.[19] While the former might be characterized by the illegal movement of convicts from outlying rural to urban areas, there are plenty of examples of prisoners who attempted to quit the colony altogether. Recent work by Duffield, for example, has emphasized the prevalence of piratical attempts at escape by seizing vessels.[20]

Regardless of the difference in scale between temporary absence and attempted escape, historians have traditionally viewed these as apolitical activities. Connell and Irving, for example, lamented the manner in which convicts sought to obtain a passage home rather than challenge the conditions under which they served.[21] Analysis of newspapers, bench books, and conduct records reveal that many if not most convicts did in fact challenge their conditions, with individuals being dragged before the courts for dissent on a daily basis and engaging in hundreds of strikes and slowdowns. For example, there were more than a hundred strikes or collective slowdowns by convicts at the coal mines on the Tasman Peninsula alone between February 1836 and July 1841. Strikes and slowdowns among convict gangs were being tried on an almost weekly basis by the 1820s. Similar protests by those assigned to farms and estates were also common if not as frequent.[22]

The political economy of absconding by convicts is illuminated by the wider context of workers' dissent in the nineteenth century. As is now recognized with regard to other workers like seamen and indentured immigrants, individual and collective absconding should be viewed as another form of work-related protest—indeed it was a prevalent form of protest among workers more generally in the nineteenth century.[23] It is no accident, for example, that labor laws in Van Diemen's Land and New South Wales empowered constables to arrest seamen suspected of deserting on suspicion without requiring a warrant.[24] A provision in the Police Act enabled the bench to sentence seamen to a road gang for a second offense, adding the prospect of further punishment, including flogging.[25] Desertion by seamen and whalers was often collective and highly organized—it had to be to leave the ship without a pass under the ever-watchful eyes of water police and roving constables. The same point applied to convicts serving on gangs or at remote farms and sheep stations.

Absconding needs to be seen as only one dimension—albeit an important one—of workers voting with their feet. Free immigrants or convicts who had served their sentence and who had fulfilled their engagement under the Master and Servants Act had the option of leaving Van Diemen's Land for the mainland colonies where generally superior wages could be found. From the mid-1840s an increasing number were doing this, causing growing concern in the press about the significant loss of skilled craft and agricultural workers.[26]

Colonial newspapers published a steady stream of letters, complaints, commentaries, and editorials about the prevalence of absconding from both government road and chain gangs and private service.[27] The *Cornwall Chronicle* complained, for example, that a sentence to a female factory failed to deter widespread running away by domestic servants in Launceston.[28] Repeated advertisements concerning absconders over a period of time (many months and even years in some cases) by both private employers and government authorities (in the case of convicts) indicate that some absconders, irrespective of whether they were convict or free, stayed at large for lengthy periods if not escaping detection and recapture altogether. Indeed, government notices were criticized for making it all too clear that many people ran away and some stayed at large for long periods. The *Launceston Examiner* reported that a female convict absconder had successfully evaded the law for six months and was arrested only after she committed a felony.[29]

Vandemonian authorities went to great lengths to recover their lost property. The description of prisoners who were thought to have left the colony altogether were sent to London where they were printed in the *Police Gazette,* or *Hue and Cry.* This periodical was first issued under the name the *Quarterly Pursuit* by the Bow Street Police Office in 1772. By the 1830s over 160,000 copies were printed each year and circulated to mayors and principal officers of every city and town in the British Isles, justices of the peace, keepers of jails and houses of correction, the metropolitan police, the War Office, Horse Patrol, and police offices as well as the commanding officers of military regiments. Copies were also circulated outside of the British Isles to each colony and further afield.[30] Runaway Australian convicts were apprehended in Valparaiso, Mauritius, Bombay, Calcutta, and Rio de Janeiro—testimony to the reach of the "open air panopticon"—and to the resistance to it.[31]

Within the colony the state used pecuniary rewards and fines to clamp down on the illicit movements of convicts without overly investing in expensive physical infrastructure. A reward of £2 was regularly provided for the capture of male, but not female, runaways. Because this could only be claimed if the absconder had been advertised in the *Government Gazette,* this otherwise dull official circular gained a surprising wide circulation.[32] The provision of bank accounts for prisoners provided the colonial administration with further means to impose financial checks and balances aimed at reducing clandestine movements. Recaptured convicts risked forfeiting their savings. Monies taken from the accounts of apprehended absconders were used to reimburse the state by covering the costs of rewards paid out to their capturers.

Would-be employers also ran risks. The standard fine for harboring runaways was £10 (although more could be levied in cases considered severe). Half of this sum was provided to informers.[33] This had a double advantage of encouraging convicts to "dob" on other prisoners while simultaneously depositing money into the informant's bank account, thereby providing them with a disincentive to put into effect any self-liberation plans of their own. The legislation was tightened in 1825. Nonetheless, harboring remained a problem in the 1820s and beyond. In 1826 the *Colonial Times* reported that magistrates were agitating for additional legislation because of the ease with which convicts could be induced to neglect their work and abscond.[34]

Despite the use of pecuniary rewards and penalties there were advantages to employing convicts who were illegally at large. In 1842, for example, a Mr. Drummin was fined £15 for hiring two absconders to split timber at "a very low wage."[35] It is likely that at times runaways formed something of a cheap labor reserve. In return for harboring absconders, some employers offered wages far below the market rate.

Labor shortages also provided opportunities for absconders. British, French, and American merchant vessels and whalers were regular visitors to the colony's ports. Deaths at sea and desertions often meant that these ships were short crewed by the time they berthed in Van Diemen's Land. Matthew Forster, the chief police magistrate, warned that absconders from road parties in the interior were attracted to town with a view of getting on board such vessels, sometimes dressed "in the garb of sailors"—a mode of disguise that in his opinion necessitated restrictions on the free movement of legitimate mariners, since if Jack Tars were allowed "to perambulate the town at all hours without passes" there was nothing to prevent convicts who were similarly "habited" mingling with them in order to make their escape.[36]

The elaborate measures put in place to police the movements of prisoners also restricted the movement of the free. Theoretically, no worker—free or unfree— was permitted to remove him- or herself from the place of employment without giving notice and obtaining the prior permission of a magistrate. While convicts could only travel legitimately if they carried a pass issued by their employer and countersigned by a magistrate, such a system made little sense unless free workers carried papers too.[37] Thus, while competition with convict workers reduced colonial wage rates, free workers found their ability to bargain with employers further restricted by the rules that governed the movement of labor in a penal colony. Thus, the master of the *Essex* was fined £10 and costs after he unwittingly hired a runaway from the Campbell Town Road Party who he claimed had shown him a certificate of discharge from the ship *Ebro* recently arrived from London. The fraud was only detected when the ship was searched by the police prior to clearing port.[38]

Several masters complained that when assigned servants ran they took their clothes with them. As a settler from the Cross Marsh bemoaned, it cost 30 shillings to buy slops for a convict servant who when kitted out might "on some frivolous pretext" abscond from his service, "carrying all his good clothes along with him." By the time the servant was apprehended and returned to his or her master, anything of value was likely to have been sold or exchanged.[39] For this reason it was not uncommon for absconders to be tried for stealing the clothes that they ran in, a charge that substantially upped the ante, increasing the severity of the sanctions that could be applied by a sentencing magistrate.

Ironically, even the state's primary anti-absconding weapons proved to have monetary value. In 1828 an alarmed principal superintendent of convicts wrote to the colonial secretary to report that a prisoner in a chain gang could secure "half a dozen" certificates of freedom "in a few days for about 20 or thirty shillings each." The difficulties in prosecuting free individuals for loss of paperwork made it difficult to stamp out such trafficking. The best the state could do was to issue periodic lists of missing certificates and issue duplicates on payment of a fee of five shillings.[40] Worse yet, some absconders struck deals with their captors, living on credit in remote stock huts until half of the £2 reward had been spent. Absconder and clandestine landlord would then walk to the nearest police office where the escapee would be cashed in, having effectively already spent a substantial proportion of the money the state had invested in their recapture.[41]

The punishments awarded to absconders underscore the extent to which the offense was perceived as a major threat. During the years 1816–39 nearly a quarter of all male convicts convicted of absconding were flogged, averaging over 55 lashes per beating—significantly more than the mean number of strokes meted out to those prosecuted for other offenses. Over a third (36 percent) were sentenced to serve in irons, a sanction applied to under 10 percent of other offenders. The average amount of time apprehended absconders were ordered to serve in fetters was also far in excess of that for non-movement-related offenses—294 days compared to 163. Many of those sentenced to hard labor in and out of chains were removed to penal stations. Even these remote places of secondary punishment did not

TABLE 8.1 Percentage male convicts punished for absconding, being absent, and other offenses (1816–1839).

	Flogged	Solitary	Road Party	Chain Gang	Treadwheel	Fined	Reprimanded or Dismissed
Absconding	24.1	3.6	17.6	36.4	1.0	0.2	1.0
Absent Without Leave	15.8	17.7	13.0	8.5	9.4	1.0	23.1
All Other Offenses	15.3	19.3	13.7	9.4	4.7	5.3	14.6

TABLE 8.2 Mean number of days punished, lashes or shillings for absconding, being absent, and other offenses (1816–1839).

	Mean lashes	Mean days cells	Mean days roads	Mean days chains	Mean days treadwheel	Mean fine (shillings)
Absconding	55.6	17.0	242.1	293.8	13.2	5.0
Absent Without Leave	32.1	6.4	98.0	97.7	9.3	8.2
Other Offence	35.5	6.0	134.5	163.2	10.9	18.5

N = Absconding	478	5.3%
Absent	1578	17.5%
All Other	6984	77.3%

SOURCE: TAHO, Con 31 and 32.

prevent further absconding. In October 1831, for example, four convicts were apprehended after escaping from Maria Island as were two who escaped Port Arthur in 1839.[42] What the press and the government never publicized were those who escaped successfully.[43] Although relatively few absconders were sentenced to solitary confinement, the mean number of days they were forced to sit in the dark on a diet of bread and water was nearly three times that awarded to those found guilty of other charges.

If absconders gambled on cutting their sentences, state sentencing strategies raised the stakes. Apprehended absconders were at significantly greater risk of having their sentences extended. While a comparatively rare sanction, a bench consisting of at least two magistrates was empowered to recommend an extension of sentence of up to three years. Nearly 15 percent of absconders had their terms of service lengthened compared to just one percent of those charged with other offenses. The message was emphatic—clandestine attempts to shorten sentences to transportation were likely to increase, rather than decrease, the amount of time served. Absconding was treated more seriously than strike action and all but the most serious attacks on overseers and many thefts.

By contrast the state viewed temporary absences as relatively minor offenses. The frequent prosecutions for being out after hours or away from a stipulated place of employment without a pass accounted for 17.5 percent of all prosecutions compared to just 5.3 percent for absconding or attempting to abscond or escape. Despite their frequency most absentees were lightly punished if punished at all. While under two percent of charges that involved absconding resulted in an acquittal or a reprimand, the equivalent figure for absenteeism was 27 percent. Absconding charges could, however, be downgraded to lesser offenses. While absconders from the public works were invariably savagely punished, cross-checking of absconding notices with the "black books" reveals that many assigned servants had their charges downgraded to the lesser offense of being absent. This was particularly the case with farmworkers and those with other valued skills, a reminder that many absconding attempts and subsequent charges were part of a wider landscape of negotiation. The state's efforts to keep convicts in place reveal much about the worth of convict labor and the wider political economy of labor extraction.

THE MORAL ECONOMY OF ABSCONDING

As historians of slavery have long recognized, stealing oneself was an important labor withdrawal strategy. Prisoners who were not paid a wage, or were forced to sign contracts to exchange their labor power for wages below those paid to free workers, may have regarded the withdrawal of those labor services as a legitimate response to labor exploitation. In this sense it is possible to draw parallels with other forms of lower-order direct action to restore what were regarded as fairer systems of exchange. Since Thompson's pioneering work in the 1960s, such forms of collective action are thought to have been commonplace reactions to the disruption of traditional forms of exchange resulting from the intrusion of external market forces.[44]

In the case of unfree labor systems the contested good was the labor of the worker. The political economy of labor exploitation rested on restricting the ability of the unfree to bargain for better conditions, whether monetary payments or better accommodation, clothing, food, and other material benefits. The actions of the unfree might increase the return to the worker, closing the gap between the monetary value of the goods they received as rations and incentives and those provided to free workers in the form of a wage. Whereas such actions may not have constituted a direct attempt to restore the liberty of the unfree, such day-to-day forms of resistance nevertheless threatened to undercut the rational of unfreedom. In this sense they might be seen as a form of quiet abolition from within—a set of practices designed to restore the remuneration for labor that prevailed before the imposition of an unfree contract. Thus, while attempts to escape the penal colony altogether might be seen as an outright rejection (or in the eyes of some, a self-motivated and therefore apolitical act), there is room to see some convict desertions as a strategic form of labor negotiation.

One might expect such forms of labor withdrawal to be particularly associated with instances where the actions of owners, or the state, were thought by convicts to erode their rights—whether a reduction of rations or an increase in work intensity or punishment. In this case absconding and absenteeism should be particularly associated with push rather than pull factors—that is, more likely to be prompted by a deterioration in conditions rather than a response to external attractions, be those opportunities to escape or to gain temporary relief in a tavern or a house of ill-repute. We should note, however, that there is no reason why both factors might not operate in conjunction.

To test this hypothesis we examine the characteristics of those convicts who appeared in the pages of the *Government Gazette* in order to explore the extent to which they differed from the profile of convicts transported to Van Diemen's Land as a whole. We also explore an annual runaways pattern to see if there was a season in which convicts were more likely to be advertised as runaways and we look at the locations from which convicts disproportionately deserted. Finally, we use convict testimony sourced from court and newspaper records to flesh out the statistical picture.

Before embarking on such an analysis it is important to explore one particular feature of the data. In convict Australia the relationship between movement offenses and master-servant relations was complicated by the regulations governing the lodging of complaints. While convicts had a theoretical right to bring grievances before a magistrates' bench they required a pass from their master in order to do so. If this was not forthcoming the prisoner could be tried for being illegally at large. Thus, in 1834 three convicts who tried to lodge a complaint about rations against their Bruny Island master had their claim dismissed as "frivolous" and were flogged for leaving their master's service.[45] Convicts with a grievance against their master worried about lodging a formal complaint with a court—often a local bench composed of employers who were friends or associates of their master. Even those in gangs seem to have had little confidence in the system. When the bench asked a probationer charged with refusing work and threatening an overseer on the Sandy Bay gang in 1841 why he had not lodged a complaint about being starved (along with others) he responded by looking very significantly at one of the magistrates and stating it would serve "little purpose doing, as there was no probability of redress, but a greater chance of severer treatment."[46]

On at least one occasion a threat by the bench to punish a convict who had brought a complaint triggered a mass withdrawal of labor. The five prisoners who left the property subsequently returned with firearms, laying siege to their former master's house.[47] Four were executed for the offense and the survivor sent to Macquarie Harbour penal station. Thus some desertions occurred only after other methods of protest had failed. When three convicts absconded from the Deloraine

Probation Station, taking a substantial part of the third-class prisoners' rations with them, the superintendent refused to make good the shortfall. Deprived of their rations the third-class prisoners laid down their tools and refused to proceed to work. The visiting magistrate attempted to deal with the strike by sentencing every prisoner to an extension of their period of probation of between three to six months. Twenty-one convicts soon absconded, prompting fears of a regional convict revolt.[48] The warning here is that it is often difficult to separate the decision to run (and the decision of master and state to prosecute) from other forms of labor negotiation and protest.

Absconding convicts were not typical of those disembarked in the penal colony as whole. On arrival in Australia those who went on to abscond were on average more than three years younger than their shipmates who did not. The difference was particularly marked among men (an age difference of 3.6 years compared to 3.1 for women). Desertion could be a physically demanding undertaking and older convicts clearly thought twice about leaving their workplace for extended periods of time.

The occupational profile of deserting convicts also differed. Convicts with prior experience in the maritime sector were 2.6 times more likely to abscond over the course of a sentence than those with a background in agriculture (Fig. 8.2). While the difference reflects the degree to which sailors and boatmen could gain a passage elsewhere as crew on an undermanned vessel, this is unlikely to be the only reason for the elevated absconding rate for convicts with nautical work experiences. As we have seen, maritime workers had a long history of using desertion as a means of terminating unfavorable contracts or bargaining for better conditions. The word strike appears to have first been used in an industrial context in 1768, when sailors "struck" (removed) the topgallant sails of merchant ships at port.[49] Former soldiers, who were 2.4 times more likely to abscond than convicts claiming rural skills, were also formerly employed in a sector where desertion was used as a common tactic. Many ended up in Van Diemen's Land and New South Wales, not because they had broken the criminal law, but because they had breached military regulations by trying to withdraw their labor and been court-martialed for their pains. Convicts' prior experience of industrial relations probably had a bearing on the type and intensity of action they undertook while under sentence in a penal colony.

The rate at which convicts from different occupational backgrounds ran also reflects their varying experiences within the Australian penal colonies. Agricultural workers were valued and as a result were flogged less often than those with other useful skills. Convicts with maritime skills were one and a half times more likely to be sentenced to a flogging than convicts from the agricultural sector. Those from the textile industry and with military backgrounds were at even greater risk of being pinned to the triangles.[50] There is a high degree of correlation between the amount of coercion applied to convicts with different work skills and the extent to which they resorted to absconding.

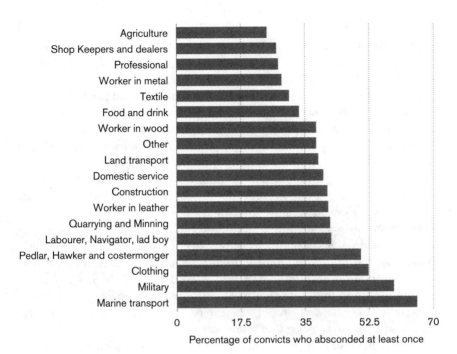

FIGURE 8.2. Absconding rates for male convicts, Van Diemen's Land, 1817–1860.

SOURCES: *Hobart Town Gazette,* Con 18, 23 and 33

While convicts ran from a wide range of locations including private assign-ment, the rate of desertion by male convicts from road parties and other punish-ment gangs was particularly high. Indeed, fluctuations in the number of convicts undergoing punishment on the public works explain 46 percent of the variation in male absconding rates over time. This is not in itself surprising. Road gangs were employed in labor-intensive tasks designed to punish through increased levels of physical exertion. Convicts reacted by voting with their feet. This suggests that much convict absconding in Van Diemen's Land was motivated by push factors—by a desire to seek relief from coercive labor extraction or a connection to wider protests designed to ameliorate conditions in gangs.

Female workers have historically run less frequently than males. A study of slave runaways in the early nineteenth-century Cape Colony, for example, revealed that 90 percent were male.[51] By contrast 22 percent of runaway notices in Van Die-men's Land were for female absconders. The state policy of splitting female con-victs from their children and the heavy-handed manner in which sexuality of pris-oners was policed almost certainly increased female mobility rates. Family ties helped to anchor workers in place. By contrast absconding rates increased when families were split apart. Although nearly two thousand children accompanied their convict mothers to Van Diemen's Land, the majority were sent to the colonial "orphan school" so that the mother, unencumbered by dependents, was free to labor as a domestic servant.[52] The policy that made the labor of convict women more exploitable also made them more mobile.

Female convicts seeking to form partnerships with men had to do so largely in secret. As Reid has demonstrated, the number of women prisoners permitted to marry fell sharply in the early 1820s at a time when demand for domestic servants was rising.[53] The many sexual offenses for which female convicts were tried have been used to underscore their depraved nature, but these were charges that could not have been brought against free workers. The attempt to maximize convict labor by minimizing family formation effectively created a whole raft of sexual offenses. It also elevated female absconding rates.

Environmental conditions may have played an important part in influencing the timing of decisions to run. Convicts tended not to abscond in the cold winter months, although this applied less to women than it did to men. Male convicts undergoing punishment were least likely to abscond in June—the Southern Hemisphere month with the shortest hours of sunlight and the most inclement weather. Conversely December was a popular time to run, suggesting that some prisoners took annual leave to coincide with traditional festivities.

The weather also reduced opportunities to extract work from prisoners who labored outdoors. Winter was the slack period in the agricultural cycle where the least demands were placed on farm servants. Even in road gangs and punishment stations the weather could curtail work efforts. At the Bridgewater Chain Gang, for example, work constructing the causeway across the Derwent was called off if the weather was too wet. The work of indoor servants, more likely to be female, was less impacted upon by such seasonal variations. The demands of heating houses in winter could elevate the amount of labor required to clean grates, and the availability of lamps and candles meant that it was possible for indoor workers to be kept at work in the hours of darkness. Their work was never called off because the weather was foul.

The time of increased labor demand for male convicts was summer, a reflection of longer days. This was particularly true for those employed on public works. For many assigned convicts peak labor came early in the new year. Although the hay harvest fell in December, the month with the most hours of sunlight, it was the wheat harvest that stretched the agricultural sector. Absconding rates among male convicts deployed in the private service rose in January as the harvest commenced and peaked in February as farmers mobilized the labor of harvest gangs (Fig. 8.3).

Male convicts absconded in particularly high rates from punishment stations, especially road gangs. As Brand observed, increases in the severity of punishment, including the use of the lash, was an important impetus for absconding.[54] Fluctuations in absconding rates over time can largely be explained by the extent to which

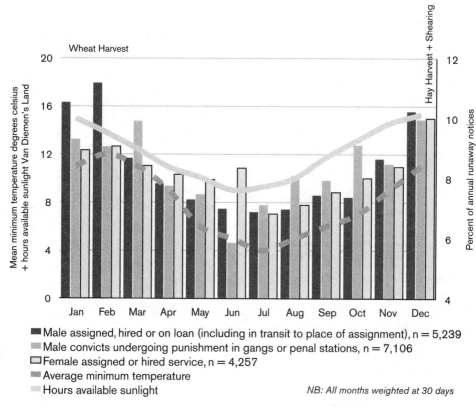

FIGURE 8.3. Month convicts absconded as recorded in runaway notices, 1824–1860.

ganging was employed to extract labor from the bodies of prisoners (Fig. 8.4). The data confirms that it was push factors that primarily drove absconding rates, rather than the lure of the brothel and the public bar. Whenever the rate of coercion increased, convicts voted with their feet and left.

While most convicts who escaped from private service ran on their own, the rate of collective absconding increased with the severity of the labor extraction process. On average each attempt to escape from a penal station involved the gazetting of more than two prisoners (Fig. 8.5). The actual rate is likely to have been greater, since some runaways were probably apprehended before the *Government Gazette* went to press. A heavy emphasis on ganging not only triggered higher running rates, but resulted in an increased collective withdrawal of labor.

The state responded by sentencing significant numbers of absconders to terms of service in chain gangs and penal stations. This action effectively curbed desertion rates but came at a cost. Irons were not a productivity aid and penal stations

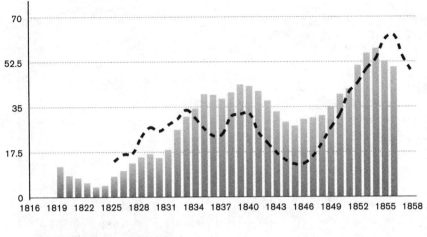

FIGURE 8.4. Voting with their feet: ganging and male absconding rates.

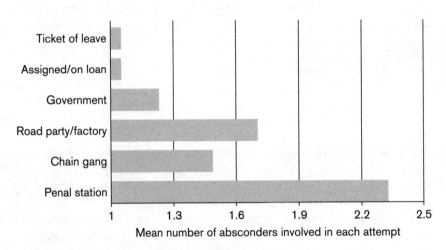

FIGURE 8.5. Collective absconding, Van Diemen's Land, 1824–1860.

were costly to maintain. In order to stamp out the distemper of running, the open-air panopticon was forced to adopt the architectural apparatus of confinement, cutting productivity.

Newspaper reports provide more evidence that work fueled running away. Edward Holloway and Andrew Phenn, who were sentenced to 50 lashes for absconding from the Sandy Bay road gang with a number of others in 1835, told the bench they had left due to the privations in the rations supplied by their overseer. This is typical of numerous cases except that in this instance the evidence of mistreatment was so compelling that the bench determined to investigate the matter further.[55]

Harsh treatment, poor rations, and inadequate clothing were common complaints when absconders were recaptured. In some cases absconding followed the failure of an earlier dissent such as a complaint to a master or a strike. At other times the actions were almost coincident. In March 1834 for instance, seven convicts belonging to the Bridgewater gang were charged with defacing their irons with intent to escape while three others were convicted of refusing to work.[56] On 6 December 1844 James Dickie, Charles Gordon, and John Porter were each charged with insubordination in endeavoring to create a riot and also breaking out of confinement at night from the Hamilton Farm.[57]

Absconding was occasionally connected to incendiarism, bushranging (a colonial term used to describe attacks and robberies committed by armed absconders), and other forms of revenge on a hated employer. In 1832 several convicts set fire to a haystack of their master Edward Gough's Verulam property near Launceston before absconding—they were apprehended but escaped conviction for incendiarism because the only evidence was the dying testimony of one of those involved.[58] The *Hobart Town Courier* urged that men sentenced by magistrates for misconduct to road or chain gangs should be kept as far as away from their master's farm as possible because they would not only run away but induce others to do so in order to attack the place where they had been employed.[59]

Absconding was a form of industrial dissent among convicts. It was practiced on a large scale and could have wider political ramifications. Indeed, for convicts absconding offered advantages compared to other forms of protest like strikes, insolence or neglect, and slowdowns where punishment and a return to the employer—with the prospect of retributive treatment—were more certain. Runaways could "melt" into a community not too distant from where they escaped, claim to be free, and, as newspaper reports indicate, remain undetected. If they could reach the mainland chances of detection were even more remote. In 1839 James Shalvey was recaptured in Sydney and sentenced to Port Arthur for two years—but even in this case he had been at large for 12 months prior to his arrest.[60] Once transportation to New South Wales ended in 1840 and demand for labor in Port Philip increased, the chances of arrest diminished further. Even if apprehended and sentenced to a road gang a worker still might be sent to another employer at the end of their sentence (especially if the original master was exasperated or had found a replacement).

Absconding, including collective absconding, should be seen as a significant aspect of convict resistance to their conditions of work along with strikes, riots, slowdowns, and other forms of protest. There is ample evidence that in many instances absconding was a direct response to grievances at work. Indeed, the data for Van Diemen's Land indicates it was the favored form of protest and for good reason as it gave aggrieved convicts the best chance of escaping a harsh master or other conditions. It was a form of protest shaped by the particular conditions of convict labor. Absconding was also a common form of protest by free workers in the first half of the nineteenth century, bound under the punitive conditions of master and servant and maritime and military labor laws. It was particularly common among specific groups of workers, most notably merchant seamen and whalers, whose work experiences and discipline most closely approximated convicts. This point sets an important context for understanding absconding by convicts.

An emphasis on absconding is also important because of the enormous challenges and costs it posed for the government and its enforcement arms (the police and the courts) and for private employers and the wider community. Absconding was disruptive to the administration of labor; it was expensive (both in terms of time and resources) to apprehend and try absconders; and, notwithstanding harsh penalties, difficult to deter. For many private employers it represented a loss of workers that could prove especially costly when skills were in short supply or seasonal demands for labor was at its peak.

Yet contradictions arose when some employers were only too happy to engage workers without inquiring too closely into whether they were free (as many claimed) or were absconders. In effect absconding convicts had realistic prospects of exchanging unfreedom for a form of semi-freedom laboring for poor wages and perks in a shadow colonial economy. There is an irony here. Penal transportation was cost effective as a form of punishment because it was able to co-opt the services of private landholders and business owners, who were provided with access to convict labor on the cheap in return for covering the costs of clothing, feeding, and housing their charges. The problem was that employers could cut their labor costs still further by hiring runaways. The state sought to address this problem by penalizing employers who engaged absconding convicts, but the effort had at best a limited deterrent effect. Thus, the market demand for labor, the mechanism that enabled the British state to minimize the costs of penal transportation, also worked to undermine the colonial government's hold on its convict charges.

There has been a tendency to treat penal transportation to the Australian colonies as a bizarre interlude in the wider history of the rise of the prison.[61] As more recent work has shown, including the contributions to this volume by Leo Lucassen, Yevan Terrien, Matthias van Rossum, and Johan Heinsen, all of the Western empires utilized the labor of convicts. The overseas deployment and exploitation of convicted labor was one of a number of overlapping mechanisms used by global capital to direct manpower to areas where workers were in short supply.[62] In the case of Australia, convict labor enabled the British to seize a continent. As

Pomeranz has argued, the sheepwalks of New South Wales and Van Diemen's Land were critical to the development of the nineteenth-century Yorkshire wool industry.[63] The penal "experiment" was thus neither unique to Australia nor detached from the wider processes of colonization.

In some ways convicts were the ideal unfree labor force. As they had already been found guilty in a court of law, it was easy to justify the levels of punishment meted out to transported workers. The thrashing of thieves attracted little attention from humanitarians. Such strategies also shaped attitudes to convict resistance. Attempts to ameliorate the conditions under which convicts served could easily be passed off as evidence that they were work-shy recidivists. Such views have prevented serious analysis of the extent to which penal workers challenged the conditions under which they toiled. Yet there is plenty of evidence that convicts did resist the colonial capitalist order. They often did so in conjunction with those who were free, but even when acting on their own they used the methods of resistance common to the subalterns of empire. Desertion was chief among these.

NOTES

1. Hamish Maxwell-Stewart, "'Like Poor Galley Slaves': Slavery and Convict Transportation," in *Legacies of Slavery: Comparative Perspectives*, ed. Marie Suzette Fernandes Dias (Newcastle: Cambridge Scholars, 2007), 56–57.

2. Stephen Nicholas, "The Care and Feeding of Convicts," in *Convict Workers: Reinterpreting Australia's Past*, ed. S. Nicholas (Cambridge University Press, Cambridge, 1988), 187, and House of Commons, *Accounts and Papers*, 13, "Crime, Police, Convicts" (1843), XLII:158.

3. Bruce Hindmarsh, "Beer and Fighting: Some Aspects of Male Convict Leisure in Van Diemen's Land," *Journal of Australian Studies* 23 (1999): 152–53.

4. David Meredith and Deborah Oxley, "Contracting Convicts: The Convict Labour Market in Van Diemen's Land 1840–1857," *Australian Economic History Review* 45, no. 1 (2005): 45–72.

5. See for example *Colonial Times*, 23 February 1841.

6. *Hobart Town Gazette and Van Diemen's Land Advertiser*, 25 February 1825.

7. See for example *Tasmanian*, 19 September 1828; *Colonial* Times, 6 August 1830; *Hobart Town Courier*, 28 July 1837; *Tasmanian Weekly Dispatch*, 4 December 1840; *Launceston Examiner*, 12 November 1842.

8. Stefan Petrow, "Policing in a Penal Colony: Governor Arthur's Police System in Van Diemen's Land, 1826–1836," *Law and History Review* 18, no. 2 (2000): 351–96.

9. Kay Daniels, *Convict Women* (Sydney: Allen and Unwin, 1998), 103–33.

10. James C. Scott, *Seeing Like a State* (New Haven, CT: Yale University Press, 1998), 53–84.

11. Robert Shoemaker and Richard Ward, "Understanding the Criminal: Record Keeping, Statistics and the Early History of Criminology in England," *British Journal of Criminology* 57, no. 6 (2017): 1442–61.

12. Hamish Maxwell-Stewart and James Bradley, "'Behold the Man': Power, Observation and the Tattooed Convict," *Australian Studies* 12, no. 1 (1997): 72–75.

13. David Roberts, "A 'Change of Place': Illegal Movement on the Bathurst Frontier, 1822–1825," *Journal of Australian Colonial History* 7 (2005): 97–122.

14. Roberts, "'Change of Place,'" 99.

15. *Hobart Town Courier,* 18 October 1848.

16. Roberts, " 'Change of Place,' " 101–2; *Courier,* 7 October 1842, 4.

17. *Colonial Times,* 19 July 1836.

18. Alan Atkinson, "Four Patterns of Convict Protest," *Labour History* 37 (1979): 36.

19. Roberts, " 'Change of Place,' " 97.

20. Ian Duffield, "Cutting Out and Taking Liberties: Australia's Convict Pirates, 1790–1829," in *Mutiny and Maritime Radicalism in the Age of Revolution: A Global Survey,* ed. C. Anderson, N. Frykman, L. H. van Voss, and M. Rediker, 197–228 (Cambridge: Cambridge University Press, 2013).

21. Robert W. Connell and Terence H. Irving, *Class Structure in Australian History, Documents, Narrative and Argument* (Melbourne: Melbourne University Press, 1984), 50.

22. Michael Quinlan, *The Origins of Worker Mobilisation in Australia 1788–1850* (New York: Routledge, 2018).

23. Kay Saunders, " 'Troublesome Servants': The Strategies of Resistance Employed by Melanesian Indentured Labourers on Plantations in Colonial Queensland," *Journal of Pacific History* 14, no. 3 (1979): 168–83; Michael Quinlan, Margaret Gardner, and Peter R. Akers, "Reconsidering the Collective Impulse: Formal Organisation and Informal Associations amongst Workers in the Australian Colonies, 1795–1850," *Labour—Le Travail* 52 (2003): 137–80; Michael Quinlan, "The Low Rumble of Informal Dissent: Shipboard Protests over Health and Safety in Australian Waters, 1790–1900," *Labour History* 102 (2012): 1–26.

24. Quinlan, "Low Rumble of Informal Dissent."

25. *Colonial Times,* 16 June 1835; *Hobart Town Courier,* 21 August 1835.

26. See for example *Cornwall Chronicle,* 20 February 1847.

27. See for example *Launceston Advertiser,* 20 September 1833.

28. *Cornwall Chronicle,* 9 February 1848.

29. *Launceston Examiner,* 28 November 1848.

30. See for example *Colonial Times,* 8 February 1831; *Courier,* 20 January 1843.

31. Hamish Maxwell-Stewart, *Closing Hell's Gates: The Death of a Convict Station* (Sydney: Allen and Unwin, 2008), 54.

32. Roberts, " 'Change of Place,' " 112.

33. *Hobart Town Gazette and Van Diemen's Land Advertiser,* 5 March 1824.

34. *Colonial Times,* 26 May 1826.

35. *Colonial Times,* 11 October 1842.

36. *Colonist and Van Diemen's Land Commercial and Agricultural Advertiser,* 31 December 1833.

37. *Hobart Town Gazette and Van Diemen's Land Advertiser,* 5 March 1824.

38. *Cornwall Chronicle,* 28 October 1840.

39. *Hobart Town Courier,* 22 November 1828.

40. TAHO, John Lakeland, 28 January 1828, CSO1-1-199, 4745: 240–44.

41. Margaret C. Dillon, "Convict Labour and Colonial Society in the Campbell Town Police District 1820–1839" (PhD thesis, University of Tasmania, 2008), 110, 140–41.

42. *Hobart Town Courier,* 1 October 1831, 11 January 1839.

43. Maxwell-Stewart, *Closing Hell's Gates,* 165–202.

44. E. P. Thompson, "The Moral Economy of the English Crowd in the Eighteenth Century," *Past and Present* 50 (1971): 76–136; James C. Scott, *The Moral Economy of the Peasant: Rebellion and Subsistence in South East Asia* (New Haven, CT: Yale University Press, 1976); John Bohstedt, *The Politics of Provisions: Food Riots, Moral Economy, and Market Transition in England, c. 1550–1850* (London: Ashgate, 2010).

45. *Colonial Times,* 28 January 1834.

46. *Colonial Times,* 23 March 1841.

47. Hamish Maxwell-Stewart, "'This is the bird that never flew': William Stewart, Major Donald MacLeod and the Launceston Advertiser," *Journal of Australian Colonial History* 2, no. 1 (2000): 1–28.

48. Tom P. Dunning and Hamish Maxwell-Stewart, "Mutiny at Deloraine: Ganging and Convict Resistance in 1840s Van Diemen's Land," *Labour History* 82 (2002): 35–47.

49. Marcus Rediker, *Between the Devil and the Deep Blue Sea: Merchant Seaman, Pirates and the Anglo-American Maritime World 1700–1750* (Cambridge: Cambridge University Press, 1987), 205.

50. Hamish Maxwell-Stewart, "Convict Labour Extraction and Transportation from Britain and Ireland 1615–1870," in *Convict Labour: A Global Regime*, ed. Christian G. de Vito and Alex Lichtenstein (Leiden: Brill, 2015), 188.

51. Nigel Worden, "Revolt in Cape Colonial Slave Society," in *Resisting Bondage Resisting Bondage in Indian Ocean Africa and Asia*, ed. Edward A. Alpers, Gwyn Campbell, and Michael Salman (London: Routledge, 2007), 10–23.

52. Lucy Frost, *Abandoned Women: Scottish Convicts Exiled beyond the Seas* (Sydney: Allen and Unwin, 2012), 80–142.

53. Kirsty Reid, *Gender, Crime and Empire: Convicts, Settlers and the State in Early Colonial Australia* (Manchester: Manchester University Press, 2007), 133–37.

54. Ian Brand et al., *The Convict Probation System: Van Diemen's Land, 1839–1854* (Hobart: Blubber Head Press, 1990), 62.

55. *Colonial Times*, 15 September 1835.

56. *Colonial Times*, 11 March 1834.

57. James Dickie, Police Number 6706, Con 33/28; Charles Gordon, Police Number 10706, Con 33/45 and John Porter, Police Number 12883, Con 33/54.

58. *Launceston Advertiser*, 22 February 1832.

59. *Hobart Town Courier*, 6 June 1834.

60. *Hobart Town Courier*, 11 January 1839.

61. Robert Hughes, *The Fatal Shore: The Epic of Australia's Founding* (London: Vintage, 1988).

62. Clare Anderson, ed., *A Global History of Convicts and Penal Colonies* (London: Bloomsbury, 2018); Hamish Maxwell-Stewart, "The Rise and Fall of Penal Transportation," in *Oxford Handbook of the History of Crime and Criminal Justice*, ed. Anya Johansen, 335–654 (Oxford: Oxford University Press, 2016).

63. Kenneth Pomeranz, *The Great Divergence: China, Europe, and the Making of the Modern World Economy* (Princeton, NJ: Princeton University Press, 2000), 276.

9

"He says that if he is not taught a trade, he will run away"

Recaptured Africans, Desertion, and Mobility in the British Caribbean, 1808–1828

Anita Rupprecht

Aquabia had been living on the tiny British West Indian island of Tortola for eight years when he made the threat that precedes the title of this chapter. Aged twelve, he had been forced aboard a Spanish slaving vessel, the *Atrevido*, probably at Bonny or Old Calabar, and survived the Middle Passage bound for Havana.[1] As it entered the Caribbean, the ship was captured by the British Navy, and escorted to Tortola where the Vice Admiralty Court condemned the vessel as an illegal trader. Aquabia was disembarked and detained in the island's barracks where he was renamed Paul. On February 22, 1815, he was indentured for fourteen years to a Tortola merchant, Richard Roberts, who made him haul bales of cotton and failed to feed him properly for years. One day, Paul stole some wine and pork so Roberts turned him out of the house and made him haul wood instead. Paul had had enough of backbreaking menial labor and being hungry. He knew that the terms of his indenture—that stipulated that he be taught a trade—were not being met, and he knew about the British Royal Commissioners who had turned up on the island to inspect the progress of the humanitarian labor policy. As soon as they arrived, he hid his good clothes, donned dirty rags, appeared before them, and made his threat. Having made use of Paul's labor for nearly a decade, Roberts responded by telling the commissioners that his bonded servant was a liar, a thief, impudent and lazy, and "that he wished to give him up." The commissioners complied with the request and transferred Paul's indenture to Ben Dougan, a free black ship's carpenter.[2]

As Clare Anderson notes, nineteenth-century "empire's variously staggered [slave] emancipations were moments that laid the ground for the production of new coerced labour forms."[3] Indeed, the British pioneered what would become a new global capitalist system of indentured labor that mobilized hundreds of thousands of workers, mostly from India and from parts of China, once slavery had ended. Paul's protest, however, illustrates the complexity of laboring conditions that existed within Caribbean society *prior* to the ending of slavery. It also indicates that the similarly staggered set of Acts to abolish the transoceanic slave trades decades prior to slavery's endings, in part, laid preparatory ground for the ways in which imperial labor would be managed once enslavement had been outlawed. Between 1807 and 1867, some 181,000 "recaptured" or "liberated" Africans arrived in the Americas where they were put to work in a wide variety of coerced laboring conditions. A further 100,000 Africans were disembarked in Sierra Leone, just over 5,000 in the Cape Colony, over 1,000 in Mauritius, and just over 24,000 in St Helena. Many were subsequently moved again from those sites.[4] The experience of indentureship differed depending on the particular site of "liberation"; nevertheless together they created a global landscape of colonial apprenticeship shaped by the irreconcilable poles of commercial capitalist interest and humanitarian governance through the nineteenth century.[5]

Paul's enforced narrative above is drawn from the documents of a Royal Commission sent to the Caribbean in 1821, twelve years before the British ended slavery. Under intensifying antislavery pressure from within and without Parliament, the commission was charged with investigating the "state" and "condition" of those Africans who, since the passing of the British Abolition Act in 1807, had been rescued from slaving vessels operating illegally in, or near, the Caribbean. The act had legislated for the destiny of those Africans, and recalibrated their identities (again), by licensing the British Navy to seize them as contraband property to be held by the crown. Once "condemned," however, under no circumstances were they to be "sold, disposed of, treated or dealt with as Slaves."[6] Local officials were authorized to "enlist the same, or any of them, into His Majesty's Land, or Sea Service, as Soldiers, Seamen, or Marines, or to bind the same or any of them, whether of full Age or not as Apprentices, for any Term not exceeding Fourteen Years." The law stipulated that the Africans were to enter into these new relationships "as if" they had done so "voluntarily."[7] Drawn up in the context of imperial war, the act thus provided an alternative to the purchase of enslaved Africans for the British armed forces in the Caribbean, and guaranteed, however inadequately, a continued supply of bound and disciplined labor for the sugar colonies.[8]

Over five years, three sets of commissioners traveled to eight sugar colonies and accounted for some 3,500 Africans who had been rescued and then enlisted into the British military services or indentured alongside the enslaved.[9] Embedded in the mass of documents assembled by the commission, Paul's threat to run and his "rescue" were thus viewed as part of the discrepant "results" of an experiment in an alternative form of coerced labor, administered publicly rather than privately, the terms of which were deemed to be necessarily reforming. But it is also evidence of the ways in which Africans made their own contributions to metropolitan debates about colonial subjecthood, servitude, and self-ownership in the years immediately prior to emancipation.

Many historians have noted that so-called "liberated Africans," who arrived in the Americas in this manner, lived lives little better than if they had been enslaved, suggesting that the difference between slavery and "apprenticeship" was in name only. Paul's testimony, however, demands that the distance between servitude and slavery be recognized, making it clear that the legal difference certainly mattered to the Africans themselves. They understood the specific terms of their indenture—that they be taught a trade—very clearly. In this particular context, Paul's threat to run was a crucial way of contesting his bondage, and a medium for negotiation and bargaining.

The following case study focuses on the culture of absconding developed by the rescued Africans who were disembarked and indentured, prior to the ending of slavery, in Tortola in the British Virgin Islands. This culture was produced and shaped by the pivotal historical moment within which it took place, by the socioeconomic and geographical particularity of its location, and by the Africans' rejection of the terms and conditions of their bonded labor. While the practice of running away enacted by Tortola's bonded servants, indentured among the enslaved prior to emancipation, cannot be understood as representative of all "liberated Africans" who arrived in the Caribbean between 1807 and 1867, not to mention those on the coasts of Africa and in the Indian Ocean, it certainly speaks loudly to the colonially targeted patterns of labor resistance generally associated with the transition from transatlantic enslavement to other forms of coerced labor migration. Worker mobility itself was a central site of struggle.

Tortola's vulnerability to the waning of British mercantilist interest in the British Caribbean sugar islands was already starkly evident in 1807. Located sixty miles east of Puerto Rico, at the northern tip of the Leewards bordering Drake's Passage, the tiny island—twelve miles long and just over three miles wide—was in severe economic decline when the first seventy traumatized Africans disembarked from the American brig *Nancy* in late November of that year.[10] Planters were abandoning their estates or removing their enslaved to other, more profitable, colonies, particularly to the new crown colonies of Trinidad and Guyana. By 1815, the enslaved population had nearly halved in forty years, standing at 5,765 people, while the white population was one quarter of what it had been. Living on the island were 296 white residents and 681 free blacks.[11] Between 1808 and 1822, planters moved ninety-five enslaved workers, and in 1825 alone, a further 1,055 were removed.[12]

Due to its strategic location and favorable anchorage, Tortola had a Vice Admiralty Court. As the English travel writer Trelawney Wentworth lamented in 1822, while the court "contributed in no inconsiderable degree to its resources and prosperity . . . the termination of the war had put a sudden and serious check to them."[13] In 1807, however, the Abolition Act had brought a new source of business to the

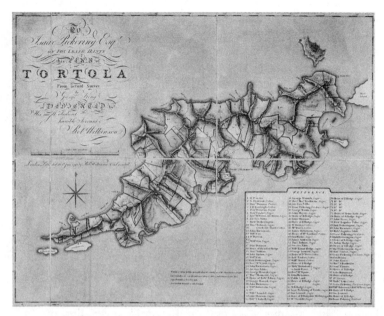

FIGURE 9.1. "To Isaac Pickering Esqr of Fox Lease Hants this plan of Tortola from actual survey by George King, 1798." This map shows the island's (total) division into 104 plantations, the location of sugar works, and contains a list of all plantation owners.

court when it became more profitable to attack slaving vessels, and for local colonials to condemn the ships and take control of their valuable cargoes of captives. Between 1807 and 1822, just over 1,300 illegally transported Africans were condemned by the court, the vast majority of whom disembarked from four large Spanish vessels—the *Manuella, Venus, Candelaria,* and *Atrevido*—all of which had been bound for Havana, in 1814 and 1815.[14] The commissioners later recorded that 248 had died in detention before they were either enlisted or indentured; 352 had been "taken into His Majesty's military and naval service," while 647 were indentured to people on the island and surrounding keys.[15]

This large group arrived during a period of severe drought that was followed, in 1819, by a devastating hurricane that laid waste to many of the island's remaining estates, damaged the harbor, sunk ships, and leveled homes in the capital, Road Town. Colonials believed the storm to have dealt "a final blow" to the island's "importance."[16] For the rest of the island's population, and for the new arrivals, the storm exacerbated further the contradictions emerging from the shifting social relations of production produced by the already parlous circumstances.

While sweeping the island's "desolate" landscape for novelty three years later, Wentworth's colonial gaze registered something of these contradictions in terms of breached boundaries and confused hierarchies: "The extensive ranges of waste land and pasturage, afford the negroes an opportunity of cultivating provisions to an almost unlimited extent," he noted, while "some of them possess several head of horned cattle, as well as goats and sheep." He observed that the slave law prohibiting cattle ownership had clearly been disregarded. More remarkably, these illegal oxen were being herded together with "the stock belonging to the estates," and even hired out to planters.[17] Wentworth ignored the grinding poverty, food shortages, and daily struggle for most of the island's population. Instead, he saw people with apparently not much to do, and inhabiting spaces where they were not supposed to be. He was clearly surprised to see the indentured Africans, whom he described disparagingly as "protégés of the government," making up most of the crowd at an auction in town. He wrote,

> At an auction we witnessed in the Road Town the number of negroes perhaps exceeded that of the white and coloured portion of the assemblage, and we were naturally led to inquire into that apparent independence in their use of their time, which their attendance seemed to bespeak.[18]

Wentworth's pompous aestheticizing was a perfect vehicle for glossing the fact that he was looking, if not at a world turning upside down, then one in certain transition. His sarcastic comment that it was only "natural" to inquire into the indentured African's "apparent independence in their use of their time," registers his recognition of the (errant) forms of autonomy and mobility that were being carved out of their bondage in the context of weakening planter authority.[19]

ARRIVAL, DETENTION, AND RESISTANCE

Africans who disembarked from illegal slave ships were detained around the Atlantic World in secure holding areas prior to their enlistment or indenture. In 1811, a specially built, walled "recruiting depot" was established in Free Town, Sierra Leone, known as the King's Yard.[20] Beginning in 1818, the *emancipados* were confined in Rio de Janeiro's house of correction, the city jail.[21] A wooden "African Depot" was erected in Key West for those arriving in the United States, encircled by a six-foot-high fence that extended into the surf.[22] The first rescued Africans to disembark in Tortola were confined in the island's barracks that came to be known locally as the "Guinea Yard." The widespread use of places of detention hinted at future contests over mobility.

The 1808 Orders in Council charged local Collectors of Customs—relatively junior colonial officials who were used to dealing in smuggled goods but not in smuggled persons—with the responsibility of recalibrating each African's identity from illegal property to involuntary laborer. Those who were deemed to be unfit for enlistment were to be placed with "prudent and humane masters and mistresses."

Bonded servants were to be provided with food, clothing, given religious instruction, and taught a trade. Fieldwork was legally prohibited.

Collectors were also tasked with the regulation of the indentureships. They were required to submit annual reports detailing all indentures and their progress. If they were unable to produce an apprentice for inspection, collectors were liable for a fine: the amount payable would be equivalent to "double the sum at which an apprentice would be valued if to be sold as a slave."[23] Practically, this stipulation was designed to deter corruption. Collectors, in collaboration with customs and court officials, were tempted, and did, funnel their charges straight back into the slave trade, especially in the early years of suppression. The measure of monetary value and equivalence also references the persistence of the rescued Africans' legal proximity to property rather than "freedom" throughout the "rescue" narrative.[24]

Collectors struggled to control the newly arrived Africans held in confinement. Those who arrived from Senegal aboard the *Nancy,* the first ship to be condemned in Tortola in 1807, had fought their captors for the entire transatlantic crossing by repeatedly attempting to break out of the vessel's hold, attacking the captain, and rising several times on the crew. Three had been killed in the fighting, others had been shot and stabbed, one had leapt overboard, and many more arrived wounded.[25] Even though they were severely depleted by their Middle Passages, many Africans carried their fury with them onto the shore. During these early days of the policy, their attempts to escape detention exposed a loophole in the hastily assembled suppression laws designed to de-commodify the Africans. Collectors of Customs, despite their new responsibilities, had no legal authority over their charges, and so were in no position to criminalize their resistance to their confinement.[26] In law, the Africans, who were no longer classified as contraband goods, and who were not yet indentured or impressed, were effectively "free" despite the fact that they were detained. From the beginning, absconding promised liberty.

At a "complete loss" as to how to force the rescued Africans to submit to his will, Antigua's collector, Wyke, appealed to the judge of the Vice Admiralty Court for permission to build "suitable apartments for occasional confinement" in order to quell "drunken and riotous" behavior, and to confine "stragglers and runaways." He complained that his struggle to "secure good order and subordination" was increasingly met by the Africans kicking down the doors of the barracks with defiant laughter.[27] The Vice Admiralty judge suggested that Wyke needed to write to the British secretary of state as his local court could only hear complaints by Africans who had already been indentured. Moreover, he noted, English apprenticeship laws did not apply in the colony.[28] Increasingly desperate, and unable to prevent the Africans from escaping his attempts to secure them, Wyke finally wrote to London asking for money to "put the Africans afloat out of harms way." On receipt of the grant, he hired a 200-ton vessel to act as a prison hulk, placed the Africans on board, and moored it out in the harbor.[29]

In Tortola, the collector also struggled to prevent the rescued Africans from disappearing from the barracks. He enlisted other Africans, or "Bombas," who spoke the "African and the English language," to help him ensure that they were neither "stolen" nor that they absconded.[30] Francis Welsch, "a free coloured man" hired by Tortola's collector to feed the Africans, reported that despite the fact that he and the Bombas counted them twice a day, they nevertheless ran, and had to be hunted down.[31] In 1825, the Tortola collector refused to accept a group of indentured Africans from the governor of St. Kitts because he was concerned about being fined if they ran away. His letter to the Colonial Office listed a string of objections to accepting any more apprentices on to the island, nearly all of which referred to his limited "powers of correction."[32] As the records of the Royal Commission make clear, the collector's anxieties were born out of hard experience. The Africans kept on running after they had been indentured.

INDENTURE AND REGULATION

The archive of this almost completely ignored Royal Commission provides an extremely rich source of information about the ways in which the indentured Africans protested their conditions. More significantly, it sheds light on the significance of desertion for the metropolitan officials, local colonials, and for Africans themselves. The lists of individuals, tallying of numbers, statistics, multiple decisions and judgments offer a vivid reminder of the ways in which instrumental economic imperative, imperial interest, and fantasies about appropriate colonial subjectivity framed official visions of alternatives to enslaved labor in the Caribbean in the years prior to emancipation.[33] In this sense, the documents show how African identity came into question as British imperialists looked for ways to control how slavery ended within what would remain a colonially administered plantation context. The records are not simply an expression of that white control fantasy, however. Their paper remains are part of an early attempt to enact it. In other words, the sources do not simply provide a commentary on what happened; rather, their most expressive significance lies in the highly contested ways in which they were produced in the colonies.

The investigative process was not orderly or coherent, and as an effort in colonial surveillance and regulation, it cannot be said to have been successful. The veneer of order and precision evinced by the "schedules" and tables is punctured by multiple instances that record dissent, rejection, bargaining, fury, and opposition. The commissioners located, counted, and interviewed the apprenticed Africans, recording their findings as judgments of character, ability, and attitude. Unsurprisingly, the archive contains no testimony written by the indentured Africans themselves, but elements of the interviews were recorded by clerks who often directly transcribed snatches of the Africans' replies to the commissioners' questions.

Moreover, copious peripheral documents, including letters, affidavits, and espe-cially the daily minute books, capture more substantially the verbatim words of the African interviewees.

On Tortola, the inquiry was held in the Custom House where the records of the original condemnations were stored. Its structure, its daily routines, and the way in which it elicited particular performances from each individual necessarily shaped the picture of labor relations that emerges from the records. That picture is particularly detailed due, in part, to the interminable, and in the end irreconcila-ble, disputes between the two commissioners. One, Thomas Moody, was a staunch defender of slavery and with long military experience in the Caribbean. The other, John Dougan, was a Tortolan ex-slaveholder turned evangelical abolitionist. If the internal procedures of the commission were fractured by personal and ideological animosity, any evidence garnered from this inquiry also needs to take into account the ways in which it disrupted external everyday relations on the island.

Colonials, increasingly anxious about the intensification of London's imperial meddling in their arbitrary, violent, and exploitative affairs, resented the imposi-tion. Like Paul, many impoverished apprentices knew that the commission was concerned with their situation, and they were eager to appear before the metro-politan officials. By the early 1820s, ideas, opinions, and rumors about the antislav-ery movement in Britain were circulating across all classes in the sugar colonies, igniting resistance and work stoppages. In Tortola, colonial hostility to the sup-posed purposes of the inquiry also influenced the nature and tenor of the informa-tion accumulated. Not long after the inquiry began, Dougan resigned precipitously from his post in exasperation with Moody's vicious racial prejudice and his demean-ing treatment of the Africans. Dougan sailed immediately for London to petition the Colonial Office but was persuaded to return. While he was away, an alarmed member of the island's Assembly warned Moody that "an Opinion was entertained in the Island that Mr. Dougan had gone home, to get the Slaves emancipated."[34]

The interview records are indelibly marked by the limited and limiting ques-tions the colonial administrators put to the indentured Africans as well as by the complex web of power and dissent that positioned the visiting metropolitan com-missioners, local colonial officials, masters, and mistresses, and the interviewees in relation to each other. While the multiple voices are orchestrated by the persistent theme of running away, they register a sense of the forms of community, collective struggle, and connection between apprentices, the enslaved and free people, both black and white, that existed beyond the inquiry room. The metropolitan over-sight imposed on the indentured Africans meant that they could not be as tightly controlled as their colonial employers desired, while the Africans themselves opened up—through their mobility and creativity—the fault lines produced by the imperial legislation explicitly designed to impose "a measure of constraint" on their masters and mistresses as well as on their own activities. Many sparse and unsatisfactory sentences register the commissioners' frustrations, and the employ-ers' defensive complaints, but they also show how the boundaries between differ-ent forms of colonial labor drawn from above were being consistently and deter-minedly *redrawn* from below.

The indentured Africans represented a new and cheap source of labor to planters, merchants, and colonial elites. Given the well-established moral economy of the island's creole enslaved, it is possible to imagine that they were viewed as a new source of refreshingly pliable labor, even if fieldwork was technically "prohibited." So many Africans had arrived in 1814 and 1815 that they had also provided an opportu-nity for poorer creoles to supplement their tiny incomes. The Africans entered a wide variety of bonded situations on the island, as across the British Caribbean. In common with similar practices elsewhere, the legal requirements stipulating the terms of the contract were bent to favor those who had social influence. As Thomas Audain, a "respectable carpenter" and Daniel Johnson, one of the island's tailors, found out to their dismay, colonial officials and "the principal planters of the island" monopolized the indenturing process. Taking first pick of the new arrivals, they con-tracted large numbers as domestic workers for their households or to profit from their labor by hiring them out. Ex-Jamaica slaveholder Abraham Mendes Belisario, the marshal of Tortola's Vice Admiralty Court, made sure that he acquired twenty-four servants from the *Manuella* for himself whom he employed as carpenters, "Domestics," "Washes," and boatmen. He then hired his indentured trainee carpen-ters back out to local tradesmen, including Thomas Audain. The wealthy Tortola planter George Forbes took twenty-nine men and women. He did not sign the indenture papers, rendering them "imperfect." He then transported the servants to his new estate on Nevis, the majority of whom he put to work in "cane-holing."[35]

Outside of the plantations, the Africans found themselves bonded among all strata of the white and black population, and even to other rescued Africans whose own indentures had expired. Many lived in urban or semi-urban situations, work-ing in menial service for the impoverished free black petty-trading population. The initial allocation of laboring positions was explicitly gendered. Female "apprentices" were employed as house servants, cooks, washerwomen, or seam-stresses, while men worked as porters, gardeners, or cleaners. Some worked as stevedores, fishermen, and mariners, and some (as the imperial law stipulated) were bound to tradesmen—coopers, carpenters, builders, cobblers, or tailors—although when this was the case, very few were actually engaged in learning the requisite skills. More often, they were employed as domestic servants and perhaps worked their employer's provision grounds, or they were hired out to carry out the menial jobs that no other member of the colony would do. Belisario hired one of his apprentices, George, to the island's jailor "to clear the prison of all filth daily." He noted that "a white or free coloured man would not do that Duty" and he would have to pay a slave.[36]

A CULTURE OF ABSCONDING

Complaints about the mobility of the indentured servants marble the commission records. The vast majority of those who absconded did so temporarily and repeatedly—each occasion lasting anything from a few weeks or months to several years. The term "runaway" describes servants who are missing, or it is stated that servants "absented" themselves for certain periods of time. The apprentices did not use the same terms to explain their actions. Where their words appear to have been directly transcribed, explanations for leaving or returning to a place of indenture are cast in terms of "staying" or "going."

Servants said that they ran away to escape physical abuse. For example, Hannah had run after being put to fieldwork and repeatedly cart-whipped.[37] George, indentured as a mariner, disappeared after he was whipped with a towline for taking too long at the market. Other servants were compelled to run from a sense of the injustice stemming from the comparison of their own labor relation to that of other workers on the island. Given that they were not enslaved, they protested the fact that they were unwaged. For example, Bonaparte was first indentured to a planter who "punished him too much." When the planter died, Bonaparte was transferred to a "free coloured mariner," Benjamin Smith. Bonaparte did not complain about his new employer who, he said, "was kind to him" but, in explaining why he had been missing for the last four months, he stated bitterly that his countrymen "tell him somebody make him fool. That he works for nothing and gets no money to put in his pocket." Smith informed the commissioners that when Bonaparte got "among his countrymen," they told him "that he is free."[38]

Cork, indentured to John Strachan, a ship's carpenter, had been absent for a month prior to his interview but turned up nevertheless. Strachen would not agree to let him have every other day to himself so Cork was effectively on strike. Cork complained that he was sleeping on the boat that he was repairing because he had nowhere else to go. As he left the interview room, he "demanded a bit per diem from his master." Presumably Cork was referring to the fact that jobbing slaves were paid "per diem." Cork did not have anywhere to sleep. Strachen had dismantled his house because, he said, Cork was "harbouring runaway negroes." He also stated that Cork's demands for flexible working hours and a regular wage were the result of the bad advice and bad company he had been keeping.[39]

The indentured servants argued that employers who had a property interest in their workers seemed to treat them more carefully. They explained angrily that, unlike themselves, the enslaved were considered to be valuable property and so owners had an interest in their welfare. Tom, called up in front of the commissioners and accused of helping his wife, Jane, escape to the next island, said, "This Tortola is very bad." He was aggrieved that his employer had not cared for Jane when she was sick. He went on to explain, those that "came to the Custom House to take Africans . . . suppose they get sick. Them say, they don't care nothing about them, because they have not paid any money for them." He said his employer had not provided clothing for his own children because "they did not belong to him." Tom divulged a sense of collective dissatisfaction and preparedness to run when he stated that if the servants were not given "a Piece of Bread to put in their Mouth" they would all run away. When asked where the servants went to when they ran, Tom answered that some had "gone into the Bush," or to St. Thomas, and that, if they were apprehended there, they would "get a Boat" and disappear. He noted that if they were beaten too much "two or three will make a Bargain to run away."[40]

Tom, like Paul in the opening example to this chapter, protested that his employment differed from what he had been led to expect. He had been indentured to a tailor, a "free coloured man" named William Phillips, and should have been trained in tailoring but Phillips had given him—with no authority—to a Mr. McCullen instead. McCullen made him herd cows. By the time Tom was interviewed, he been on the run for two and a half years, and was living in the home of a "free coloured woman" called Catherine Bennett. He sustained himself by collecting and selling wood. Rebecca, a fellow apprentice, provided his clothes.

The desire for autonomy, to be able to choose when, and if, to work at all, was often stronger than the threat of punishment. Acting on that desire was possible given the opportunities for petty trading and self-hiring. Bristol, indentured to George Patinelli, never stayed with him for more than a week at a time even though the merchant had jailed him repeatedly. Patinelli complained that "he is industrious when he works for himself but he will not work for his master." Another merchant, Luke Greenwood, reported that his servant Sam is "disobedient, industrious for himself; has quitted and gone to a foreign colony three or four times."[41] Abraham used the commission to try to negotiate his time between the duties stipulated by his indenture and his own desires for independence. He said that he "wished to serve his mistress" but "he wanted a little time to serve himself." Mrs. Hunter thought he was "very insolent."[42]

As these testimonies indicate, indentured servants who absconded had assessed their situation in comparison to others and decided to labor temporarily "elsewhere" for personal gain. They either took short-term waged work or they engaged in trading. The apprentices tilled abandoned land for themselves, or they worked the provision plots with the enslaved while many of them marketed surplus foodstuffs, and sometimes stock. Others collected firewood and grass to sell. Colonial employers were infuriated by these independent activities even if they did not interfere with the servant's primary occupation. For example, Belisario, the island's provost marshal, expected "gratitude" for his "kind treatment" of Frederick, and for the "expense" of training him as a carpenter. He profited from his skilled labor but Frederick also found time to raise his own stock to sell for himself. Belisario was outraged by what he called Frederick's "disobedience of orders, contumacy and insolent conduct." The employer's intense hostility to *African* self-sufficiency can be read in relation to racialized labor hierarchies and to the implications of the island's colonial decline. Such activities visibly undermined colonial authority, thereby further exacerbating the inherent antagonism of the master-unfree labor relationship. Determined to maintain boundaries and enforce subordination, employers interpreted the autonomous activities, and the circulation of knowledge about them, as spreading discontent, emboldening other servants, and unsettling the enslaved.

The servants made comparative judgments about the relative merits of their employers, and manipulated their situation to escape onerous oversight and to improve their contractual conditions. This possibility was facilitated by a network of local knowledge, supported by the fact that all strata of the island's free community employed indentured Africans. For example, Frederick maneuvered himself out of his indenture to Belisario and into a more flexible situation by behaving so badly that Belisario decided to give him up as he was nothing but a "burden." Before Belisario could find someone equally overbearing to whom he could transfer the indenture, Frederick approached Sally Keys, a free black woman, known for her sympathy toward the apprentices, and asked her if she would sign his indenture documents. Keys had no employment for Frederick and reported to the authorities that she agreed to the transfer "out of Charity." Keys, in fact, owed Frederick money and had agreed to take on the bond when "he offered to pay the Expense of the Indenture himself through her rather than not be taken by her." Thus, having paid for his own indenture—to Keys who did not expect "gratitude"—Frederick disappeared to St. Thomas a week later to sell his stock. Although Keys later denied it, the rumor quickly spread that she had given Frederick the "Liberty to work out at St. Thomas," prompting the rest of Belisario's indentured servants to lobby for the same concession.

While Frederick was missing, Harry, Belisario's "Head Carpenter" and also a leading figure among the apprentices, had a row with his violent foreman, shouting, "I wish you tell Massa to give me up."[43] Tom, another apprenticed carpenter, was heard to say, "I wish I could tand [*sic*] like Frederick" which meant the same thing. Both men recognized the success of Frederick's maneuver that had, in effect, allowed him to re-indenture himself (to himself) in circumstances that now granted him the mobility and autonomy to work where, when, and in what occupation he wished.

The majority of those apprentices who absconded from their employers did not go far—a reminder that island geography and the racialized violence of Caribbean slave society made full flight an extremely dangerous act for newly arrived Africans who were vulnerable to kidnap and re-enslavement. The port of Charlotte Amalie, on the nearby Danish island of St. Thomas, was less than twenty miles away, however. As a thriving and cosmopolitan free port, it operated as one of the busiest maritime crossroads in the Caribbean in sharp contrast to sleepy Tortola. It was also a place where anyone on the run could find shelter and work.

Attempts to regulate the mobility of the indentured Africans meant that time-limited passes were issued to Tortola's apprentices for the purposes of hiring out or self-hiring in St. Thomas. Yet many simply outstayed their duration, thereby turning a legitimate visit into an illegitimate one. The dense traffic across the calm waters between the Dutch and British islands meant that it was relatively easy to gain a covert passage. Sailing with some of Tortola's boatmen could be risky as two of Belisario's apprenticed "Washes," June and Venus, found out when they approached the Master of a Shallop for a passage to St. Thomas. The Master reported their attempt to Belisario but, undeterred, they tried again, and with the assistance of Jane's husband, Tom, were finally successful.[44] Apprentices sometimes stole boats to escape but more often they shipped with enslaved Danish fishermen or boatmen from the quays, for a small fee. Women found work as domestics and hucksters while, for men, the docks offered copious opportunities for employment in loading and unloading vessels, in warehousing and transporting goods, and as local maritime crew. Like Frederick, other apprentices absconded in order to sell their produce in Charlotte Amalie's busy market center that drew enslaved and freed people from across the islands to trade in surplus fruit, vegetables, stock, grass, and firewood. In such a busy and itinerant context, local employers tended to ignore the legal status and domicile of those who offered their short-term labor. While St. Thomas provided opportunities for marketing or short-term work, it also provided space for relaxation. Tortolan colonials who spotted runaways taking time out in St. Thomas saw them as engaging in outrageous practices such as standing "at the Corner of Houses and walking through the Streets" and "generally sitting down supporting their Head with their Hands."[45] Apprentices ran to the "foreign colony" for a variety of reasons, all of which provided some relief from the coercion, control, and surveillance associated with their indentures.

Nevertheless, absconding to St. Thomas was not without risks. Tortola's planters, overseers, and public officials also regularly visited the port, and were able to identify missing servants. If information networks and social connections were crucial in aiding the indentured servant's mobility, these were also of use to masters, mistresses, and officials who sought to apprehend the abscondee. In the 1820s there was no press on Tortola by which to advertise runaways. Notices were posted in Road Town but the exchange of information was a key mechanism of surveillance. Overseers were asked to apprehend and return indentured Africans should they find them on their estates. On hearing reports of sightings in St. Thomas, many employers pursued their absent servants, or sent Tortola's police after them. If identified as runaways by the Danish officials, they were liable to be jailed, put to the chain gang, or sent back to Tortola. Moreover, a thriving slave market existed in nearby "Porto Rico," rendering St. Thomas of interest to slave smugglers. Unidentified, footloose, saltwater Africans were inviting targets.

For those on the run, these various dangers were not unconnected. James, a serial runaway, escaped from Tortola's jail and fled to St. Thomas. There, he was convicted again for robbery and served his sentence, but refused to produce his indenture papers. As a result, he was advertised to be sold by public vendue for one dollar. Mr. Aaron Wolff offered the dollar, and immediately took him to "Porto Rico" where he was sold again at a tidy profit. The Danish governor explained that "[James] could not be looked upon in another light than as a runaway slave, who, not claimed by anyone, was sold off, in order not to remain a burden to the colony."[46]

Under the imperial stipulations of the indenture policies, masters and mistresses who could not keep track of their bonded servants were liable to have the contracts withdrawn. Hence the arrival of the commission prompted vigorous attempts to retrieve the missing servants. Thomas had been in St. Thomas for two years when the constable came looking for him. He was caught, and escaped again. He was then apprehended, locked up, and brought from the jail to report to the commission. He immediately ran again after telling the commissioners that many others had done exactly the same as soon as "their names were in the book."[47] Other servants returned voluntarily to speak at the commission, some believing that they were to be made free, others knowing that it was a place to, at least, protest their conditions. Hull and Nelson had served out their fourteen years as apprentices. They traveled from other islands, and waited for five days for the fact to be recorded and recognized.[48]

In Tortola, as elsewhere, white colonials indentured the kidnapped Africans to supplement their enslaved labor force, or to appropriate their labor value by hiring them out, but they also resented their presence, universally reporting them to be a threat to already unstable racial and social hierarchies. Time and again they suggested that the apprentices were actively disliked by both the enslaved and the free creoles due to their saltwater difference and their protected status. This colonial attitude echoed across the Caribbean islands on which kidnapped Africans were placed. Belisario's apprentice carpenter, Tom, suggested that identifications and prejudices were more complicated when he said of his fellow apprentices, "some stands with Black people and some stands with White people." Tensions certainly existed between the laboring constituencies on Tortola given the daily struggle for meager subsistence. African apprentices who raised a few hogs, goats, and poultry for sale were in direct competition with enslaved and freed peoples, and disputes, sometimes violent, erupted, for example when animals trespassed into provision plots or yards. Tom reported that the "Creoles" thought "that them Africans come to take the country." George Stephens, a "free coloured man," had called Tom a "Guinea Negro," and threatened to shoot all the stock belonging to the African apprentices, saying he did not "give a damn about the master and all the whites and blacks."[49]

Elsewhere in the commission records, a different picture of social relationships forged across the racialized laboring constituencies emerges. Solidarities, kinship relations, and affective relationships were established between the enslaved, bonded, and free in the name of a common material interest, and resistance to exploitation. Hull, indentured to a mason, for example, lived with his enslaved wife and children on a sugar estate in St. John. Christina Wheateley, another indentured African, was married to Jem Hodge, the head slave on an estate.[50] Cottrine appeared before the commissioners with no indenture papers to prove her status. She reported that she was living with Daniel Bruce, a slave, and cultivating his plot.[51] Reverend Curtin, who infamously defended the Woods, owners of Mary Prince, observed that apprenticed Africans absconded to live with the enslaved on plantations in Antigua too. He described this common activity as "living by trespass."[52]

The condemnatory phrase "living by trespass" is a reminder of Stephanie Camp's use of the concept "rival geography" for her intricate analysis of the ways in which bondspeople of the American slave South used their mobility to challenge the spatial formations of the plantation. As an everyday practice of resistance and dissent, she vividly illustrates how persistent "truancy" (as opposed to full flight) contested the laws, curfews, boundaries, and labor routines that governed the plantation, creating an endemic problem of labor discipline in the old South. As she notes, as truants "slipped between their own and others' quarters, woods, swamps, outbuildings, and farms they plaited these diverse spaces into a shared rival geography that provided space and time not only for relief from exploitation, control and surveillance but also for independent activity."[53] Unlike the southern states, Tortola's plantation society was decaying, its plantation topography no longer so extremely defined and policed. Moreover, mobility for most of Tortola's apprenticed Africans was not entirely dictated by the spaces of the plantation. Cumulatively, their various acts of absconding constituted a complementary and overlapping "rival geography." It was a geography that helped to stretch and blur the ones defined by slavery insofar as they "plaited" urban street corners, rural provision plots, dock sides, market stalls, building sites, laundry rooms, doss houses, and the spaces of the plantation. Alongside the abiding issue of "steady" labor discipline, the subversive nature of their actions can be seen as a running theme in the commission records concerning the apprenticed Africans' inappropriate use of public space, whether that use was connected to their "absconding" or not.

Opportunities for running away were structured and facilitated by a collective sense of rival geography. Facilitating those opportunities was even a source of income for some. For example, Dennis, an enslaved man, forged passes that he sold on credit to apprentices wishing to get to St. Thomas.[54] Community networks of covert support and assistance blurred laboring boundaries, and enabled desperate servants to organize themselves to be able to run. Jane, employed as a house servant to a white woman in town, ran away and was discovered living with "Mama

Sally," an enslaved woman belonging to Sally Keys. Jane, however, wanted to get to St. Thomas so she stole her indenture papers. She was able to give them to Harry, Belisario's carpenter, for safekeeping. Harry was known for aiding runaways, giving shelter to those who were destitute, and turning up to "beg" for those who were jailed for absconding.[55] It was also well known that apprentices went to him "to consult among themselves what to do and how to act."[56]

Mama Sally also harbored Jennet, who refused to travel to the quays with her employer, Mrs. Frett, who tried to "catch her" before she ran to St. Thomas and hired herself as a nanny. Meanwhile, Mama Sally cared for Jennet's sick child until it died.[57] Maria—a washer who repeatedly ran—absconded to nearby Scrub Island with a runaway slave.[58] Adeline—a cook—ran from her employer for sixteen months, and was "harboured by Aunty Bella, a Creole slave" on the Hetherington plantation.[59] William, not well enough to work as a domestic, ran away and was "harboured by a free coloured man in town."[60] Mimey, indentured on Pickering's plantation, absented herself for a year to live "an irregular kind of life" on Buck's Island with "a free black man named George Sharp."[61]

RESISTANCE AND TRANSITION

Running away from *and* returning to Tortola were both affected by the arrival of the Royal Commissioners on the island, signaling that the Africans were conscious of the nature of their situation in relation to metropolitan legal shifts in the imperial management of Caribbean labor relations, and the complexity of the local consequences of these changes. The commission was not the cause of running, however. The reasons for running and the ways in which it could be achieved were already well established by the time the commissioners arrived. The Africans used the commission to protest their situation verbally. They were also unafraid to let it be known that they used their bodies in protest too—absenting themselves errantly, unpredictably, and exorbitantly.

Unlike in Sierra Leone, Tortola's indentured Africans developed no formal collective voice with which to petition for their better treatment, but a common view of their struggle is exactly what these commission documents record. The indentured Africans did not engage in collectively organized flight; their testimonies offer evidence of many individual or small group acts of running away. Yet their patterns and repetitions suggest the development of a wider culture of absconding—structured by a set of pathways—constructed, actively maintained, and supported by cross-community networks and solidarities, and by the proximity of a relatively accessible and nearby and busy foreign port.

This particular and local culture of absconding developed in response to, and was shaped by, the social contradictions produced by Tortola's dramatic economic decline as a result of its peripheral location in the British Atlantic sugar economy, and by the effects of post-abolition imperial policy in the Caribbean. The kidnapped Africans arrived in a context of extreme economic hardship for the laboring poor, and worsening material conditions for the enslaved. Unlike the planters, the poor—whether enslaved, free, or African apprentices—were not in a position to abandon the colony. Weakened planter authority, enhanced bargaining power, a complex set of kinship connections forged over time, the extensive development of provisioning plots, and embedded understandings of customary land rights constituted, however, albeit in highly contingent and contentious ways, conditions in which a collective struggle for survival, *and* for independence and autonomy, could be waged from below.

In 1828, during the last phase of the antislavery campaigns, a circular dispatch was sent to all colonial governors in the Caribbean directing them to issue freedom papers to all rescued Africans whose indentures had expired. These papers dictated that freedom was still some way off. For an additional seven years, the right to remain in place was secure as long as the "bearer's Conduct merits this Indulgence." Evidence of criminality or destitution rendered the owner subject to transportation or to be "constrained to labor for [their] Subsistence."[62] In 1831, Tortola's Collector of Customs successfully negotiated a grant for the purchase of a piece of land on which to found a settlement for the captured Africans. It was called Kingstown. Designed as a benevolent measure of protection, it also sought to circumscribe the African's mobility, and to separate their homes from the rest of the local population. Moreover, the money was granted on the condition that the land would not pass into the ownership of the Africans themselves.[63]

The distinct, and condensed, confluence of circumstances in Tortola facilitated the development of a generalized resistance to coerced labor, both to indenture, with its similarities to the labor conditions of slavery, and to the coercion characteristic of the wage-labor form. This characteristic form of resistance—rooted in an insistence on mobility—contributed to class formation and struggle across the British Caribbean after emancipation. The patterns of desertion or running away by the kidnapped Africans illuminate the contradictory consequences of the move from the private to the public management of work as the imperial state began to control the direction of Caribbean labor in the run-up to emancipation. These patterns thus speak to the significance of ruling-class division in shaping the possibilities for resistance. In the Caribbean, for example, the determination of the plantocracy to resist the metropolitan decision to end slave labor relations exposed fault-lines that could be exploited when Parliament moved to curtail planter's power over labor. The patterns reveal a deeper set of historical continuities, convergences, *and* blind-spots in the wider imperial reallocation of colonial labor within which Caribbean emancipation was implicated but which it did not completely define. Moreover, the practices of desertion further illuminate the ways in which both enslavement and its abolition were predicated on elaborate transatlantic imperial legal structures that were designed to police mobility, and which bound Africans to new forms of coerced servitude before and after the abolition of transatlantic slavery.

The ancient practice of indenture—variously deployed and repurposed over time—was central to the historical expansion of global capitalism. In the seventeenth century the practice had tied the first colonial laborers in the Americas, providing the context for the development of racialized chattel slavery.[64] It was tested again on the "rescued" or "liberated" Africans after the British outlawed the transatlantic slave trade in 1807. By the early nineteenth century, hiring out had also become an essential part of the British Caribbean labor system, especially in economically failing colonies such as Tortola.[65] Indenturing and sometimes hiring out illegally trafficked Africans, and the increased hiring out of the enslaved, both demonstrate how shifts in the nature of coerced labor relations took shape deep inside the Atlantic capitalist system itself. The forms of labor that then emerged bound ex-slaves and others to new forms of servitude before and after the final abolition of slavery. Indenture or "apprenticeship" stood for emancipation in the British Caribbean between 1833 and 1838, and it then set terms for the next phase in the development of the nineteenth-century global imperial labor system as subsequent huge waves of indentured Indian and Chinese workers were mobilized for the continued expansion of colonies in the Caribbean and Asia.[66]

Thanks to Britain's meticulous bureaucratic imperial machine, the archive of the British Royal Commission examined here bears witness to the fact that running away shaped early nineteenth-century Black Atlantic resistance not only to enslavement—as has been well documented—but also to bonded servitude and to proletarianization. The commission records reveal the ways in which forcibly transported Africans arriving in the Caribbean prior to 1833, under the auspices of the British Navy rather than the slave traders, represented their own lives, figured their freedoms, and imagined their own labor beyond the confines of the incarcerating narratives within which they found themselves. Most generally—by documenting a particularly localized moment of global labor transition—the records testify to the centrality of desertion in shaping the wider dialectics of struggle integral to the development of capitalism.

NOTES

1. Voyage 41853, *Atrevido* (1814), Transatlantic Slave Trade Database at www.slavevoyages.org /voyage/41853/variables.

2. Reports by Commissioners of Inquiry into State of Africans apprenticed in West Indies. Papers relating to Captured Negroes, *Parliamentary Papers* [hereafter *PP*], 1825 (114) XXV.193, 244. When Africans were disembarked from condemned slave ships, their original names were documented alongside their new European names, although it was noted that sometimes the Africans had been already been renamed on the slave ships. Hereafter, I cite the European names given to the rescued Africans once

disembarked in the Caribbean because they are the ones used throughout the original colonial sources to which I refer. The sources do not reveal by which names the Africans addressed each other.

3. Clare Anderson, "After Emancipation: Empires and Imperial Formations," in *Emancipation and the Remaking of the British Imperial World*, ed. Catherine Hall et al. (Manchester: Manchester University Press, 2014), 113. For a comparative analysis of the introduction of Indian indentured labor in the British Caribbean post-emancipation and the simultaneous and connected development of the Indian plantation sector see Prabhu P. Mohapatra, "Assam and the West Indies: Immobilising Plantation Labor," in *Masters, Servants, and Magistrates in Britain and the Empire, 1562–1955*, ed. Douglas Hay and Paul Craven (Chapel Hill: University of North Carolina Press, 2005), 455–80.

4. For the size, origin, and movement of the liberated African diaspora see Daniel Domingues da Silva et al., "The Diaspora of Africans Liberated from Slave Ships in the Nineteenth Century," *Journal of African History* 55 (2014): 347–69.

5. Maeve Ryan, "'A Moral Millstone?': British Humanitarian Governance and the Policy of Liberated African Apprenticeship, 1808–1848," *Slavery and Abolition* 37, no. 2 (2016): 3.

6. "An Act to Abolish the Slave Trade," 47 Geo III Sess. 2, c. 36.

7. 47 Geo III Sess. 2, c. 36.

8. It is impossible to calculate the number of Africans captured and condemned in the Vice Admiralty Courts in the West Indies accurately. It is estimated that over 40,000 were settled in British Caribbean territories over the sixty years of the suppression campaigns. Rosanne Adderley, *"New Negroes from Africa": Slave Trade Abolition and Free African Settlement in the Nineteenth-Century Caribbean* (Indianapolis: Indiana University Press, 2006), 2. See also Domingues de Silva et al., "Diaspora of Africans"; Johnson U. J. Asiegbu, *Slavery and the Politics of Liberation, 1787–1861: A Study of Liberated African Emigration and British Anti-Slavery Policy* (London: Longmans, 1969), 1–33; Howard Johnson, "The Liberated Africans in the Bahamas," *Immigrants and Minorities* 7, no. 1 (1988): 16–40; Alvin O. Thompson, "African 'Recaptives' under Apprenticeship in the British West Indies, 1807–1828," *Immigrants and Minorities* 9, no. 2 (1990): 123–44.

9. According to accounts laid before the British Parliament in 1821, "there appeared to be 3,207 Captured Negroes in the West Indies," National Archives of the UK [hereafter TNA] CO 320/5. In 1824, Commissioners Bowles and Gannon were appointed to go to Nevis, St. Kitts, and Antigua, and Wyndham, Burdett, and Kinchela were appointed to investigate the Winkel Establishment of Crown Slaves at Berbice. See Alvin O. Thompson, *Profitable Servants: Crown Slaves in Berbice, Guyana 1803–1831* (Barbados: University of the West Indies Press, 2002), 113–14. For the primary documents for the entire commission see TNA CO 318/82–83, CO318/85–93.

10. Voyage 36948, *Nancy* (1807), Transatlantic Slave Trade Database at www.slavevoyages.org /voyage/36948/variables.

11. TNA CO 239/9, "John Stobo's Statistics on the British Virgin Islands."

12. Isaac Dookhan, *A History of the British Virgin Islands, 1672–1970* (Essex: Caribbean University Press, 1975), 93.

13. Trelawney Wentworth, *The West India Sketch Book*, vol. 1 (London, 1834), 235.

14. Voyage 41854, *Venus*, (1814), Transatlantic Slave Trade Database at www.slavevoyages.org /voyage/41854/variables; Voyage 41816, *Candelaria* (1814) at www.slavevoyages.org/voyage/41816/variables; Voyage 41855, *Manuela* (1814) at www.slavevoyages.org/voyage/41855/variables.

15. *PP*, 1825 (114) XXV.193, No. 3, "Separate Report of Thomas Moody," 52.

16. Wentworth, *West India Sketch Book*, 236.

17. Wentworth, *West India Sketch Book*, 178.

18. Wentworth, *West India Sketch Book*, 220.

19. Ira Berlin and Philip D. Morgan, eds., *The Slaves' Economy: Independent Production by Slaves in the Americas* (London: Frank Cass, 1991).

20. Christopher Fyfe, *A History of Sierra Leone* (New York: Oxford University Press, 1962), 130, 133–34, 137–38.

21. Robert Conrad, "Neither Slave nor Free: The Emancipados of Brazil, 1818–1868," *Hispanic American Historical Review* 53, no. 1 (February 1973): 50–70, 57–58.

22. Sharla M. Fett, *Recaptured Africans: Surviving Slave Ships, Detention and Dislocation in the Final Years of the Slave Trade* (Chapel Hill: University of North Carolina Press, 2017), 80.

23. "Abstract of the Acts of Parliament for Abolishing the Slave Trade, and of the Orders in Council Founded on Them" (London: African Institution, 1810), 40.

24. For the corrupt operations of Tortola's Vice Admiralty Court and of its colonial port officials see Lauren Benton, "This Melancholy Labyrinth: The Trial of Author Hodge and the Boundaries of Imperial Law, 1790–1820," *Alabama Law Review* 64 (2012).

25. Elizabeth Donnen, *Documents Illustrative of the History of the Slave Trade to America*, vol. 3, *New England and the Middle Colonies* (Washington, DC: Carnegie Institution of Washington, 1932), 400–401.

26. TNA CO239/15. In July 1825, Orders in Council closed this legal loophole by allowing Africans to be indentured to the collector himself.

27. "Information Received from the Island of Antigua Respecting Acts if Insubordination by Liberated Africans," *PP*, 1826 (351) XXVI.453, 3.

28. Ibid., 5.

29. Ibid., 6.

30. "Bombas" were African captives who were encouraged to help keep order over others on Danish slave ships. The same word was used for Black overseers in the field. See Lief Svalesen, *The Slave Ship Fredensborg* (Bloomington: Indiana University Press, 2000), 86, 177, 185. The use of the word in Tortola is most probably due to the proximity of the Danish Virgin Islands.

31. "Reports by the Commissioners of Inquiry into the State of Slaves in H. M. Colonies under the Acts Abolishing the Slave Trade (Tortola)," *PP*, 1828, (535) XXVI.123, 6–7.

32. TNA CO 235/15.

33. The commissioners attempted to record each apprentice's name, both African and English, their "nation," "apparent" age, height, any "distinguishing marks," their "state of bodily health," the date of indenture, whether the indenture contract was "perfect" or imperfect," to whom they have been indentured, and the "trade, craft or employment" in which each apprentice was engaged.

34. TNA CO 318/81, "Minute Book," 91.

35. "Mr. Gannon's Report on the State and Condition of the Apprenticed Africans at Antigua," *PP* 1826–7 (355) XXII, 17.

36. TNA CO 318/81, "Minute Book."

37. *PP*, 1825 (114) XXV.193, No. 1, "Schedules," 172.

38. Ibid., 68.

39. Ibid., 196.

40. TNA CO 318/81, "Minute Book."

41. Ibid., 62.

42. Ibid., 74.

43. *PP*, 1825 (114) XXV.193, No. 1, "Schedules," 224.

44. TNA CO 318/81, "Minute Book."

45. Ibid.

46. *PP*, 1825 (114) XXV.193, No. 1, "Schedules," 207.

47. Ibid., 140.

48. TNA CO 318/81, "Minute Book."

49. *PP*, 1825 (114) XXV.193, No. 1, "Schedules," 339.

50. *PP*, 1825 (114) XXV.193, No. 3, "Moody's Separate Report", 96.

51. Ibid., 70.

52. "Report of the Committee of the House of Lords," *Anti-Slavery Reporter* 5 (1833): 509.

53. Stephanie Camp, *Closer to Freedom: Enslaved Women and Everyday Resistance in the Plantation South* (Chapel Hill: University of North Carolina Press, 2004), 36.

54. *PP*, 1825 (114) XXV.193, no. 1, "Schedules," 72.

55. Ibid., 56, 130.

56. Ibid., 224.

57. Ibid.,104.

58. Ibid., 306.

59. Ibid., 306.

60. Ibid., 252.

61. Ibid., 310.

62. Alvin O. Thompson, "African 'Recaptives' under Apprenticeship in the British West Indies, 1807–1828," *Immigrants and Minorities* 9, no. 2 (1990): 140.

63. TNA CO 239/25.

64. Hilary McD. Beckles, *The First Black Slave Society: Britain's "Barbarity Time" in Barbados, 1636–1876* (Mona: University of West Indies Press, 2016).

65. Heather Cateau, "Re-examining the Labor Matrix in the British Caribbean 1750–1850," in Hall et al., *Emancipation*, 98–112.

66. David Northrup, *Indentured Labour in the Age of Imperialism, 1834–1922* (Cambridge: Cambridge University Press, 1995); Madhavi Kale, *Fragments of Empire: Capital, Slavery and Indian Indentured Labour in the British Caribbean* (Philadelphia: University of Pennsylvania Press, 2010).

10

Lurking but Working

City Maroons in Antebellum New Orleans

Mary Niall Mitchell

When a young enslaved woman named Jane, living in New Orleans, left her owner on a Sunday morning in January of 1844, she was not wearing any shoes. This might have been, in part, because she did not plan to go very far. After her departure from the home of her enslaver, a mile or so upriver from the city's French Quarter, she had been seen two or three times at nearby markets: one on Poydras Street and the other on St. Mary's Street. This bit of intelligence was printed in the advertisement her owner placed in the New Orleans *Daily Picayune* seeking her return (see Figure 10.1). Like other central markets in the city, these two fed the local populace and served as a source of income for both free and enslaved people. The markets may have been a place where Jane hoped to blend in without notice. They were hives of activity, abuzz with buying and selling, but they were also rife with gossip. If Jane wanted to disappear, she was not doing a very good job of it. But then Jane's goal may have been something different.[1]

The reason we know part of Jane's story is that her owner placed the ad seeking her return in the local newspaper. Enslavers seeking the return of their property and jailers who had apprehended suspected fugitives both placed fugitive ads. In their efforts to apprehend runaways or identify owners (in the case of jailers) they created brief biographical portraits of people who had rejected enslavement by running away. They included any combination of details, from appearance, personality, linguistic ability, and skills, to previous owners, histories of sale, or places to which the fugitive was likely to flee.[2]

Some of those advertised in New Orleans papers may have been seeking a more permanent freedom by escaping to free territory, which, from New Orleans, typically required travel by boat via the Mississippi River, Atlantic Seaboard, or the Gulf

FIGURE 10.1. Advertisement in search of Jane, New Orleans *Daily Picayune*, March 2, 1844.

$10 REWARD.—Absconded on Sunday morning last, the Negress JANE, aged about 19 years, stout made and short in height, very black, and rather talkative; dressed in a blue cottonade frock, no shoes; has been seen for two or three mornings past in the Poydras and St. Mary Market. All persons are cautioned from employing or harboring her. The above reward will be paid on delivering the said slave at the Work House, 2d Municipality, or at the corner of St. Andrew and Tainturer streets, one square from the head of Camp street.   m2 2t*

of Mexico. New Orleans's enslaved residents, however, lacked what runaways living in an Upper South city like Baltimore had: proximity to a free state. So the question of permanent flight had to be weighed against one's likelihood of surviving a long ocean voyage or avoiding detection and capture along the river. The standard closure to most of these ads spoke to this issue: "captains of vessels, steamboats, and others are cautioned against harboring said slave under the penalties of the law." In the context of New Orleans, this tagline was especially pertinent. It acknowledged the regular interaction between enslaved people and maritime workers, and the potential for their collaboration. And it hinted at the fact that ready employment along the river, near the city, is what many fugitives may have sought.

Among those who appeared in fugitive advertisements, in fact, there was a substantial subset of people who seem to have sought a more temporary freedom, or at least a less direct route to liberation. The significant numbers of ads containing fugitives who were spotted in and around the city—those who were "lurking" about (to use the parlance of slaveholders)—suggest that remaining in New Orleans had its advantages for those who ran, in terms of existing networks of family and friends, accessing known economic opportunities, and concealing oneself for periods of time in a crowded port city. Jane and other enslaved people who absented themselves from their enslavers, then, may have been seeking an impermanent but self-supported respite from those who claimed them as property.[3]

When Jane ran away, New Orleans was the Deep South's largest city and home to the nation's largest slave market.[4] The city, colonized by France in 1718 but American-controlled by the early nineteenth century, still had a large French-speaking Creole population, free and enslaved. But the forced migration of thousands of enslaved African Americans from the Upper to the Lower South beginning in 1820, combined with rapid Americanization as more Americans moved in to seek their fortunes in cotton and slaves, and a sizable Irish immigration, brought an influx of English-speaking people. The small but growing port city became a southern metropolis in just a few decades (see Figure 10.2).[5] In 1830, the combined "colored" population in the city, free and enslaved, made up 57 percent of its 49,000 inhabitants. But by 1850, this group comprised only 23 percent of a city that had more than doubled in size, to some 119,000 people. The working class of the

FIGURE 10.2. Norman's plan of New Orleans and environs, 1845.

city reflected this rapid expansion and diversity—it had become an economic stratum of thousands of men and women, white and black, immigrant and native born, free and enslaved.[6] This essay focuses on the period from roughly 1830 to 1850, when the demographics and size of New Orleans made "lurking but working" a feasible practice for many enslaved people.

The city grew in tandem with the domestic slave trade, as the drive for cotton production increased the traffic in enslaved people.[7] While it is difficult to quantify the economic effects of running away—particularly among those who absconded for brief periods—it is significant to note that the expansion of the domestic slave trade can be tracked by increasing numbers of fugitive advertisements in New Orleans. This is especially clear in the pages of the New Orleans *Argus* between 1828 and 1830 (which carried the bulk of the city's runaway ads at the time) where nearly four thousand notices appeared. In addition to enslavers in search of their human property, local jailers in the city and the surrounding parishes posted ads seeking to return alleged fugitives to their enslavers.

Arguably the most common image of a runaway slave in the United States is of a fugitive fleeing on foot from a southern plantation and toward free soil in the northern states. But not all of those who ran were heading north.[8] This idea of a direct path toward freedom, perhaps, also stems from the published narratives of fugitive slaves such as Frederick Douglass and Harriet Jacobs, both of whom were enslaved in the Upper South. In the Deep South, however, southern cities were frequent destinations for fugitives. There, they could blend into large, dense populations of enslaved and free people of color.[9] In the case of New Orleans, runaways could also escape by boat to the free states or onto the Atlantic or the Gulf and into the Caribbean. Others who found themselves sold into the slave markets in New Orleans, separated from family in the Upper South, tried to return there. All of these possible trajectories surface in the fugitive advertisements in New Orleans's newspapers. But those who remained in the city—evading their enslaver's claims upon them like maroons living on the edges of plantations—seemed to have a different set of goals, as well as a different set of challenges before them.

Historians have studied *marronage* among enslaved people in the Atlantic World as primarily a plantation phenomenon and a practice that could take one of two forms. *Grand marronage* refers to the creation of communities of fugitive slaves in hard-to-reach swamps and mountainous areas that skirted plantation regions. The largest and most well-studied maroon settlements were in the Caribbean and Latin America, although recent work has highlighted the presence of maroons in North America as well. *Petit marronage,* on the other hand, has often been used to describe the practice of enslaved people who wanted a temporary respite from the plantation—perhaps to avoid the wrath of an overseer until tempers cooled, or to visit family, in secret, on other plantations. Following these definitions, *grand marronage* was a full rejection of enslavement whereas *petit marronage* was a form of day-to-day resistance and negotiation between enslaved and enslaver.[10]

Sylviane Diouf, who has written the most recent study of maroons in North America, argues that the distinction between "*petit*" and "*grand*" *marronage* does not take into account the geography of enslavement. Diouf proposes instead that we think of a "maroon landscape" where spaces of slavery and freedom were interdependent and in "borderland" spaces often blurred. The city of New Orleans was one such landscape. City maroons in New Orleans were deserters in the sense that they abandoned their owners, yet they did not quit the urban spaces in which they lived.[11]

In such a borderland space, fugitive slaves could be self-sustaining. Indeed, what separated the men, women, and children who were suspected of "lurking about the city" from those fugitives who "lurked" on the edge of rural plantations was that city maroons could almost always support themselves. They participated in the commerce of the city while eluding capture. Further, in advertisements for city maroons in New Orleans, runaways were seldom accused of *stealing* much. Those who left with more than the clothes on their back, like 35-year-old Venice who "took all her clothes with her when she left," were the exception, at least in terms of what slave owners reported.[12] Many fugitives were traveling light and not traveling very far. And the fact that they did not steal may have indicated that they wanted to avoid punishment when they returned.

Based on fugitive slave ads for this period, it seems that antebellum New Orleans had a sizable, shifting urban maroon population living alongside free and enslaved residents, although precisely how large it was is difficult to determine. These city maroons had their own trajectories and expectations about where they needed or wanted to be, which was indicated in the ads by the frequent use of the term "lurking." In rural areas, the term "lurking" appeared in correspondence and in print when planters thought that an enslaved person was still near the bounds of the plantation, or that he or she might be "lurking" near another plantation to be close to family. Anthony Kaye, in his study of southern antebellum neighborhoods, noted that runaways could be a burden on friends and relatives who had to feed them. The dangers of stealing food from plantations were undeniable.[13]

In the city, "lurking" did not translate as an inability to work. Rather, the very activity of "lurking" in an urban setting was one that fugitives did *while* working. Urban "lurking" was sustainable because fugitives could labor alongside members of the free working classes. Moses and William McCullen, for instance, were marooned from urban slavery while continuing to engage, from day to day, with the society that sheltered that system. In 1828, Moses, who "walks and speaks like a sailor," was supposed to be "lurking about the city." That same year, William McCullen was "lurking about" the home of his former owner in another part of town. Albert or Alfred who "lurked about the lake for sometime; has since been heard of in the city."[14]

The experience of a sample of New Orleans's urban maroons suggests that we must add to slavery's atlas yet another type of maroon landscape. Historians have noted that cities functioned as a "borderland" for enslaved people who fled nearby plantations to find work or a network of support.[15] But for those who lived in New Orleans and absented themselves from their master's supervision, their borderland was often, at most, a few streets away from their enslaver. In fact, judging from the extended run of certain ads, some city maroons were often missing for weeks or months, suggesting that they were not using flight as a tool for negotiation with owners (a strategy associated with *petit marronage*). Rather, that they aimed to live freely, within the city, for as long as they could manage it. Although some of these runaways could have planned a permanent escape when the opportunity arose, there are enough of these alleged desertions *in situ* to suggest that this was a common practice among the city's enslaved. Ultimately, we cannot know how successful these runaways were in eluding their owners. Probably many more failed to remain at large than succeeded. But the ads speak to strategies of individual and collective resistance among enslaved people in the Deep South that have been mostly uncharted.

If the effects of this kind of marronage upon the economics of antebellum slavery are difficult to quantify, they are not hard to grasp in terms of power. Enslaved people who deserted their owners rejected their enslaved status and claimed their freedom, however fleeting, through self-directed movement and concealment. They also denied slaveholders income from their labor and "stole" valuable human property. Fugitives who continued to live within and around the city made the boundary between enslaved and free appear porous and even fluid. With each escape, however temporary, they demonstrated, publicly, the limits of slaveholders' power.

Enslavers in the city knew that some degree of mobility among the people they owned was necessary in order to make urban slaveholding sustainable. But they also knew that such mobility made the system more vulnerable to desertions. Take Cassey (also called Catherine) as an example. According to the ad placed by her owner, P. Reynaud, in 1844, Cassey was "well known in the city." For many years she had been the property of a man in nearby St. James Parish and just before Reynaud purchased her, she had been enslaved to "Mlle Belle," a free woman of color in New Orleans. Cassey was between 40 and 45 years of age and missing her front teeth. She also had a swollen place on her head "by an accident on the railroad," which indicates one of two forms of transport that Cassey probably used on a regular basis. When she left Reynaud's house Cassey she was wearing colorful clothes that might have distinguished her from most plantation workers: a light blue print frock, yellow striped apron, red shawl, and a green and yellow handkerchief around her head. Reynaud, who offered $100 for Cassey's return, did not report that she had left with any additional clothing or provisions, suggesting perhaps that she did not plan to go far. But it is the final detail Reynaud provides that indicates Cassey's customary mobility and her possible whereabouts: "Said servant has long been in the habit of selling in the streets and on board of steamboats as a Marchande."[16]

When enslaved people ran away in an urban setting, Cassey demonstrated, they often took one especially valuable thing with them: a skill or expertise. Cassey was a seasoned marketer and likely supporting herself by doing what she knew how to do. Similarly, a "Dark Griff Boy" of twenty who ran away from William Reed near Jackson Street had been "employed latterly in blacksmithing" and a woman named Susan, "originally from South Carolina" with "the Charleston brogue or accent in her speech," was a seamstress, and had been missing for at least four months, being "no doubt harbored in the city."[17] Many others, as we will see, used the river's economy and steady demand for labor to sustain themselves after they fled their enslaver.

Like Cassey, before becoming maroons, most people listed in fugitive ads who had been residents of New Orleans for any length of time were accustomed to a fair amount of mobility within and between neighborhoods and along the Mississippi River. City maroons aimed to sustain that mobility while rejecting enslavement. Although they continued to share the cityscape with slave owners, police, free whites, and free people of color, they followed their own trajectories. They may have been "beyond the master's eye," to use historian Richard Wade's phrase, but as maroons they were often right under his nose.[18]

Drawing from the ads, we can only speculate about the reasons why city maroons fled their master's household. While some of the reasons dovetail with those of fugitives from rural places, their options were somewhat different from those in isolated areas and their strategies for survival were rooted in an urban existence. As historian Walter Johnson has noted, for most enslaved people, "escape was part of their daily lives in slavery." They left their enslavement behind temporarily through drink, song, socializing, hunting, and "passing the time that slaveholders thought belonged to them."[19] Living in a busy city like New Orleans, opportunities for such temporary escape were fairly frequent. And yet many enslaved city dwellers chose the more dangerous path of disappearing for long stretches of time.

Separation from their families and friends was a frequent reason for flight. Because New Orleans was fast becoming the hub of the antebellum slave market in these years, many ads tell stories of families separated over long distances. A woman named Rachel fled wearing "an iron collar with three prongs, with a small bell attached to each prong," a torture device that indicates Rachel was a flight risk. Her owner speculated that she would try to return to Frankfort, Kentucky, where she surely had people. Two men, Phil and Sam, ran away together from a plantation downriver and were suspected of heading "either towards North Alabama or Georgia" from which they likely had been sold and where their community remained.[20] We also know from other sources, including ex-slave narratives from the nineteenth and twentieth centuries, as well as court records, that the *threat* of sale led enslaved people to run. Individual ads often chronicle a string of recent owners in the city and nearby parishes, demonstrating that the escapee had been separated at some point, or multiple points, from friends and family. Lucinda, for instance, "formerly belonged to Messrs. Hyde & Leeds" and "has ranaway frequently before, for a short period, and been harboured in the upper fauxbourg." Jack (or John) Perry left his enslaver at the City Hotel and was thought to be "loitering in the lower part of the city, as he has a number of acquaintances there; or he may try to get on some of the steamboats going up the river." Perry had reached the city seven years prior from St. Louis and had been recently purchased from an owner in rural St. Mary Parish.[21]

There is also evidence of family separation *within* the city. Fanny, for instance, left her owner, taking her seven-year-old daughter with her. She was suspected of staying with another daughter on Girod Street. Fanny had last been seen at the St. Mary Market, adjacent to the river. Another woman, Sarah Lockwood, described as "a creole; aged about twenty-one years" was suspected of being pregnant when she fled. According to the ad placed in search of her "she is supposed to be concealed by free persons of color, who are related to her."[22] For women such as Fanny and Sarah, then, flight was part of a plan to reach family across town. Again, testimony from court cases supports evidence of families struggling to remain together and the expectations of slaveholders that they would do so. Some acts of sale even came with the caveat that an enslaved man would, at times, leave to visit his wife.[23]

Published slave narratives such as Harriet Jacobs's *Incidents in the Life of a Slave Girl* make plain that abuse by owners was a clear incentive for enslaved people to run. But because fugitive ads were the accounts of owners and jailers, stories of abuse at the hands of enslavers seldom surface in them, unless that abuse took the form of the collar Rachel wore or it had left identifiable scars or other deformities, all of which would aid in the recognition of a runaway. Many of the enslaved people advertised in the New Orleans papers had some amount of scarring on their faces or hands and some were missing parts of fingers or ears—all evidence of abuse combined with grinding work. Owners would not admit to abusing their property in the newspaper and jailers, relying on testimony from those they captured, did not include narratives of abuse.

Common to nearly all of those who were suspected of still "lurking" about the city, however, no matter what had driven them to flee, was that they clearly had the means to support themselves. The rapidly growing city provided ample opportunities for those with skills in building, working on the water and on the docks, marketing, and other activities. In this borderland between slavery and freedom, those who were "lurking" but working knew well how to navigate the city's streets, canals, and other vibrant social spaces.

By the 1840s, New Orleans behaved as much like Rio de Janeiro as it did Charleston or Baltimore. It was a city where enslaved people interacted daily with free people, black and white, drinking with them, trading with them, working alongside them, and inhabiting the same neighborhoods. When they decided to absent themselves from their owners but remain in the city, they relied upon a set of knowledge peculiar to people who lived in a place surrounded by water, full of markets and commerce, still echoing, even then, with Spanish, French, German, and English. City maroons relied upon the bustle of the port of New Orleans itself to keep away from those who claimed them as property (see Figure 10.3).

Mobility was critical to participation in this marketplace, and fugitives were exploiting the city's rapidly expanding urban economy. They knew the value of their labor to the day-to-day commerce of the city, since both "skilled" and "unskilled" enslaved people were frequently hired out to others by their owners.[24] City maroons took this practice a step further, participating in the economy as day laborers for support of themselves alone. Like free laborers, they went where work could be had, whether that was along the river levee, the canals, or the markets. Even as owners sought to reclaim their bodies and their labor, in fact, city maroons made it clear that in a city like New Orleans, enslaved people were as much a part of the wage economy as they were captive in the slave economy.

FIGURE 10.3. Bird's-eye view of New Orleans drawn from nature on stone by John Bachman, ca. 1851.

The talents maroons needed in order to survive as fugitives served to reinforce their place within the city's working class. One of the most prominent of these was the ability to perform "skilled" labor. James, for instance, who ran away in 1828, was a shoemaker and "was seen the first few days of his absence, at a shoemaker's in the back part of the city." Davis was a blacksmith "and may have been seen at Mr. Lannai's, in Toulouse Street, where he commonly worked." In 1840, both Aaron, a painter, and Griffin, a carpenter, were suspected of using their skills to find work in the city at a time (both owners noted) when there was plenty of construction work available; as Griffin's owner put it, the fugitive was no doubt "employed about some of the buildings going up in the city." A man named Philander, aged 40, "by trade a house carpenter," fled from the nearby parish of East Feliciana. His owner, however, had "heard of him in New Orleans, and believe he is working at his trade in that city."[25]

Linguistic skills, too, were an advantage. Those who could speak both French and English could move more easily between the American and Creole sections of the city in search of work. Through the 1840s, linguistic ability was an important descriptor of fugitives. Ellick (or Alexander) spoke English, French, and Spanish. A 22-year-old man named Narry who fled from his owner's house on Rampart Street spoke both French and English and had been "seen at different times about [the nearby municipality] of Lafayette."[26] Whether an enslaved person spoke

English or French, and how well, however, was not just a means to identify them. It was a skill with which they could navigate the city. A nineteen-year-old man named Peter, for instance, had been missing for three months when his owner placed an ad in the newspaper seeking his return. Peter had been spotted at two lines of transport into and out of the city: the New Basin Canal above the French Quarter in the American section, and on the Pontchartrain Railroad in the Faubourg Marigny below the Quarter. Both connected the city to Lake Pontchartrain and would have presented plenty of opportunity for work. Peter's skills in French and English likely helped him find employment uptown and downtown.[27]

To be a successful maroon in this environment, one also needed detailed knowledge of the city itself: its neighborhoods, taverns, markets, and waterways. Perhaps the clearest indication that enslaved people in New Orleans practiced marronage on a regular basis was the frequent suggestion that they were hiding out or being harbored in one of the "faubourgs" or municipalities. To read the ads, it is clear that family and friends living in the less developed reaches of the city—especially in the "lower faubourg" below the French Quarter (what is now the Marigny) and the "upper faubourg" upriver from the Quarter—were harboring most of these runaways.[28] Such ads are testament to the mobility and self-direction of enslaved city-dwellers, male and female, and the communities they created. Jack aka John Perry, for instance, fled his owner at the City Hotel on Common Street in 1840. His owner speculated: "it is possible he is loitering in the lower part of the city as he has a number of acquaintances there." Sixteen-year-old Eliza "carried away with her many clothes" and her owner suspected that "she may pass herself for free . . . . It is thought she has been seduced by some persons, who keep her hid in some of the fauxbourgs." The same was suspected of 19-year-old Sarah Ann and 45-year-old Hannah, the latter of whom "absented herself without cause" in February of 1844, even though her owner was still looking for her in July. Lucinda, 26, "ran away frequently before, for a short-period, and been harboured in the upper fauxbourg."[29] E. Forstall posted an ad for a woman named Mary in July of 1828, four months after she had fled. Mary was in her late twenties, without her front teeth. She spoke French and English "with the same facility." She had a six-month-old baby whom she often carried with her. Mary was "very intimate" with a man named William who belonged to a Mdme. Gaudin. Forstall hinted where William and Mary might be: "both of them have had for a long time relations with the negro fishermen at the Bayou."[30]

What is clear in the examples of Mary and Fanny (p. 205) is that city marronage was a form of flight that women could attempt with small children in tow, suggesting networks of friends or family. Although a majority of the ads explored here involve male fugitives, there was a steady flow of women on the pages of the newspapers who had left their enslavers. In 1846, for instance, of the hundreds of advertisements for fugitives in that year, there were at least 36 women listed, and those ads ran often for weeks at a time. Most of the women were between the ages of 18 and 40, and although not every ad mentioned the presence of family, these women surely had children somewhere.[31] More certain, however, is that they could draw on a community network in the city for protection. "Hannah/Ann Lee," for instance, left with a pass in her hand, given to her by her owner, that allowed her to hire herself out for a month, but then never returned. Cora was suspected of forging a pass for herself. Both used the plausibility of enslaved women being hired out to take their leave. Other ads featuring women suggest the presence of deep community ties, or at least a community presence beyond the household of their enslavers in their daily lives. Jane, for instance, was described as a "Creole" who spoke English and French—a native of the city, in other words—making it highly likely that she was being sheltered by family. The slaveholder who advertised for Kitty suggested that relations between enslaved people and the local community could work in positive and negative ways. In addition to a reward for her recovery, he offered $150 for the apprehension of those who sheltered her and an additional $80 for the capture of anyone who endeavored to "run her out of the city."[32]

As New Orleans grew, so too did the neighborhoods where these women might have been hiding. By the 1840s, the city was divided into three municipalities with many runaways hiding in what was called the Second Municipality, which marked the furthest reaches of the city upriver—at that time, just above Canal Street and the French Quarter—and was predominantly American not Creole. This may have been a way to escape the surveillance of Creole enslavers in the French Quarter by frequenting one of the less-settled parts of the city. In 1844, a "griffe girl" named Mary aka Mary Ann was "supposed to be in the Second Municipality." Betsy, described as "mulatto" and said to be 35 to 40 years old, was also there, or so her owner thought: "She is well known in this city, and is supposed to be harbored by some one in the Second Municipality." Ellis, "about 40 years of age," ran away from his master who lived in the French Quarter and was believed to be "lurking about in the Second Municipality." William "is well known in the city and has been seen lately in the Second Municipality, particularly in the neighborhood of a cotton-press in the upper part of Magazine street." And John "was well acquainted in the city, particularly in the upper part of the Second Municipality and Lafayette" (a town just beyond the upper city limits).[33]

But the Second Municipality was a haven for other reasons as well. From the 1840s into the 1860s, it became the site of "cabarets and drinking dens" where enslaved people could "obtain liquor in any quantity, and at all time, day and night."[34] From the earliest decades of the nineteenth century, in fact, taverns and boardinghouses were spaces where enslaved people, poor whites, and free blacks interacted, and were therefore threats to the social order in the view of authorities. An 1808 ordinance passed by the city council reflects the anxiety such spaces caused for local leaders and especially enslavers. It was aimed at the sorts of public spaces where working-class people regularly socialized: "inns, public boarding houses, coffee-houses, billiard houses, taverns, and other places of entertainment in the City, Suburbs, and Liberties." Enslaved people could only purchase alcohol with the written permission of their owner. According to historian Rashauna Johnson, when "New Englanders and Germans, Irishmen and Africans congregated in the city's spaces," liquor was "the social lubricant that set their social betters on edge."[35]

With the sudden rise in immigration into the city from Germany and Ireland, the polyglot nature of the city's working class, and the taverns and boardinghouses they frequented, were becoming increasingly irrepressible. By 1837, the *New Orleans Bee* could report: "not a street nor corner can be passed without encountering these magazines of degradation. That spring up in all directions with inconceivable rapidity, within the last few years they have augmented in almost unparalleled ratio, and are fortified and sustained by the thousands who flock to them."[36] A white visitor to New Orleans from Savannah noted as late as the 1850s the existence of domiciles under the control of enslaved people: "In this city, hundreds of such places might be pointed out, in which the slave is the keeper of the house—a slave over whom the master pretends to exercise no control."[37]

Looking closely at spaces of interaction between the free working class and enslaved people has long been important to social historians studying the depth and scope of resistance to Atlantic World capitalism.[38] In terms of urban slavery, too, we can view fugitive slaves not as people outside of the daily workings of society, but rather, deep in the mix of sailors, marketeers, stevedores, domestic workers, and carpenters. In the public space of the city, enslaved people created their own landscape, with pockets of refuge and leisure with the city. Ellick, also known as Alexander, left a steamboat and was missing for several months at least, from February to June, being spotted on occasion at the Levee and "at the Coffee House on the corner of Front Levee and Conti Streets." Similarly, Isaac alias "John Brice" took advantage of these spaces. While his owner, named Carter, seemed convinced that Isaac would try to find work on the levee, where he was "well known," he also relayed in the advertisement that Isaac "frequents grog-shops and negro gambling houses." A month later, Carter was still looking for Isaac.[39]

Another destination for city maroons by the 1840s was the large St. Mary Market, built in 1836 just above the French Quarter (where the Convention Center stands today) as part of the general expansion of markets throughout the city.[40] Women seem especially likely to have been "seen" at the market. Fanny, described above, was suspected of staying with her daughter on Girod Street, but she had last been seen at the St. Mary Market. And recall that after Jane had left her owner's house on Camp Street she had been seen at two different markets, the Poydras and the St. Mary "for two or three mornings past." [41]

The markets were part of a more complex network of economic interaction, conducted at the riverfront, lakefront, canals, and bayous that rimmed the city.

These waterways were a favored place of public retreat and labor opportunities for many fugitives, mostly male but not exclusively.[42] John Dygs had been hired to a steamboat by his New Orleans owner when he disappeared. Another woman, Sarah, who left the Marigny home of her owner, was also "known to frequent steamboats." And recall that Cassey, too, was in the "habit" of working on steamships as a marchande. Albert aka Alfred who "had been heard of in the city" was "a good barber and steward and may have gone up the river on a steamboat." A young man named Wilson was surely using his skills as a marchand after running away. He had "been seen many times near Carrollton, and on board steamboats."[43]

Others who had skills as domestic workers could also make a living waiting on passengers aboard steamships. Turner, for instance, "was accustomed to wait about the house, can cook, is artful, and will no doubt alter his name; was last seen on a steamboat, but it is believed is yet concealed in the city." Jack, according to his enslaver, was "a house servant, and has never done anything else" and "no doubt he will try to get on some steamboat as waiter."[44] As these slaveholders well knew, the heavily trafficked Mississippi River was the chosen path to freedom for many people enslaved in New Orleans. Indeed, many court cases regarding runaways involved enslaved people who had been hired out to the owners of steamboats and then fled, leading the owner to sue the steamship captain or his company.[45]

If hopping a steamship was one strategy to avoid recapture, another that surfaces in the ads involved fugitives passing themselves off as free. The case of Harry, who was accused of doing just that, also demonstrates the multitude of spaces he frequented. According to his owner, Harry was "known to many in this city as having been formerly the coachman of Mr. J. B. Digges" but had changed his name and "passes himself off as a free man" and even had forged papers. After having been employed on steamboats "in the port" he was arrested on the levee but escaped. Since then he had been "frequently seen within the last week about the steamboat landing."[46] About another man, Edmond, his owner explained "it is supposed he has free papers with him, as he has been seen with papers of some description in his possession." A 27-year-old man, John, who ran away from his owner's house on Baronne Street, was also suspected of "passing himself as a free boy."[47]

Just by performing certain jobs in the city, in fact, some fugitives were more likely to *appear* free. In light of the numbers of free women of color who worked in New Orleans as laundresses, for instance, posing as a washerwoman was a logical strategy for Ary [Mary?]. Her owner wrote, "it is likely that she will pass herself off for a washerwoman; as she was in the habit of washing about the city three years ago."[48] Indeed, the idea that enslaved people could more easily disappear into a city with nearly 20,000 free black residents in 1840 is a notion rooted in fixed racial ideology about the appearance of people of African descent. What gets lost, however, is that fugitives were not just impersonating free black people (or in the case of very light-skinned runaways, free white people); they were also impersonating free *workers* and making themselves part of the city's working class.[49] This became easier to do as the nineteenth century reached its midpoint and thousands of Irish and German immigrants came into the city.

By the 1830s, this increasingly ethnically diverse working-class population, combined with the growing numbers of enslaved people being brought to New Orleans markets from the Upper South, created an ever-growing problem of social control for city officials. The resistance of city maroons must be understood in this light: increasingly stringent efforts on the part of authorities to control the diverse population of New Orleans. Prior to 1837, for example, the city's incarcerated population was a motley crew of free and enslaved, black and white. With the construction of a new facility that year, white and black prisoners were housed separately.[50] Efforts at control would become increasingly difficult through the 1840s and 1850s, as the population rapidly expanded and as the lucrative nature of the domestic slave trade drove more individuals into the South's largest slave market for sale.

As many historians have argued, the impact of day-to-day resistance on the part of enslaved people upon the institution of slavery is never easy to measure.[51] It was precisely the daily nature of their unwillingness to submit that makes it hard to transform their resistance into a cause-and-effect equation. Those who chose to live as maroons in the neighborhoods and markets and along the bayous and levees of the city did not, on their own, bring an end to urban slavery. But they nonetheless deprived slaveholders of profits and taxed the system of surveillance within the city for every day they eluded recapture. Consider Ned, a man of about 45 who ran away from a plantation near the city. He "was for a long time engaged in a wood yard near Carrollton (in what is now the 'Uptown area of' New Orleans) where he is well known." The ad's subscriber was certain Ned was employed nearby, doing what he knew how to do and at the same time filling a regular demand in the city for firewood, particularly by steamboats. Ned, he speculated, "is probably employed in cutting wood" in the swamp "back of the city or on the levee above or below town."[52] As a fugitive slave who had deserted the plantation on which he had been forced to labor, and who was working for himself, Ned was *literally* fueling the economic life of the city, the constant flow of vessels that brought goods, free passengers, and enslaved people downriver to New Orleans. Men and women like Ned participated in the economic system as if they were free workers while undermining the institution of slavery on which that economy was built. Hiding out and yet remaining in the city to be spotted or gossiped about, maroons spent the time and money of their owners seeking their return.

The stories of city maroons suggest that we need a revised map of urban slavery that takes into account their place on the terrain of global capitalism and its expansion in the nineteenth century. Their efforts at autonomy and self-sufficiency, no matter how temporary or long-lived, shaped the economies of international port cities such as New Orleans—urban spaces built from a combination of enslaved and wage labor via forced and voluntary migration, respectively. Their decision to flee their owners but to remain in the city complicates this history of labor migration even further. Finding city maroons and situating them within the specific landscape of New Orleans also reminds us that the spatial history of slavery is varied and complicated and that it goes well beyond the patriarchal household of the plantation. Jane, Cassey, Ned, and their fellow fugitives pushed again, and again, against the boundaries of ownership using their wits, their skills, their social networks, the city itself, and of course their feet.

NOTES

1. Jane, New Orleans *Daily Picayune* (hereafter NODP), March 2, 1844.

2. I am collecting fugitive slave ads, with the help of students, for Freedom on the Move (FOTM), a collaborative digital database of runaway ads housed at Cornell University. My historian co-collaborators on FOTM are Ed Baptist, Vanessa Holden, Hasan Jeffries, and Joshua Rothman.

3. Historians John Hope Franklin and Loren Schweninger wrote about fugitives running to cities from plantation areas. The city maroons highlighted here, however, were urban residents before their escape. Franklin and Schweninger, *Runaway Slaves: Rebels on the Plantation* (New York: Oxford University Press, 1999), chap. 6

4. See Walter Johnson, *Soul by Soul: Life inside the Antebellum Slave Market* (Cambridge, MA: Harvard University Press, 1998).

5. On slavery and capitalism in the antebellum South see Edward E. Baptist, *The Half Has Never Been Told: Slavery and the Making of American Capitalism* (New York: Basic Books, 2014); Joshua Rothman, *Flush Times and Fever Dreams: A Story of Capitalism and Slavery in the Age of Jackson* (Athens: University of Georgia Press, 2012); and Walter Johnson, *River of Dark Dreams: Slavery and Empire in the Cotton Kingdom* (Cambridge, MA: Harvard University Press, 2013).

6. Richard Campanella, *Bienville's Dilemma: A Historical Geography of New Orleans* (Lafayette: Center for Louisiana Studies, 2008), 34, 169.

7. See Baptist, *Half Has Never Been Told,* 178.

8. Franklin and Schweninger, *Runaway Slaves,* chap. 5.

9. Frederick Douglass, *Narrative of the Life of Frederick Douglass, an American Slave. Written by Himself* (Boston: Anti-Slavery Office, 1845); Harriet Jacobs, *Incidents in the Life of a Slave Girl. Written by Herself* (Boston, 1861); Richard Wade, *Slavery in Cities, The South 1820–1860* (New York: Oxford University Press, 1964); Seth Rockman, *Scraping By: Wage Labor, Slavery, and Survival in Early Baltimore* (Baltimore: Johns Hopkins University Press, 2009).

10. Richard Price defines *petit marronage* as "repetitive or periodic truancy with temporary goals such as visiting a relative or lover on a plantation." According to Price, throughout the Americas "planters seemed to have accepted [*petit marronage*] as part of the system" and "temporary flight of this type was clearly an everyday part of plantation life in the southern United States." Richard Price, *Maroon Societies: Rebel Slave Communities in the Americas* (New York: Alfred A. Knopf, 2013) [originally published by Johns Hopkins University Press, 1979], introduction. *Grand marronage* was most common in Caribbean colonial societies such as Cuba and Haiti; see, for instance, Gabino La Rosa Corzo, *Runaway Slave Settlements in Cuba: Resistance and Repression,* trans. Mary Todd (Chapel Hill: University of North Carolina Press, 1988). For an analysis of the role of maroons in the Haitian Revolution, see Carolyn Fick, *The Making of Haiti: The San Domingue Revolution from Below* (Knoxville: University of Tennessee Press, 1990). For an exploration of marronage in both Africa and the Americas see Gad

Neuman, ed., *Out of the House of Bondage: Runaways, Resistance and Marronage in Africa and the New World* (New York: Routledge, 2016).

11. Sylviane Diouf, *Slavery's Exiles: The Story of the American Maroons* (New York: NYU Press, 2014), chap. 3. In her introduction, Diouf reminds us of Steven Hahn's suggestion that free black populations in the antebellum North, to which fugitives often ran, also constituted a type of "maroon" community. See Steven Hahn, *The Political Worlds of Slavery and Freedom* (Cambridge, MA: Harvard University Press, 2009), 22. Franklin and Schweninger, *Runaway Slaves,* chap. 6.

12. Venice, NODP, December 30, 1840.

13. On traversing the highly surveilled "carceral landscape" of the antebellum plantation South see Johnson, *River of Dark Dreams,* chap. 8; Anthony Kaye, *Joining Places: Slave Neighborhoods in the Old South* (Chapel Hill: University of North Carolina Press, 2009), 131–36.

14. Moses, New Orleans *Argus* (hereafter NOAR) July 8, 1828; William McCullen, NOAR, June 24, 1828; Alfred, NODP, July 13, 1838.

15. See Franklin and Schweininger, *Runaway Slaves,* chap. 6.; Rockman, *Scraping By,* 20–21; Christopher Phillips, *Freedom's Port: The African American Community of Baltimore* (Chicago: University of Chicago Press, 1997), chap. 3.

16. Cassey or Catherine, NODP, Jan 2, 1844.

17. "Dark Griff Boy," NODP, March 19, 1845; Susan, NODP, May 25, 1845.

18. Wade, *Slavery in Cities,* 143.

19. Johnson, *Soul by Soul,* 195.

20. Rachel, NODP, February 17, 1844; Phil and Sam, NODP, June 11, 1845.

21. Lucinda, NOAR, March 14, 1828; Jack or John Perry, NODP, December 18, 1840. For the hundreds of cases involving enslaved and free people of color in Louisiana, drawn from the Supreme Court records of the state, see the work of Judith Schafer, especially *Slavery, the Civil Law, and the Supreme Court of Louisiana* (Baton Rouge: LSU Press, 1997) and *Becoming Free, Remaining Free: Manumission and Enslavement in New Orleans, 1846–1862* (Baton Rouge: LSU Press, 2003).

22. Fanny, NODP, March 9, 1844; Sarah Lockwood, NODP, May 23, 1845.

23. See examples from Johnson, *Soul by Soul,* 194–95.

24. On slave hiring see Jonathan Martin, *Divided Mastery: Slave Hiring in the American South* (Cambridge. MA: Harvard University Press, 2004).

25. James and Andrew, NOAR, May 23, 1828; Davis, NOAR, June 10, 1828; Aaron, NODP, November 24, 1840; Griffin, NODP, December 3 1840; Philander, NODP, June 15, 1845.

26. Narry, NODP, February 28, 1845.

27. Peter, NODP, May 2, 1844.

28. The Marigny, founded by Bernard Marigny, began in 1805 as an answer to the growing housing shortage in the city. But by 1820, free people of color constituted some 40 percent of the neighborhood's growing population, most of them women, and many of these property holders and boardinghouse owners. On the development of Faubourg Marigny see Rashauna Johnson, *Slavery's Metropolis: Unfree Labor in New Orleans during the Age of Revolutions* (New York: Cambridge University Press, 2016), 89–100, esp. 98.

29. Jack or John Perry, NODP, December 18, 1840; Eliza, NOAR, April 23, 1828; Sarah Ann, NODP, April 10, 1844; Hannah, NODP, July 7, 1844; Lucinda, NOAR, March 14, 1828.

30. Mary, NOAR, July 26, 1828.

31. On women of childbearing age being separated from children by the domestic slave trade from Upper South to Lower South see Baptist, *Half Has Never Been Told,* 105–9.

32. Hannah / Ann Lee, NODP, February 18, 1846; Cora, NODP, March 29, 1846; Jane, NODP, April 30, 1846; Kitty, NODP, March 31, 1846.

33. Mary aka MaryAnn, NODP, May 2, 1844; Betsy, NODP, March 6, 1844; Ellis, NODP, November 1, 1840; William, NODP, June 10, 1845; John aka Phil, NODP, November 12, 1844.

34. *New Orleans Bee*, June 22, 1855. Quoted in Wade, *Slavery in Cities*, p. 151.

35. Johnson, *Slavery's Metropolis*, 105. For the 1808 ordinance, see Johnson's discussion on p. 104 and the original document: New Orleans City Council: "An Ordinance Concerning the Police of Inns, Public Boarding-Houses, Coffee-Houses, Billard-Houses, Taverns and Other Places of Entertainment Within the City, Suburbs and Liberties of the City of New-Orleans," in *Police Code, or Collection of the Ordinances of Police Made by the City Council of New Orleans* (New Orleans: J. Renard, Printer of the Corporation, 1808). Early American Imprints, Series 2, no. 15740, http://infoweb.newsbank.com.

36. *New Orleans Bee*, November 8, 1837. Quoted in Wade, *Slavery in Cities*, 150. On the significance of grog shops and taverns in New Orleans just after the Louisiana Purchase and the Haitian Revolution see Rashawna Johnson, "'*Laissez les bons temps roulez!*' and Other Concealments: Households, Taverns, and Irregular Intimacies in Antebellum New Orleans," in *Interconnections: Gender and Race in American History*, ed. Carol Faulkner and Alison M. Parker (Rochester: University of Rochester Press, 2012), chap. 2. See also Johnson, *Slavery's Metropolis*, 104–12.

37. *Savannah Republican*, February 3, 1859. Quoted in Wade, *Slavery in Cities*, 146.

38. Peter Linebaugh and Marcus Rediker, *The Many-Headed Hydra: Sailors, Slaves, Commoners, and the Hidden History of the Revolutionary Atlantic* (Boston: Beacon Press, 2000).

39. Ellick, NODP, June 2, 1846; Isaac, NODP, April 17, 1845; Isaac, NODP, May 4, 1845.

40. Campanella, *Bienville's Dilemma*, 32.

41. Fanny, NODP, March 9, 1844; Jane, NODP, March 2, 1844.

42. On river escapes by steamboat see Thomas C. Buchanan, *Black Life on the Mississippi: Slaves, Free Blacks and the Western Steamboat World* (Chapel Hill: University of North Carolina Press, 2004), chap. 4.

43. John Dygs, NODP, May 10, 1845; Sarah, NODP, April 5, 1845; Albert aka Alfred, NODP, July 13, 1838; Wilson, NODP, April 4, 1844.

44. Turner, NODP, June 7, 1838; Jack, NODP, May 22, 1845.

45. See Schafer, *Slavery*, chap. 4.

46. Harry, NODP, January 2, 1840.

47. Edmond, NODP, May 11; John, NODP, January 1, 1850. Sometimes jailers would post ads stating that an enslaved person "claimed to be free." Free people of color were vulnerable to capture, as the case of William Johnson attests. Johnson was arrested by police in the 2nd Municipality while walking down the street. The city placed nighttime curfews on enslaved people, but not free people of color. Johnson sued and won his case, though many others were surely not as lucky. Johnson, f.m.c. v. Petric, No. 3158, Third District Court of New Orleans, 10 December 1850. See Schafer, *Becoming Free, Remaining Free*, 105.

48. Ary, NODP, January 3, 1840.

49. Campbell Gibson and Kay Jung, *Historical Census Statistics on Population Totals by Race, 1790 to 1990, and by Hispanic Origin, 1970 to 1990, for Large Cities and Other Urban Places in the United States*, Population Division, Working Paper No. 76 (Washington, DC: U.S. Census Bureau), 2005, www.census.gov/population/www/documentation/twps0076/twps0076.pdf (accessed June 17, 2017). For examples of court cases on this issue see Williamson v. Norton (*Western World*), No. 2427, 7 La. Ann. 393 (1852) and Spalding v. Taylor (*St. Missouri*), No. 5628, 1 La. Ann. 195 (1846). Both cited in Schafer, *Slavery*, 109–10.

50. Johnson, *Slavery's Metropolis*, 160.

51. For a summary and reanalysis of day-to-day resistance see Walter Johnson, "On Agency," *Journal of Social History* 37, no. 1, special issue (Autumn 2003): 113–24.

52. Ned, NODP, September 29, 1846.

11

Runaway Slaves, Vigilance Committees, and the Pedagogy of Revolutionary Abolitionism, 1835–1863

Jesse Olsavsky

In 1872, William Still, a Philadelphia abolitionist and self-taught son of a runaway slave, reminisced upon the role of runaways in inspiring and teaching the antislavery movement: "While the grand little army of abolitionists was waging its untiring warfare for freedom . . . no agency encouraged them like the heroism of fugitives. The pulse of the four million slaves, and their desire for freedom, were better felt through 'The Underground Railroad,' than through any other channel."[1] Still knew what he was talking about. As a public agitator, he worked personally with many of the rank-and-file in "the grand little army of abolitionists." More importantly, as the head of a clandestine group known as the Philadelphia Vigilance Committee, Still had helped over nine hundred slaves desert the plantations and free themselves. Still listened to runaways' stories of work, oppression, and resistance. He wrote those stories down. He learned from fugitives of all ages, genders, and shades of experience, and encouraged them to teach others about the horrors of slavery. As Still and many others involved in vigilance committees understood it, runaway slaves were the teachers of the abolitionist movement. They inspired through their irrepressible desire for freedom. They educated through intimate dialogue with antislavery activists. Their "underground" mobility provided the foundation for abolitionism's "aboveground" mobilizations.

William Still had been part of a vast network of militant abolitionists who organized vigilance committees in northern cities, particularly on the East Coast. Organized first in the 1830s, vigilance committees were secret organizations, composed of antislavery activists from all backgrounds, who illegally aided hundreds of fugitive slaves in their exodus from slavery. They offered runaways food, clothing, advice, and transportation to Canada (as well as to Trinidad, England, and

Haiti). They also worked to protect free black communities from slave catchers, who would unscrupulously capture any black person, free or fugitive, and sell them into slavery. The committees raised funds, coordinated with each other, wrote public propaganda, and built secret networks in the South and among the black working class and other allies in order to facilitate the mass movement of slaves out of the South. In short, the committees were the militant, highly organized urban wing of the Underground Railroad. Unlike other antislavery activists, vigilance committee members worked closely with fugitive slaves and the major antislavery societies. Vigilance committee activists like Still were thus ideally positioned to learn from runaways and to recruit them into the movement. Collectively runaways and committee members put the wider abolitionist movement into closer touch with the desires, knowledge, resistance strategies, and "the pulse of the four million slaves."

This essay narrates the history of the Philadelphia Vigilance Committee (PVC), the Boston Vigilance Committee (BVC), the New York Vigilance Committee (NYVC), and the hundreds of fugitives they aided. Vigilance committee members took detailed notes on their interviews with fugitives.[2] They and the fugitives they aided also contributed to the vast protest literature of abolition by writing histories, slave narratives, novels, newspaper articles, and autobiographies. Based upon this rich array of evidence, this essay will sketch, first, a brief portrait of fugitive slaves who reached vigilance committees in the period from 1835–60, specifically showing the relationship of flight to the expansion and intensification of labor exploitation in the South. To grasp the movement to overthrow slavery requires an examination of the experiences of the enslaved, the structures they defied, and the knowledge they acquired and imparted. Second, the essay will outline the varied interactions among runaways, vigilance committees, and the wider antislavery movement in order to show how the enslaved people who passed through the committees taught the movement how to write, act, organize, and use both moral and physical force to fight the slave power. Vigilance committees and mobile slaves thus made the antislavery vanguard revolutionary.[3] The first long wave of mass desertion, better known as the Underground Railroad, helped to cause the Civil War and paved the way for the greater desertion that overthrew slavery in the 1860s.

RUNAWAYS, THEIR ALLIES, AND THE POLITICAL ECONOMY OF DESERTION

The scholarly literature on runaway slaves in the United States is vast and well documented, though it often delimits the importance of northward flight and its relation to the South's changing political economy. Much good research has focused on temporary runaways, maroons, or other deserters who remained in the South. However, most scholars of temporary flight and *marronage* wrongly see these forms of resistance as fundamentally disconnected from the Underground Railroad.[4] The historiography of the Underground Railroad still romanticizes daring feats of flight from slavery, rarely connecting those adventure stories to slaves' wider experience of labor and life or to the political economy of flight.[5] The documents left by vigilance committees offer a more comprehensive picture of slave desertion. Slaves and abolitionists saw that increased repression and the swiftly transforming political economy of the South spurred an increase in runaways. A "motley crew" of allies in the North and the South further assisted this rising movement of people by connecting vigilance committees to the working-class networks of desertion forged by slaves. Slaves and abolitionists experienced and understood the Underground Railroad as merely one aspect of a wider phenomenon—the autonomous mobility of the enslaved. They viewed temporary flight, *marronage,* desertion northward, and the networks facilitating this as an interconnected counterforce to what abolitionists called "the slave power."

When fugitives reached vigilance committees, abolitionists interviewed runaways rigorously about their lives in servitude. The purpose of these interviews was to expose imposters, reunite family members who had fled separately, and learn about the repressive institutions of slavery and methods for resisting it. Some runaways, who had never before told their tales of oppression, felt it to be a humanizing experience.[6] The records of the vigilance committees indicate that they aided as many as 7,000 runaways. Of these, detailed documentation exists for 1,700, most of which comes from the records of the PVC in the 1850s (the PVC manuscripts are the most detailed and fully preserved). According to these records only one percent of runaways came from the Deep South. A handful came from as far away as Brazil.[7] Most came from the upper states of Maryland, Virginia, and North Carolina—proximity to the North made escape much easier. About one-fourth of runaways came from rural plantations; the rest worked in urban areas, and were particularly concentrated in the cities of Baltimore, Richmond, and Norfolk (21% of the total came from these cities to Philadelphia). Women composed 22% of the runaways documented by the PVC,[8] 21% by the BVC, and 23% by the NYVC.[9] Most fugitives escaped alone or in pairs, though some escaped in families or groups as large as thirty.[10] The PVC noted 165 runaways came by water; the rest came by land.[11] The vast majority of runaways who reached New York and Boston "came by water, as stowaways on vessels."[12]

Slaves fled northward in increasing numbers from the 1830s onward due to the sheer brutality and repression of the slave system. Nearly all the narratives of slaves that passed through vigilance committees mention beatings, whippings, and precarious family lives. A few female slaves were candid and courageous enough to discuss with mainly male committee members about sexual violence inflicted by slaveholders.[13] Following Nat Turner's Rebellion (1831), the ruling class of the South closed itself off from various forms of gradual emancipation. They banned religious meetings and increased slave patrols. Fugitives who fled in the 1830s specifically mention this wave of violent repression as a primary reason for their flight.[14] As "Mrs. Coleman Freeman" put it, "I came away from North Carolina in consequence of persecution. There was a rebellion among slaves in Virginia, under Nat Turner, near where I was."[15] Aware of an increasing fugitive problem, and afraid of growing free black communities, authorities in southern cities kept black populations under heavy surveillance through enlarged police forces, and strict regulation of a system of passes and free papers.[16] Although these measures hardly deterred slaves, flight to nearby cities did become less simple and less secure; it was best to take one's chances going north.[17] As one Richmond slave, conversing with an abolitionist, put it, "now it seems as if the laws are becoming worse and worse for us every day; we can't enjoy anything now; we can't have the social meetings as we used to have; the colored people think about it a good deal. They run away every good chance they can get."[18]

The most significant reason for increasing escapes has to do with the expansion and intensification of slavery. In the Upper South the plantation complex expanded minimally. Expansion mainly took place in the Cotton Kingdom of the Deep South, and served as the violent foundations for the expansion of American empire.[19] But the Upper South provided the fuel for this monstrous expansion: labor power. The planters of Maryland and Virginia sold laborers to slave traders and cotton planters in droves, dividing families, and using fear of sale southwards to discipline their own workforces. Harriet Beecher Stowe described this monstrous trade as one of "the locomotive tendencies of the nineteenth century."[20] Slaves in the Upper South had a 10 percent chance of being sold southward, and nearly every enslaved person had a relative, spouse, or friend who had been sold away.[21] Of the runaways interviewed by Still nearly half justified running way due to fear of being sold or that close family or friends had already been sold. Some had been sold multiple times before fleeing.[22] Fugitives escaped from slave traders while on their way southward.[23] One runaway, Madison Washington, who had received aid and inspiration from the PVC, was recaptured in Virginia attempting to rescue his wife, and sold South. On that forced journey by ship to the New Orleans market, Washington (and 135 other captives) launched a successful slave-ship rebellion aboard the *Creole,* and navigated their ship to freedom in the Bahamas.[24]

Although plantation slavery in the Upper South expanded only slightly, slavery in the region became industrialized, commercialized, and waged. Slaveholders, often short on cash, hired out slaves to the burgeoning industries and service sectors of the cities. Hired-out slaves worked as porters, draymen, chambermaids, and house servants.[25] But they also worked in industrial settings, such as iron foundries, coal mines, and tobacco factories. Before deserting, one runaway had spent nineteen years "hired out, sometimes as waiter, sometimes in a tobacco factory, and for five years in the *coal mines.*"[26] As the records of vigilance committees attest, hiring-out practices encouraged northward flight.[27] Life in cities increased opportunities for freedom, knowledge, and interaction with free black communities. As the centers of the coastal trade, southern cities facilitated easy interaction between slaves and abolitionist sailors.[28] In fact, fugitives from rural plantations sometimes complained that city slaves had easier lives and better opportunities for escape.[29] However, cities also created new conditions for exploitation and oppression. Fugitive abolitionists singled out tobacco factories, the Upper South's largest industrial enterprise, as places of exceptional violence.[30] In the factories, male and female slaves faced sixteen-hour days, industrial work discipline, and constant thrashings from overseers. Like all other hired-out slaves, they paid most (or all) of their hard-earned wages to their masters.[31] Approximately one of four slaves who reached vigilance committees had been hired out, and about three percent came from the tobacco factories.[32]

Slaves had to find allies in their flight to freedom,[33] usually black women and men in cities, who had experiences of racism or slavery (though Quakers and a few ship captains also helped out).[34] These allies in turn collaborated with the vigilance committees. Free black workers in the South communicated with slaves and told them the safest routes to the committees. Ex-slave Thomas Smallwood and his wife, Elizabeth, took fugitives by wagon, sometimes a dozen at a time, from the Upper South to the PVC.[35] Leonard Grimes served a two-year prison sentence for doing the same thing in Washington, DC. Afterwards he made his way to Boston and became a leading member of the BVC.[36] The PVC worked with a group of market women in Baltimore who forged freedom papers and directed fugitives to the committee.[37] Sailors on trading vessels also proved crucial, helping runaways stow away, sometimes without the knowledge of their captains.[38] George Latimer stowed away in such fashion, and later became an informant for the BVC.[39] David Ruggles (head of the NYVC) had once worked as a sailor, and pioneered the use of maritime networks to push forward what he called the "mighty revolution" of emancipation.[40] In northern cities, committees relied on dockers, porters, and other black workers who served as informants.[41] The BVC worked with a "colored woman," an Irish "laborer," and a ship captain who sneaked on board harbored ships, and "found out if there was any fugitive on board."[42] These mainly proletarian abolitionists directed the runaways to the vigilance committees, who then offered food, clothing, advice, transportation, and / or work.[43] In short, as one abolitionist writer put it, the committees "displayed the most diversified assemblage of characters, but this diversity secured its greater efficiency."[44]

The records of vigilance committees show that abolitionists and fugitives conceived the autonomous mobility of the enslaved—in all its forms—as a fundamental means to resist coerced labor. Abolitionists learned that "the social desires of slaves" to freely move, visit friends, or absent themselves from work established "the secret and rapid modes of communication" that made the Underground Railroad possible.[45] Temporary flight, escape to cities, and forms of *petit marronage* in the swamps and backwoods flowed into one another, and often became the first steps toward the bolder flight north. As many runaways related, they would temporarily desert to the wilderness until friends in cities could secure them passage on vessels headed to free states.[46] Nor was the Underground Railroad disconnected from *marronage* in Virginia's Dismal Swamp. Slaves ran to the Dismal Swamp, and finding it less safe from slave catchers than they had hoped, fled north.[47] "Agents" working in the South for the vigilance committees sometimes told runaways to seek aid from the maroons until safe passage north could be found for them.[48] The black abolitionist Stephen Myers (Albany VC), for instance, believed that the Underground Railroad and *marronage* were two primary vectors of resistance to the slave empire. As he put it, "the North Star is clearly unconstitutional, as decidedly so as the Dismal Swamp."[49] Abolitionists understood this mobility as unique and potentially revolutionary. Yet they also understood it as commonplace practice within a global history of desertion. They knew that Caribbean maroons had done similar things to good effect.[50] The runaway slave Lewis Clarke (helped by the BVC) stressed that even "the natives of India fled to the Jungles . . . to escape the barbarous cruelty of Warren Hastings," the brutal governor of colonial Bengal.[51]

RUNAWAYS, VIGILANCE COMMITTEES, AND ABOLITIONIST EDUCATION

Until recently, scholarship on the Underground Railroad hardly considered the role of vigilance committees in the secretive Underground Railroad or in the public antislavery movement. Most scholarship on the Underground Railroad has focused either on the Railroad's degree of organization or on its impact upon national debates over the 1850 fugitive slave law.[52] But just as importantly, though often overlooked, radical abolitionists used vigilance committees to talk with the mass base of their own liberation movement—slaves. They learned from each other. Runaways taught by shaping the abolitionist critique of slavery and revealing new vectors of resistance to it. They promoted a radical diversity of people and ideas within the movement, further affirming abolitionists' intersectional commitments to all the other reforms under the sun. They helped reconfigure the tactics of abolition by pushing the movement from "moral suasion" to illegal direct action, practical aid to the enslaved, and the use of violent means. In short, by building connections between subaltern slave resistance and public agitation, runaways made the mobility of slaves the basis for the revolutionary mobilization to overturn slavery.

Conservative contemporary writers usually claimed that "most abolitionists know little or nothing of slavery and slaveholders." Yet one such writer admitted that abolitionist information "is learned from excited, caressed, and tempted fugitives."[53] The committees facilitated new interactions that had been previously rare within the antislavery ranks. More than that, they created an open space in which learning among runaways, abolitionists, and other marginalized groups could bloom. Praising the NYVC for its openness and inclusivity, one runaway slave exclaimed that "she had no confidence in other societies."[54] Dialogues gave runaways a sense of the earnestness and urgency of radical abolitionists, and motivated them to educate themselves further and become voices for their oppressed sisters and brothers.[55] Involved in education reform and fascinated by novel forms of pedagogy, abolitionists used the metaphor of the school to describe their own learning experiences in the committees. T. W. Higginson explained that "it has been my privilege to live in the best society all my life—namely that of abolitionists and fugitive slaves . . . . Nothing short of knowing them could be called a liberal education."[56] The black abolitionist William Cooper Nell (BVC) described the vigilance committees as a "school indeed for learning" in which runaways did most of the teaching.[57]

First and foremost, fugitives taught abolitionists by entering the ranks of the antislavery vanguard. Due to conviction and a little encouragement from abolitionists, runaways attended meetings, read newspapers, donated money, or engaged in other antislavery activities. Although William Still advised most freed people to go to Canada, he actively encouraged activism among Canadian fugitives through an extensive correspondence, patronage of Afro-Canadian newspapers, and occasional Canadian lecture tours.[58] Knowing intimately the workings of the Underground Railroad, a handful of fugitives rose to leadership positions in vigilance committees.[59] Others taught abolitionists through speaking and writing. Vigilance committees recruited runaways to become paid lecturers and agents for the movement.[60] Some of these runaways went on national speaking tours and three went on popular international tours.[61] One fugitive woman aided by the NYVC composed and performed moving "antislavery songs."[62] On the matter of antislavery eloquence, Thomas Wentworth Higginson (BVC) wrote that "my own teachers were the slave women who came shyly before the audience," but spoke words of fire.[63] Thirty-four runaways who passed through the committees, or worked with them— including Frederick Douglass and Harriet Jacobs—wrote stirring autobiographies that advanced the abolitionist critique of slavery. Committee members hailed them as significant and revolutionary contributions to world literature.[64] A PVC member remarked in 1849 that the revolutionary heroism related by runaways in their narratives "exceeded" anything "done on the barricades of Paris."[65]

Fugitives in dialogue with committee members crafted trenchant analyses of American slavery. Runaways systematized their experiences into a sociology of slavery. Peter Randolph, who was helped by the BVC, had many conversations with committee members. However, he related, "as I listened and conversed with these earnest men, I was impressed with the idea that they were not familiar with all the relations that existed between master and slave."[66] He therefore wrote a pamphlet that gave a scientific account of class relations in the South, the customs of slaves, and the differing lives of rural slaves on the plantations and city slaves hired out or "employed in factories."[67] Fugitives genuinely cared about the creation of new knowledge. Henry Watson (helped by the BVC) wrote his narrative not for religious or personal reasons, but to "throw some light upon the condition of slaves in Mississippi; the narration of other fugitives having their scenes in other states."[68] Female fugitives divulged the specific plights of enslaved women—the double burdens of work and motherhood, sexual violence, the difficulties of escape.[69] The black feminist writer Frances Harper (PVC) based her popular poems "The Slave Mother" and "The Fugitive's Wife" on her discussion with enslaved women.[70]

Abolitionists learned from fugitives of slavery's violence, of its deep entrenchment in American life, and of the importance of desertion and resistance. Richard Hildreth (BVC), in his book *Despotism in America,* argued that slavery was America's *national* institution, at the heart of its imperial expansion, upheld by violence, and fraught with desertion and the perpetual "whisper of an insurrection."[71] The Underground Railroad "conductor" Jonathan Walker—knowing that desertion challenged the slave-based economic expansion of the United States—asserted that American empire required the immobilization of the enslaved. Desertion northward, he argued, made free states into "a hunting ground for slaveholders," backed by the government, northern "gentleman of property and standing," and racist apathy. Because slaves "fled to the Indians for protection . . . whites therefore demanded the expulsion of the Indians." Flight to freedom westward necessitated "a war of conquest and extermination waged and carried on against the republic of Mexico."[72] Confinement became the metaphor for slavery. Slaves and abolitionists alike referred to the slave empire as "the prison house."

Inspired by the stories of resistance in the Dismal Swamp, committee members began to narrate the story of the maroons, which they expanded into historical accounts of *marronage.* Information on the maroons was hard to come by. As one BVC member noted, few slave patrols penetrated deeply into the swamp, and slaveholders rarely divulged information on slave resistance.[73] Instead, another abolitionist wrote, in a study of the Virginia maroons, the only knowledge of life in the swamp came from "the uniform testimony of the runaways."[74] At a meeting of the Pennsylvania Antislavery Society, PVC members narrated "an account given of some fugitive slaves fresh from the dismal swamp."[75] Edmund Jackson and William Cooper Nell of the BVC published accounts of the Virginia Maroons, comparing them to the Underground Railroad and the international history of *marronage.*[76] Thomas Wentworth Higginson (BVC) expanded those analyses into a series of essays on slave rebellion and *marronage* throughout the Americas.[77] Harriet Beecher Stowe rethought her own conceptions of slavery through interactions with the activists, fugitive and freeborn, of the BVC. She talked with them, read and wrote introductions to their descriptions of the Dismal Swamp, and absorbed their fierce criticisms of *Uncle Tom's Cabin*.[78] As a result, the protagonist of her next popular antislavery novel was a Virginia maroon who helped runaways, claimed to be the son of Denmark Vesey, and fiercely advocated slave revolution.[79] Such literature inspired abolitionists of all stripes. A well-read runaway praised Nell's "solid historical facts ... [that] brought forward much to our credit that might have been entirely lost."[80]

By connecting public antislavery agitation to the resistance of the enslaved, vigilance committees transformed the tactics of the wider antislavery movement. They did so first by making fugitive aid an accepted and encouraged tactic among the major antislavery societies. In the 1830s and early 1840s, committees boasted about their autonomy from the sectarian politics of the major antislavery societies.[81] The societies desired to reform the master; the committees sought to rescue the slave.[82] But as more slaves fled and fewer masters reformed, overburdened, underfunded committees began to argue that their preferential option for the enslaved should be a foundation of the movement.[83] Committee members urged more support at meetings of the antislavery societies. At an 1843 antislavery meeting, with delegations from northern states, Charles Torrey and a band of fugitives moved "that the *South* should be represented in the delegation of certain fugitives."[84] In some instances, fugitive slaves organized their own antislavery meetings, which free abolitionists also attended.[85] By the late 1840s, the PVC, BVC, and NYVC had integrated themselves with the antislavery societies. They received their funds and used their offices and resources. Committee leaders often held important positions within antislavery societies.[86] As a result, abolitionists became more involved in fugitive aid. William Parker, a runaway residing in southeastern Pennsylvania, secretly aided runaways autonomously of vigilance committees and antislavery organizations. By the late 1840s abolitionists began actively collaborating with him. Speaking of those abolitionists, Parker wrote, "[I] have always found them men and women with hearts .... They are indeed and in truth, the poor slave's friend. To shelter him, to help him on to freedom, I have ever found them ready."[87] Thus, by the time of the passage of the more draconian Fugitive Slave Law of 1850, vigilance committees, fugitives, and their allies had already put in place the public and clandestine mechanisms to respond to the crisis.

Fugitives and vigilance committees spearheaded the abolitionist turn to violent means in the 1850s. Runaways, knowing that Christian "nonresistance" would not prevent them being returned to slavery, defended their right to bear arms against slave catchers. Of the runaways interviewed by Still, 40 fled slavery armed, and 14 engaged in violent confrontations with slave catchers.[88] Jermain Loguen, runaway and head of the Syracuse VC, wrote, "My hands will fight a slaveholder .... I am a fugitive slave, and you know that we have strange notions about many things."[89] Fugitives taught these "strange notions" to committee members, who in turn taught them to the rest of the movement. Runaways urged William Still to be more aggressive in his Underground Railroad work. One runaway even urged him to organize slave insurrections.[90] Helping runaway William Craft elude slave catchers, Henry Bowditch (BVC) learned the ways of militant abolitionism when Craft handed him a pistol and ordered him to use it if necessary.[91] The committees further pushed the movement to violence through a number of high-profile slave rescues. In 1851, runaway William Parker—leading a band of fugitives, militant Quakers, and a black PVC agent—fought a pitched battle with slave catchers at Christiana, Pennsylvania. Contemporaries described the event as a "servile insurrection," and attempted to try the combatants for treason.[92] In the same year, the Syracuse VC and BVC helped in successful rescues of fugitives from court houses and prisons.[93] In 1854, armed BVC members attempted to rescue fugitive Anthony Burns from his jail cell. They killed one police officer, but failed to free Burns.[94]

Conversing on plans for slave insurrection in 1858, Thomas Wentworth Higginson (BVC) wrote to Lysander Spooner (BVC) "in Revolutions the practical end always comes first and the theory afterwards."[95] Abolitionist theories of slave revolution, interestingly enough, did not come directly from acts of slave insurrection, but from the existing practices of slave mobility. Edmund Jackson (BVC), for instance, argued "that through the exodus of repeated slave insurrections, the oppressed are destined by inscrutable laws to eventually secure their freedom."[96] His use of the term *exodus* suggests his understanding of the process of revolt in terms of desertion and movement. Runaway John Henry Hill, in an 1857 letter to William Still urging the use of "fire and sword" to overthrow slavery, described slave rebellions as "insurrectionary movements among slaves" (interestingly, the word "*social movement*" had only just been coined in 1850 by European social theorist Lorenz von Stein, suggesting that runaway slaves were independently formulating their own theory of the social movement).[97] Others thought similarly. Fugitive slaves brought their experiences of slavery to bear in some of the first histories of Vesey's Rebellion and the Haitian Revolution.[98] James McCune Smith—black abolitionist, Underground Railroad worker, and collaborator with many committee members—wrote a history of the Haitian Revolution which argued that runaways and maroons helped spark the revolution.[99] Other committee members wrote their own histories of the Haitian Revolution, as well as pioneering histories of *marronage* and slave insurrection.[100]

Theories and histories quickly congealed into plans and praxis. Thomas Wentworth Higginson believed that establishing maroon communities in the Alleghenies, "like the maroons of Jamaica and Surinam," would provide a base for future slave insurrections.[101] Lysander Spooner (BVC) devised an elaborate plan (never carried out) of slave revolution based upon the experience of the Underground Railroad. His plan called for the establishment of "vigilance committees" on southern plantations. These vigilance committees would sabotage production, collect arms, and train for battle. At the opportune moment slaves would rise up in revolt, seize plantations, and redistribute the land.[102] More significantly, John Brown described his foreboding plans for slave revolution as "[Underground] Railroad business on a *somewhat extended* scale."[103]

Vigilance committees built up the resources and knowledge necessary for John Brown's attempt to move beyond the Underground Railroad to slave revolt. In the 1850s Brown had involved himself in the underground networks of fugitive aid forged by the committees, discussing his tentative plans for insurrection with runaways like Frederick Douglass, Jermain Loguen, and Harriet Tubman.[104] At the home of runaway slave Lewis Hayden (BVC), Brown "brooded and schemed for the slave."[105] In 1858, BVC members formed a group known as the "Secret Six" who financed and advised Brown and his motley band of militant abolitionists, runaways, and European revolutionaries.[106] Immediately prior to his raid in Virginia, Brown had extensive discussions with PVC members on the best routes and "the persons who were actually to be relied upon" in the South.[107] One PVC member even organized an auxiliary "colored military company" for the coming trials.[108] The knowledge, tactics, and networks mobilized by the committees made Brown's plans possible, but in the end they could not make them successful. Nevertheless, committees crafted Brown's disastrous failures into stunning victories. Underground Railroad networks helped some of Brown's conspirators flee authorities.[109] Committee members wrote powerful pamphlets and eulogies praising Brown and defending slaves' right to flight and insurrection. Other committee members organized the highly publicized procession of Brown's corpse to burial in New York, creating the legend of "John Brown's Body."[110] Fugitives and vigilance committees translated practices of desertion into theories of resistance. They then attempted to reconfigure those theories into practices of slave revolution that—quixotic though they were—heightened contradictions and helped to cause the American Civil War.

When Civil War broke out, fugitives and vigilance committees knew that those still in slavery had a tremendous role to play in making the Civil War a war against slavery. At the war's beginning, one BVC member argued that the counterrevolution of southern planters closely resembled the planter counterrevolution in 1790s Saint Domingue. By fleeing and fighting amidst the turmoil of war, abolitionist Elizur Wright argued, slaves would force the U.S. government to pass immediate emancipation laws, as had happened in France in 1794.[111] Precisely this happened, and no event precipitated emancipation and radical reconstruction more profoundly than the mass desertion of the black worker.[112] Fugitives and committee members took part in these auspicious events. Moncure Conway, the son of a Virginia slaveholder, and sometime fellow traveler with the BVC, had been secretly helping a few of his father's slaves flee to Ohio throughout the 1850s. Once the Civil War erupted, Conway, finding that the rest of his father's slaves had suddenly deserted to Union lines, also helped them get to Ohio.[113] Fugitives enlisted in the Union Army. Two fugitives helped by the PVC became soldiers, and later radical reconstruction politicians in North Carolina (one of them, Abraham Galloway, was the first person to publicly advocate armed self-defense against the Ku Klux Klan).[114] Thomas Wentworth Higginson (BVC) commanded the first United States regiment composed of deserters from the plantations. In the 1850s, Higginson, with the encouragement of militant abolitionists and revolutionary runaways, had been an impatient advocate of slave revolt. But from the fugitive soldiers out of the much deeper reaches of the South he "learned the patient self-control of those who had waited till the course of events should open a better way. When it came they accepted it."[115] In short, as W. E. B. Dubois suggested long ago, politics followed in the footsteps of the fugitive slave from the Underground Railroad to the mass desertions of the Civil War.[116]

The mobilizations of slaves and abolitionists before, during, and after the Civil War immediately changed the vectors of global capitalism. Frustrated with the United States government's inability to curtail the northward flight of fugitives, an insurgent, powerful capitalist class of slave owners briefly attempted to separate itself from the rest of the country, to establish a vast slave empire. But after military defeat, and after witnessing the specter of radical, interracial "abolition democracy" during Reconstruction, northern and southern capitalists reunited and became more powerful than ever. Industrialism, western expansion, and the rise of the "new" South remade the United States into the world's largest capitalist economy by 1890. Having lost a vast pool of dark, highly exploitable labor in the wake of emancipation in the Americas, Europe and America's rulers turned to labor in Africa and Asia, inaugurating the high era of colonialism. As Dubois explained, "the abolition of American Slavery started the transportation of capital from white to black countries where slavery prevailed, with the same tremendous and awful consequences upon the laboring classes of the world which we see about us today. When raw material could not be raised in a country like the United States, it could be raised in the tropics and semi-tropics under a dictatorship of industry, commerce, and manufacture."[117]

Runaways used their mobility to create new class alliances among the ruled, forging connections with middle-class intellectuals, reformers, and revolutionaries, to whom they offered knowledge of slavery, effective strategies of resistance, as well as new propaganda, new literary sensibilities, and new ideas.[118] They made mobility the driving force behind antislavery theory and practice. Fugitive slaves had some white proletarian allies in their freedom struggles, but their numbers were few, and longer-term interracial class solidarities failed to emerge. As global imperialism revamped itself in the post–Civil War era, and as white American workers continued to reap the benefits of white supremacy, the descendants of slaves found their condition more like that of the colonized than their fellow American workers.[119] Thus, when William Lloyd Garrison (BVC) preached to an all-black audience in 1840 to show their sympathy and solidarity with colonized people the world over, he anticipated the types of real and imagined international working-class solidarities that were to emerge in the following century.[120]

NOTES

1. William Still, *The Underground Rail Road: A Record of Facts, Authentic Narratives, Letters Sec. Narrating the Hardships, Hair-breadth Escapes and Death Struggles of the Slaves in Their Efforts for Freedom, as Related by Themselves and Others or Witnessed by the Author; Together with Sketches of Some of the Largest Stockholders and Most Liberal Aiders and Advisers of the Road* (Philadelphia, 1872), xviii.

2. Still, *Underground Rail Road*; Sydney Howard Gay, "Record of Fugitives," Sydney Howard Gay Papers, Columbia University; Francis Jackson, *Account Book of Francis Jackson, Treasurer, the Vigilance Committee of Boston* (Boston: Library of the Bostonian Society, 1924); Joseph A. Borome, "The Vigilant Committee of Philadelphia," *Pennsylvania Magazine of History and Biography* 92, no. 3 (1968): 320–51; John White Browne, "Boston Committee of Vigilance: Agent's Records, 1846–1847," Wendell Phillips Papers, Houghton Library, Harvard; "Records of the Vigilance Committee of Boston," Antislavery Collection, Boston Public Library; "Boston Anti-Man Hunting League Records," Massachusetts Historical Society.

3. For treatments of the antislavery movement as a revolutionary movement, see W. E. B. Dubois, *Black Reconstruction in America, 1860–1880* (New York: Free Press, 1992); Herbert Aptheker, *Abolitionism: A Revolutionary Movement* (Boston: Twayne, 1979); Manisha Sinha, *The Slave's Cause: A History of Abolition* (New Haven, CT: Yale University Press, 2016).

4. See, for example, John Hope Franklin and Loren Schweninger, *Runaway Slaves: Rebels on the Plantation* (New York: Oxford University Press, 1999); Syviane Diouf, *Slavery's Exiles: The Story of the American Maroons* (New York: New York University Press, 2014); see also Herbert Aptheker, "Maroons within the Present Limits of the United States," in *Maroon Societies: Rebel Slave Communities in the Americas,* ed. Richard Price (Baltimore: Johns Hopkins University Press, 1979), 151–69.

5. Among the fine recent treatments of the Underground Railroad are David Blight, ed., *Passages to Freedom: The Underground Railroad in History and Memory* (New York: HarperCollins, 2004); Fergus M. Bordewich, *Bound for Canaan: The Epic Story of the Underground Railroad* (New York: HarperCollins, 2005); Eric Foner, *Gateway to Freedom: The Hidden History of the Underground Railroad* (New York: Norton, 2015).

6. Henry Brown, *Narrative of the Life of Henry Box Brown, Written by Himself* (Manchester: Lee and Glynn, 1851), 59; Lucretia Mott to Joseph Rugdale, 28 March 1849, in Beverly Wilson Palmer, ed., *Selected Letters of Lucretia Coffin Mott* (Urbana: University of Illinois Press, 2002), 180; Harriet Jacobs, *Incidents in the Life of a Slave Girl,* ed. Lydia Maria Child (Boston: 1861), 245.

7. "Vigilance Committee Records, 1846–1847," Massachusetts Historical Society; Mahommah Baquaqua, *Biography of Mahomma G. Baquaqua. . .* (Detroit: George E. Pomeroy, 1854).

8. Still, *Underground Rail Road.*

9. Jackson, *Account Book of Francis Jackson*; Gay, "Record of Fugitives."

10. Joshua Coffin to Maria W. Chapman, 26 September 1842, Antislavery Collection, Boston Public Library.

11. Still, *Underground Rail Road.*

12. Thomas Wentworth Higginson to Wilbur Siebert, 24 July 1896, Siebert Papers, Ohio Historical Society.

13. Jacobs, *Life of a Slave Girl,* 244; Still, *Underground Rail Road,* 80–82; Thomas Wentworth Higginson, "Obeying the Higher Law" and "The Black Troops: Intensely Human" in *The Magnificent*

Activist: The Writings of Thomas Wentworth Higginson, 1823–1911, ed. Howard N. Meyer (Boston: Da Capo Press, 2000), 65, 181–82.

14. Jacobs, *Life of a Slave Girl;* James L. Smith, *Autobiography of James L. Smith* (Norwich, CT: Press of the Bulletin Company, 1881), 30; Henry Brown, *Narrative of the Life of Henry Box Brown, Written by Himself* (Manchester: Lee and Glynn, 1851), 19.

15. Benjamin Drew, *The Refugee: Or the Narratives of Fugitive Slaves in Canada Related by Themselves* (Boston: John P. Jewett, 1856), 332.

16. Still, *Underground Rail Road*, 92; "Daybook of the Richmond Police Guard," Alderman Library, University of Virginia; Frederick Law Olmsted, *A Journey in the Seaboard Slave States, with Remarks on Their Economy* (New York: Dix and Edwards, 1856), 20.

17. J. M. McKim, "The Slave's Ultima Ratio," *The Liberty Bell: By Friends of Freedom* (Boston: National Antislavery Bazaar, 1857), 326.

18. James Redpath, *The Roving Editor; or, Talks with Slaves in the Southern States* (A. B. Burdick, 1859), 17.

19. Edward Baptist, *The Half Has Never Been Told: Slavery and the Making of American Capitalism* (New York: Basic Books, 2014).

20. Harriet Beecher Stowe, *Uncle Tom's Cabin; or, Life among the Lowly* (New York: Harper and Rowe, 1958), 73.

21. Michael Tadman, *Speculators and Slaves: Masters, Traders, and Slaves in the Old South* (Madison: University of Wisconsin Press, 1989), 45.

22. Still, *Underground Rail Road*, 61.

23. Ibid., 291–93.

24. "Newspaper Scrapbook, 1880–1899," Charles L. Blockson Collection, Temple University. Interestingly, Washington learned from abolitionists and in turn (through his militant actions) inspired abolitionists. See Anita Rupprecht, "'All We Have Done, We Have Done for Freedom': The *Creole* Slave-Ship Revolt (1841) and the Revolutionary Atlantic," *International Review of Social History* 58 (2013): 253–77; Stanley Harrold, "Romanticizing Slave Revolt: Madison Washington, the *Creole* Mutiny and Abolitionist Celebration of Violent Means," in *Antislavery Violence: Sectional, Racial, and Cultural Conflict in Antebellum America*, ed. John R. McKivigan and Stanley Harrold (Knoxville: University of Tennessee Press, 1999), 89–108; William Wells Brown, *The Black Man: His Antecedents, His Genius, and His Achievements* (Boston: Robert F. Walcutt, 1865), 75–86.

25. Barbara Fields, *Slavery and Freedom on the Middle Ground: Maryland during the Nineteenth Century* (New Haven, CT: Yale University Press, 1985); Seth Rockman, *Scraping By: Wage Labor, Slavery, and Survival in Early Baltimore* (Baltimore: Johns Hopkins University Press, 2009).

26. Still, *Underground Railroad*, 111–12.

27. Still, *Underground Rail Road*, 115.

28. Henry A. Wise, "Wealth, Resources, and Hopes of Virginia," *Debow's Review* 23, no. 1 (1857): 66.

29. Peter Randolph, *From Slave Cabin to Pulpit* (Boston: James H. Earl, 1893), 191–93; H. C. Bruce, *The New Man: Twenty Nine Years a Slave, Twenty Nine Years a Freeman* (York Pennsylvania: P. Anstadt and Sons, 1895), 34.

30. Henry Brown, *Narrative of the Life of Henry Box Brown, Written by Himself* (Manchester: Lee and Glynn, 1851), 22; Kate R. Pickard, *The Kidnapped and the Ransomed, Being the Personal Recollections of Peter Still and His Wife Vina after Forty Years of Slavery* (Syracuse: William T. Hamilton, 1856), 107.

31. *Richmond Enquirer*, 14 May 1852. See also Joseph Clarke Robert, *The Tobacco Kingdom: Plantation, Market, and Factory in Virginia and North Carolina* (Gloucester, MA: Peter Smith, 1965); Suzanne Gehring Schnittman, "Slavery in Virginia's Urban Tobacco Industry, 1840–1860" (PhD diss., University of Rochester, 1986).

32. Still, *Underground Rail Road.*

33. More work needs to be done on unearthing these proletarian networks, particularly in the South. Some works that do start to write this history are Stanley Harrold, *Subversives: Antislavery Community in Washington, D.C., 1828–1865* (Baton Rouge: LSU Press, 2003); T. Stephen Whitman, *Challenging Slavery in the Chesapeake: Black and White Resistance to Human Bondage, 1775–1865* (Baltimore: Maryland Historical Society, 2007); David Cecelski, *Waterman's Song: Slavery and Freedom in Maritime North Carolina* (Chapel Hill: University of North Carolina Press, 2001).

34. Quakers and a few more audacious ship captains also provided crucial aid to fugitives. R. C. Smedley, *History of the Underground Railroad in Chester and the Neighboring Counties of Pennsylvania* (Lancaster, PA, 1883); Daniel Drayton, *Personal Memoirs of Daniel Drayton* (New York: American and Foreign Antislavery Society, 1853).

35. Thomas Smallwood, *A Narrative of Thomas Smallwood, (Colored Man): Giving an Account of His Birth—The Period He Was Held in Slavery—and Removal to Canada, Etc., Together with an Account of the Underground Railroad* (Toronto: James Stephens, 1851).

36. Charles Emery Stevens, *Anthony Burns: A History* (Boston: John Jewett, 1856), 203–9.

37. Smedley, *History of the Underground Railroad,* 355; Robert Purvis to Wilbur Siebert, 23 December 1895, Siebert Papers, Ohio Historical Society. Baltimore was often the first stop for fugitives.

38. *Address of the Committee Appointed by a Public Meeting Held at Faneuil Hall, September 26 for the Purpose of Considering the Recent Case of Kidnapping from Our Soil* (Boston: White and Potter, 1846), 3; Francis Jackson, "Fugitive Slaves," in *The Liberty Bell: By Friends of Freedom* (Boston: National Anti-Slavery Bazaar, 1858), 29–43; Jacobs, *Life of a Slave Girl,* 241; Stevens, *Anthony Burns,* 176; John Andrew Jackson, *The Experience of a Slave in South Carolina* (London: Passmore and Alabastor, 1867), 26.

39. Jackson, *Account Book of Francis Jackson.*

40. Graham Russel Hodges, *David Ruggles: A Radical Black Abolitionist and the Underground Railroad in New York City* (Chapel Hill: University of North Carolina Press, 2010); *Fifth Annual Report of the New York Committee of Vigilance for the Year 1842, with Interesting Facts Relative to the Proceedings* (New York: G. Vale, 1842), 29–30.

41. Still, *Underground Rail Road,* 57.

42. Thomas Wentworth Higginson to Wilbur Siebert, 24 July 1896, Siebert Papers, Ohio Historical Society; For more on the maritime dimensions of the BVC, see Austin Bearse, *Reminisces of Fugitive Slave Law Days in Boston* (Boston: Warren Richardson, 1880); "Statement of Stockholders Loss in Yacht Flirt," Antislavery Collection, Boston Public Library; Boston Anti-Man-Hunting League Records, 1846–1887, Massachusetts Historical Society.

43. S. J. Celestine Edward, *From Slavery to a Bishopric, or the Life of Bishop Walter Hawkins of the Methodist Episcopal Church of Canada* (London: John Kensit, 1891), 65; Kate R. Pickard, *Kidnapped and the Ransomed,* 244.

44. Stevens, *Anthony Burns,* 29–31.

45. Redpath, *Roving Editor,* 284; Still, *Underground Rail Road,* 115.

46. Still, *Underground Rail Road,* 32, 88, 192, 294; Gay "Record of Fugitives," (Notebook 1) 16, 21, 31, (Notebook 2), 36; Drew, *Refugee,* 186.

47. "Pennsylvania Antislavery Society Records, 1837–1856," Historical Society Pennsylvania, 256; William Mitchell, *The Underground Railroad* (London: William Tweedie, 1860), 73; J. M. McKim, "Slave's Ultima Ratio," 325; Still, *Underground Rail Road,* 43.

48. Still, *Underground Rail Road,* 169.

49. Stephen Myers to Francis Jackson, 22 May 1858, Antislavery Collection, Boston Public Library.

50. Thomas Wentworth Higginson, *Army Life in a Black Regiment* (Boston: Fields and Osgood, 1870), 248.

51. Lewis Clarke and Milton Clarke, *The Narratives of the Sufferings of Lewis and Milton Clarke* (Boston: Bela Marsh, 1846), 10.

52. Foner, *Gateway to Freedom;* Hodges, *David Ruggles.* Both of these works focus on the New York Vigilance Committee; Richard Blackett, *The Captive's Quest for Freedom: Fugitive Slaves, the 1850 Fugitive Slave Law, and the Politics of Slavery* (New York: Cambridge University Press, 2018).

53. F. G. De Fontaine, *American Abolitionism from 1787 to 1861* (New York: D. Appleton, 1861), 6.

54. Nathaniel P. Rogers, *Collection from the Miscellaneous Writings of Nathaniel Peabody Rogers* (Boston: Benjamin B. Mussey, 1849), 138.

55. Lewis Hayden to Wendell Phillips, 21 February 1848, Wendell Phillips Papers, Houghton Library; Still, *Underground Rail Road,* 134–36.

56. Thomas Wentworth Higginson, *Contemporaries* (Boston: Houghton and Mifflin, 1899), 227.

57. William Cooper Nell to Amy Kirby Post, 5 December 1850, in *William Cooper Nell: Nineteenth-Century African American Abolitionist, Historian, Integrationist, Selected Writing, 1832–1874,* ed. Dorothy Porter and Constance Uzelac (Baltimore: Black Classic Press, 2002), 180.

58. *Public Ledger,* 21 January 1860; Still, *Underground Rail Road.*

59. Most notably Lewis Hayden (BVC) and Jermain Loguen (Syracuse VC). J. W. Loguen, *The Rev. J. W. Loguen As a Slave and As a Freeman* (Syracuse, NY: J. G. K. Truair, 1859); Harriet Beecher Stowe, *The Key to "Uncle Tom's Cabin," Presenting Original Facts Upon Which the Story Is Founded* (Boston, 1853), 154–55.

60. Sidney Howard Gay to Caroline Weston, 4 January 1847, Sidney Howard Gay Papers, Columbia University; "American Anti-Slavery Society Ledger, 1844–1863," New York Public Library.

61. Brown, *Life of Henry Box Brown;* William Craft, *Running a Thousand Miles for Freedom; Or, the Escape of William and Ellen Craft* (London: William Tweedie, 1860); R. J. M. Blackett, *Building an Antislavery Wall: Black Americans in the Atlantic Abolitionist Movement, 1830–1860* (Baton Rouge: LSU Press, 1983).

62. *Sketch of the Life of Charles B. Ray* (New York: J. J. Little, 1887), 65–66.

63. Thomas Wentworth Higginson, *Cheerful Yesterdays* (Boston: Houghton and Mifflin, 1898), 328.

64. *The Liberator,* 21 April 1865.

65. J. Miller McKim to Sidney Howard Gay, 14 November 1849, Antislavery Collection, Boston Public Library.

66. Randolph, *From Slave Cabin to Pulpit,* 31.

67. Peter Randolph, "Sketches of Slave Life" (1855), in *From Slave Cabin to Pulpit,* 147–217.

68. Henry Watson, *Narrative of Henry Watson, A Fugitive Slave* (Boston: Bela Marsh, 1850), 40.

69. Jacobs, *Life of a Slave Girl.*

70. Frances Ellen Watkins Harper, *A Brighter Coming Day: A Frances Ellen Watkins Harper Reader* (New York: Feminist Press, 1990), 58, 72.

71. Richard Hildreth, *Despotism in America: An Inquiry Into the Nature, Results, and Legal Basis of the Slaveholding System in the United States* (Boston: John P. Jewett, 1854).

72. Jonathan Walker, *A Brief View of American Chattelized Humanity and Its Supports* (Boston: Dow and Jackson, 1847), 20, 24–26.

73. Edmund Jackson, "The Virginia Maroons," in *The Liberty Bell: By Friends of Freedom* (Boston: Massachusetts Antislavery Fair, 1852), 146–47.

74. Redpath, *Roving Editor,* 288.

75. Pennsylvania Antislavery Society Records, vol. 3, 256, Historical Society of Pennsylvania.

76. Jackson, "Virginia Maroons," 143–51; William Cooper Nell, *The Colored Patriots of the American Revolution* (Boston: Robert F. Walcutt), 227–29.

77. See Thomas Wentworth Higginson, *Travelers and Outlaws* (Boston, 1889).

78. Stowe wrote an introduction to Nell's work. Harriet Beecher Stowe to Richard Henry Dana, 6 March 1851, Dana Family Papers, Massachusetts Historical Society; Harriet Beecher Stowe, *A Key to Uncle Tom's Cabin* (Boston 1853), 154–55; Bearse, *Reminisces of Fugitive Slave Law Days,* 8.

79. Harriet Beecher Stowe, *Dred; A Tale of the Great Dismal Swamp* (Boston, 1855).

80. F. N. Boney et al., eds., *God Made Man, Man Made the Slave: The Autobiography of George Teamoh* (Macon, GA: Mercer University Press, 1992), 114.

81. *The First Annual Report of the New York Committee of Vigilance, for the Year 1837 Together with Facts Relative to Their Proceedings* (New York: Piercy and Reed, 1837), 12.

82. Aileen Kraditor, *Means and Ends in American Abolitionism: Garrison and His Critics on Strategy and Tactics, 1834–1840* (New York: Pantheon, 1989), 241.

83. Interestingly, these debates were most fierce within the Pennsylvania Female Antislavery Society. See "Minutes of the Philadelphia Female Antislavery Society," PAS Papers, Historical Society of Pennsylvania.

84. C. S. Brown, *Memoir of Abel Brown* (C. S. Brown, 1874), 173–74.

85. "Fugitive Slaves' Appeal!! To the Clergy of Massachusetts at the Meeting of Fugitive Slaves Held in Boston, 1850," Siebert Papers, Ohio Historical Society; *North Star*, 5 April 1850; *The Liberator*, 13 September 1850.

86. Pennsylvania Antislavery Society Records, vol. 1, 61, Historical Society of Pennsylvania; Foner, *Gateway to Freedom*, 82; *In Memoriam: Testimonials to the Life and Character of the Late Francis Jackson* (Boston: R. F. Wallcut, 1861); Lewis Tappan, *The Life of Arthur Tappan* (New York: Hurd and Houghton, 1870), 181–82; *Eighteenth Annual Report of the Massachusetts Antislavery Society* (Boston: Dow and Jackson, 1850), 47–49.

87. William Parker, "The Freedman's Story," in *Atlantic Monthly: A Magazine of Literature, Science, Art, and Politics* 17 (Boston: Ticknor and Fields, 1866), 160–61.

88. Still, *Underground Rail Road.*

89. Quoted in Carol M. Hunter, *To Set the Captives Free: Reverend Jermain Wesley Loguen and the Struggle for Freedom in Central New York, 1835–1872* (New York: Garland, 1993), 79.

90. Still, *Underground Rail Road*, 46, 143.

91. Vincent Y. Bowditch, *Life and Correspondence of Henry Ingersoll Bowditch* (Boston: Houghton and Mifflin, 1902), 207.

92. Parker, "Freedman's Story," 281–82; W. V. Hensel, *The Christiana Riot and the Treason Trials of 1851* (Lancaster, PA: New Era, 1911).

93. Loguen, *Rev. J. W. Loguen*, 399–424; Gary Collison, *Shadrach Minkins: From Fugitive Slave to Citizen* (Cambridge, MA: Harvard University Press, 1998).

94. Stevens, *Anthony Burns*; Albert J. von Frank, *The Trials of Anthony Burns: Freedom and Slavery in Emerson's Boston* (Cambridge, MA: Harvard University Press, 1998).

95. Thomas Wentworth Higginson to Lysander Spooner, 30 November 1858; see also Herbert Aptheker, "Militant Abolitionism," in *Herbert Aptheker on Race and Democracy: A Reader*, ed. Eric Foner and Manning Marable (Champaign: University of Illinois Press, 2006), 57–97.

96. Edmund Jackson, "Servile Insurrections" (Boston: National Antislavery Bazaar, 1851), 164.

97. Still, *Underground Railroad*, 143; Lorenz von Stein, *The History of the Social Movement in France, 1789–1850*, trans. Kaethe Mengelberg (Totawa, NJ: Bedminster Press, 1964).

98. Henry Bibb, *The Late Contemplated Insurrection in Charleston, S. C., with the Execution of Thirty-Six of the Patriots* (New York: 1850); William Wells Brown, *St. Domingo: Its Revolutions and Its Patriots* (Boston: Bela Marsh, 1855).

99. James McCune Smith, *A Lecture on the Haytien Revolution with a Sketch of the Character of Toussaint L'Ouverture* (New York: Daniel Fanshaw, 1841), 8.

100. Wendell Phillips, "Toussaint L'Ouverture," in *Speeches, Lectures, and Addresses: First Series* (Boston: Lothrop, Lee, and Shephard, 1891), 468–95; Joshua Coffin, *An Account of Some of the Principal Slave Insurrections, and Others, which Have Occurred or Been Attempted In the United States and Elsewhere, during the Last Two Centuries* (New York: American Antislavery Society, 1860); Higginson, *Travelers and Outlaws.*

101. Thomas Wentworth Higginson, *Letters and Journals of Thomas Wentworth Higginson* (Boston: Mary Thacher Higginson, 1921), 87.

102. Lysander Spooner, "To the Non-slaveholders of the South," draft manuscript, Antislavery Collection, Boston Public Library.

103. Quoted in Higginson, *Cheerful Yesterdays*, 218.

104. Frederick Douglass, *The Life and Times of Frederick Douglass* (New York: Dover, 2003), 225–31; Sarah H. Bradford, *Scenes in the Life of Harriet Tubman* (Auburn, NY: W. J. Moses, 1869), 81–82; Hunter, *Set the Captives Free*, 189.

105. Archibald Grimke, "Anti-Slavery Boston," in *New England Magazine* 3 (September 1890–February 1891): 458.

106. Jeffrey Rossbach, *Ambivalent Conspirators: John Brown, the Secret Six and a Theory of Slave Violence* (Philadelphia: University of Pennsylvania Press, 1982).

107. W. E. B. Dubois, *John Brown* (New York: International, 1962), 248; Richard T. Hinton, *John Brown and His Men: With Some Account of the Routes They Traveled to Reach Harper's Ferry* (New York: Funk and Wagnalls, 1894), 170.

108. William Henry Johnson, *Autobiography of William Henry Johnson* (Albany: Argus, 1900), 31.

109. Douglass, *Life and Times of Frederick Douglass*, 231; Franklin Benjamin Sanborn, *The Life of Henry David Thoreau* (Louisa Sanborn, 1917), 469.

110. William Henry Furness, *Put Up Thy Sword: A Discourse Delivered before Theodore Parker's Society, at the Music Hall, Boston, Sunday, March 11, 1860* (Boston: R. F. Walcutt, 1860); Theodore Parker, *John Brown's Expedition Reviewed* (Boston: Fraternity, 1860); Wendell Phillips, "The Burial of John Brown," in *Speeches, Lectures, and Addresses*, 289–94; Henry David Thoreau, "The Last Days of John Brown," in *Thoreau: Political Writings*, ed. Nancy L. Rosenblum (New York: Cambridge University Press, 1996), 163–70; H. H. Furness, "Retrospective of William Henry Furness," Furness Family Papers, 1765–1937, University of Pennsylvania Special Collections.

111. Elizur Wright, *The Lessons of St. Domingo: How To Make the War Short and the Peace Righteous* (Boston: Williams, 1861).

112. See W. E. B. Dubois, *Black Reconstruction in America, 1860–1880* (New York: Free Press, 1992).

113. Moncure Conway, *Testimonies Concerning Slavery* (London: Chapman and Hall, 1865), 103; Moncure Conway, *Autobiography, Memories, and Experiences* (Boston: Houghton Mifflin, 1904), 357–63.

114. Still, *Underground Rail Road*, 150–52, 187. For more on Galloway during Reconstruction, see David Cecelski, "A Radical and Jacobinical Spirit: Abraham Galloway and the Struggle for Freedom in the Maritime South," in *The Waterman's Song: Slavery and Freedom in Maritime North Carolina* (Chapel Hill: University of North Carolina Press, 2001), 179–203.

115. Higginson, *Army Life*, 248.

116. Dubois, *Black Reconstruction*, 81.

117. Dubois, *Black Reconstruction*, 48.

118. The most profound analysis of how the Underground Railroad spurred American literary and political creativity is still C. L. R. James, "American Intellectuals in the Nineteenth Century," in *American Civilization* (Cambridge, MA: Blackwell, 1993), 50–99.

119. In fact, black thinkers working in the abolitionist intellectual tradition saw the structural reasons for this quite early on. T. Thomas Fortune, *Black and White: Land, Labor, and Politics in the South* (New York: Fords, Howard, and Hulbert, 1880).

120. Wendell Phillips Garrison and Francis Jackson Garrison, *William Lloyd Garrison: The Story of His Life as Told by His Children*, vol. 2 (Boston: Houghton Mifflin, 1889), 408.

SELECTED REFERENCES

Adderley, Rosanne. *"New Negroes from Africa": Slave Trade Abolition and Free African Settlement in the Nineteenth-Century Caribbean.* Indianapolis: Indiana University Press, 2006.

Ágoston, Gábor. *Guns for the Sultan: Military Power and the Weapons Industry in the Ottoman Empire.* Cambridge: Cambridge University Press, 2005.

Akenson, Donald. *If the Irish Ran the World: Montserrat, 1630–1730.* Montreal: McGill-Queen's University Press, 1997.

Allen, Theodore. *The Invention of the White Race.* New York: Verso, 1993.

Anderson, Clare, ed. *A Global History of Convicts and Penal Colonies.* London: Bloomsbury, 2018.

———, Niklas Frykman, Lex Heerma van Voss, and Marcus Rediker, eds. *Mutiny and Maritime Radicalism during the Age of Revolution: A Global Survey.* Cambridge: Cambridge University Press, 2013.

Aptheker, Herbert. *Abolitionism: A Revolutionary Movement.* Boston: Twayne, 1979.

Asiegbu, Johnson U. J. *Slavery and the Politics of Liberation, 1787–1861: A Study of Liberated African Emigration and British Anti-Slavery Policy.* London: Longmans, 1969.

Auvray, Michel. *Objecteurs, Insoumis, Déserteurs: Histoire des Réfractaires en France.* Paris: Éditions Stock, 1983.

Baay, Reggie. *Daar werd iets gruwelijks verricht: Slavernij in Nederlands-Indië.* Amsterdam: Athenaeum, 2015.

Balvay, Arnaud. *L'épée et la plume: Amérindiens et soldats des troupes de la marine en Louisiane et au Pays d'en haut (1683–1763).* Québec: Presses de l'Université Laval, 2006.

Banaji, Jairus. *Theory as History: Essays on Modes of Production and Exploitation.* Chicago: Haymarket Books, 2011.

Banks, James A., and Cheryl A. Banks. *March toward Freedom: A History of Black Americans.* New York: Fearon, 1970.

Baptist, Edward E. *The Half Has Never Been Told: Slavery and the Making of American Capitalism.* New York: Basic Books, 2014.

Baseler, Marilyn C. *"Asylum for Mankind": America, 1607–1800.* Ithaca, NY: Cornell University Press, 1998.

Beckles, Hilary McD. *The First Black Slave Society: Britain's "Barbarity Time" in Barbados, 1636–1876.* Mona: University of West Indies Press, 2016.

Berlin, Ira, and Philip D. Morgan, eds. *The Slaves' Economy: Independent Production by Slaves in the Americas.* London: Frank Cass, 1991.

Bernier, François. *Travels in the Mogul Empire AD 1656–1668,* 2nd ed. Reprinted by Delhi: Low Price, 1989. First published 1934.

Blackett, Richard J. M. *Building an Antislavery Wall: Black Americans in the Atlantic Abolitionist Movement, 1830–1860.* Baton Rouge: Louisiana State University Press, 1983.

———. *The Captive's Quest for Freedom: Fugitive Slaves, the 1850 Fugitive Slave Law, and the Politics of Slavery.* Cambridge: Cambridge University Press, 2018.

Blake, John W. *West Africa: Quest for God and Gold 1454–1578.* London: Curzon Press, 1977.

Blight, David, ed. *Passages to Freedom: The Underground Railroad in History and Memory.* New York: HarperCollins, 2004.

Bohstedt, John. *The Politics of Provisions: Food Riots, Moral Economy, and Market Transition in England c. 1550–1850.* Burlington, VT: Ashgate, 2010.

Boney, F. N., Richard L. Hume, and Rafia Zafar, eds. *God Made Man, Man Made the Slave: The Autobiography of George Teamoh.* Macon, GA: Mercer University Press, 1992.

Bordewich, Fergus M. *Bound for Canaan: The Epic Story of the Underground Railroad.* New York: HarperCollins, 2005.

Bosma, Ulbe, Elise van Nederveen Meerkerk, et al., eds. *Mediating Labour: Worldwide Labour Intermediation in the Nineteenth and Twentieth Centuries.* Special issue of the *International Review of Social History.* Cambridge: Cambridge University Press, 2012.

Boucher, Philip. *France and the American Tropics to 1700.* Baltimore: Johns Hopkins University Press, 2008.

Boxer, Charles R. *The Dutch Seaborne Empire.* London: Hutchinson, 1965.

———. *Jan Compagnie in War and Peace, 1602–1799.* Hong Kong: Heinemann Asia, 1979.

Brand, Ian, Charles Joseph La Trobe, Michael N. Sprod, and James Boyd. *The Convict Probation System, Van Diemen's Land, 1839–1854.* Hobart, Tasmania: Blubber Head Press, 1990.

Brandon, Pepijn. *War, Capital, and the Dutch State (1588–1795).* Leiden: Brill, 2015.

Brasseaux, Carl A. *France's Forgotten Legion Service: Records of French Military and Administrative Personnel Stationed in the Mississippi Valley and Gulf Coast Region, 1699–1769.* Baton Rouge: Louisiana State University Press, 2000.

Bridenbaugh, Carl, and Roberta Bridenbaugh. *No Peace beyond the Line.* New York: Oxford University Press, 1972.

Bruijn, J. R., and E. S. Eyck van Heslinga. *Muiterij: Oproer en berechting op schepen van de VOC.* Haarlem: De Boer Maritiem 1980.

Buchanan, Thomas C. *Black Life on the Mississippi: Slaves, Free Blacks and the Western Steamboat World.* Chapel Hill: University of North Carolina Press, 2004.

Burbank, Jane, and Frederic Cooper. *Empires in World History: Power and the Politics of Difference.* Princeton, NJ: Princeton University Press, 2010.

Burds, Jeffrey. *Peasant Dreams and Market Politics: Labor Migration and the Russian Village, 1861–1905*. Pittsburgh: University of Pittsburgh Press, 1998.

Camp, Stephanie. *Closer to Freedom: Enslaved Women and Everyday Resistance in the Plantation South*. Chapel Hill: University of North Carolina Press, 2004.

Campanella, Richard. *Bienville's Dilemma: A Historical Geography of New Orleans*. Lafayette: Center for Louisiana Studies, 2008.

Campos, Joaquim Joseph A. *History of the Portuguese in Bengal*. Delhi: Facsimile, 2018. First published 1919 by Butterworth & Co.

Castro Henriques, Isabel. *São Tomé e Príncipe: A Invenção de Uma Sociedade*. Lisboa: Vega, 2000.

———. *Os Pilares da Diferença, Relações Portugal-África, Séculos XV–XX*. Lisboa: Centro de História, 2004.

Cecelski, David. *Waterman's Song: Slavery and Freedom in Maritime North Carolina*. Chapel Hill: University of North Carolina Press, 2001.

Christopher, Emma. *Slave Ship Sailors and Their Captive Cargoes, 1720–1807*. Cambridge: Cambridge University Press, 2006.

Coates, Timothy J. *Convicts and Orphan: Forced and State-Sponsored Colonization in the Portuguese Empire, 1550–1755*. Stanford, CA: Stanford University Press, 2001.

———. *Convict Labor in the Portuguese Empire, 1740–1932: Redefining the Empire with Forced Labor and New Imperialism*. Leiden: Brill, 2014.

Collis, Maurice. *The Land of the Great Image: Being Experiences of Friar Manrique in Arakan*. New York: New Directions, 1985. First published 1943 by Alfred A. Knopf.

Collison, Gary. *Shadrach Minkins: From Fugitive Slave to Citizen*. Cambridge, MA: Harvard University Press, 1998.

Connell, Robert W., and Terence H. Irving. *Class Structure in Australian History, Documents, Narrative and Argument*. Melbourne: Melbourne University Press, 1984.

Corvisier, André. *L'armée française de la fin du XVIIIe siècle au ministère de Choiseul: Le soldat*. Paris: Presses universitaires de France, 1964.

Crouse, Nellis. *French Pioneers in the West Indies*. New York: Columbia University Press, 1940.

Curtin, Philip. *The Atlantic Slave Trade: A Census*. Madison: University of Wisconsin Press, 1969.

———. *The Rise and Fall of the Plantation Complex*. Cambridge: Cambridge University Press, 1990.

Dalgas, Ingeborg. *De Bremerholmske Jernfanger og Fangevogtere på Fæstningen Christiansø 1725–1735*. Aarhus, 2014.

Daniels, Kay. *Convict Women*. Sydney: Allen and Unwin, 1998.

Davis, Robert C. *Christian Slaves, Muslim Masters: White Slavery in the Mediterranean, the Barbary Coast, and Italy, 1500–1800*. New York: Palgrave Macmillan, 2003.

Dawdy, Shannon Lee. *Building the Devil's Empire: French Colonial New Orleans*. Chicago: University of Chicago Press, 2008.

de Vauban, Sébastien Le Prestre, and Michèle Virol. *Les oisivetés de monsieur de Vauban, ou ramas de plusieurs mémoires de sa façon sur différents sujets*. Ceyzérieu, France: Editions Champ Vallon, 2007.

De Vito, Christian G., and Alex Lichtenstein, eds. *Global Convict Labour*. Leiden: Brill, 2015.

de Zwart, Pim. *Globalization and the Colonial Origins of the Great Divergence: Intercontinental Trade and Living Standards in the Dutch East India Company's Commercial Empire, c. 1600–1800*. Leiden: Brill, 2016.

Diouf, Sylviane. *Slavery's Exiles: The Story of the American Maroons*. New York: NYU Press, 2014.

Disney, Anthony R. *Twilight of the Pepper Empire: Portuguese Trade in Southwest India in the Early Seventeenth Century*. Cambridge, MA: Harvard University Press, 1978.

do Couto, Diogo. *Dialog of a Veteran Soldier, Discussing the Frauds and Realities of Portuguese India*. Translated and edited by Timothy Coates. Dartmouth, MA: Tagus Press, 2016.

Dookhan, Isaac. *A History of the British Virgin Islands, 1672–1970*. Essex: Caribbean University Press, 1975.

Du Bois, W. E. B. *Black Reconstruction*. New York: Harcourt, Brace, 1935.

———. *John Brown*. New York: International, 1962.

Dunn, Richard. *Sugar and Slaves*. New York: Norton, 1972.

Dunning, Tom P., and Hamish Maxwell-Stewart. "Mutiny at Deloraine: Ganging and Convict Resistance in 1840s Van Diemen's Land." *Labour History*, no. 82 (2002): 35–47.

Eltis, David. *The Rise of African Slavery in the Americas*. Cambridge: Cambridge University Press, 2000.

Fett, Sharla M. *Recaptured Africans: Surviving Slave Ships, Detention and Dislocation in the Final Years of the Slave Trade*. Chapel Hill: University of North Carolina Press, 2017.

Feys, Torsten. *The Battle for the Migrants: The Introduction of Steamshipping on the North Atlantic and Its Impact on the European Exodus*. St. John's, Newfoundland: International Maritime Economic History Association, 2013.

Fick, Carolyn. *The Making of Haiti: The San Domingue Revolution from Below*. Knoxville: University of Tennessee Press, 1990.

Fields, Barbara. *Slavery and Freedom on the Middle Ground: Maryland during the Nineteenth Century*. New Haven, CT: Yale University Press, 1985.

Foner, Eric. *Gateway to Freedom: The Hidden History of the Underground Railroad*. New York: W. W. Norton, 2015.

Forrest, Alan. *Conscripts and Deserters: The Army and French Society during the Revolution and Empire*. New York and Oxford: Oxford University Press, 1989.

Franklin, John Hope, and Loren Schweninger. *Runaway Slaves: Rebels on the Plantation*. New York: Oxford, 1999.

Frost, Lucy. *Abandoned Women: Scottish Convicts Exiled beyond the Seas*. Sydney: Allen and Unwin, 2012.

Frykman, Niklas, Lex Heerma van Voss, and Marcus Rediker, eds. *Mutiny and Maritime Radicalism in the Age of Revolution: A Global Survey*. Cambridge: Cambridge University Press, 2014.

Fyfe, Christopher. *A History of Sierra Leone*. New York: Oxford University Press, 1962.

Gaastra, F. S. *De Geschiedenis van de VOC*. Zutphen: Walburg Pers, 1991.

Gabaccia, Donna R., and Dirk Hoerder, eds. *Connecting Seas and Connected Ocean Rims: Indian, Atlantic and Pacific Oceans and China Seas Migrations from the 1830s to the 1930s*. Leiden and Boston: Brill, 2011.

Gad, Finn. *Grønlands Historie II: 1700–1782*. Copenhagen: Nyt Nordisk Forlag, 1969.

Garfield, Robert. *A History of São Tomé Island.* San Francisco: Mellen Research University Press, 1992.

Garraway, Doris. *The Libertine Colony: Creolization in the Early French Caribbean.* Durham, NC: Duke University Press, 2005.

Gaspar, David Barry. *Bondmen and Rebels: A Study of Master-Slave Relations in Antigua.* Durham, NC: Duke University Press, 1993.

Godinho, Manuel. *Intrepid Itinerant: Manuel Godinho and His Journey from India to Portugal, 1663.* Oxford: Bombay, 1990.

Guy, Richard J. *First Spaces of Colonialism: The Architecture of Dutch East India Company Ships.* PhD diss., Cornell University, 2012.

Steven Hahn. *The Political Worlds of Slavery and Freedom.* Cambridge, MA: Harvard University Press, 2009.

Hall, Catherine, Nicholas Draper, and Keith McClelland, eds. *Emancipation and the Remaking of the British Imperial World.* Manchester: Manchester University Press, 2014.

Hall, Neville A. T. *Slave Society in the Danish West Indies: St. Thomas, St. John and St. Croix.* Mona, Cave Hill, and St. Augustine: University of the West Indies Press, 1992.

Hall, N. A. T. "Maritime Maroons: Grand Marronage from the Danish West Indies." In *Origins of the Black Atlantic,* edited by L. Dubois and J. S. Scott, 47–68. New York and London: Routledge.

Hanna, Mark. *Pirates Nests and the Rise of the English Empire, 1570–1740.* Chapel Hill: University of North Carolina Press, 2017.

Harlow, Vincent, ed. *Colonising Expeditions to the West Indies and Guiana.* London: Hakluyt Society, 1925.

Harper, Frances Ellen Watkins. *A Brighter Coming Day: A Frances Ellen Watkins Harper Reader.* New York: Feminist Press, 1990.

Harrold, Stanley. *Subversives: Antislavery Community in Washington, D. C., 1828–1865.* Baton Rouge: Louisiana State University Press, 2003.

Hay, Douglas, and Paul Craven, eds. *Masters, Servants, and Magistrates in Britain and the Empire, 1562–1955.* Chapel Hill: University of North Carolina Press, 2005.

Heese, H. F. *Reg en Onreg: Kaapse Regspraak in die Agtiende Eeu.* C-Reeks: Narvorsingspublikasies, No. 6. Bellville: Insituut vir Histories Narvorsing, Universiteit van Wes-Kaapland, 1994.

Heinsen, Johan. "Dissonance in the Danish Atlantic." *Atlantic Studies* 13, no. 2 (2016): 187–205.

———. *Det første fængsel.* Aarhus: Aarhus University Press, 2018.

———. *Mutiny in the Danish Atlantic World: Convicts, Sailors and a Dissonant Empire.* London: Bloomsbury, 2017.

Held, David, Anthony G. McGrew, David Goldblatt, and Jonathan Perration. *Global Transformations: Politics, Economics and Culture.* Cambridge: Polity Press, 1999.

Higham, C. S. S. *The Development of the Leeward Islands under the Restoration.* Cambridge: Cambridge University Press, 1921.

Hirschman, Albert O. *Exit, Voice, and Loyalty: Responses to Decline in Firms, Organizations, and States.* Cambridge, MA: Harvard University Press, 1970.

Hochstadt, Steve. *Mobility and Modernity: Migration in Germany, 1820–1989.* Ann Arbor: University of Michigan Press, 1999.

Hodges, Graham Russel, ed. *The Black Loyalist Directory: African Americans in Exile after the American Revolution*. New York: Garland, 1996.

———. *David Ruggles: A Radical Black Abolitionist and the Underground Railroad in New York City*. Chapel Hill: University of North Carolina Press, 2010.

Hoerder, Dirk. *Cultures in Contact: World Migrations in the Second Millennium*. Durham, NC: Duke University Press, 2002.

Hofmeester, Karin, and Pim de Zwart, eds. *Colonialism, Institutional Change and Shifts in Global Labour Relations*. Amsterdam: Amsterdam University Press, 2018.

Hughes, Robert. *The Fatal Shore: The Epic of Australia's Founding*. London: Vintage, 1988.

Hulme, Peter, and Neil Whitehead, eds. *Wild Majesty: Encounters with Caribs from Columbus to the Present Day*. Oxford: Oxford University Press, 1992.

Hunter, Carol M. *To Set the Captives Free: Reverend Jermain Wesley Loguen and the Struggle for Freedom in Central New York, 1835–1872*. New York: Garland, 1993.

Ingersoll, Thomas N. *Mammon and Manon in Early New Orleans: The First Slave Society in the Deep South, 1718–1819*. Knoxville: University of Tennessee Press, 1999.

Jaffer, Aaron. *Lascars and Indian Ocean Seafaring, 1780–1860: Shipboard Life, Unrest and Mutiny*. Rochester: Boydell Press, 2015.

James, C. L. R. *The Black Jacobins*. New York: Vintage, 1989.

Johnson, Rashawna. *Slavery's Metropolis: Unfree Labor in New Orleans during the Age of Revolutions*. New York: Cambridge University Press, 2016.

Johnson, Walter. *River of Dark Dreams: Slavery and Empire in the Cotton Kingdom*. Cambridge, MA: Harvard University Press, 2013.

———. *Soul by Soul: Life Inside the Antebellum Slave Market*. Cambridge, MA: Harvard University Press, 1998.

Kale, Madhavi. *Fragments of Empire: Capital, Slavery and Indian Indentured Labour in the British Caribbean*. Philadelphia: University of Pennsylvania Press, 2010.

Kaye, Anthony. *Joining Places: Slave Neighborhoods in the Old South*. Chapel Hill: University of North Carolina Press, 2009.

Kealy, George S. *Toronto Workers Respond to Industrial Capitalism, 1867–1892*. Toronto: University of Toronto Press, 1980.

Keeling, Drew. *The Business of Transatlantic Migration between Europe and the USA, 1900–1914*. Zürich: Chronos, 2012.

Ketting, Herman. *Leven, werk en rebellie aan boord van Oost-Indiëvaarders (1595–1650)*. Amsterdam: Aksant, 2002.

Klein, Herbert S. *The Atlantic Slave Trade*. Cambridge: Cambridge University Press, 1999.

Knaap, G. J. *Kruidnagelen en Christenen: De Verenigde Oost-Indische Compagnie en de bevolking van Ambon 1656–1696*. Dordrecht: Foris, 1987.

Kolchin, Peter. *American Slavery, 1619–1877*. New York: Hill and Wang, 1993.

———. *Unfree Labor: American Slavery and Russian Serfdom*. Cambridge, MA: Harvard University Press, 1987.

Kolsky, Elizabeth. *Colonial Justice in British India*. New Delhi: Cambridge University Press, 2010.

Komlos, John. *Nutrition and Economic Development in the Eighteenth-Century Habsburg Monarchy*. Princeton, NJ: Princeton University Press, 1989.

Kraditor, Aileen. *Means and Ends in American Abolitionism: Garrison and His Critics on Strategy and Tactics, 1834–1840*. New York: Pantheon, 1989.

Krogh, Tyge. *Oplysningstiden og det Magiske*. Copenhagen: Samleren 2000.

Kusch, Frank. *Draft Dodgers in Canada from the Vietnam War*. Westport, CT: Praeger, 2001.

La Rosa Corzo, Gabino. *Runaway Slave Settlements in Cuba: Resistance and Repression*. Translated by Mary Todd. Chapel Hill: University of North Carolina Press, 1988.

LeBaron, Genevieve. *The Global Business of Forced Labour: Report of Findings*. Sheffield: SPERI, 2018.

Lequin, Frank. "Het Personeel van de Verenigde Oost-Indische Compagne in de Achttiende Eeuw, Meer in Het Bijzonder in de Vestiging Bengalen, Deel I." PhD diss., Leiden University, 1982.

Linebaugh, Peter. *The London Hanged: Crime and Civil Society in the Eighteenth Century*. 2nd ed. London: Verso, 2003.

—— and Marcus Rediker. *The Many-Headed Hydra: Sailors, Slaves, Commoners, and the Hidden History of the Revolutionary Atlantic*. New York: Verso, 2000.

Lucassen, Jan. *Migrant Labour in Europe: The Drift to the North Sea*. London: Croom Helm, 1987.

——. "Outlines of a History of Labour." Research paper. Amsterdam: International Institute of Social History, 2013.

——, ed. *Global Labour History: A State of the Art*. Bern: Peter Lang, 2006.

Lucassen, Jan, and Leo Lucassen, eds. *Migration, Migration History, History: Old Paradigms and New Perspectives*. Bern: Peter Lang, 1997.

Lucassen, Jan, and Leo Lucassen. *The Mobility Transition in Europe Revisited, 1500–1900: Sources and Methods*. Amsterdam: International Institute of Social History, IISH Research Papers, 2010.

Lucassen, Jan, and Leo Lucassen, eds. *Globalising Migration History: The Eurasian Experience (16th–21st Centuries*. Leiden: Brill, 2014.

Lucassen, Jan, Leo Lucassen, and Patrick Manning, eds. *Migration History in World History: Multidisciplinary Approaches*. Leiden: Brill, 2010.

Lucassen, Leo. *Zigeuner: Die Geschichte eines Polizeilichen Ordnungsbegriffes in Deutschland 1700–1945*. Köln: Böhlau, 1996.

Lynn, John A. *Giant of the Grand Siècle: The French Army, 1610–1715*. Cambridge: Cambridge University Press, 2006.

Macpherson, C. B. *The Political Theory of Possessive Individualism*. Oxford: Oxford University Press, 1962.

Manning, Patrick. *Migration in World History*. 2nd ed. New York: Routledge, 2013.

Manuel Caldeira, Arlindo. *Mulheres, Sexualidade e Casamento em São Tomé e Príncipe (séculos XV–XVIII)*. Lisboa: Cosmos, 1999.

Marley, David. *Wars of the Americas*. Santa Barbara, CA: ABC-CLIO, 1998.

Martin, Jonathan. *Divided Mastery: Slave Hiring in the American South*. Cambridge, MA: Harvard University Press, 2004.

Maxwell-Stewart, Hamish. *Closing Hell's Gates*. Sidney: Allen and Unwin, 2008.

——. "Convict Labour Extraction and Transportation from Britain and Ireland, 1615–1870." In *Global Convict Labour*, edited by Christian G. De Vito and Alex Lichtenstein, 168–96. Leiden: Brill, 2015.

———. "'Like Poor Galley Slaves': Slavery and Convict Transportation." In *Legacies of Slavery: Comparative Perspectives,* edited by Marie Suzette Fernandes Dias, 56–57. Newcastle: Cambridge Scholars, 2007.

———. "The Rise and Fall of Penal Transportation." In *Oxford Handbook of the History of Crime and Criminal Justice,* edited by Anya Johansen, 635–54. Oxford: Oxford University Press.

———. "'This is the bird that never flew': William Stewart, Major Donald MacLeod and the Launceston Advertiser." *Journal of Australian Colonial History* 2, no. 1 (2000): 1–28.

Maxwell-Stewart, Hamish, and J. Bradley. "'Behold the Man': Power, Observation and the Tattooed Convict." *Australian Studies* 12, no. 1 (1997): 72–75.

Miller, Joseph. *Way of Death.* Madison: University of Wisconsin Press, 1988.

Mims, Stewart. *Colbert's West India Policy.* New Haven, CT: Yale University Press, 1912.

Mitchell, Laura. *Belongings: Property, Family, and Identity in Colonial South Africa.* New York: Columbia University Press, 2009.

Mitchell, Mary Niall. "The Real Ida May: A Fugitive Tale in the Archives." *Massachusetts Historical Review* 15 (Fall 2013): 54–88.

Moch, Leslie Page. *Paths to the City: Regional Migration in Nineteenth-Century France.* Beverly Hills: Sage, 1983.

———. *Moving Europeans: Migration in Western Europe since 1650.* Bloomington: Indiana University Press, 2003.

Moreland, W. H. *Relations of Golconda in the Early Seventeenth Century.* London: Hakluyt Society, 1931.

Münkler, Herbert. *Imperien: Die Logik der Weltherrschaft vom Alten Rom bis zu den Vereinigten Staaten.* Berlin: Rowohlt, 2005.

Newitt, Malyn. *A History of Portuguese Overseas Expansion, 1400–1668.* London: Routledge, 2005.

Neuman, Gad, ed. *Out of the House of Bondage: Runaways, Resistance and Marronage in Africa and the New World.* New York: Routledge, 2016.

Niemeijer, H. E. *Batavia: Een koloniale samenleving in de 17de eeuw.* Amsterdam: Uitgeverij Balans, 2005.

Noiriel, Gérard. *La Tyrannie du National: Le Droit d'Asile en Europe (1793–1993).* Paris: Calmann-Lévy, 1991.

Northrup, David. *Indentured Labour in the Age of Imperialism, 1834–1922.* Cambridge: Cambridge University Press, 1995.

Pargas, Damian A. *Slavery and Forced Migration in the Antebellum South.* Cambridge: Cambridge University Press, 2014.

Parmentier, Jan. *"De Holle Compagnie": Smokkel en Legale Handel onder Zuidnederlandse Vlag in Bengalen, ca. 1720–1744.* Hilversum: Verloren, 1992.

Pérez-Mallaína, Pablo E. *Spain's Men of the Sea: Daily Life on the Indies Fleets in the Sixteenth Century.* Baltimore: Johns Hopkins University Press, 1998.

Pesantubbee, Michelene E. *Choctaw Women in a Chaotic World: The Clash of Cultures in the Colonial Southeast.* Albuquerque: University of New Mexico Press, 2005.

Pestana, Carla. *The English Atlantic in an Age of Revolution.* Cambridge, MA: Harvard University Press, 2004.

Phillips, Christopher. *Freedom's Port: The African American Community of Baltimore*. Chicago: University of Chicago Press, 1997.

Pieroni, Geraldo, and Timothy Coates. *Castro Marim: Da Vila do Couto à Vila do Sal*. Lisboa: Sa da Costa, 2002.

Pike, Ruth. *Penal Servitude in Early Modern Spain*. Madison: University of Wisconsin Press, 1983.

Pomeranz, Kenneth. *The Great Divergence: China, Europe, and the Making of the Modern World Economy*. Princeton, NJ: Princeton University Press, 2000.

Price, Richard. *Maroon Societies: Rebel Slave Communities in the Americas*. New York: Alfred A. Knopf, 2013.

Pritchard, James S. *In Search of Empire: The French in the Americas, 1670–1730*. New York: Cambridge University Press, 2004.

Quinlan, Michael. *The Origins of Worker Mobilisation in Australia 1788–1850*. New York: Routledge, 2018.

Raven-Hart, Rowland. *Cape Good Hope / 1652–1702 / The First 50 Years of Dutch Colonisation as Seen by Callers*. Cape Town: A. A. Balkema, 1971.

Ray, Aniruddha. *Adventurers, Landowners and Rebels, c. 1575–c. 1715*. New Delhi: Munshiram Manoharlal, 1998.

Rediker, Marcus. *Between the Devil and the Deep Blue Sea: Merchant Seamen, Pirates and the Anglo-American Maritime World, 1700–1750*. Cambridge: Cambridge University Press, 1989.

———. *Outlaws of the Atlantic: Sailors, Pirates and Motley Crews in the Age of Sail*. Boston: Beacon Press, 2014.

Reid, Kirsty. *Gender, Crime and Empire: Convicts, Settlers and the State in Early Colonial Australia*. Manchester: Manchester University Press, 2007.

Richards, John F. *The Mughal Empire: The New Cambridge History of India, Vol. 1.5*. New Delhi: Cambridge University Press, 1993.

Robert, Joseph Clarke. *The Tobacco Kingdom: Plantation, Market, and Factory in Virginia and North Carolina*. Gloucester, MA: Peter Smith, 1965.

Rockman, Seth. *Scraping By: Wage Labor, Slavery, and Survival in Early Baltimore*. Baltimore: Johns Hopkins University Press, 2009.

Rodrigues Silveira, Francisco. *Memórias de um Soldado da índia*. Edited by A. de S. S. Costa Lobo. Lisbon: Imprensa Nacional, 1987. First published 1877.

Ross, Robert. *Cape of Torments: Slavery and Resistance in South Africa*. London: Routledge and Kegan Paul, 1983.

Rossbach, Jeffrey. *Ambivalent Conspirators: John Brown, the Secret Six and a Theory of Slave Violence*. Philadelphia: University of Pennsylvania Press, 1982.

Rothman, Joshua. *Flush Times and Fever Dreams: A Story of Capitalism and Slavery in the Age of Jackson*. Athens: University of Georgia Press, 2012.

Rowland, Dunbar, A. G. Sanders, and Patricia Galloway, eds. *Mississippi Provincial Archives: French Dominion*. Baton Rouge: Louisiana State University Press, 1984.

Rupprecht, Anita. "'All We Have Done, We Have Done for Freedom': The *Creole* Slave-Ship Revolt (1841) and the Revolutionary Atlantic." *International Review of Social History* 58 (2013): 253–77.

———. "From Slavery to Indenture: Scripts for Slavery's Endings." In *Emancipation and the Remaking of the British Imperial World,* edited by Catherine Hall, Nicholas Draper, and Keith McClellan. Manchester: Manchester University Press, 2014.

———. " 'When he gets among his Countrymen, they tell him that he is free': Slave Trade Abolition, Indentured Africans and a Royal Commission." *Slavery and Abolition* 33, no. 3 (September 2012): 418–56.

Rusche, Georg, and Otto Kirchheimer. *Punishment and Social Structure.* Reprinted by New York: Russell and Russell, 1968. First published 1939.

Saggs, H. W. F. Saggs. *Babylonians.* Berkeley: University of California Press, 2000.

Sandmo, Erling. *Voldssamfunnets Undergang: Om Disciplineringen av Norge på 1600-tallet.* Oslo: Universitetsforlaget, 2002.

Schafer, Judith. *Becoming Free, Remaining Free: Manumission and Enslavement in New Orleans, 1846–1862.* Baton Rouge: Louisiana State University Press, 2003.

———. *Slavery, the Civil Law, and the Supreme Court of Louisiana.* Baton Rouge: Louisiana State University Press, 1997.

Schnittman, Suzanne Gehring. "Slavery in Virginia's Urban Tobacco Industry, 1840–1860." PhD diss., University of Rochester, 1986.

Schwartz, Stuart, ed. *Tropical Babylons: Sugar and the Making of the Atlantic World, 1450–1680.* Chapel Hill: University of North Carolina Press, 2004.

Scott, Julius. *Common Wind: Afro-American Organization in the Revolution against Slavery.* New York: Verso, 2018.

Scott, James C. *The Art of Not Being Governed: An Anarchist History of Upland Southeast Asia.* New Haven: Yale University Press, 2009.

———. *Domination and the Arts of Resistance: Hidden Transcripts.* New Haven, CT: Yale University Press, 1990.

———. *The Moral Economy of the Peasant: Rebellion and Subsistence in South East Asia.* New Haven, CT: Yale University Press, 1976.

———. *Seeing Like a State.* New Haven, CT: Yale University Press, 1998.

———. *Weapons of the Weak: Everyday Forms of Peasant Resistance.* New Haven, CT: Yale University Press, 1985.

Scully, Pamela. *Liberating the Family? Gender and British Slave Emancipation in the Rural Western Cape, South Africa, 1823–1853.* Cape Town: David Philip, 1997.

Seuanes Serafim, Cristina Maria. *As Ilhas de São Tomé no Século XVII.* Lisboa: Universidade Nova de Lisboa, 2000.

Shaw, Jenny. *Everyday Life in the Early English Caribbean.* Athens: University of Georgia Press, 2013.

Shell, Robert. *Children of Bondage: A Social History of the Slave Society at the Cape of Good Hope, 1652–1838.* Johannesburg: University of the Witwatersrand Press, 2001.

Sinha, Manisha. *The Slave's Cause: A History of Abolition.* New Haven, CT: Yale University Press, 2016.

Sleigh, Dan, and Piet Westra. *De Opstand op het Slavenschip Meermin.* Amsterdam: Cossee, 2012.

Smith, Abbot Emerson. *Colonists in Bondage: White Servitude and Convict Labor in America, 1607–1776.* Chapel Hill: University of North Carolina Press, 1947.

Smith, Carole A. *Guatemalan Indians and the State: 1540 to 1988*. Austin: University of Texas Press, 1990.

Stanziani, Alessandro. *Bondage: Labor and Rights in Eurasia from the Sixteenth to the Early Twentieth Centuries*. New York: Berghahn Books, 2014.

———. *Sailors, Slaves, and Immigrants: Bondage in the Indian Ocean World, 1750–1914*. New York: Palgrave, 2014.

Stein, Burton. *The New Cambridge History of India*, Vol. 1:2, *Vijayanagara*. Cambridge: Cambridge University Press, 1992.

Steinfeld, Robert J. *The Invention of Free Labor: The Employment Relation in English and American Law and Culture, 1350–1870*. Chapel Hill: University of North Carolina Press, 1991.

Stern, Philip J. *The Company-State: Corporate Sovereignty and the Early Modern Foundations of the British Empire in India*. Oxford: Oxford University Press, 2011.

Subramanyam, Sanjay. *Improvising Empire: Portuguese Trade and Settlement in the Bay of Bengal 1500–1700*. Delhi: Oxford, 1990.

———. *The Portuguese Empire in Asia 1500–1700*. New York: Longman, 1993.

Svalesen, Leif. *The Slave Ship Fredensborg*. Bloomington: Indiana University Press, 2000.

Sweet, James H. *Domingos Álvares, African Healing, and the Intellectual History of the Atlantic World*. Chapel Hill: University of North Carolina Press, 2011.

Tadman, Michael. *Speculators and Slaves: Masters, Traders, and Slaves in the Old South*. Madison: University of Wisconsin Press, 1989.

Taylor, Alan. *American Colonies*. New York: Viking, 2001.

Thompson, Alvin O. *Profitable Servants: Crown Slaves in Berbice, Guyana 1803–1831*. Barbados: University of the West Indies Press, 2002.

Toth, Stephen A. *Beyond Papillon: The French Overseas Penal Colonies, 1854–1952*. Lincoln: University of Nebraska Press, 2006.

Trenschel, Kate. *Under the Influence: Working-Class Drinking, Temperance, and Cultural Revolution in Russia, 1895–1932*. Pittsburgh: University of Pittsburgh Press, 2006.

Ulrich, Nicole. "Abolition from Below: The 1808 Revolt in the Cape Colony." In *Humanitarian Intervention" and Changing Labour Relations: Long-term Consequences of the British Act on the Abolition of the Slave Trade, 1807*, edited by Marcel van der Linden, 193–222. Leiden: Brill, 2011.

———. "Between Reform and Revolution: The Cape's Popular Classes Under British Rule During the Age of Revolution, c. 1803- 1814." In *Facing Empire*, edited by Kate Fullagar and Michael McDonnel, 163–91. Baltimore: John Hopkins University Press, 2018.

———. "Cape of Storms: Rethinking Popular Protest in Eighteenth Century South Africa." *New Contree* no. 73 (2015): 16–39.

———. "Dr. Anders Sparrman: Travelling with the Labouring Poor in the Late Eighteenth-Century Cape." *South African Historical Journal* 61, no. 4 (2009): 731–49.

———. "From Servants to British Subjects: Citizenship, Khoesan Labour, and the Making of the Modern Colonial State, 1652–1815." In *Citizenship, Belonging, and Political Community in Africa: Dialogue between Past and Present*, edited by Emma Hunter, 43–73. Athens: Ohio University Press, 2016.

————. "Popular-Community in Eighteenth-Century Southern Africa: Family, Fellowship, Alternative Networks, and Mutual Aid at the Cape of Good Hope, 1652–1795." *Journal of Southern African Studies* 40, no. 6 (2015): 1139–57.

Usner, Daniel H. *Indians, Settlers and Slaves in a Frontier Exchange Economy: The Lower Mississippi Valley before 1783.* Chapel Hill: University of North Carolina Press, 1992.

Van der Linden, Marcel. *Workers of the World: Essays toward a Global Labor History.* Leiden: Brill, 2008.

Van Rossum, Matthias. *Kleurrijke tragiek: De geschiedenis van slavernij in Azië onder de VOC.* Hilversum: Verloren, 2015.

————. *Werkers van de Wereld: Globalisering, Arbeid en Interculturele Ontmoetingen Tussen Aziatische en Europese Zeelieden in dienst van de VOC, 1600–1800.* Hilversum: Verloren, 2014.

———— and Jeannette Kamp, eds. *Desertion in the Early Modern World.* London: Bloomsbury, 2016.

Vanvugt, Ewald. *Nieuw Zwartboek van Nederland Overzee.* Amsterdam: Aspekt, 2011.

von Frank, Albert J. *The Trials of Anthony Burns: Freedom and Slavery in Emerson's Boston.* Cambridge, MA: Harvard University Press, 1998.

von Stein, Lorenz. *The History of the Social Movement in France, 1789–1850.* Translated by Kaethe Mengelberg. Totawa, NJ: Bedminster Press, 1964.

Wade, Richard. *Slavery in Cities: The South 1820–1860.* New York: Oxford University Press, 1964.

Warren, Stephen. *The Worlds the Shawnees Made: Migration and Violence in Early America.* Chapel Hill: University of North Carolina Press, 2014.

Whitman, T. Stephen. *Challenging Slavery in the Chesapeake: Black and White Resistance to Human Bondage, 1775–1865.* Baltimore: Maryland Historical Society, 2007.

Wiedemann, Thomas. *Greek and Roman Slavery.* Baltimore: Johns Hopkins University Press, 1981.

Worden, Nigel. *Slavery in Dutch South Africa.* Cambridge: Cambridge University Press, 1985.

Worden, Nigel, and Gerald Groenewald. *Trials of Slavery: Selected Documents Concerning Slaves from the Criminal Records of the Council of Justice at the Cape of Good Hope, 1705–1794.* Cape Town: Van Riebeeck Society, Second Series, No. 36, 2005.

Worden, Nigel, Elizabeth van Heyningen, and Vivian Bickford-Smith. *Cape Town: The Making of a City: An Illustrated History.* Cape Town: David Philips, 2004.

Zacek, Natalie. *Settler Society in the English Leeward Islands, 1670–1776.* New York: Cambridge University Press, 2010.

Zürcher, Erik-Jan, ed. *Fighting for a Living: A Comparative History of Military Labour, 1500–2000.* Amsterdam: Amsterdam University Press, 2013.

CONTRIBUTORS

TITAS CHAKRABORTY is Assistant Professor of History at Duke Kunshan University, China. Her research and teaching interests are South Asian and World History with special attention to labor, migration, and gender. Prior to joining Duke Kunshan University she was a Postdoctoral Research Fellow at the Institute of Historical Studies, University of Texas at Austin, and a Visiting Assistant Professor at Oberlin College. Her work has appeared in the *International Review of Social History*. Her current book project, "Work and Ascendancy of the English East India Company in Bengal, 1650–1819," explores how the conflict between the English East India Company and its workers shaped its attitude toward labor in Bengal.

TIMOTHY COATES is Professor of History Emeritus from the College of Charleston, where he taught Latin American and global history for many years. He has authored three monographs on forced labor in the Portuguese World, most recently *Convict Labor in the Portuguese Empire, 1740–1932* with Brill in 2014. He also translated the 1612 classic work on Portuguese Asia, Diogo do Couto's *O Soldado Prático*, published in 2014 as *Dialog of a Veteran Soldier*. He is currently completing a translation of Frei Vicente do Salvador's 1627 *History of Brazil*.

JAMES F. DATOR is Assistant Professor of History at Goucher College. His current book project, "'To See the World in a Grain of Sand': Liberty and Slavery in the Leeward Caribbean, 1689–1739," explores the transimperial history of the Leeward Islands from below.

LEX HEERMA VAN VOSS is a historian of work. He is Director of the Huygens Institute for the History of the Netherlands and Professor of the History of Social Security at Utrecht University. He co-edited *Selling Sex in the City: A Global History of Prostitution, 1600s–2000s* (Brill, 2017).

JOHAN HEINSEN is Associate Professor at Aalborg University, Denmark. He studies the social history of maritime and penal institutions in early modern Denmark. His publications include the monographs *Mutiny in the Danish Atlantic World* (Bloomsbury, 2017) and *Det første fængsel* (Aarhus University Press, 2018).

LEO LUCASSEN is Director of Research of the International Institute of Social History (IISH) in Amsterdam and Professor of Global Labour and Migration History at the University of Leiden. Among his publications are *The Immigrant Threat: Old and New Migrants in Western Europe since 1850* (University of Illinois Press, 2005). He is also co-editor of *The Encyclopedia of Migration and Minorities in Europe: From the 17th Century to the Present* (Cambridge University Press, 2011) and *Globalizing Migration History: The Eurasian Experience* (Brill, 2014).

HAMISH MAXWELL-STEWART is Professor of History at the University of Tasmania, Australia. He has authored a number of books and many articles on convict transportation including *Closing Hell's Gates: The Death of a Penal Station* (Allen and Unwin, 2008). He is currently working on a large project exploring the impact of forced labor migration on life course outcomes and intergenerational inequality.

MARY NIALL MITCHELL is Ethel & Herman L. Midlo Endowed Chair in History at the University of New Orleans and co-director of the Midlo Center for New Orleans Studies. She is the author of *Raising Freedom's Child: Black Children and Visions of the Future after Slavery* (NYU Press, 2008) and has published online for *The Atlantic, Harper's,* the *New York Times,* and *The History Channel.* She is a lead historian on *Freedom on the Move,* a digitized crowd-sourced database of fugitive slave advertisements housed at Cornell University.

JESSE OLSAVSKY is a PhD candidate at the University of Pittsburgh. He is currently writing a dissertation titled "'Fire and Sword Will Do More Good': Fugitives, Vigilance Committees, and the Making of Revolutionary Abolitionism, 1835–1859." He has published articles and reviews in such journals as *Slavery and Abolition, Black Scholar,* and *International Review of Social History.*

MICHAEL QUINLAN is Emeritus Professor at the University of New South Wales, Australia. He is the author of *The Origins of Worker Mobilisation: Australia 1788–1850* (Routledge, 2017). He is currently working with Hamish Maxwell-Stewart on a history of convict resistance in Eastern Australia.

MARCUS REDIKER is Distinguished Professor of Atlantic History at the University of Pittsburgh. His books have won numerous awards and been translated into fifteen languages. His most recent book is *The Fearless Benjamin Lay: The Quaker Dwarf Who Became the First Revolutionary Abolitionist* (Beacon Press, 2017). He is the producer of the documentary *Ghosts of Amistad: In the Footsteps of the Rebels* (director, Tony Buba) about the meaning of the *Amistad* slave ship revolt of 1839 in contemporary Sierra Leone.

ANITA RUPPRECHT is Principal Lecturer in the School of Humanities, University of Brighton, UK. Her research focuses on the history and representation of transatlantic slavery, abolition and emancipation. She has published articles in *Slavery and Abolition, Race & Class, History Workshop Journal,* and *International Review of Social History.*

YEVAN TERRIEN is a PhD candidate in Atlantic History at the University of Pittsburgh. The archival research for his dissertation, "Exiles and Fugitives: Labor, Mobility, and Power in French Colonial Louisiana, ca. 1700–1770," has been supported by the McNeil Center for Early American Studies, the New Orleans Center for the Gulf South, and the Newberry,

Huntington, and John Carter Brown libraries. His work has appeared in the journal *Atlantic Studies* and in the volume *New Orleans, the Founding Era*, ed. Erin Greenwald (Historic New Orleans Collection, 2018).

NICOLE ULRICH is Senior Lecturer in the History Department at Rhodes University, South Africa. Her research focuses on the radicalism of laborers and the poor in colonial (and apartheid) southern Africa, examined within broader transnational or comparative contexts. She has published research articles in *International Review of Social History, Journal of Southern African Studies, Journal of Contemporary African Studies,* and *South African Historical Journal* as well as numerous book chapters, with the most recent appearing in Kate Fullagar and Mike McDonnell, eds., *Facing Empire: Indigenous Histories in the Revolutionary Age, 1760–1840* (John Hopkins University Press, 2018) and Kirk Helliker and Lucien van der Walt, eds., *Politics at a Distance from the State: Radical and African Perspectives* (Routledge, 2018).

MATTHIAS VAN ROSSUM is Senior Researcher at the International Institute of Social History (IISH). He specializes in global labor history and has published on maritime labor, convicts, slavery, and slave trade, as well as labor conflicts and resistance. He completed a research project on slave trade and slave labor in South and Southeast Asia ("Between Local Debts and Global Markets," NWO Veni Grant, 2016–2019) and is co-applicant to a research project on racialization in the Dutch early modern empire (Resilient Diversity, NWO VC Grant, 2017–2021).

CREDITS

by the agents A. Guerber & Co. Photograph. https://www.loc.gov/item
/93500720/

Fig. 10.3   Möllhausen, Henry, Benjamin Moore Norman, and Shields & Hammond.
Norman's plan of New Orleans & environs. [S.l, 1845] Map. https://www.loc.gov
/item/98687133/

INDEX

THE CALIFORNIA WORLD HISTORY LIBRARY
Edited by Edmund Burke III, Kenneth Pomeranz, and Patricia Seed